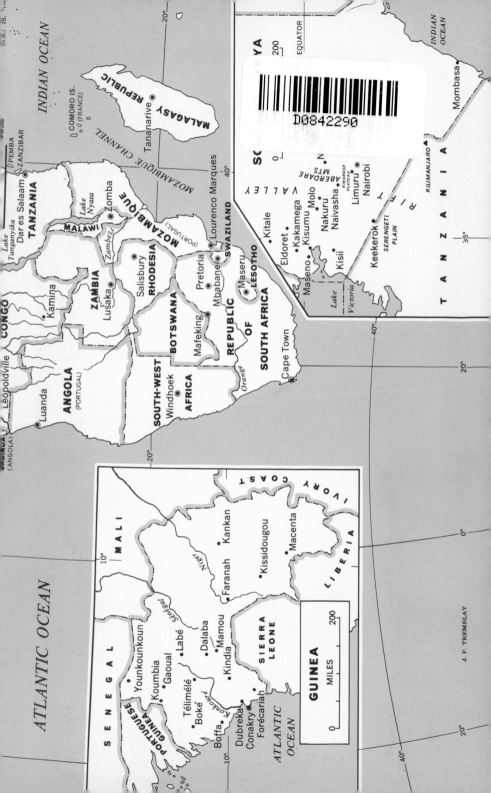

THE REDS AND THE BLACKS

THE REDS AND

THE BLACKS

A Personal Adventure

●

WILLIAM ATTWOOD

HARPER & ROW, PUBLISHERS

NEW YORK
EVANSTON
AND LONDON

To CHESTER BOWLES

The lines on page 8 are from "Stopping by Woods on a Snowy Evening" from *Complete Poems of Robert Frost*. Copyright 1923 by Holt, Rinehart and Winston, Inc. Copyright 1951 by Robert Frost. Reprinted by permission of Holt, Rinehart and Winston, Inc.

The lines on page 237 are from "Odinga"—copyright 1965 by Ogden Nash. First published in *The New Republic*, 1965.

The lines on page 281 are from *Out of Africa*, by Isak Dinesen. Copyright 1937 and renewed 1965 by Rungstedlundfonden. Reprinted by permission of Random House, Inc.

FIRST EDITION

LIBRARY OF CONGRESS CATALOG CARD NUMBER: 67-15746

B-R

Contents

●

Illustrations follow page 118

A Message to the Reader

•

> What a man knows at fifty that he did not know at twenty
> is, for the most part, incommunicable. . . . The knowledge he
> has acquired with age is not the knowledge of formulas, or
> forms of words, but of people, places, actions—a knowledge
> not gained by words but by touch, sight, sound, victories, fail-
> ures, sleeplessness, devotion, love—the human experiences of
> this earth and of oneself and other men.
>
> —Adlai Stevenson at Princeton, June, 1954

I'm not yet fifty, and you're probably over twenty, but
what Stevenson was telling the Princeton seniors has some rele-
vance to this book. For it will be about some of the things I
learned in Africa, and in our government, during more than five
years as an American ambassador working for two Presidents.
When a man reaches middle age and then learns something really
new about the world, the people in it and himself, he needs to
write about it even though so much of it seems, as Stevenson said,
incommunicable.

I said "needs to write" because there are other things I'd rather
be doing for the next couple of months. Writing a book is hard,
lonely work, and you don't do it unless you have to. Either you
need the money or you feel you have such a good story to tell
that you can't keep it to yourself any longer. In my case, it's the
story.

The reason for this introduction is to tell the reader what to expect in the pages that follow. Anybody who buys a book these days is, I think, entitled to a personal word from the author before spending the kind of money books cost. The blurb on the cover gives some idea of what's inside, but it's actually a commercial. Anyone who reads this introduction will really know what I intend to do and whether he wants to go along on this safari through Africa's political bush and Washington's bureaucratic jungles. At the end of these few pages he may decide to put the book back on the shelf, but at least he'll know what he's missing.

As the title suggests, this book is essentially about what I saw of Soviet and Chinese efforts to penetrate and subvert Africa and what we and the Africans and others did to counter these efforts. In both Guinea and Kenya I was up against the opposition at close enough range to understand why it has so far failed. Those who are interested in an eyewitness account of Communist tactics in a vast, turbulent and largely unreported continent won't be disappointed.

However, as the subtitle suggests, this book is not only about cold warfare in a hot climate. I went from journalism to diplomacy via the politics of the 1960 campaign, working for Adlai Stevenson and Jack Kennedy, so I hope to tell something of how our government works, how power is acquired and exercised and what has to be done in Washington to get results.

Africa is a big place, more than three times the size of the United States, and I traveled through twenty-one of its thirty-eight countries; readers who like to visit strange places and hear the noises of tom-toms and wild animals will not be short-changed. But statistics will be kept to a minimum. There are reference books galore about Africa these days, and I don't want to clutter up a personal narrative with the kind of data you can find in your local library.

Impressions and opinions, yes—about people and policies and the conduct of our foreign affairs, not just in Africa but in Vietnam, Cuba and elsewhere; for I've acquired some strong views in these five years. Some of these views will surprise my liberal friends, who may not understand how an old Stevenson Democrat can have such admiration for Lyndon Johnson; some will seem disloyal— such as the harsh things I'll be saying, as a journalist, about the press; and some will appear paradoxical—such as my conviction that we must dismantle the Agency for International Development if we are to save and strengthen our vitally important foreign assistance program. Yet all the views and conclusions will be based on the hard and illuminating experience you get only from struggling with real problems in the real world, and from lying awake at night in faraway places.

There will be a good many heroes but no real villains in this book, not human ones anyway. There's the System, but I won't go into that now. If I have to knock somebody, I'll omit his name.

Be prepared to shed some illusions. Did you know that walking around city streets at night is safer in Africa than in America? That Nairobi's automated parking facilities are more modern than New York's? That one encounters less race feeling, as a white man, in black Africa than in multiracial America? That it's possible to be a U.S. ambassador for more than five years without ever wearing a hat or a pair of striped pants? This book will, I hope, cast some new light on the world of modern diplomacy and on this African continent which, as President Johnson recently said, "has never been so dark as our ignorance of it."

I wondered how to start and especially how to structure the cryptic and random jottings of a long diary. With a summary of African political history? With a chapter on Communist objectives in the underdeveloped world? Or should I first explain how the State Department functions and how ambassadors are chosen? Thinking about it, I decided that the best way to write a story like this—a story of six years in a man's life—was to start at the beginning and tell what happened, more or less the way the old explorers used to write about their expeditions from the moment they disappeared into the jungle until the day they staggered out, gaunt but happy, months or years later.

The conclusions and the strong views come at the end. You may or may not agree with me, but at least you will understand how I came to feel as I do. For you will share quite a few adventures with me, as well as some frustrations. I have run out of inner tubes in the forests of central Guinea, ridden zebroids through a blizzard on the equatorial slops of Mount Kenya and spent Christmas in Timbuktu.

I met all kinds of interesting people—Soviet intelligence agents; Congolese confidence men; Masai warriors whose favorite cocktail is a blend of blood, milk and urine; itinerant Congressmen and whisky-drinking missionaries; even a Mongolian ambassador's secretary who used to read Kafka in French. I went swimming every afternoon for a year with eleven Chinese Communists—and was never greeted. I had long, lively talks with passionate ideologists like President Sékou Touré and wise old men like President Jomo Kenyatta (Ruark fans are in for a shock). I sweated out the Stanleyville air drop and, two days later, stood at an embassy window, more in sorrow than in anger, to watch a mob brandishing anti-American signs and setting fire to parked cars.

In Washington, I conferred with the tweedy pipe-smokers who inhabit the air-conditioned grottoes of the CIA building. I went to Georgetown parties and watched the New Frontiersmen at play. From time to time, I walked into the Oval Room of the White House to be greeted by two different Presidents, and noted the changes. I was sitting with Adlai Stevenson looking at the television screen on that terrible afternoon when one of them was shot.

Except for a permanent limp (mine) and some temporary amoebas (my son's), our family came through this long adventure relatively unscathed. We even added a daughter to the family roster. And we came away with an abiding affection for Africa and its people, a deep respect for the overworked and underpaid men and women who staff our Foreign Service, a backlog of indignation at public ignorance and crippling bureaucratic foolishness, a renewed pride in being Americans in this century, and a wonderful hand-lettered sign, snatched from some well-wishers as I left Nairobi airport, reading "Yankee Don't Go Home."

But this really belongs at the end of the story. The beginning, for me, was flying from Washington to New York on an Eastern Airlines shuttle one evening in December, 1959, with Adlai Stevenson as my seatmate.

I

How It Started: Adlai and JFK

•

This chapter is about politics—more specifically, about what I saw of Democratic politics in the 1960 campaign. If I hadn't decided to become a speech-writer—if Stevenson had decided to block Kennedy's nomination—if Johnson hadn't been on the ticket—if Kennedy had fumbled one of three key plays in the fall—then I would never have become an ambassador.

So the first year begins and ends in Washington.

The 1960 campaign was no exception to the rule that contests for the Presidency usually get under way well over a year before the election. I had gone to Washington in December on business for *Look* magazine, of which I was then foreign editor, and some friends of Kennedy told me he was already certain of five hundred convention delegates, even though he had not yet announced his candidacy. And he was already annoyed that Stevenson had so far not given him any assurances of support against the only three other serious contenders—Johnson, Symington and Humphrey.

Stevenson was also in Washington that day, and we arranged to fly back to New York together to discuss some articles he would do about his forthcoming trip to South America. We drove to the airport with Senator Monroney, who was worried that Truman and Acheson, by advocating a hard-line foreign policy, were going to make it easy for the Republicans to pre-empt the peace issue in an election year; he wanted Stevenson to assert himself as the Democratic party's spokesman in a series of major speeches and thereby commit the candidate—whoever he might be—to a liberal position on the big issues.

Stevenson agreed it might be useful and said he would plan his spring speaking schedule with this in mind. Later, on the plane, he acknowledged that delivering political speeches in the spring of an election year would make him look like a candidate. But I gathered from the way he talked that he didn't approve of Kennedy as the Democratic standard-bearer against Nixon and that he more or less expected the convention would have to turn to him again as the only man able to keep the party united.

"I don't know what will happen," he said, "but I ought to be ready. I suppose I'm too old to change my ways of campaigning, but I do want to be better organized this time."

He then asked me if I would take a leave of absence to prepare speech material for him to use during the spring and, if necessary, for the campaign against Nixon. I said I would think it over and let him know in a few weeks.

Having worked with Stevenson before (particularly during a grueling trip around the world with him in 1953) and having watched his chaotic 1956 campaign, I wasn't especially enthusiastic about joining him for another harrowing and, even worse, perhaps futile try for the Presidency. But if some of the political pros were right in thinking that Kennedy's youth, religion and relative inexperience were insuperable handicaps, then there might in fact be no alternative to Stevenson in July. Johnson would alienate too many Negroes and liberals, and Humphrey too many conservative Democrats; Symington would be a respectable but uninspiring compromise. And if it had to be Stevenson, I agreed with him that he should be well prepared, with the issues clarified and the speeches on tap, in order to stand a chance in November.

Also, 1960 was no time for anyone who cared about America's role in the world, and who had watched the gradual erosion of our influence, to stand on the sidelines. For eight years, from McCarthy on through Sputnik, I had seen the consequences of drift and indecision in an administration that substituted words for action and public relations for policy. As a nation, we seemed to have lost our energy at a time when the Communist powers were flexing their muscles; we were becoming irrelevant bystanders in a revolutionary world, everywhere defending the status quo while others were making history. And as an American who often traveled abroad, I was embarrassed by the gratuitous moralizing and hollow threats of John Foster Dulles; the indifference in high places to such explosive issues as nuclear testing and civil rights; the tendency to support any tinhorn dictator so long as he made anti-Communist noises; and the official complacency about our deteriorating cities, our overcrowded schools, our chronically unemployed, our sick and our aged. We had a tired President who preferred to reign rather than to lead and, in Richard Nixon, a crown prince whose public utterances were such a mixture of platitude and invective as to disqualify him from the most powerful office in the world. Yet he was running for it, and I knew how hard he could run.

So I had to get involved in this election—the most important, I still think, of this century. Win or lose, I wanted to be able to tell my children someday that I'd done what I could. But I still had my doubts about the Stevenson exercise.

These were partly resolved, late in December, by Tom Finletter, a New York lawyer who was organizing support for Stevenson among some Eastern liberals—including a few disenchanted Republicans. He urged me to take a leave—there was money available to match my *Look* salary—and to work with Stevenson on some hard-hitting speeches. These would be needed in the campaign whether he was the candidate or not. Chester Bowles, who had not yet joined the Kennedy camp, also thought Stevenson might get the nomination by default but agreed he would have to be much more decisive to beat Nixon. Other Democratic friends felt the same way.

I therefore told Stevenson on January 20 that I would take a leave until November, not to help him get the nomination but to help defeat Nixon. He seemed gratified, though harried and distracted as usual, and outlined the themes of five speeches he planned for the spring, most of them concerned with foreign policy. He was about to leave for South America—partly, I think, to avoid inquisitive reporters—and would say nothing about politics until he returned in April. (His law partner, Bill Blair, who was going along, told me he was half-inclined to declare his candidacy but feared the humiliation of later losing the nomination.)

Meanwhile, I had lunched with Kennedy and the *Look* editorial board in New York. I had met him before but never to talk politics. When he asked me who I was for, I told him I was for anybody who could beat Nixon. He smiled and said the only other possible candidates now were Stevenson and Symington but that neither of them had a chance against Nixon.

Having made my decision and knowing the press would play up any signs that Stevenson was challenging Kennedy, I called on Ted Sorensen in February to tell him what Stevenson's intentions were (make speeches but endorse nobody) and my role (provide him with material and help *any* Democrat win after July). I emphasized that Stevenson, to my knowledge, was not personally involved in a stop-Kennedy drive. Sorensen was cordial but understandably suspicious. He was sorry we'd be "enemies" but glad we'd be "on the same side" after July.

In March the *Wall Street Journal* came out with a lead story called "Adlai's Third Try," in which he was described as "itching to run" and encouraging the behind-the-scenes efforts of his New York and Washington backers—among them Finletter, George Ball and Senator Monroney. The story was right about his backers —they were getting very busy—but wrong about their getting much encouragement from the noncandidate. Yet they were determined to make him one. I remember suggesting to the New York group that Stevenson publicly back Kennedy if he won the Wisconsin primary; otherwise he might find himself leading, willy-nilly, a stop-Kennedy drive that would probably fail and might split the party. They didn't agree. There was no love for Kennedy among the dedicated and twice-frustrated Stevensonians. Even Eleanor Roosevelt, who told me that Stevenson, unlike her husband, "didn't understand the problems of the common man because he didn't enjoy mingling with them," wanted him to fight for the nomination.

Early in April I flew to Barbados to show Stevenson a draft of a speech he was to make at the University of Virginia. At first he found it too political for an academic audience. "I don't want to get into this thing again," he said almost plaintively. But with

Arthur Schlesinger's help, we managed to produce a finished version that would satisfy the scholars without sparing the Republicans. The speech got good headlines ("Adlai Lashes Out at GOP"), but Kennedy had won in Wisconsin and was on his way to victory in West Virginia. Stevenson began toning down the political content of his subsequent speeches; he might even have followed the advice of his law partners—Blair, Newt Minow and Bill Wirtz—and come out for Kennedy if the U-2 incident in May and the breakdown of the Paris Conference had not suddenly given a fresh impetus to the Stevenson movement. With the cold war apparently heating up again, the voters would be inclined to turn to the man with experience in foreign affairs. Stevenson, it was argued, could hold his own against Nixon on this issue; Kennedy could not. Walter Lippmann, among others, suggested a Stevenson-Kennedy ticket. By mid-May, Draft Stevenson clubs were mushrooming across the country.

On May 18 I met Stevenson at his farm in Libertyville after talking to Ball and Lippmann in Washington. They wanted him to hit the administration hard on the U-2 blunder. He was angry enough to agree, and we concocted a speech accusing Eisenhower of handing Khrushchev "a crowbar and sledgehammer" to wreck the Paris Conference. After we had watched Khrushchev on television, the phone began ringing. Lyndon Johnson called about issuing a joint Democratic party statement—and about the chances of stopping Kennedy. Mrs. Roosevelt called too. "She wants to throw me to the wolves," said Stevenson when he came back to the living room. "But can Kennedy be stopped now?" I said I didn't know, but if he really wanted to try, the time to start was now. "I'm not sure I can beat Nixon," he went on, "and I know I can't if we come out of that convention with blood on the floor."

When I left him in the morning, he was still musing, still uncertain. And when Kennedy (now concerned about the changed international situation) came to the farm three days later to ask his support in exchange for any job he wanted, Stevenson politely declined, saying it would "look like a deal." He told me later he was "not sure" if he even wanted to be Secretary of State under Kennedy.

The danger of a Stevenson-Kennedy split—fatal to whoever

was the nominee—was now real. In Washington, Ben Bradlee, a close friend of Kennedy's, told me that, in his present mood, "Jack will walk out of the convention if he doesn't get the nomination." He suggested I meet with Kennedy if only to maintain communications. (Bill Blair, who was close to Kennedy, had gone off to Europe on holiday after West Virginia, calling Stevenson's stance "hypocritical.")

On June 14 the Kennedys and I had dinner with the Bradlees at their Georgetown home. After some small talk over cocktails, Kennedy turned to me and came right to the point: What the hell was Adlai up to? (The day before, Stevenson had denied Mrs. Roosevelt's assertion that he *was* a candidate.) I explained that Stevenson wanted to remain available in case of a deadlock to keep the party united but, despite the urging of his supporters, would do nothing to get the nomination or prevent Kennedy or anyone else from getting it. Kennedy replied that he had the nomination virtually sewed up and that Stevenson's actions, or nonactions, were only helping Johnson and Symington. Kennedy implied that if by some chance he didn't win, his delegates would probably go to Symington. As for a Stevenson-Kennedy ticket, that was out.

I said I understood why he had to say that now, but that if the delegates did end up by choosing Stevenson, they would surely draft him for the second spot.

"I wouldn't take it," he said in a flat, hard voice. "I'm campaigning for the Presidency, period."

Not even knowing it would make Nixon's election inevitable?

Jackie, who had taken no part in the political dialogue, then spoke up with feeling. "Let Adlai get beaten alone!" she said. "If you don't believe Jack, I'll cut my wrists and write an oath in blood that he'll refuse to run with Stevenson!"

I told her I was now convinced. After a few more unflattering remarks by Kennedy about Stevenson's political acumen, the conversation turned to the campaign. He was glad I'd been working on a campaign strategy memo because he'd been too busy with the primaries to think about Nixon. He especially needed new foreign policy ideas. He admitted, ruefully, that the Irish Catholic hierarchy was for Nixon, and was worried about the Negro vote. I urged him to cultivate the CORE leaders (he had not heard of

CORE). He assumed I'd want to work on the campaign. I said I would but wanted him and his staff to know I would be doing it only to beat Nixon and not because I wanted a job in his administration, especially a White House job.

By the end of the evening, Kennedy was relaxed and jovial, practicing chip shots on the rug with a golf club and asking us whether he should make Bowles or Stevenson Secretary of State. When he left, standing in the doorway behind Jackie with his arms around her, he said I'd be getting a call after the convention; meanwhile, he hoped Stevenson would do nothing he'd regret.

Stevenson phoned the next day, asking me for a memo on my talk with Kennedy. I gave it to him in Chicago. When he finished reading it, his only reaction was: "How could I ever go to work for such an arrogant young man?"

But I think the Kennedy message did help Stevenson resist the mounting pressure from his friends (now including Hubert Humphrey) that he make a move for the nomination. To Humphrey he had replied that he would "gladly accept" the nomination if the delegates, who knew him, wanted him, but would not seek it or give encouragement to his supporters; and that he would "work with all his heart and energy" to help elect whatever candidate the convention chose.

His supporters remained undaunted and undismayed. With Ike forced by anti-American riots to cancel his trip to Japan, foreign policy was in the spotlight, and Stevenson was indirectly encouraging his ardent amateurs with stronger speeches on this issue. (Handing me one draft, he suggested I cut out his own "philosophical lamentations" and "put some bite into it.") And he was disturbed but flattered by the activities of the Draft Stevenson clubs ("I didn't know young people still cared about me"). I was mainly disturbed, especially after talking to the Lexington Democratic Club in New York in June: the audience froze when I said some kind words about Kennedy.

Stevenson came to Los Angeles four days before the nominating speeches. He might still have prevented a Kennedy nomination then by saying "I want it" and acting like a candidate. Fortunately he didn't. But neither did he yield to the pleas of his law partners and his friends in the Kennedy camp that he deliver Kennedy's nominating speech. All through the turmoil, he remained curiously and (to almost everyone) exasperatingly cool and detached. The day before the nomination and just before making his tumultuous and dramatic appearance on the convention floor, he asked me to prepare a draft introducing and praising Kennedy at a post-convention rally. I must have looked surprised because he smiled and said, "Well, that's the way it's going to turn out."

That night, after the California caucus had revealed unexpected pro-Stevenson sentiment, a group of exhilarated Stevenson delegates met to map out the next day's stop-Kennedy strategy on the floor. Even Bill Wirtz, who wanted Stevenson to back Kennedy, was swept along in the excitement. The prospect of surprising the pollsters, the pundits and the professionals was somehow intoxicating. Stevenson himself turned up late in the evening and made a few graceful but noncommittal remarks. But when he ended with a quote of Robert Frost—"I have promises to keep and miles to go before I sleep"—the assembled delegates happily assumed he had decided to do battle and was going to spend the rest of the night mobilizing support. They were wrong. A few minutes later I went up to his suite and found him already in his pajamas.

Kennedy's nomination came as a relief to all but the hordes of bitter and resentful Stevenson demonstrators. Even though Kennedy pointedly omitted any reference to the noncandidate in his acceptance speech, Stevenson seemed cheerful after the proceedings and called the nominee in the morning for an appointment. Kennedy graciously offered to come to Stevenson's suite. Unlike some of his lieutenants, who never forgave Stevenson (nor fully trusted any Democrat who hadn't been on their side from the beginning), Kennedy himself bore no grudges. Things were going to be all right, and there wasn't any blood on the floor.

Before leaving Los Angeles, Stevenson told me he'd agreed to make ten speeches for Kennedy (as it turned out, he made more than seventy-five) and wanted me to prepare some material. While I was doing this, back in Connecticut, I got a call from Kennedy headquarters inviting me to join his speech-writing staff. After a talk with Sorensen, I went to Washington in August and moved into a cubicle between Bob Yoakum and Joe Kraft and started knocking out memos and speech drafts in a sweaty bedlam of jangling phones, carpenters' hammers and chattering female volunteers. After three frenetic days, I met Kennedy in the cool of Joe Alsop's Georgetown garden. He didn't seem to attach much importance to our speech-writing factory. He felt that foreign policy would be the No. 1 issue—for a while. "But as I see it," he said, "the only issue by October will be just Nixon or me."

A couple of days later he told us assembled speech-writers that all he really needed were some memos with the key facts and all the good quotes and anecdotes we could dig or dream up. Yet the factory was now set up and speech drafts by the ream were conveyed to Sorensen's office, where they generally disappeared.

Stevenson came to Washington at the end of August. I met him at the airport with George Ball and Bob Kennedy, and we went on to Bowles's house to go over a series of one-paragraph position memos on various foreign policy issues (Berlin, Laos, Cuba and so on) that Ball and I had composed to help the candidate sound consistent as the campaign wore on. Stevenson was planning a cross-country speaking tour in October and suggested I come along. I told him I'd ask Kennedy, whose airborne caravan I was joining in California in mid-September for a swing through Texas and back to New York.

It was on this trip that Kennedy had his dramatic televised confrontation with the Protestant ministers in Houston. It came at the end of a hard day's campaigning—seven stops and a dozen speeches that started at breakfast in El Paso with Lyndon Johnson. Even I was tired and I hadn't made a speech or shaken a hand all day. Watching him facing the hard-eyed clergymen under the hot lights and coolly fielding their loaded questions, I suddenly felt proud about the Kennedy staff badge on my jacket. His performance at Houston was one of the turning points of the campaign; it buried the religious issue for millions of voters. The other two were his first television debate (which convinced more millions that he was a forceful and articulate leader) and his phone call to Mrs. Martin Luther King when her husband was jailed in Georgia (which captured the imagination and support of hitherto indifferent Negro voters).

But one disturbing revelation of this September trip was that the Stevenson cultists were still sulking. They weren't out ringing doorbells or licking envelopes for Kennedy. Most were passive;

some were even planning to sit out the election. There were plenty of them, and nobody but Adlai could crank them up.

On the flight from St. Louis to New York, I suggested to Kennedy that I'd be more useful traveling with Stevenson and helping him stir up his loyal legions. He agreed, and from New York I flew to Chicago, where Stevenson was about to embark on his tour. I brought with me an all-purpose speech that evoked nostalgic memories of 1952 and 1956 and ended with a clarion call for victory at last with a candidate who stood for all they had bled for together in the past.

Stevenson wasn't used to campaigning for somebody else; he kept saying he was tired, and I had to remember to pin Kennedy buttons on his lapel before every speech (they would drop off and he'd never notice). But I think his feeling about Nixon, whom he detested as much as any man in public life, was what kept him going day after day—with only Bill Blair, Bill Wirtz and me to handle the complicated logistics of the tour. And his own version of the all-purpose speech seemed to have the desired effect. All the Stevensonians wanted was just to hear Adlai himself say he was really for Jack.

In Sacramento (good Stevenson territory) Wirtz and I drafted a speech that let Nixon have it with all barrels—something Kennedy himself correctly refrained from doing. Stevenson liked it but wondered if it wasn't perhaps too rough. We resolved his doubts by saying it had already been released to the press. And the crowd, most of them still flaunting Adlai-for-President buttons, roared with delight as he poured it on. But when he left the hall and met the reporters outside, a voice in the dark asked, "Governor, since when have you become Jack Kennedy's hatchet man?" And that was the last time he delivered *that* speech.

Curiously enough—in the light of what was to happen six months later—his one contact with Kennedy during October was a phone call he made from North Carolina to Wisconsin after a statement had been issued by the Kennedy staff implying support for an invasion of Cuba by exile forces. He wanted to know what the party line was. Kennedy told him the statement was a mistake and suggested he "get us back on the high ground" in a CBS interview the next day. By "high ground" he meant letting the

Organization of American States take the lead in coping with the problem of Cuba.

Looking back, I think Stevenson's campaigning helped; it certainly stirred up a good many liberal Democrats and may have provided the slim but vital margins of victory in Illinois, Minnesota and New Jersey. (A few more Sacramento-style speeches might have carried California too.) At any rate, I tottered back to Connecticut to debate Bill Buckley and watch the interminable election returns with the satisfaction that I'd done what I could in a good cause and, if we lost, wouldn't have to apologize someday to my kids.

The long campaign over, I returned to my magazine job, feeling both restless and deflated after this excursion into politics. I had enjoyed the action, and I had learned to like and respect professional politicians as a tough, warm and intensely human breed of men. Yet government service did not appeal to me, even on the New Frontier. I decided I needed a vacation, but first I wanted to do an article previewing Kennedy's foreign policy before the inauguration.

So I found myself back in Washington in December, just a year after that fateful plane ride with Stevenson. On the way I'd stopped to see Stevenson in New York and met Blair in his hotel suite. Stevenson had just been offered the UN job, and Blair was urging him to take it despite his disappointment at not becoming Secretary of State. Stevenson finally agreed when Kennedy told him he'd have a voice in policy-making and that Dean Rusk, whom he knew, was getting the top job. He still had reservations, but told me later, "I'd probably have felt frustrated six months from now if I hadn't said yes."

In Washington, I checked out a draft of my article with Sorensen and saw some friends from the campaign. Many assumed I'd be joining Stevenson's staff at the UN. (He did ask me, but I declined.) Bowles, who had just been appointed Under Secretary of State, talked to me about taking a job in the State Department, but that didn't tempt me either. Then he went on to say that he was looking for some energetic younger men to become ambassadors in several of the volatile and newly independent countries of Asia and

Africa where protocol was less important than sensitivity and drive. He said he'd appreciate my sending him the names of some likely candidates, and to let him know if I changed my mind about coming to work in Washington.

On December 19 I sent Bowles some names and added: "For my part I am less and less inclined—since my return to *Look*—to enter the government either at the UN or in Washington unless the job has real responsibility. However, if you ever need an ambassador to Guinea, I'd like a chance to apply."

The last sentence was no more than a casual afterthought (until you become an ambassador you can never quite conceive of yourself as one)—an afterthought because I remembered Guinea from a visit in 1947 and its President, Sékou Touré, as a man with the courage to say no to De Gaulle; and casual because I didn't even bother to note it in my diary and in fact left two days later for a family holiday in Guadeloupe—black, French-speaking and tropical and hardly the place to go if you're planning to move to West Africa.

We came home January 9. Bowles called that evening while my wife, Sim, was ironing and I was watching the snow fall and wondering if the commuter train would be running in the morning. He asked about my foreign policy piece and then added, "By the way, I think you're all set for Guinea." I'd forgotten but suddenly remembered.

"When do I go?" I asked.

"Probably not before April," he said. "You'll have to spend some time in Washington first."

When he hung up, I said to Sim, "I'll be damned. We're going to Africa." She looked up from her ironing and said, "Fine. Just tell me when to start packing."

Ten days later, now really snowbound, I watched the inaugural on television and heard the President speak:

Let the word go forth from this time and place, to friend and foe alike, that the torch has been passed to a new generation of Americans, born in this century, tempered by war, disciplined by a hard and bitter peace, proud of our ancient heritage, and unwilling to witness or permit the slow undoing of those human rights to which this nation has always been committed, and to which we are committed today at home and around the world.

I was one of those Americans, and I was glad now to have joined the New Frontier.

Wanting some confirmation of what Bowles had told me, I went to Washington early in February and saw Pierre Salinger at the White House. He said the President had approved me for any ambassadorship Bowles had in mind. If I didn't care for Guinea, how about Morocco or Thailand? He suggested I go to Bowles and tell him what I wanted.

Driving over to the State Department, I thought of Rabat, overlooking the Atlantic and sparkling in the sun; Bangkok with its canals and pagodas and oriental charm; and Conakry, the dilapidated capital of hot, humid Guinea—the country the Communists now considered their African Cuba. And I made up my mind. I told Bowles that my choice was still Guinea.

"Good," he said. "I don't think you'll regret it."

It was going to be a lot tougher than I thought. But Chet was right. Sim and I never did regret it.

II

The View from Foggy Bottom

•

The White House announced my appointment on February 17, and I flew to Washington a couple of weeks later to start my briefings while the FBI completed my security investigation. (Their agents are certainly conscientious: when Stevenson was named Ambassador to the UN they called me, as one of his friends, to ask my opinion of his loyalty, integrity and discretion.) Meanwhile, I had been talking to some Africans at the UN, who warned me that the continent was in a violent mood since the assassination of Patrice Lumumba in the Congo on January 17. Sékou Touré had gone so far as to send Kennedy an angry telegram accusing us of having had a hand in it. (The President wisely refrained from raising the emotional temperature by replying immediately, preferring to wait until I got over there.) I had also seen our retiring Ambassador, a Negro educator named John Morrow, who had just returned from Guinea disheartened by his inability even to see Touré in recent weeks and by the lack of support or understanding he'd received from the outgoing administration. The top executives of Olin Mathieson, with $75 million invested in the processing of Guinean bauxite, were also downcast and apprehensive; Soviet President Brezhnev, during a triumphal tour of Guinea, had just awarded Touré the Lenin Peace Prize (Fidel Castro had been similarly honored the year before); and Soviet bloc technicians were now serving as advisers to the Guinean Government and pressing for the expropriation of all foreign firms in the name of "socialism."

The outlook was hardly bright, but even the Olin people had

faith in Touré's goodwill and common sense—if we could only get through to him.

Before reporting to the State Department, I had also had a chance to read the report of a task force assigned by Kennedy in December to study African policy. Its conclusions were encouraging. It recognized African aspirations for independence, self-determination, nonalignment, equal rights and economic development. It recommended that U.S. support for Africa's basic needs— education, agricultural development, technical assistance and capital formation—be coordinated with other friendly nations, and favored encouraging U.S. private investment with tax inducements. It suggested we respond affirmatively to reasonable requests but opposed using aid as political bribery for cold war purposes. It advocated greater unity and cooperation among African nations, in their own interest, as against the political polarization developing between the so-called moderate and radical states. It rejected the Eurafrica idea, then prevalent in Western capitals, that Africa was still a semidependency of Europe and that America should not intrude, even though the Russians and Chinese were doing so. But it stressed that our "intrusion" should be low-key, practical and in harmony with the wishes of Africa's own nationalist leaders.

The task force recommendations, like the appointment of Governor G. Mennen Williams as Assistant Secretary of State for African Affairs, were a sign that we were going to take a new and serious look at Africa. It was about time. State's African Bureau had long been neglected and understaffed despite the fact that nineteen new African nations had come into being since 1956 (there would be twelve more by 1967). All these states had votes in the UN; their leaders—mostly young men—were determined to move from a colonial, feudal and, in places, prehistoric society into the industrial atomic age as quickly as possible. There was no point any more in protesting that they weren't ready for independence; for independence had come, and, as Gladstone once said, "The only preparation for liberty is liberty."

Not only that; the continent they represented, three and a half times the size of the United States, was no longer a blank space on the map. Its hydroelectric potential was sufficient to light the world, and it now produced commercially seventy-five of the earth's eighty most important minerals, with much of its resources still unsurveyed. And the people of Africa, more than 270 million of them, were in revolutionary ferment—suddenly aware, thanks to modern communications, that life could be better, that poverty and disease need not be their eternal fate, that being black did not mean being the white man's servant forever.

But if Africa was now discovering the outside world, we in America had barely started discovering Africa, even though more than twenty million Americans were of African descent. The stock image of Africa was—and for the most part still is—a vision of vast jungles populated by cannibals, witch doctors, Mau Mau savages, lions, gorillas, Tarzan, Jane and Dr. Schweitzer. It's about as accurate as saying an episode of "Gunsmoke" portrays life in America today. But images die hard, especially when fostered by imaginative entertainers like Edgar Rice Burroughs and Robert Ruark.

The fact remained that getting acquainted with this continent and its people—and quickly—was essential if we were to have any influence on this suddenly surging tide of African history. By 1961 a start had been made; in former French West Africa, where I found just one U.S. consulate in 1947, we now had eleven embassies. Although they were understaffed, at least Washington was finally getting some firsthand information that wasn't filtered through European capitals. But, as I learned from the Foreign Service officers manning the Bureau of African Affairs, our policy, if you could call it one, was still to tailor our actions in Africa to the wishes of our often shortsighted NATO partners (who were still saying in the fifties that independence for Africa was at least a generation away).

White House interest in Africa had been minimal. While Khrushchev glad-handed African leaders at the UN in 1960, Eisenhower went on a golfing holiday. With new African embassies opening in Washington, Eisenhower's chief of protocol was notorious for complaining about having to invite "these niggers" to receptions. Ike himself was a problem when African visitors appeared at the White House; on one occasion he got the Ethiopian and Korean envoys mixed up; on another, trying to think of something to say, he innocently remarked to an African chief of state that African elephants, unlike their Indian cousins, couldn't be trained to work. (The African, inferring a racial slur, was indignant.)

All in all, our policy-makers seemed oblivious of the fact that ignoring the awakening African giant today might cost us dearly later, just as our perennial indifference to Latin America's real problems gave Fidel Castro his chance.

And while we dawdled, the Russians, and to a lesser extent the Chinese, were already getting very busy in Africa. This was the decade when Khrushchev's salesmen replaced Stalin's soldiers as the instruments of Soviet imperialism, and Africa looked to them like virgin—and promising—territory.

So it might be useful, before we make the Washington scene, to quickly review what the Communists were up to in Africa, and why.

Until 1954, Soviet Africanists, whose chief theoretician was Professor I. I. Potekhin, clung to the orthodox Stalinist view that a proletarian (i.e., Communist) revolution led by the "working class" was essential to the "liberation" of colonial territories. They had no use for nationalist leaders who did not follow the pure Marxist gospel. As early as 1920, Lenin decreed that nationalist leaders be supported "only on condition that the elements of future proletarian parties in these countries, which will be Communist not only in name, will be brought together and educated to understand their special task—the task to fight the bourgeois-democratic movements within their own nation." This policy of helping Communists, and only Communists, in Asia and Africa persisted for nearly thirty-five years.

But soon after Stalin's death, Khrushchev amended it, at least tactically, in the light of historical facts. For independence was coming to colonial territories not by revolution but by peaceful means, and he saw that militant methods would only isolate local Communist parties (which in Africa were mostly led by Europeans). Marxist-Leninist doctrine had to be reconciled, at least outwardly, with reality, if the new Soviet policy of peaceful coexistence were to make any headway among the young neutralist countries. Khrushchev himself started the process in 1955 in India by graciously "rehabilitating" Ghandi as a true revolutionary. Professor Potekhin quickly got the message, stopped denouncing "bourgeois-nationalists" and was soon reporting blandly that the "working class" in Africa "is still young and lacks political consciousness." His colleagues now praised nationalism (a dirty word within the Soviet empire) and, in the former colonies, called for "full democratic rights and freedoms" (which were nonexistent in their own country).

In short, Lenin's ultimate aim of world revolution directed from Moscow was still Khrushchev's goal, but the means for achieving it had been updated. The new tactics in Africa included subversion through aid, trade and indoctrination. Between 1954 and 1962, the Soviet bloc (Russia and the East European satellites) extended about $550 million in grants and credits to Black (sub-Saharan) Africa, most of it going to six countries. (Soviet aid to all non-Communist countries during this period was $5 billion—about 40 percent of it for military assistance—and was now being committed at the rate of $300 million a year.) One purpose of the credits, which usually carried a minimal 2.5 percent interest rate, was to tie up the recipient country's exports (in repayment) and thereby reduce its economic and political relations with the West. Another purpose was to permit the influx of agents, posing as technicians on Soviet projects, whose off-duty mission was to win recruits to the Communist cause. Nor should we overlook the crash program that, by 1962, had brought some thirteen thousand presumably impressionable foreign students—half of them from Black Africa—to Communist countries for carefully guided courses of study.

If the Russians, their East European satellites and, more recently, the Chinese were prepared to spend this much of their limited resources in faraway and unfamiliar lands, then they must have had a good strategic reason. And the reason, as they perceived it even through their own distorted dogmatic lenses, was that continents like Africa were now in the throes of revolutionary change, and the opportunity to become the leaders of the revolution—the architects of change—was too tempting to pass up.

Nevertheless, as Walter Lippmann pointed out in 1961,

The wave of the future is not Communist domination of the world. The wave of the future is social reform and social revolution driving toward the goal of national independence and equality of personal status. . . . If we make our policy one of opposition to the world-wide movement of social change, we shall lose the cold war and Mr. Khrushchev's hopes will be realized. If, on the other hand, we befriend and support with active measures the movements of social change, their leaders will not submit to Moscow . . . because what they want is independence.

Luckily we had a President who understood the challenge and the choice before us. As a Senator, before he was even a Presidential candidate, he had declared, "If African progress falters because of lack of capital and education, if these new states and emerging peoples turn bitter in their taste of independence, then the reason will be that the Western powers, by indifference or lack of imagination, have failed to see that it is their own future that is also at stake."

I checked into the State Department on March 7 and was assigned a desk, soon piled high with classified papers about Guinea, in AFW—the Office of West African Affairs. It took me several days to find my way around the corridors—and several weeks before I began looking up when somebody said "Mr. Ambassador" —but I was soon settled in with a coolly deferential escort officer making appointments for me all over town. My new colleagues were cordial and helpful. But Foreign Service officers are braced for an influx of political appointees after every Presidential election (normally 20 percent of our ambassadors come from private life), and I could understand how they felt about my showing up. Every ambassadorship filled by an outsider means one less chance for them to get to the top. Yet those of us who came in with Kennedy—men like Ed Reischauer, Jim Loeb, John Bartlow Martin, Phil Kaiser, Ken Galbraith, Lincoln Gordon, Bill Blair and Ted Moscoso—were not the amateurs in foreign affairs that the State Department was accustomed to put up with after previous Presidential inaugurals. We gained acceptance in the Establishment—grudging though it was at times—because we'd been out in the world, spoke the necessary languages, were conversant with foreign affairs and held views that we could articulate with conviction. In short, we could hold our own with the old hands; in time we even became categorized in departmental nomenclature as "noncareer professionals."

My job now was to soak up as much information as I could about Guinea in a few weeks, and in between departmental briefings, interagency calls, medical tests and administrative paperwork. Perhaps I'd better distill some of my findings, for I've learned to assume that hardly anyone knows anything about Guinea. (I'll never forget Dick Watts, the drama critic, telling me of the shocked retort of some of his friends, all cosmopolitan New York liberals, when he remarked that he lived across the street from the Guinea Mission to the UN: "Really, Dick! Can't you say *Italian?*")

Guinea is about the size of Oregon, but the resemblance ends there. Its topography includes a hot and humid coastal plain (200 inches of rain a year), some lightly forested highlands rising from this plain, a broad plateau of dry savanna beyond the hills and a big clump of rain forest down by the Liberian border. Guinea's three million people—about 90 percent Moslem and 85 percent illiterate, and with an average life span of thirty years—mostly work at subsistence farming. (They are also West Africa's best dancers and musicians.) They speak some two dozen tribal languages, but French is the one taught in the schools.

The French took over Guinea in the 1880's during the colonial scramble for African real estate, subjugated the local kings and chiefs and started banana plantations in the coastal plain. Much later, they discovered bauxite—the mineral that makes aluminum —and built the most modern alumina plant in Africa with more than half the capital provided by U.S., German, British and Swiss firms. Today Guinea is estimated to possess a third of the world's known reserves of bauxite. With several rivers pouring out of the highlands into the Atlantic, Guinea also has hydroelectric power to spare.

In 1950 Guinea was the only one of France's African colonies to reject membership in one of De Gaulle's pet projects, a French "community" of African states. In a referendum run by the French, the Guineans went out and voted for full independence by a nine-to-one majority. The result was a tribute to the organizing skill of Sékou Touré, a thirty-eight-year-old trade union leader whose Democratic Party of Guinea (PDG) had been harassed but never crushed by the French authorities. De Gaulle angrily decided to make an example of Guinea as a warning to the other French African leaders not to follow suit (which they did anyway two years later). He ordered all French administrators, teachers, doctors and technicians out of Guinea. Before leaving, they destroyed documents, ripped out telephones, smashed light bulbs and stripped the police of uniforms and weapons. Touré's Guinea had been condemned to death. Desperate, he turned to other countries, including the U.S., for help. But Washington, fearful of offending De Gaulle, did nothing; six months dragged by before we even sent an ambassador to Conakry.

The Communist bloc had no such compunctions. Seeing a chance to establish an African beachhead, they moved fast. The first ambassador to arrive in Guinea was a Bulgarian. The Russians, Czechs, Poles, Hungarians and Chinese—and even Mongolians—came soon after. By 1961 more than a thousand Communist bloc technicians were in Guinea, advising, surveying and breaking ground on projects included in a $100 million Soviet bloc aid package. Most of these projects were designed to serve Soviet rather than Guinean needs: a jet airport (to be used as a refueling stop to Latin America); a 100 kilowatt radio station and outsized printing plant (to subvert neighboring countries); a municipal loudspeaker system (to brainwash the populace); weapons, uniforms and instructors for the army (to keep the lid on). The Russians took over management of Guinea's newly nationalized diamond mines and were displaying considerable interest in its huge deposits of bauxite.

A look at Soviet bloc and Chinese activities in Guinea in the first two weeks of 1961 alone will give you an idea of how busy they were:

Jan. 1: A Soviet artist gives Sékou Touré a portrait of his grandfather (and Guinea's national hero), Chief Samori.

Jan. 2: The East German Labor Front donates office equipment to Guinea's trade unions and movie projectors and money to start a Communist labor school.

Jan. 6: East Germany announces it is buying about 40 percent of Guinea's banana crop and 20 percent of its palm oil harvest.

Jan. 10: A Soviet-Guinean trade agreement is signed in Conakry. Czechoslovakia says Guinea is now the biggest customer of its state export organization. A program of cultural and scientific cooperation with the Soviet Union is renewed for another year; it includes a Soviet film week, the assigning of fifteen Russian instructors to Guinean institutions and the sending of thirty-five specialized Guinean students to study in Moscow.

Jan. 11: Two Polish fishing boats and several instructors arrive in Conakry to set up a joint fishing company. Polish experts are en route to train Guinean port personnel.

Jan. 12: Czech trade officials announce they will supply office equipment to Guinea and will fly meat products to Guinea in ten hours.

Jan. 15: A Chinese economic exhibition opens in Conakry and is visited by delegations from several African nations.

When your opponent in a chess game suddenly moves a key piece forward, you should try to figure out why he did it and how to counter it. But American policy toward Guinea remained passive. While expressing sympathy for Guinea's difficulties, we took no action that might look as if we were being nice to De Gaulle's bad boys. The Bureau of Western European Affairs was in fact dictating our African policy.

In 1960 we did sign a bilateral aid agreement with Guinea, but it had not yet been implemented when I got there. If Guinea was to survive as a nation, Touré had no choice after independence but to let the Communist powers move in. A drowning man, it has been said, will even clutch at a razor.

In Washington I found a widespread disposition to "write Guinea off" as being "hopelessly down the drain." Touré had not only accepted aid from the Communists but had thanked them for it; ergo, he must be pro-Communist, and rather than give him any alternative, we should isolate him and help those docile African leaders who said nice things about the West.

But trying to divide Africa's new leaders into good guys and bad guys was, at best, a shortsighted policy. So-called good guys often turned out to be weak or corrupt, and the bad guys tough and enduring. Touré in 1961 was a strong leader of a potentially wealthy country and a popular hero throughout most of Africa because of the way he had stood up to De Gaulle and survived; in short, not a man to "write off" if we wanted to exert some influence in Africa.

Nor could I accept the defeatist argument that any country was "down the drain" just because the Soviets got there first. If the New Frontier meant anything, it meant that America had stopped sitting back and giving up when problems got difficult—whether down in Mississippi, up in space or out in the world. What distinguished Kennedy appointees from most career civil servants in 1961 Washington was their inclination to say "Why not?" instead of "Better not" when a new initiative was suggested.

So far as Guinea was concerned, I was suggesting that we at least make an effort to find out if Touré was in fact an African nationalist or a Communist fellow traveler before ostracizing him. My background reading had already indicated that Touré valued his reputation as an African leader too much to tarnish it by becoming a Soviet stooge; that his past experience in left-wing French politics had taught him enough about Communist tactics to know that economic dependence led to political control; and that he had courage and integrity. I intended to test these tentative conclusions after I got there.

Meanwhile, I was busy learning the bureaucratic ropes and meeting people in all the various government departments and agencies concerned with our operations abroad—Commerce, Labor, Agriculture, Defense, CIA, the White House, USIA, ICA (now AID) and the fledgling Peace Corps. Almost everywhere I found friends, from the campaign and before, whom the New Frontier had lured to Washington: Ed Murrow and Don Wilson at USIA, Adam Yarmolinsky at the Pentagon, Averell Harriman at State, Sarge Shriver at the Peace Corps, Luther Hodges at Commerce. Kennedy had also recruited all Adlai Stevenson's law partners—Blair (Ambassador to Denmark), Wirtz (Under Secretary of Labor), Ed Day (Postmaster General), Minow (FCC Chairman)—as well as his leading preconvention backers, Ball (Under Secretary of State) and Finletter (Ambassador to NATO). And I was finding out that the only way to get things done fast in Washington is to know at least one key man you can call by his first name in every government agency.

I was also picking up the local jargon. I could soon tell the difference between an Embtel in the TOICA series (telegram sent from an embassy to the International Cooperation Administration in Washington) and a Depcirctel in the USITO series (circular telegraphic message from Washington to USIS posts); between Titles One, Two, Three and Four surplus food shipments under PL 480 (too complicated to explain here); and between a DCM (Deputy Chief of Mission), a CAO (Cultural Affairs Officer) and a NIACT (a telegram important enough to wake somebody up at night for).

For those who aren't familiar with the State Department, let me quickly explain the pyramid of authority. Just below the Secretary of State in the hierarchy came two Under Secretaries—one for Political and one for Economic Affairs. There were also Deputy Under Secretaries for Political Affairs and Administration. Along with the Director General of the Foreign Service and some ambassadors at large, these people occupied the seventh floor, where the offices were carpeted and the walls paneled. Next, on the sixth floor, came the sixteen Assistant Secretaries, one for each geographical area and others for functional bureaus, such as Public Affairs and Cultural Affairs. Under them, and their deputies, were the Office Directors (fifth floor, fewer carpets, smaller couches, shared waiting rooms), who, with their staffs, handled subregions like East Africa, Central America or Northern Europe. Finally came the desk officers—generally one for each country—who were the most important cogs in the whole machinery. They got the incoming messages first, informed the necessary people in the pyramid, proposed the action, got the clearances and drafted the replies.

Desk officers are usually FSO-3's and -4's. This means they are halfway up the career ladder. Foreign Service officers start at Class 8 and work their way up to Class 1. If they're lucky, they go on to career minister or career ambassador; not many do—we have only seven CA's and fifty-two CM's. But whatever their rank, none, except perhaps the top brass on the seventh floor, work so hard or so long as the desk officers for countries where things are happening.

In general, I found support at the top echelon for making a greater effort in Guinea. I remember Harriman, then sixty-nine but as young in spirit as anybody in town, telling a gathering of New

Frontier insiders at Arthur Schlesinger's house that this administration could not ask me to go to Guinea without assurances that
I'd get the backing I needed to be effective, and that he'd personally make sure I got it. With Kennedy in the White House, ac-
tivism was in style, and even in the State Department you could
sense a kind of subdued enthusiasm in the middle and lower ranks
of Foreign Service officers.

On March 23 I appeared before the Senate Foreign Relations
Committee for confirmation. The questioning was gentle. Senator
Capehart did want to know if I was a Democrat and how much I
had contributed to the campaign. I told him I had contributed a
good deal of effort but had been paid for it; as for being a Democrat, I said I was not beyond redemption since I'd cast my first
vote for Willkie. "I'm glad he lost," grunted Capehart, and the
hearing was over.

Two days later I called on the President with four other newly
appointed ambassadors. As we left, he suggested I come back
alone for a talk about Guinea. That evening a French UN official
(and African expert) told me he'd just talked with Kennedy for an
hour and had never been asked so many intelligent questions about
Africa by any American. It felt good to have a boss who knew the
score.

Blair and I were sworn in on April 6, with Ball officiating and
dozens of friends watching the proceedings. After the ceremony, I
asked Bob Kennedy if Sim, who was staying in Washington overnight, could meet the President before we took off. He told me to
call Ken O'Donnell, who was now Appointments Secretary.
O'Donnell said the President's schedule was too tight just now. But
Bradlee, who dined at the White House that night, called later to
say the President would see us at eight. I'd learned something to
remember later on: if you really had to get to Kennedy, the best
way was to by-pass the protective White House staff. At any rate,
unlike most ambassadors' wives, Sim had a chance to say good-bye
to him in the Cabinet Room, and she appreciated it.

On April 9 I met the Guinean Ambassador to the UN, Telli
Diallo. (Our paths were to cross many times in the next five years,
sometimes dramatically.) I found him sharp, articulate and outwardly candid. A former judge in the colonial administration, he
spoke impeccable French, which he used to good effect in attack-

ing U.S. policy at the UN. (Stevenson complained to me that in his speeches Diallo and the Guineans sounded like "worse S.O.B.'s than the Russians.") But his advice to me made sense: be frank, even blunt, with Touré and bear in mind that education is Guinea's first priority. I told him we were sympathetic to Guinea's problems but did not intend to help build a Soviet colony in Africa. He agreed emphatically. As for our foreign policy, I suggested that it was changing—in substituting quiet diplomacy for public pronouncements, in preparing for arms control, and now in accepting rather than denouncing neutralism, as in Laos. Diallo said Touré must be convinced that we were not just cold warriors, that we "understood" him. At least Diallo—who was generally known by his first name—and I seemed to understand each other.

Back in Washington, I talked to World Bank officials about getting Guinea to join the International Monetary Fund; said goodbye to Governor Williams, who was complaining about "wheels within wheels" in the African Bureau, and called on ICA Director Henry Labouisse, who promised to try and scrape up some aid money for Guinea—just in case.

My last day was typically hectic. With my security clearance out of the way, I spent the morning getting briefed at CIA. (They conducted no operations in Guinea but did want information on Soviet bloc activities.) I was glad that Allen Dulles, at least, didn't think Guinea was a lost cause. What I didn't know then was that one of the most important and welcome results of the imminent Cuban invasion would be that ambassadors, by a Presidential directive of May 29, were to get the authority to supervise CIA operations in the field.

After seeing some aluminum industry executives, who were pressing for a U.S. Government loan and guarantee to develop Guinea's bauxite deposits, I made farewell calls on Secretary Rusk; on Ball, who thought we should underwrite the construction of a dam and aluminum smelter in Guinea; on Henry Tasca, Williams' deputy, who agreed with me that schools were more urgent than dams and promised to "find a way" to meet my requests for aid funds; on Roger Jones, the Deputy Under Secretary for Administration, who approved my plea for an embassy Jeep and told me to "yell for anything I wanted" (and yell I had to); and on my new friends and colleagues in the African Bureau, where I now felt I belonged.

I also saw the President alone and gave him a short memo about how things looked in Guinea. He asked a few perceptive questions and suggested I write him some letters from Africa. He also said I should tell Touré that, while he appreciated his emotional reaction to Lumumba's assassination, the President of the United States was shocked by the telegram Touré had sent him.

Saying good-bye, I told the President (no longer "Jack") that whether or not we succeeded in the field depended to a great extent on what his administration accomplished at home. Like the New Deal, the New Frontier could capture the imagination of people all over the world who were looking to America for strong and sensitive leadership.

The President seemed relaxed and confident, and I didn't suspect the Bay of Pigs operation was only six days away. When I learned about it, halfway across the Atlantic, I remember thinking that if it didn't succeed in forty-eight hours, I and every other New Frontier emissary would be starting out with one strike against us. I certainly didn't need another strike where I was going; for all I knew we had struck out already.

III

Vive la Révolution!

•

In the morning, when we boarded the Air France jet at Orly Airport, chill gusts of April-in-Paris rain swept the runway; that evening we were sitting on the terrace of a concrete bungalow watching the Atlantic turning orange in the tropical sunset, oil palms stirring in the offshore breeze and fruit bats darting across a violet sky.

We had changed planes in Dakar, and flown into Conakry on a French DC-4. Tony Ross, the DCM, and two smiling Foreign Ministry officials—who called me "Excellence"—met the plane; the rest of the embassy staff, about twenty strong, were on hand to greet me in the two-story terminal building. I glanced around but saw no placards telling Kennedy to get out of Cuba or me to get out of Guinea. So when a couple of French and British reporters asked me how I felt, I just replied, "Optimistic." My official car, a black and beflagged Mercury, was parked outside and we were in a hurry to see our new home.

Conakry proper is on a peninsula connected to the mainland by a narrow causeway. But the town's population had doubled (to 100,000) in the last few years and now overflowed onto the mainland. Driving from the airport, seven miles out, to our house, about halfway to town, we went through a suburban sprawl of tin-roofed shacks and thatched huts swarming with people—the men mostly in sport shirts and shorts, the women in long, gaily colored skirts and the children often in nothing.

Our house was on a two-acre plot of palm-shaded land facing the ocean and bore little resemblance to the ambassadorial residences you may have seen in Washington, Europe or Latin America. It consisted of a tiled living and dining area extending onto a terrace, three small air-conditioned bedrooms—one of which was used to store perishable groceries—two bathrooms and a cramped kitchen. There were no windowpanes in the living area, so when the mosquitoes (mostly malarial) appeared after sundown, our only refuge was the bedroom. Still, the gate at the lower end of the garden opened onto the only stretch of sand along Conakry's rocky coast, and the sea breeze felt good as we walked through the house.

We dined early. Afterward, while Sim got acquainted with our cook and two houseboys (all named Mamadou), and the kids— ten-year-old Peter and eight-year-old Jan—went searching for crabs along the shore, I stretched out in a canvas chair to watch the sunset and the palms and the fruit bats and to ponder what to say to the embassy staff. Officially, I had been an ambassador for more than two weeks. But for the first time a telegram had gone out to the State Department over my signature. What it said was: "Assumed charge 1730 April 22." What it meant was: I was on my own.

Our embassy—technically, chancery—was a newly rented, two-story, whitewashed building on a quiet side street near the center of town. In some ways, Conakry seemed more like an outsized village than a capital city: here and there, a few modernistic but slightly scabrous office and apartment buildings rose above the green canopy of mango and *fromager* trees like some world's fair structures that had been left up too long; the other buildings, like the mildewed colonial villas along the sea front, were low-roofed, the traffic sparse, the crowds on the sidewalks as unhurried as the occupants of an Alabama courthouse square at midday. The government ministries were mostly within walking distance of each other and of the Presidential palace, an unpretentious edifice that looked the same as when I met the French Governor there in 1947—except that the red, yellow and green tricolor of independent Guinea now hung from the flagpole.

The American Embassy staff consisted of the DCM, who was about my age; one economic, one labor, one consular and two political officers; an administrative officer and four other Americans to handle our finance and housekeeping; a USIS officer; three communications clerks, five secretaries and a dozen or so African drivers, bookkeepers and maintenance personnel. As embassies go, we were about as skeletonized as we could get considering the reporting and paperwork Washington required.

Since there was no room in the embassy big enough to hold all the Americans at once, we all assembled, wives included, in Ross's garden in the afternoon. Like any random group of Foreign Service people, they were a cross-section of America, their backgrounds as varied as their home towns and their accents. (If your image of the State Department is one of buttoned-down Ivy League personnel, erase it.) They were here in Conakry as a result of anonymous and unexpected travel orders, and I could sense they were puzzled by my arrival. Why should anybody, who didn't have to, come to Guinea?

So I told them why I'd volunteered for this assignment, that I had not come to vegetate under the palms and that the President himself wanted us to make an effort here and wished us well. I knew that Conakry was (rightly) classed as a hardship post, and I promised to do what I could to improve our living and working conditions: an embassy nurse would be arriving shortly (there was only one practicing European doctor in town); bulk orders of food would be imported under my name (meat and canned goods were hard to find locally); and maybe we could even get some American films for private showings. But I added that anybody who just couldn't take it should let me know—I'd be sending them all a personal and confidential questionnaire about their problems—and I'd get them transferred. Meanwhile, I expected everyone who didn't speak adequate French to perfect it and get to know Guineans, because there was no room for deadwood on a staff this size. Now that the home office no longer considered Guinea just another tropical whistle stop, we were going to be busy, not merely watching and reporting what others were doing but hopefully playing a small part in the history of our time.

No one, as it turned out, asked to or had to be transferred. The answers to my questionnaire showed that morale was better than I'd expected. As I learned in the Pacific war, Americans don't mind roughing it when they feel there's a reason for it. The essential thing, as Picasso once said, is to create enthusiasm.

While I waited to present my credentials to the President—until then an ambassador has no official status—Sim and I got settled in at home and at the office. She found shopping arduous; some fruits and vegetables could be found in the open-air markets, but shop counters were usually bare except for odd items like canned Russian crabmeat or Bulgarian brandy. At least she never had to wait. When Africans saw her they invariably insisted that she go to the head of the line "as a guest in our country." And the fact that she spoke fluent French and dressed neatly made a good impression in contrast to the dowdy, inarticulate Russian and Czech housewives whom the Africans openly scorned as "uncultured."

Our neighbors in the suburbs were a cosmopolitan lot. On one side we had the Hungarian Ambassador, an old Communist activist who had lost an arm in Spain, whose buxom wife watered her garden each morning in a transparent nightgown and whose pneumatic teen-age daughter had a weakness for young Guineans; beyond them was the Chinese Embassy, where grim-faced young men could be seen doing their daily calisthenics with the Ambassador behind a high cyclone fence. On the other side, we had the more neighborly West Germans (too neighborly—Frau Schroeder once walked into our room while I was emerging from the shower); then Jim Podboy, the young Texaco representative, and beyond him, the Russian Ambassador. All of us used the strip of beach—surely the most international in Africa—along with assorted Czech, Israeli, French and Haitian teachers and their Guinean pupils from the high school across the road.

At the embassy I found a backlog of papers to be read and signed—a sizable part of every ambassador's day is spent signing documents and initialing telegrams—and a flock of housekeeping problems: no less than forty-four embassy appliances, including half our air-conditioners, were out of order; the labor officer (who entertained Africans) had no porch furniture while the general services assistant (who did not) had three sets; the reception hall needed a place for guests to sit down, a magazine rack and a receptionist. Things like that. I was finding out that a conscientious ambassador at a small post has to be part drill sergeant, part chaplain and part cruise director.

I also called on the Foreign Minister, an amiable but nervous crony of Touré's named Louis-Lansana Beavogui, who told me they had awaited my arrival "with impatience" and that the President would receive me on April 26. Apparently this was a new local speed record for presenting credentials. I thanked him and asked that meanwhile he do something about a Polish stowaway who had walked off an East German freighter the night before and was now parked in our embassy.

Touré's protocol chief turned up at the embassy on the appointed day with a Mercedes flying Guinean and American flags and an escort of six motorcycles. We roared into the palace grounds, where an honor guard in Czech uniforms presented arms. Inside, Sékou Touré came down the stairs wearing a white Guinean *boubou* (a kind of billowing, ankle-length robe), a cap and Moslem sandals. After shaking hands, we sat down and I handed him the credentials while we sipped fruit juice. A microphone was set up and I delivered my memorized speech. I said I was here as the representative of a young President of a nation that remembered its own revolutionary past and had fought for its own independence nearly two centuries ago; and that I was glad to return to a country that had helped pioneer African independence. I concluded that the bonds that united Africa and America were stronger than our occasional misunderstandings and expressed the hope we could work together in an atmosphere of frankness and mutual comprehension.

My remarks must have pleased him because they were broadcast on all the day's news programs—quite an achievement since Communist advisers in the Information Ministry virtually dictated what went on the air.

We talked briefly. I passed on Kennedy's message about the Lumumba telegram. Touré just nodded and remarked that Africans like himself naturally became emotional about the murder of African leaders. He recalled meeting Kennedy in Africa the year before and agreed to my suggestion that we have a long, frank talk as soon as possible.

A crowd of Guineans was massed around the residence when we got home. Word had somehow reached the suburbs via the marvelously swift African grapevine that I was calling on the President, and people had come to see the motorcycles.

With my credentials accepted, I could now start calling on government ministers and my fellow diplomats. The calls would be timely, for I had just received an urgent message that would require my returning to Washington in mid-May with an up-to-date assessment of the situation in Guinea.

At the risk of oversimplifying a complicated and somewhat technical subject, here was the problem: A consortium of Canadian and American aluminum companies had contractually agreed, before Guinea's independence, to develop the extensive bauxite deposits near the town of Boké. The first step was to be the construction of port facilities and a railroad; the second was an alumina plant, to be completed by 1964. The total investment required was nearly $200 million. Eventually, so the Guineans hoped, the project would expand into a national aluminum industry with the addition of a smelter, and a dam and hydroelectric station on the Konkouré River to power it.

More than $10 million had already been spent on infrastructure, but some companies had pulled out of the consortium and others were cooling off. French Guinea looked safe; independent Guinea did not. Before fulfilling the original agreement, which the Guinean Government had endorsed, the remaining companies now wanted Washington to guarantee the total investment to enable them to raise more capital. Otherwise they threatened to pull out, leaving the Russians, now busily surveying the dam site, in a position to take over the project—and with it, a third of the world's bauxite reserves.

Before making a decision on the guarantee, George Ball wanted me to take a reading of the political temperature; meanwhile, Phil Habib, a Foreign Service officer from the Bureau of Economic Affairs (E), was being sent over to help us size up the economics of the problem.

So my official calls would have more than protocol value. And I had plenty to make. No less than 30 countries—seven Western, eleven African or neutralist and twelve Communist—had resident envoys in Conakry. (Add their staffs, and you could figure that one out of every 250 people in town was some kind of a diplomat.) Fortunately, I could skip some, since we didn't recognize China, North Vietnam, North Korea, Mongolia or East Germany.

But there were also nearly twenty government ministers and high PDG officials to visit.

I saw most of them for the first time in the reviewing stand for the May Day celebrations, where we literally sweated out a four-hour parade (there seemed to be more marchers than spectators) and a forty-five-minute oration by Touré calling for hard work and sacrifice and ending with an impassioned *"Vive la Révolution!"* That evening, after a long afternoon of more speeches in trade union headquarters, we were treated to a made-in-Moscow, anti-American film about the Congo. Some of the Guineans near us seemed embarrassed when the lights went on, but I only remarked, over a glass of warm Russian champagne, that the film was very interesting, though I was surprised that an independent, nonaligned country should have to resort to Communist propaganda at its own celebration. The word got around. And by bringing along four American visitors from a touring Foreign Service seminar group, I was able to provoke some stares and speculations among my Communist colleagues; there was no harm in letting them wonder what we were up to.

Touré, in thanking the Russians at the parade for the Lenin Peace Prize, had added that he got the award "even though Guinea was not a Communist country." Yet the tone of the May Day festivities was decidedly unfriendly to the West. Lunching with Jim Bell, of *Time,* at the Hôtel de France the next day (the dining room, to the dismay of the Guinean maître d'hôtel, was full of Russian technicians in soiled undershirts), I had to admit that we had no place to go but up.

Habib arrived on May 2 and I had just started my calls when Touré summoned me to the palace. I found him waiting in his shabby second-floor office with Saifoulaye Diallo, Guinea's No. 2 man, a tall reserved Fulah chief's son and no great friend of the West. Our meeting lasted an hour and a half. The gist of my message to him, which took about twenty minutes, was that we had new leadership in Washington, we now understood African aspirations and we were ready to help Guinea strengthen its independence and stay nonaligned, but not if Guinea was going to exchange one form of colonialism for another. After citing some pro-Communist statements by his ministers and the slanted news

on the Guinean radio as evidence, to some, that he was a puppet of
the Soviet bloc, I said I personally had no preconceptions about
him or Guinea but was here to learn and to report the truth to
Washington. The main thing was that we talk frankly to each
other.

Touré heard me out attentively. After a long pause and a cigarette, he launched into an eloquent and often impassioned account
of Guinea's turbulent history since 1958. He said he understood
De Gaulle, who had been misinformed about Guinea and whose
vanity had been hurt. But while he bore no grudge against the
French, he would never crawl back to them on his knees. (I
couldn't help feeling that he spoke a little like De Gaulle—his
words came out in structured paragraphs and you could almost
hear the punctuation.) He also talked of his revolutionary dream
of an African nation run by Africans with the children all in
school, the women all emancipated and the population all happily
at work in a society combining African communal traditions and
modern technology. Such a nation could never be Communist, he
said, for the Guinean "revolution" rejected atheism, historical
materialism, the class struggle and the idea of an elite and all-
powerful party. In Guinea there would always be free discussion at
all levels of the PDG. He had accepted aid from the Communist
powers because none other had been offered. But he would never
take orders from anyone. And he spoke with feeling about African
unity and of the continent's role as a bridge and buffer between
East and West. His manner combined the truculence and pride of
the very poor, the verbosity of the self-educated and the dignity of
a born leader—but he could also laugh. He struck me as a vision-
ary beset by unmanageable problems but also as a tough guy who
spoke his own mind. I liked him. We agreed to meet again to
discuss Guinea's immediate needs.

While Habib drove up to Boké, I called on the cabinet ministers. They were mostly men in their thirties and early forties,
friendly and courteous on the whole but usually ill at ease when I
entered their cramped and dilapidated offices. It was understand-
able. Being black, poor and insecure in their jobs (two years before,
they most likely had been grammar school teachers or post office
clerks), they could hardly be expected to greet the representative
(maybe a racist) of the most powerful nation in the world with the

assurance and equanimity of a Dean Rusk or Robert McNamara. Some concealed their shyness with a hard shell of arrogance, others slowly relaxed with small talk.

Many of them seemed practical-minded, looking for solutions to Guinea's problems and disturbed by Guinea's dependence on the Soviets. I also gathered they were irritated by the cocky, back-slapping manner of the Russian Ambassador, Daniel Solod; one referred to the Soviet bloc technicians as "robots." A few were frankly apologetic about the Lenin Peace Prize award, seeing it as a ploy—which it was—to make Touré seem like an obedient vassal.

Other ministers radiated suspicion and even hostility. They had been given the VIP brainwashing treatment in Moscow and Peking and were clearly convinced that the Communist road was the shortcut to economic development. (Hadn't Russia and China leaped from poverty to power in a few years?) For them, Western colonialism was not the dying horse we knew it to be but still a predatory monster against which they must be constantly on guard —with the help of their new Communist friends. Their suspicions had been confirmed by a plot the year before, in which some Frenchmen were implicated, to overthrow Sékou Touré. They saw Americans as big brothers to the French, and racist to boot. (I recalled how surprised Africans were in 1947 when I shook hands with them—the French had told them that no white American would have anything to do with a Negro.) And they were con-vinced that American aid was a device to "take over" Africa from the French and British.

There was no point in arguing—yet. To questions about aid, I merely observed that the Soviet projects unfortunately seemed rather expensive and impractical; as for U.S. aid, I admitted it was not wholly disinterested, since we did want to strengthen Africa so it could resist foreign domination, and I had seen what that was like in Eastern Europe.

Among Western diplomats and commercial representatives, I found a general feeling that Touré was a genuine nationalist look-ing for a way out of the tightening Soviet embrace. (The French Ambassador said there was little France could do now since De Gaulle had convinced himself Touré was a Communist.) By and large, the African diplomats hoped for an American initiative here, since a Soviet Guinea would pose a threat to neighboring countries. They also confirmed that Guinea, because of the 1958 decision to go it alone, was still regarded with admiration and pride by young African leaders; thus, what happened in Guinea would have an impact all over the continent.

As for the Communist envoys, they all received me cordially, but after the usual vodka and slivovitz toasts to peace and friendship, I heard only complaints about the rigors of living in Guinea and the incompetence of Africans. Solod was on leave, but the Soviet Chargé, an amiable, rumpled young man named Ivan Marchuk, confessed he was developing an ulcer and commiserated with me over being sent here. At least, he said, this was a very informal post, where we could talk freely, East and West, without a lot of reporters following us around.

I did infer from the East Europeans that they weren't happy about undertaking aid programs in Guinea out of their strained resources just to provide some camouflage for the Russians.

Before leaving for Washington, I saw Touré again, this time with Habib. We talked politics, bauxite and aid. He said Guinea's first task after independence was to create a sense of nationhood. Tribalism and feudalism had to be eliminated. Therefore political action had first priority. Without organization and the will to work for the common good, there could be no economic progress. That phase was over; now economic development had priority. I suggested that the capital needed for development would be easier to obtain if Guinea joined the International Monetary Fund. He appeared suspicious of it as being an instrument of "colonialists," and was surprised to hear that Yugoslavia was a member. He hoped the Western consortium would honor its commitment to build an aluminum industry here and stressed the vital importance to Guinea of the Konkouré dam. He confirmed that the Russians were surveying the site, but said he would prefer a Western initiative since the existing aluminum plant was already a European and American venture. As for U.S. aid, he said: "We need everything. Look, here I am the President of the country and I have to go downstairs to get water. There isn't enough pressure for me to get water out of the faucet on the second floor. You see what I mean? But don't think we are beggars. If you have some concrete proposals, we will gladly talk about them, but we are not asking you for anything." I said we were going to Washington and that I'd be seeing him in a couple of weeks. He said he hoped President Kennedy would come and visit Guinea, and asked me to extend an invitation.

During this talk I again raised the question of the slanted news programs on the Guinean radio, merely pointing out that it would be hard for me to convince people in Washington that Guinea was nonaligned when the state-owned radio station followed the Communist line. He said nothing, but the next day issued orders that Communist material would no longer be used in reporting news about America or Europe.

Washington had been kept informed of all our talks, but we needed a paper that summed up our conclusions. We wrote it in Dakar, where we had a day and a night between planes. (A different Africa—the beach was littered with Bikini-clad French girls, and the swanky Hotel N'Gor was designed so that each room had windows facing the ocean on one side and the gleaming white modern city on the other.)

Our report concluded that the time was ripe for a U.S. effort in Guinea. Either we should go all out and underwrite the Konkouré aluminum complex or propose an alternative that would provide enough power for some light industry. In any case, support for Guinea's needs in technical training, agriculture and education was essential. Without some evidence that America was prepared to lend him a hand, Touré would be under increasing and probably irresistible pressure from his radical ministers to go all the way with the Communists just to keep Guinea afloat. Nationalization, under Soviet management, of FRIA, the $150 million Western-owned aluminum plant, would be a likely consequence. Guinea's slide to satellite status would be irreversible, and the Soviets would have what they wanted and were paying big money for—a solid base for subversion on the West African coast. On the other hand, a favorable change in the political climate should be better insurance for the aluminum companies, and do more to encourage further investment, than U.S. Government loans and guarantees at this time.

In Washington we first met with George Ball and members of his staff. The consensus was that we should avoid a massive commitment just now; instead, we might propose building a small dam and hydroelectric plant which would not preclude its possible expansion later. To this we should add a modest but diversified aid package tailored to Guinea's basic needs. Habib and I drew up the proposal, and I asked Olin's executives if their engineers could come up with a rough estimate of what such a dam would cost. Ball meanwhile informed Kennedy we had a feasible proposal in the works; the President said he'd discuss it with us after returning from Canada.

The next few days, for me, were an education in bureaucracy. We blocked out an aid package amounting to some $9 million. And Olin did come through in record time—the dam could be built for about $15 million. But government agencies, unlike private industry, aren't conditioned to move fast. Objection after objection, roadblock after roadblock, loomed up day after day in meeting after meeting of our rump "task force." If the man from AFW approved of something, somebody from ICA or E or the Budget Bureau would question it, or a clearance had to be obtained from their superiors. I had never heard so many "yes buts" since my kids were seven years old. (At one point I was able to break a deadlock only by remarking that I had no interest in returning to Guinea if my hands were tied, and would just as soon resign.)

So Habib and I lobbied. I left copies of our revised report where it would start ripples—with Bowles, with Henry Tasco and Wayne Fredericks, with New Frontier friends at ICA, with Arthur Schlesinger and Walt Rostow at the White House. Habib moved it around the Establishment. Changes were suggested, fought over, modified and made. Eventually, at a meeting in Bowles's office, with fifteen reluctant bureaucrats around the table, we got grudging agreement in principle on doing something—but only after Bowles, who had served in India, backed me up with a tough lecture on the need for fast action in the field.

We weren't through yet. In order to present our proposal to Touré, I had to have instructions. Habib, by now exhilarated by the exercise of slashing away at the vines of red tape, suggested we write them before I left; otherwise the vines would close in again and I'd end up with nothing to say in Conakry. So we wrote out what I wanted to be told to do and hand-carried the paper up and down the corridors from office to office, asking for clearances (a dozen different people had to initial it) and waiting until we got them. The procedure was unorthodox and unprecedented, caused some resentment, but worked. By May 23 we had a final draft of my instructions and needed only the task force's approval.

First I wanted to see the President. I called O'Donnell, but he said there was no time on his schedule. So I phoned the President's secretary, Mrs. Lincoln, directly and got an appointment for 9:30 in the morning. Sitting in his rocking chair, the President asked some pointed questions about the situation in Guinea and the extent of pro-Communist influence. I showed him our report on the situation and told him of our legwork during the past week. He nodded understandingly. "I've been finding out how hard it is to run foreign policy in a government like ours," he said. "We just aren't able to move quickly like the Soviets." He approved the aid package, which would come to $25 million over a two-year period—"if they can find the money." And he agreed that Sargent Shriver (to whom I'd already talked) should go to Guinea in his place in response to Touré's invitation.

After talking to McGeorge Bundy—at the President's suggestion—I returned to the State Department to find the task force already arguing over the draft of my instructions. With things about to get unraveled, I picked up the phone, called Rostow at the White House and, with the task force silently attentive, told him about my talk with the President and said we nevertheless seemed to be running into problems. It didn't take too long after that to get the instructions approved, and I left Washington that night.

We now had a program, and I'd even managed to recruit a good man, Gene Abrams, as acting aid director. (ICA had nominated someone with suitable rank but unsuitable qualifications; fortunately, a friend from the campaign was in a position at ICA to cancel his appointment and assign Abrams to Guinea.) And I'd learned that you *can* get things done in Washington—if you're determined enough and prepared to resign (which is one advantage that a political appointee has over a career ambassador).

The next step was to see how Touré would react to a proposal that did not include the big dam.

Back in Conakry, where the ocean breeze was welcome after the smoke-filled conference rooms of Foggy Bottom, I got word he wanted to see me the next day. After briefing the staff, I went over to the palace, where I found Touré with Beavogui and some of his then more radical economic advisers, among these his stepbrother, Ismael Touré. Reports of a Washington news conference, at which I had rejected the then prevalent view that Touré was a sinister Communist agent, had filtered back to Conakry, and Touré greeted me warmly as *"cher ami."*

I then outlined our aid package: a dam and power station that would double Guinea's hydroelectric power; construction of six small plants for processing consumer goods; a turbine and generator to meet Conakry's power requirements; a vocational training program for Guinean workers; faculty and equipment for a public administration school; construction and staffing of a teacher-training institute; expansion of existing English-language programs and scholarships in the U.S. for Guinean students; technical assistance for increasing corn and rice production; a commodity import program whereby U.S. goods could be purchased with Guinean francs and these used to pay for local costs of aid projects; the provision of forty Peace Corps volunteers in the fields of education, health and public works.

I added that Shriver would be coming to Guinea shortly, as President Kennedy's personal representative, and the Peace Corps program could be discussed then. Meanwhile, our one condition was that we counted on Guinea's full cooperation and participation in all aspects of our program. (We also hoped that he would at least talk to World Bank officials about joining the IMF.) If the Guinean Government was agreeable, American experts would be here in the summer to make the necessary surveys so that project agreements could be signed as soon as possible.

When I was finished, Touré smiled and said, "We agree with everything." No one else had any comment. I said we'd be sending him a copy of the proposal in French.

We were now in business. But the bureaucrats and Francophiles in the department hadn't quite given up. The next day I found a telegram telling me to hold off talking to Touré until the department sampled the reactions of some of the other so-called "moderate" West African leaders. The idea was, I suppose, that we'd back off if they objected. By now it was academic; I'd had my meeting with Touré.

But I was glad when the returns finally came in. Touré's African neighbors thought a U.S. aid program in Guinea was a good idea. I heard later that a good many people in Washington were surprised. They might not have been had they spent more time talking to Africans instead of to their European counterparts.

IV

Vive le Président Kennedy!

•

Two days before Sargent Shriver landed in Conakry, Guinea's only newspaper, *Horoya,* came out with an article accusing the Peace Corps of being nothing but a front for the CIA. Not many people saw the article because the police confiscated every copy of the paper an hour after it went on sale. It was the first time I'd seen a government suppress a government-owned newspaper. But Guinea was a country where anything could happen and very often did. This was one way of telling us the welcome mat was out.

Shriver flew more than seven thousand miles round trip, just to spend two days in Conakry. He came both as Director of the Peace Corps and as the personal representative of the President of the United States. His title didn't mean as much to the Guineans as the fact that he was Kennedy's brother-in-law; family ties are all-important in Africa and a chief's relative is always more of a VIP than a Secretary of State.

Four cabinet ministers were on hand to greet him at the airport. His schedule called for lunch with Sékou Touré, afternoon visits to schools and hospitals, an outdoor reception which I was hosting and a private meeting with Touré the next day. But the schedule began snowballing halfway through lunch. After some small talk, Shriver—through an interpreter—started discussing the 1960 campaign, and Touré then told him how he had managed to win the 1958 referendum on independence. The conversation became a dialogue between two politicians talking shop, and the language barrier all but disappeared, as it usually does when professionals—

whatever their profession—get together. When we finally left to go and see the schools, Touré said, "Well, make it fast because I want you back here to meet the whole government at 5:30."

All the ministers and the top PDG officials, about twenty in all, were assembled around a big table when we returned. Shriver said a few words in French; Touré followed with a lecture on his political philosophy and Guinea's needs ("Attwood here can tell you the electric lights go out every night because we don't have enough current"); and Shriver then improvised in English, hitting all the right notes for an audience that was both curious and suspicious about Americans. He spoke with candor and sincerity —two qualities Africans especially appreciate after years of double-talk from white men. In reply to Touré's chip-on-the-shoulder remark that Guinea was a "socialist" country, he retorted that America really had the most socialistic society on earth because our workers have the world's highest standard of living and there is less class distinction than in any other country, including those who called themselves socialist. At that, the ice was broken with friendly laughter and a ripple of applause.

Shriver went on to stress the duty of the rich nations of the earth to help the poor and quoted Kennedy's inaugural speech pledging our aid to people struggling against poverty "not because the Communists may be doing it, not because we seek their votes, but because it is right." When he finished, Touré put his arm around him and announced another change in our schedule; he would be calling for us at 7 A.M. for a tour of the countryside.

My reception lasted too late—the government unexpectedly sent us a military band—and seven o'clock in Guinea is when the dawn is just breaking. But Touré's motorcade, headed by his white Cadillac convertible, appeared right on time, and we headed out of town on Guinea's one paved highway with flags flying and sirens scattering the traffic. People ran out of their round thatched huts to wave and cheer as we passed by. At every stop—we made five —local officials ceremonially met us in front of platforms festooned with palm fronds and plastic American flags (I didn't even know they had any). Crowds had been assembled in the village squares, appropriate speeches had been prepared overnight, and musicians, dancers, schoolboys and military bands were all on hand as though our visit had been arranged weeks, and not just hours, in advance.

Guinea's economy might be in a shambles, but Touré's grass-roots political organization was obviously in very good shape indeed.

By the time we reached Forécariah, a town twenty miles down a dirt road off the highway, Touré was so delighted with Shriver's ad lib remarks and shirt-sleeve platform manner (the pro admiring the pro) that he got up beside him and led the crowd in a cheer that had never before been heard in Guinea. *"Vive les États-Unis,"* he shouted, *"et vive le Président Kennedy!"*

I couldn't help thinking that we'd come a long way since his January telegram to Kennedy about Lumumba.

After a big African meal (rice, *fonio,* chicken, roast baby lamb and hot sauces), we drove home while the car radio broadcast a play-by-play report of our tour in French and four local languages. Back in Conakry, a quick meeting with three ministers at the guest house settled our Peace Corps business: Guinea would welcome some volunteers in education and public health. This was important; getting the Peace Corps accepted in a country reputed to be under Communist influence, at a time when Moscow and Peking were making a major propaganda effort to discredit it, was a breakthrough that would make it politically easier for other African countries to follow suit.

Shriver left in the evening laden with gifts after a last French-style embrace by Touré. At the airport he taped an interview which was broadcast the next day and provoked the Russians into protesting that the national airwaves were being used to disseminate American propaganda.

The Soviet squawk was conclusive and satisfying evidence that Shriver's visit had been successful. And I've described it in some detail because no report of the visit was ever printed in the American press. While the Stars and Stripes were flying in Forécariah, Guinea was being portrayed back home as a Communist police state where Americans hardly dared go out in the streets. (An Associated Press story in May, written in London under a Conakry dateline, described our embassy officers as harassed and intimidated, while *U.S. News & World Report* captioned a picture of an apartment building occupied by American, West German and British embassy personnel as being the headquarters of Guinea's Soviet overlords.)

Suspicion there was. When an American track coach arrived in June to train Guinean athletes, the airport police promptly seized his javelins because they looked like spears—and spears were weapons. Their experience with the French had conditioned Guinea's leaders to political intrigue and left them hypersensitive to "colonialist" plots. Many had also studied in France under Marxist teachers and come home with distorted views of rapacious American capitalism and hairy tales of dollar diplomacy which they passed on to their fellow Africans.

Breaking through this crust of ignorance and suspicion was a full-time job for our embassy staff. Fortunately, most educated Guineans loved to talk politics. And we were lucky to have a political officer named Phil Heller who had been a socialist and labor union organizer in the thirties and who knew Marxist jargon well enough to refute their theories in their own terms. Africans were disarmed by his diffident and unassuming manner, which they did not expect from an American, and fascinated by his gentle but incisive arguments. The fact that America had trade unions and unemployment compensation and social security, that sons of "the working class" could go to college, even that Negroes could own cars, was news to many Guineans. But once their curiosity was aroused, and so long as you heard them out patiently and without irritation, they always came back for more. I remember being cornered at a Czech party by two fiery young "intellectuals" who were so surprised I didn't walk away from their anti-American tirade that they invited themselves to dinner "to continue our discussion." Our readiness to engage in free-wheeling political debate was a big advantage we had over Communist diplomats, who didn't dare deviate from the strict party line—what George Orwell called "duckspeak."

Nor did I have the handicap of being a Negro, like my predecessor. For I soon discovered something which is still not fully appreciated in Washington—that Africans are generally suspicious of Negro American diplomats. They assume that Negroes are second-class citizens in the United States, and conclude that Washington is being deviously patronizing, and clearly race-conscious, in sending them more or less dark-skinned ambassadors. John Morrow left Guinea discouraged and frustrated, partly because he didn't get the support he needed in Washington and partly because Guineans (as they told me later) distrusted him. After Morrow left, Touré (the grandson of a chief who fought the French) went so far as to tell a Western diplomat that he was glad Kennedy wasn't sending another Negro to Guinea, and added: "What makes the Americans think we care for these sons of slaves?"

We did have a Negro Public Affairs Officer—which was all right. Africans can understand a Negro serving in the U.S. Government, and in fact are favorably impressed to see Americans of both races working side by side; what bothers them, because they sense it is artificial, is having Negroes appointed to top jobs in Africa unless the latter have special qualifications.

Wil Petty, our PAO, was effective and energetic. A former army officer, artist and journalist, he was good at dispelling myths about race relations back home. But he was handicapped by the fact that our USIS library was shut down by the government on the ground that a sovereign country (that didn't have a good library of its own) couldn't allow "foreign cultural centers" to operate on its soil. The Communists got around the ban by subsidizing a local bookstore called the "Librairie Africaine" whose shelves and tables were stacked with cheap editions of voluminous works by Lenin and Mao Tse-tung and magazines featuring happy North Korean cover girls driving tractors. We held onto our USIS office—a big store front on the Avenue de la République—because we could still use it for English-language classes and photographic displays of life in America.

Movies were of course more effective than still pictures. With our Fourth of July reception coming up, I asked Petty to find a good short film about the United States that we could show to what would be a captive audience of guests. Since there was nothing suitable in his film library, he queried Washington. Two weeks later, a can of film arrived in the diplomatic pouch. It turned out to be *The Life of Theodore Roosevelt,* produced in 1958 by the Department of Defense, and replete with still pictures of San Juan Hill (sure to evoke memories of the Bay of Pigs) and Teddy in a colonial pith helmet leading overburdened black porters through the African bush. It was hard to conceive of anything less appropriate, but the fact was that the U.S. Government in 1961 did not have a single film in French showing the exciting diversity of our land and our people.

THE REDS AND THE BLACKS

Luckily, a short French-dubbed color film of the inauguration arrived by chance on July 2, so we made out all right. Kennedy's reminder that "Those who foolishly sought power by riding the back of the tiger ended up inside" was not lost on our Guinean guests.

While I was getting acquainted with Guinea's educated elite, Sim was meeting more of the people who didn't read or write or care about the kind of politics that was unrelated to their everyday lives. Whenever our servants' children got boils or stomach-aches or infected cuts, she would visit their homes with our first-aid kit and soon find herself treating their neighbors' kids too. Doctors and medicines were scarce, and Conakry's two hospitals over-crowded with emergency cases, so her services were pathetically appreciated. Shy young mothers and round-eyed children would emerge from their huts, cluster around her in the dusty courtyards, waiting for a swab of disinfectant or a Vioform tablet. At first the children screamed—they'd never been close to anybody whose skin wasn't dark brown—but they soon got used to her. And the gratitude and simple courtesy of their parents, unaccustomed as they were to a "European" in their midst, were something we would remember long after we left Guinea.

These visits to what used to be called the "native quarter" also taught us something about West African society. Like most new-comers to this part of the world, we were often tempted to com-plain about or even ridicule the indolence and maddening ineffi-ciency of most Africans. But after a while you begin to appreciate the effect on people of a tropical climate, chronic malnutrition and endemic diseases. Most children in Guinea die before they are ten; the strength of the survivors is constantly sapped by protein and vitamin deficiency, yaws, malaria, dysentery and heat—just as the strength of West Africa's once flourishing kingdoms was sapped for centuries by the slave trade. The wonder is that people got any work done at all.

Nor should we disparage African society as primitive without noting—as we did in Conakry—that, poor as they are, Africans share what they have. No visiting friend or relative (and all tribal clansmen are "brothers" or "sisters") is ever turned away from the family cook pot. A child whose parents die is immediately absorbed into another family; orphanages are unknown. In short, an African has a sense of belonging to a communal society in which there are no outcasts—and no juvenile delinquents. Maybe this is primitive, and maybe we've got something to learn too.

Of course, urbanization and supratribal nationalism are inevitably loosening the tribal ties which up to now have been the cement of African society. Knowing this, Touré was deliberately building his national political party, the PDG, from a grass-roots base in the hope that the next generation would be able to transfer its former tribal allegiance and sense of communality to the nation as a whole.

In our wanderings around the town we also found more stoicism than grumbling about Guinea's run-down economy and shortages of consumer goods. Africans can put up with a lot of privation when they have something to eat and the sun is shining and there are tom-toms and *balafons* to dance to on Saturday nights. But we discovered there was a limit even to their patience when the East German loudspeakers that had been erected on every street corner were switched on, shattering the quiet with Cuban music and political oratory. Even government officials couldn't put up with the din. After two days, the noise was silenced for good, and Guinea was left with a $100,000 bill for the PA system—to be paid for in agricultural exports. (By way of contrast, the West Germans had, for half the price, built a small but efficient fish-smoking plant for Conakry that was the talk of the town and was more than paying for itself.)

We saw another and more dramatic example of the efficacy of Western methods when we drove upcountry to the FRIA alumina factory. After jouncing ninety miles over dirt roads through the sparsely settled bush, we rounded a bend and saw what seemed like a mirage—ten-story apartment houses, suburban villas, a hospital (and even a country club) surrounding a complex of quarries and processing plants. In this man-made oasis, more than four hundred French engineers, some with families, along with a nine-hundred-man African labor force, were living and working and producing half a million tons of alumina a year. Two-thirds of the proceeds covered the operating and amortization costs; the other third, about $10 million a year, provided the Guinean Government with its principal source of foreign exchange and a measure of financial independence from its barter agreements with the Soviet bloc. For Guinea, FRIA was a visible (and profitable) symbol of the efficiency of cooperative capitalism. The French plant manager told me some local politicians and union leaders now and then tried to give him a hard time; but the African workers liked their wages, housing, medical care and vocational training programs, and the government liked its foreign exchange too well to risk destroying a going concern by nationalizing it. "They talk a lot about socialism," he said, "but what they really want is something that works. And FRIA works."

The rains started in June, hard, drenching downpours that lasted four or five days at a time and turned the ocean brown with silt. They would continue into September; during this time there wasn't much for our staff to do outside of office hours. The two-court tennis club closed down; inland roads became impassable; the ancient ferry that plied between the port and the offshore island beaches developed engine trouble; even bridge games were interrupted by gusts of rain whipping into our windowpaneless living rooms. At least I had returned from Washington with a cola machine for the embassy and a promise that we'd receive an occasional film through the Armed Services Motion Picture Service; also, we had broken the customs bottleneck and were moving stuff through the port over my signature. And you'd be surprised what a cola machine, a few crates of canned groceries and the mere prospect of a movie can do for morale at a place without any of the commissaries, Post Exchanges, golf courses, recreation centers and night clubs of the American installations you see in Europe.

The rainy season did not discourage visitors. Twenty soaked and bedraggled American college students appeared at the embassy one day in a Guinean Army Russian truck. They were Operation Crossroads volunteers, here to complete construction of a social center in Mamou, one hundred miles inland, that a similar group had begun and left unfinished during the last rainy season. The Guinean Ministry of Youth, Sports and Culture had forgotten they were coming but managed to provide them with a truck and an empty two-room house. The students, especially the girls, were determined to push on to Mamou, but the Guineans were equally determined to give them the Visiting Youth Delegation treatment

—for which the ministry's personnel had been trained by its Soviet advisers. I finally persuaded the Crossroaders to work out a compromise—three weeks on the road exchanging handshakes and bouquets with local youth groups, and three weeks with the shovels and mortar at Mamou. This was done: a few rows of cement blocks were added to the building (I don't think it was ever finished), and a few more Guineans were exposed to the unexpected (to them) sight of white and Negro Americans working together. And, of course, the boys and girls learned something about Africa.

We also got used to unlikely visitors appearing at our house at unlikely hours. One night, a weather-beaten old American engineer in wrinkled chinos drove up in a cab; he had flown in from Bamako without a visa or a hotel reservation, talked his way past the airport police and now needed a bed. Early one morning, another American, young, bearded, sandaled and unwashed, was deposited on our doorstep by two embarrassed policemen; he was a hitchhiker doing Africa on two dollars a day and had asked for a night's lodging in the Conakry jail. Another time, Ruth Shachter, a visiting African scholar from Boston University, was carried in by two Africans after collapsing with a sudden fever at the airport. We put her up for a few days in the room with the groceries (sudden fevers happened all the time in Guinea, and the one doctor had no time for anything so minor), along with two embassy clerks who had just come down with hepatitis. Luckily, we'd sent our kids off to summer camp in Switzerland.

Meanwhile, our aid program had run into the opposition of certain cabinet ministers still under Communist influence. The Russians were lobbying against a larger American presence in Guinea and warning their contacts in the government to beware of aid "with strings" from imperialist America. We had anticipated these arguments in private conversation with Guineans by pointing out that we obviously weren't giving them something for nothing— that helping Guinea achieve political and economic stability had indirect benefits for us and the world, and that a prosperous Guinea could in turn help its less fortunate neighbors, thus taking some of the load from us. All this appealed to their pride and allayed some suspicions, but we were still competing with adversaries who had set aside nearly $100 million for subverting Guinea and weren't going to write it off without a fight. Soviet influence was spreading, especially among students and trade unionists, and I knew from what I'd seen in Eastern Europe how rough they could play it when they were challenged on what they regarded as their own turf.

Touré had appointed a commission, headed by Ismael, to go over our proposals in more detail. In mid-July, Ross and I met him and two other ministers to discuss our aid package. Ismael Touré was bright, disciplined and articulate; he had an engineering degree from the University of Dakar. But the Russians—perhaps because they saw his potential—had been cultivating him assiduously and with some success. He seemed ill at ease with us.

I decided not to mince words. An article had just appeared in *Horoya* attacking U.S. aid as a Trojan horse for American imperialism. I asked him if this article, in the official party newspaper, reflected the views of the government; if so, there was nothing for us to discuss—we weren't helping anybody who didn't want us around.

Ismael assured me *Horoya* didn't speak for the government and blamed the article on certain "young men" on the staff. He said they liked our aid package, except for the small dam. He hinted that a Russian offer to build the big one was imminent but said they would prefer the West to undertake it.

I said that I doubted very much the Russians would want to spend that much money in Guinea and asked him why he supposed they were so anxious to "help."

"Because they want to strengthen our independence and reinforce our neutralism," he replied.

I suggested they be careful, casually mentioning that "neutralists" like Nagy in Hungary, Masaryk in Czechoslovakia and Cienfuegos in Cuba had all been murdered when they balked at carrying out the Kremlin's instructions.

No one took offense. Ismael just remarked that the government would deal firmly with anyone who tried to undermine Guinea's sovereignty. He even reassured me that a PDG delegation was going to the Russian Communist Party Congress as a "courtesy visit"—nothing more. I told him I would query Washington about the dam, and was glad when the reply came through to drop the dam and go ahead with the rest of cheaper and more practical aid projects. If nothing else, we had made the point that we were not all that eager to come into Guinea and could not be blackmailed into building a dam by threats that the Russians might.

Soon after my talk with Ismael, Sim and I went down the coast to Lagos for an African chiefs of mission conference. We flew to Accra and drove down the rest of the way—across Togo and Dahomey to Nigeria—with our Ambassador to Ghana, Francis Russell, and his wife. The roads were good, the Hotel Benin in Togo luxurious, and the scenery picture-book African—coconut palms, grass huts, outdoor markets. But every couple of hours we ran into a frontier where Africans with British swagger sticks or French *kepis*—depending on the country—studied our passports with the dutiful concentration of bibliophiles examining first editions. These frontier posts—eight in one day's drive—dramatized the colonial Balkanization of Africa, in which lines drawn on a map made no sense in terms of ethnic divisions or economic viability. (Bad international communications were another awkward legacy of colonialism. Neither the French nor the British bothered to develop a road network linking their adjacent colonies, and as late as 1963 the only way you could phone Freetown from Conakry, a distance of eighty miles, was via Paris and London.)

We reached Lagos in the evening, after being pushed and pulled through a flash flood by the obliging inhabitants of a roadside village. After driving through miles of suburban shantytowns, the Federal Palace Hotel, facing the bay, looked inviting as a conference site.

Bowles headed the team of Washington officials and presided at the plenary meetings. His speech at the opening session emphasized the importance of Africa (good news to ambassadors who had been wondering why they'd been banished to places like Ouagadougou and Bangui); and he restated, in eloquent terms, our new policy of supporting and influencing change, rather than resisting it, all over the world. Even the old pros among the fifty-odd mission chiefs and their deputies around the room were impressed and inspired.

All conferences are at least 50 percent a waste of time, and this one was no exception. Speeches ran on and on. The ICA and CU

(Cultural Affairs) people were the worst offenders because of their infatuation with bureaucratese. After one barely intelligible lecture, three of us composed some new lyrics for the national anthem, the first stanza of which went: "O say can C.U./In the FY's ahead/Give us guidelines we need/To establish criteria."

Useless papers and documents proliferated and kept the mimeographers busy. One of my favorite (unclassified) items was entitled "Program Planning"; its second paragraph read as follows:

2. *Study Program Guidance*
   A. Determine that country program plans have been developed giving full consideration to:
      (1) Basic guidelines and assumptions covering overall U.S. program policy.
      (2) Realistic program data and program projections.

But the conference did give us a chance, between formal sessions, to get acquainted and compare notes. The caliber of the State Department participants was high, and I was impressed by the younger Foreign Service officers, like Leon Poullada from Togo and Arch Calhoun from Chad, who had just been made ambassadors in spite of the seniority system. We had the makings of a good team in Africa.

And we found ourselves in general agreement that our African clients were becoming more pragmatic; with few exceptions, everyone reported that the stated priorities in their countries were no longer the impractical symbols of sovereignty proclaimed four years before—the steel mills and the global airlines—but education, rural development, communications and light industry. The hotheaded preindependence nationalist leaders, now in power, were coming down to earth.

And we also agreed that U.S. aid in these fields was essential if we were expected to exercise any constructive leverage on the political leadership of a continent that would be in revolution for a long time to come. (As someone remarked, if you put any American in an African situation, living like an African in the modern world, you'd turn him into a flaming revolutionary.) There was no point in making enemies of the angry young men now at the top; preventing Soviet and Chinese imperialism from gaining a foothold in Africa was an important part of our job, and we should not be diverted into taking sides between "moderate" and "radical" nationalists. The danger was that the radical nationalists would be unable or unwilling, because of ignorance or inexperience, to stand up to Communist subversion until it was too late.

In a final report to the President summing up our collective views, we stressed the importance of taking a clear-cut position on Portuguese colonialism and South African racism. (The only dissenting opinions came from our consuls in Angola and Mozambique, who supported Portugal's colonial policies; but they were about to be transferred.) For it was clear that African nationalism would tend to be radical and emotional so long as Africans were deprived of basic human rights anywhere on their continent, and that the West would suffer in the long run from its identification with the master-racists of southern Africa.

The heart of the matter was that the South Africans and Portuguese were not only morally wrong but, in the long run, on the losing side. As one chief of mission observed, "You can stand up for principles and disregard the course of history, and you may win. Or you can disregard principles and go with the course of history, and you may win. But if you disregard both principles and the course of history, you are bound to lose."

We were all tired on the long drive back, this time on past Accra to Kumasi through the dense and towering rain forest and across the Ivory Coast border down to Abidjan. I developed a chronic headache on the trip and felt feverish when we finally flew back to Conakry. The local French doctor diagnosed it as a touch of malaria. Before going home to bed, I remember dictating a letter to the President about some things I'd learned in Africa these past three months. Weak as I felt leaving the office, I didn't figure I'd be away from my desk very long. Malaria was a common and transient ailment in West Africa. But within two days I could no longer walk or even sit up. An ambulance took me to the airport, and I was carried aboard an Air France DC-4 like a side of beef. Three hours later, at the French military hospital in Dakar, the doctors changed the diagnosis to polio.

V

Mr. Solod Goes Home

•

At the risk of sounding like the *Reader's Digest* ("Be Glad You Had Polio"), I have to admit there are certain advantages to being hospitalized. You get a chance to read the kind of books you normally never have time for, you can talk to friends, and you can even think.

In Bethesda Naval Hospital, where I spent more than two months in a room on the sixteenth floor, there was plenty of time for thinking. Polio is a disease that induces thought if only because you never know how crippled it will leave you, and you find yourself making contingency plans for different kinds of lives. I could neither sit up nor roll over when I arrived, and my left leg was as useless as a strand of spaghetti. The doctors were pessimistic, but the therapists—sympathetic young navy corpsmen—cheered me on as I struggled with weights and harnesses, and rejoiced with me as paralyzed muscles began to move and as I slowly graduated from stretcher to wheelchair and from crutches to cane.

You also find out who your best friends are when you're really sick. There are those who write and others who don't bother; and there are those who come to the hospital, week after week, tired as they are after a long day at the office. The friends who cheered me most, of course, were the ones, like Ben Bradlee, Tom Sorensen and Fletcher Knebel, who had had polio and recovered. For what you need most is reassurance that the daily agony of physiotherapy will make you well again.

And you develop a certain intolerance about other people's troubles. Lying helpless in a bed (or forgotten in a bathtub with the bell out of reach), you can't help feeling that anybody who can get up from a chair and walk across the room hasn't a thing to complain about.

In the evenings, after Sim had gone, young navy doctors, interns and nurses would come in to talk or play chess. They were curious about Africa and their questions were what I expected: Did we live in a house or a hut? Weren't we afraid of cannibals? How did we keep the wild animals away at night? Some of the doctors also asked me about Britain's national health service, fearful that "socialized medicine" would spread to our country and ruin medical standards and the doctor-patient relationship. When I pointed out that in Bethesda I was getting the best care I'd ever received and that our relationship was just fine, even though I wasn't paying any bills for it, they were always stumped for an answer.

My floor (they called it a deck) was reserved for the brass. As an ambassador, I ranked as a rear admiral in the building (ship), and my neighbors were mostly Senators and Congressmen. Talking to them, especially the Republicans, I was surprised by how readily they accepted our responsibility to lend a helping hand to people who needed schools and medicines and technical advice. They approved of what I told them we were trying to do in Guinea. Yet most of those I met voted regularly against foreign aid bills because they believed the money was being wasted in handouts to corrupt and grasping politicians. I could only conclude that government agencies like ICA (now AID) are unable to state their case in terms of human needs which Congressmen can in turn explain to their constituents. This failure was, and still is, inexcusable—and incomprehensible.

At the end of October I was well enough to become an outpatient. Sim and I moved into John Lindsay's house in Georgetown, returning to the hospital every morning for therapy; in the afternoon she helped me make my way around the block on crutches. My first solo outing was going to a White House lunch in honor of President Leopold Senghor of Senegal. Kennedy was in good form, remarking, in a toast, that Montesquieu had stressed the importance of the legislative branch controlling the executive and that the French hadn't followed his advice, while we seemed to be following it too much. Later, I was able to tell him that the doctors had agreed I could return to Guinea in December.

It didn't seem possible that only a year had gone by since election night.

By mid-November I was getting around with just a cane and agreed to speak to the Princeton Club of Washington about African neutralism. In talking with my hospital visitors, I'd come to feel that one reason we Americans had a hard time understanding what was going on in Africa was that we weren't able to relate that revolution to our own national experience. Yet there were similarities worth noting, and I decided to make these the theme of my speech.

Being Washingtonians, most of my audience had had opportunities to meet some of the new African diplomats at official receptions. So I read them this quotation:

He leaves his country with a heart swollen with pride; on arriving here, he at once finds we are not so engrossed by his country and the great people who inhabit it as he had supposed, and this begins to annoy him. . . . He is afraid of ranking himself too high; still more is afraid of being ranked too low . . . he is like a man beset by traps; society is not a recreation for him but a serious toil; he weighs your least actions, interrogates your looks, and scrutinizes what you say lest there should be some hidden allusion to affront him. . . . he is full of scruples and at the same time of pretensions; he wishes to do enough but fears to do too much, and as he does not know very well the limits of the one or the other, he keeps up a haughty and embarrassed air of reserve.

The author of this quotation was not describing an African in 1961 Washington; the author, Alexis de Tocqueville, was writing about Americans in Europe in the 1830's.

Let me quote a few more paragraphs from the rest of this speech:

We start out with a big potential advantage in Africa. And we have actual advantages as well, such as the fact that Africa is not only geographically closer to the West than to the East but culturally more intimately identified with the West. Most of the leaders of Africa today speak French and English, not Russian or Chinese. Our problem now is how to convince them that their interests and ours coincide and that it is to their advantage to cooperate with us rather than with the Soviets.

I think we must begin by displaying patience and understanding as well as firmness. For we are dealing with the teen-agers of the family of nations, and, like most teen-agers, these young nations are sometimes high-strung, unpredictable and exasperating. Condemning them, lecturing them or scolding them can often do more harm than good. Our first step should be to try to understand them, to put ourselves in their shoes. And I suggest we can do this best by first looking back to our own past, to our own youth, as a nation.

For example, we are often inclined to criticize the neutrals for being radicals in a world where we would prefer political stability. Yet it is not much more than a century ago that we were considered radicals, the angry young men of the world community. This is what Prince Metternich once had to say about Americans:

> In fostering revolutions wherever they show themselves, in regretting those that have failed, in extending a helping hand to those which seem to prosper, the Americans lend new strength to the apostles of sedition and reanimate the courage of every conspirator.

We also criticize the neutrals because they seem unwilling to line up with us against the tyrants of our century. Yet, soon after we became independent, the most dangerous tyrant at large in Europe was Napoleon, and I doubt very much whether the British could have succeeded in enlisting us in any crusade against him.

We criticize them for accepting Soviet aid and Soviet technicians. But many of these new countries are in a desperate economic plight, and if help is not forthcoming from the West, we should not blame them for accepting it from the East. Let's not forget that when we were fighting for our independence as a revolutionary young democracy, we had no compunction about accepting military assistance from Louis XVI.

We sometimes criticize them for refusing to choose sides in the cold war and for equating our minor faults with Communism's major sins. Yet let's not forget that neutrality was basic to our foreign policy right up to 1939. This was so because all during the nineteenth century we were less concerned with the quarrels and concerns of the outside world than we were with developing our resources, exploring our continent and building up our nation.

We are also inclined to criticize the neutralists—and particularly the Africans—for immaturity, implying that they do not seem ready for self-government. The violence in the Congo has shocked many Americans. Yet we should remember that our Civil War was one of the bloodiest in history and was waged in part for the same reason that underlies the fighting in the Congo—to decide whether a nation is to remain united or whether a part of the nation has a right to secede. And let us also bear in mind that the violence which makes headlines in our newspapers is not typical of Africa as a whole and that in six years 165 million people have made the transition to independence with less bloodshed than takes place annually on American highways.

We are sometimes critical of certain nations because they do not show proper gratitude for the aid we give them and for the fact that American power remains their chief protection against Communist domination. We should remember that back in the nineteenth century we gave little if any thanks to England for the British loans that built our railroads and for protecting our hemisphere against possible intervention by other countries. We proclaimed the Monroe Doctrine, but it was the British fleet which made it effective. The British protected us much as we protect the neutrals today, but they expected no gratitude, and got none. In fact, during most of the nineteenth century it was good politics for an American running for office to twist the lion's tail.

So I suggest that we be as mature today in dealing with the neutralists of the twentieth century as the British were in dealing with us.

In return for our help and our protection we should ask only that they assert their independence in the face of Soviet imperialism. At the moment, of course, many of the young leaders of these new countries are still too preoccupied with the vestiges and the memory of Western imperialism to recognize the menace of the new imperialism from the East. That is why the crisis in Berlin seems as remote to them as Waterloo seemed remote to us 150 years ago. But in time and with patience we can help them see the world as it is and where the danger lies.

I didn't know it at the time, but as I was speaking in Washington, Guinea was in the process of finding out just where the danger was lying. The consequences were to be dramatic.

For some time, discontent had been growing among Guinea's self-styled "intellectuals"—teachers, certain trade union leaders and students who had returned from France and the Communist countries. They resented the power and relative affluence of the political "in" group, some of whom lacked formal education. (The Minister of Social Affairs, a woman, could neither read nor write, though she could deliver a good speech.) Moreover, many of the intellectuals had been deeply influenced by Communist theories and blamed Guinea's economic plight on the fact that a true "socialist" state had not yet come into being. They saw themselves as an elite who could, if given a chance, transform Guinea into a model of state-controlled efficiency.

In this they were discreetly—and, as it turned out, not so discreetly—encouraged by Soviet bloc diplomats at whose homes they were given a sympathetic hearing and tactical advice. Like missionaries, the Communists could not pass up any opportunity to promote their gospel or to cultivate likely converts. Moreover, they were becoming somewhat disenchanted by Touré's heretical brand of socialism, by his repeated references to Guinea's "positive neutrality" and, more recently, by his flagrant (to them) overtures to the United States. For a recipient of the Lenin Peace Prize, he was getting pretty far out of line, and they were beginning to foresee the time, if alternate leadership could meanwhile be developed, when he might in fact become expendable.

In November some of the more impatient intellectuals and trade union leaders issued a manifesto critical of the government. They were dismissed and arrested after a free-for-all in which students demonstrating on their behalf clashed with the police; several were shot in the melee, the Conakry High School was shut down and strict censorship imposed.

In the investigation that followed, the Ministry of Internal Security discovered evidence that the ringleaders had been in contact with the Soviet and Czech embassies. The dilemma now confronting Touré and his entourage was what to do about it. Guinea's economy had become heavily dependent on the Soviet bloc, and a good deal of its administrative machinery was kept creaking along, after a fashion, by Communist advisers. A break with the Soviet bloc now might have consequences similar to Guinea's break with France in 1958. On the other hand, a foreign "plot" was always a useful device, politically, to get the people diverted from their economic plight.

Just about the last thing Guinea's leaders wanted, while they wrestled with their problem, was to have the U.S. Navy in town. Thus, in November, when two American naval vessels suddenly but innocently appeared in port on a prearranged goodwill visit—the crews all set to play basketball and hand out ball-point pens—the reception they got was on the frosty side. The visit was cut short, and the commander no doubt reported to his superiors that the natives in this corner of Africa appeared hostile. Actually, the natives were in a sweat.

The news from Guinea made me impatient to get back. The hospital finally discharged me on December 8 with a couple of hundred pounds of weights for systematic daily exercising (this I'd be doing for another year). And Sim and I persuaded George Ball and Adlai Stevenson, who were concerned about my hobbling back to the bush, that Conakry, with no stairs to climb, no long corridors to navigate and year-round swimming, was as good a place as any in which to convalesce.

So we flew to Dakar on December 12, missed the connection to Conakry and chartered an air taxi in order to get there in time to meet Luther Hodges, the Secretary of Commerce, who was passing through town. I met him in the evening at the VIP guest house with a group of ministers. All seemed glad to see me up and around—and back. (Two of them had come to Bethesda when I was flat on my back and told me they never expected to see me in Conakry again.) We talked about FRIA's problems—the Guineans wanted a slightly larger share of the proceeds—and Hodges had a letter for Touré from the President. But the Guineans, though cordial, appeared nervous and distracted. Touré sent word he could not receive us at the palace but would come over. We waited for an hour, but he didn't show up until after we had left for dinner. The tension was almost palpable; I felt as though I were at the house of a couple who were about to get divorced, the husband drinking heavily and the guests making small talk and wondering if there'd be a scene.

Tension was high in the town too. The police sentries stationed at embassy residences were suddenly removed and sent to guard the homes of government officials. Diplomats were forbidden to leave the city limits or to invite government officials to their homes without permission from the Foreign Ministry. Rumors were more extravagant than usual. At a reception at the palace on December 14, I ran into Seydou Conté, Guinea's new Ambassador in Washington. A quick-witted, French-educated surgeon, he had been one of Guinea's most outspoken pro-Communists until Touré sent him as his envoy to Moscow; nearly two years in Russia had cured him; the reality he saw was different from the theory he'd been taught in Paris. I asked him if the current rumor—that Ambassador Solod was being kicked out—was true. I had noted that Solod was not present at the reception.

Conté grinned. "That may be putting it a little strongly," he said. "I believe there's a more diplomatic phrase."

Solod boarded a plane to Moscow the next day. There was no public announcement, but the grapevine spread the news just as if there had been.

I called the palace right away and got an appointment with Touré for the eighteenth. I asked Gene Abrams, who had been setting up an AID office, to come along.

Touré met us in his outer office, alone, and we sat down in the shabby, plastic-covered chairs. He asked about my leg—it had taken me a while to negotiate the stairs—and I asked him if he was getting any water out of his faucet yet. He wasn't. Abrams then explained that our aid program was snarled in local red tape, with various ministers competing with each other for the projects. We cited the relative magnitude of our aid package—about $9 million in loans and grants—and suggested he appoint an aid coordinator to work with us with full authority to carry out the program. Touré agreed (I doubt if he had fully appreciated what we were prepared to do) and proposed Alassane Diop, one of the most capable men in the cabinet, to act as coordinator.

Abrams and I did most of the talking; Touré merely listened and nodded. He appeared somber and darkly brooding. Finally I alluded to his "difficulties" with the Soviet bloc and asked about Solod. "All I can tell you," he replied, "is that we caught him red-handed."

"Well," I said, "if they start putting the squeeze on you now, call me up. I can't promise anything, but we'll do what we can to help you out."

Touré smiled for the first time. When we got up to leave, he said, "I may be calling you."

I made this offer on my own, knowing that Washington would have approved, but also would have been bureaucratically unable to get the approval to me in time had I requested it. I figured it might strengthen Touré's hand with those of his associates who opposed, or feared, a showdown with the Soviets. And it may have. A week later, addressing the annual PDG Congress, Touré for the first time directly and angrily accused "Eastern embassies" of being implicated in a plot to overthrow his government.

Christmas in Conakry was a far cry from our last Christmas in Connecticut. We found a sprig of something that looked like hemlock, trimmed it with red ribbon and invited the Egyptian Ambassador, a bachelor, and the Yugoslav Ambassador, whose family had gone home sick, over to dinner along with two embassy secretaries. We sat on the terrace, grateful for the evening breeze, while the children opened their presents and a group of wandering minstrels —consisting mostly of drunken Ghanaian fishermen beating tin cans and tom-toms—serenaded us with their versions of old English carols.

Ilija Topaloski, the Yugoslav, thought there was a good deal more to the "plot" than had surfaced. He said that Solod—whom I had never met, since he was on leave before I was taken sick—had been too sure of himself; like De Gaulle in 1958, the Russians overestimated their popularity—perhaps they were both deceived by the cheering crowds mobilized by the PDG for all visiting dignitaries—and they had underestimated Touré's determination to run his own show.

Topaloski also disclosed that the Guineans had accepted a Yugoslav offer to add a turbine to Conakry's hydroelectric plant just a few weeks before accepting ours. I told him we'd therefore withdraw our offer and use the money for something else; it would be useful for the Guineans to find out we weren't competing to do them favors. Topaloski was pleased. The Yugoslavs weren't doing much in Guinea, but what they were providing was practical and productive: small brick and furniture factories, assistance in town planning, doctors to staff the hospitals. In return for their assistance they hoped to win support for Tito's "Third Force" neutralist bloc, but this posed no threat to Guinea's independence nor to our own national interests.

And the need for practical assistance was becoming ever more apparent. Food shortages in the city were frequent as produce trucks broke down for lack of maintenance. Not only did the lights go out every evening as the circuits got overloaded, but the phones, always erratic, now stopped working altogether. We heard that a bulldozer had inadvertently severed the underground cables since no one knew exactly where the cables were (the French had walked off with the charts in 1958).

Meanwhile, as if nothing had happened, a Soviet trade exhibition was being erected on the fair grounds. It was to be formally opened on January 6, and a high-powered Soviet delegation, headed by Anastas Mikoyan, arrived the day before—ostensibly for the fair but actually to patch up relations. There was none of the usual fanfare; in fact, the arrival of Ed Murrow, then USIA Director, the day before got bigger play on the radio. Touré refused to receive Mikoyan. He joined him on the rostrum for the ceremony at the fair site, to which the Diplomatic Corps was also invited. Mikoyan spoke first; as we heard his speech being translated into French, it was obvious he had been badly briefed about African sensibilities. He bragged about the achievements of Communism, violently attacked the West in general and France in particular—over Algeria (the French Ambassador got up and walked out)—and bluntly told the Guineans that they had better adopt the Communist system and cooperate with the Soviet Union if they wanted to get anywhere.

This heavy-handed attempt to drag "nonaligned" Guinea into the cold war could not have been more ill-timed. While Mikoyan was speaking, we could see Touré crossing out parts of his prepared text—they were the ones saying nice things about Russia. When his turn came, he replied courteously, but briefly, and pointedly reminded the Russians that "revolutions can neither be imported nor exported." As for Guinea's domestic policies, he said these would be "socialist only as they correspond to our special conditions."

The exhibition was as big a fiasco as the ceremony. On display were quantities of unidentified heavy machinery, furs, vodka, alarm clocks, toilet articles (including contraceptives) and even travel brochures in English about motoring in the Soviet Union. None of the stuff on display was for sale, and the Russian attendants, who spoke no French, couldn't explain why to their visitors. Walking around, Murrow compared it to a party where the host tries to impress his guests by taking everything out of his attic, closets, bathroom and bureau drawers and dumping it on the living room rug.

Touré finally received Mikoyan and complained about the quality of Soviet bloc aid, citing the East German loudspeakers and abandoned outdoor theater (Mikoyan later chewed out the East Germans). Touré was also annoyed by Soviet barter practices; he had found out from President Nasser that the Russians were sending Guinea marked-up Egyptian textiles which they had obtained in exchange for arms delivered to Cairo. He did agree to accept a new Soviet Ambassador, a short, squat economist named Dmitri Degtyar who came along with Mikoyan, but later kept him waiting seven weeks before letting him present his credentials. Degtyar's appointment—he spoke no French and had never been an ambassador—was a sign that the Russians had slowed their political offensive in Guinea for the time being and were now more concerned with salvaging what they could from their abortive aid commitments.

Mikoyan left after a reception at the palace where he was subjected to nearly four hours of Guinean drumming and dances. Murrow, who came along with us, called it "Sékou's revenge."

By the spring of 1962 the political atmosphere in Conakry was far different from what it had been a few months before. Ministers known for their pro-Western sympathies no longer hesitated to be seen with us. Radio programs were blandly neutral. The Communist bookstore went out of business. Even some French Communist teachers who had stayed on after independence began drifting away, complaining that Touré had become a fascist. And the May Day film show featured a West German documentary instead of Soviet propaganda. (There were also a couple of shorts about the opening of the Soviet radio station and the East German printing plant, but the Guinean narrator omitted mentioning who had built them.)

It had been an interesting year. Ben Bradlee told me later that Kennedy had jokingly remarked that it was too bad I hadn't gotten back to Guinea before Solod was expelled—so that I could have claimed credit for it. I did get back, three days before, but if anybody deserved the lion's share of the credit for what happened to the Russians, it was the Russians themselves.

Let's pause in our narrative and examine the reasons. For those Americans who think we make all the mistakes, the next chapter may come as a surprise.

VI

Malice in Blunderland

•

Whenever I run into somebody who's heard about Guinea
—which is not very often—I am almost sure to be asked about
Russian snowplows. The snowplow story originated in 1961 when
an observant reporter saw some mechanized brush cutters being
unloaded from a Soviet freighter in Conakry; the driver's cabin was
glassed in and heated, and they looked like—well, snowplows. The
story had that iceboxes-for-the-Eskimos twist that was irresistible
to anybody writing about Guinea ever after. Even if it wasn't quite
true, it symbolized, in a small but vivid way, the sort of things the
Soviet bloc was doing on a big scale.

Similarly, Ambassador Solod's expulsion was the kind of story
which echoed all over Africa. The fact that Sékou Touré, of all
people, should take such drastic and unprecedented action convinced a good many African leaders that the charges of subversion
were even graver than alleged and that the Russians were indeed
people to beware of. It was the kind of story that, like the snowplows, got wide circulation without being fully understood or appreciated.

The events of December, 1961, resulted from a combination of
several factors: Soviet overconfidence—Moscow figured the Guineans hated the West for what had happened in 1958 and would
wholeheartedly and naïvely embrace their saviors from the East;
Soviet inexperience—Russians and East Europeans weren't used
to dealing with people who had little or no understanding of economics, technology or even of the importance of being punctual;
Soviet cupidity—they couldn't resist unloading cheap goods on the

"natives" in return for some products they could resell for hard cash; African suspicion and shrewdness—they'd been fooled by white men before and were on their guard; African inefficiency—which is difficult to exaggerate; and finally, the readiness of the United States and West Germany, in particular, to be helpful in practical ways—which encouraged the serious Guineans, who did not want a break with the West, to assert themselves.

The Soviet thrust in Guinea followed the French pull-out. The Russians knew what they wanted in Guinea: an African Communist showcase, which would hopefully induce certain African leaders to follow Guinea's example, and a base of operations against those leaders who remained, in their lexicon, neo-colonialist puppets. To achieve their objective they offered the Guineans the kind of things that would both cater to their desire for the trappings of sovereignty and also serve wider Soviet purposes. Thus by 1961 Conakry was swarming with Soviet bloc technicians and engineers occupied with building a Polytechnic Institute for sixteen hundred students (though there were not more than fifty Guineans qualified to attend); a printing plant that eventually operated at less than 5 percent of capacity; a 100-kw radio station for external transmission (which never worked properly since it was erected over a vein of iron ore); a million-dollar outdoor theater (half-completed and abandoned); the city-wide PA system (switched off); a sea-front hotel (still under construction three years after ground-breaking); a 25,000-seat sports stadium (for a city of 100,000 people); and a national airline equipped with nine Ilyushins (usually grounded), pilots who couldn't speak French and sophisticated radar equipment (there were no fogs) that slowly deteriorated in the damp heat.

The Guineans, meeting Santa Claus for the first time, accepted everything he brought in his bag. The presents looked so dazzling that no one paused to consider whether Guinea needed them or could afford them. For their part, the Soviets paid scant attention to cost factors or feasibility surveys; gaining a foothold was the objective, and politicians, not accountants, were calling the shots. If the Guineans asked for something, the standing instructions evidently were: Give it to them. So the Russians often plunged into projects that fizzled out but still cost money—such as an unsuccessful experimental rice plantation ($4 million) and a railroad survey (nearly $1 million) which only proved the unadaptability of Russian rolling stock to Guinean track beds. A Soviet tomato cannery up in Mamou was constructed without regard to the absence of tomatoes ⌐r water in the area. A Czech-built shoe factory had a capacity twice that of Guinea's possible requirements.

Surplus and superannuated Russian weapons also equipped Guinea's three-thousand-man army. Things like mobile antitank guns served no useful purpose but looked good, rolling along on white-walled tires, at parades. Also, they provided the Russians with an excuse for stationing a forty-five-man military training mission at Camp Alpha Yaya, out by the airport.

Soviet and Chinese credits for commodity purchases brought a weird hodgepodge of articles into Conakry. Some were ordered by inexperienced clerks in the anarchic state trading organization; one, told to buy some corrugated-iron sheets for new housing, ordered enough to roof over the entire population of Guinea. We found warehouses piled high with Chinese oriental rugs and embroidered handbags. Other warehouses contained innumerable toilet bowls—with no bathrooms to put them in—enough canned Russian crabmeat to last fifty years and six tons of quill pens. Exotic-looking machinery rusted on the docks, and vacant lots were filled with broken-down and abandoned trucks and buses.

The trucks were mostly Russian and the buses Hungarian. But they were turned over to Guinean drivers who had no notion of maintenance and in any case could probably not read the service manuals—even if they had been printed in French. When the vehicles ground to a stop for lack of lubrication or spare parts, the Guineans just shoved them into the ditch and complained that they were junk.

Yet all these and many other imports came in under well-publicized barter trade agreements and had to be paid for somehow. So off to Eastern Europe in exchange went a good part of Guinea's banana, coffee and pineapple crops that might otherwise have earned some hard currency. And when you swap so many trucks for so many tons of bananas, the world market price for the bananas can—and with the Russians often did—get conveniently lost in the bookkeeping. Thus, Guinea ended up paying more for bloc imports than they were worth.

Like the Russians, the Czechs and Hungarians also resold Guinean products for hard currency. Guinean coffee was re-exported from Prague to New York, and Guinean bauxite—twenty thousand tons of it—was sold by Hungary to West Germany.

It had taken the Guineans a couple of years to find out that aid from the East was not as "disinterested" as advertised. By 1962 they had become wary of all aid or trade deals they could not understand. And rather than admit their own shortcomings—for example, they had asked for foreign teachers without making arrangements for paying or housing them—they were inclined to stall over or even drop projects that seemed tricky or complicated.

The Guineans had also been badly burned by heeding the advice of Soviet bloc economists and establishing, as early as 1961, a national currency independent of the franc zone. The new Guinean franc was nonconvertible and useless outside the country, where the black market rate of exchange was five times the official valuation of 250 to the dollar. As a result, quantities of goods and foodstuffs that people needed never got to Conakry's shops and markets; they were smuggled out and sold for real cash in neighboring Liberia or Sierra Leone. The new bills and coins were made in Czechoslovakia and looked just about as worthless as they actually were. The bank notes were, in fact, overprinted and issued to Czech technicians sent to Guinea. I doubt if the Guinean Ministry of Finance ever really knew how many bills were in circulation.

Nevertheless, having proclaimed that an "independent" currency was another milestone on the revolutionary road to real sovereignty, Touré found it impossible to backpedal and ask the French to take him back into the franc zone. So the economy developed chronic anemia as a result of ignorance, impulsiveness and bad advice from Guinea's barter-minded Communist advisers.

The fifteen hundred-odd technicans from the Soviet bloc were frequently cited in news stories about Guinea as a sign that the country was down the drain so far as the West was concerned. Readers of imaginative fiction like *The Ugly American* pictured these technicans as dedicated and disciplined missionaries winning converts to Communism by skill, guile and linguistic prowess. But the reality, as might be expected, bore little resemblance to the fiction. By and large, the nondiplomatic Russian and East European colony consisted of people who, like draftees, had been shipped to

Guinea and were performing their particular job—whether in a
school, a clinic or a construction job—dutifully but without enthusiasm. We got to know a good many, not only on our travels
around the country but also in Conakry, for I invited a group of
Czechs, Russians, Poles and Bulgarians who lived nearby to use
our garden path as an access to the beach, something their own
ambassadors wouldn't allow. Far from being missionaries, they
didn't even believe in their own system. I remember how surprised
some French Communist teachers were when they invited a few of
their new Czech colleagues over for drinks; in the course of the
evening, one of the hosts told the Czechs, "You can relax with us.
We may be French, but we are all Communists." A Czech teacher
replied, "Well, we're not"—and the party broke up.

In general, the transplanted East Europeans liked it well enough
in Guinea; the pay was good by their standards (the cost to
Guinea was about $7,000 per technician), and they said they felt
freer than in their own countries. (Many, I know, would have
defected if they had not all had either wives, children or parents
back home who were in effect being held hostage until they returned.) But, unlike Americans, they had little pride and no dis-
cernible *esprit de corps* about their mission. Even though the
United States was the "imperialist enemy," some Polish and Hungarian engineers were delighted to be assigned by the Guinean Ministry of Public Works to help out on an American aid project.

All were spied on by their own embassy security officers. Social
contacts with Africans and foreigners were controlled. (Many
Africans concluded they were stand-offish because they were
racists.) Four or five young Russians who liked to listen to jazz
records at the home of one of our clerks suddenly stopped coming;
they sent word they could no longer go out in the evening. The
Africans, of course, quickly noticed that all the "Easterners" (also
known as "Popovs") were on a tight leash. There was little off-
duty socializing at the working level, partly because the bloc technicians didn't encourage it and partly because few spoke adequate
French; at the high school several Russian teachers even had to
conduct their classes through interpreters.

Educated Africans found the Popovs crude compared to the
well-dressed, well-housed and well-read French they were accustomed to. I remember seeing a Russian telling the African desk

clerk at the Grand Hotel in Bamako that there'd be a new arrival in the evening. "I suppose that means you'll still be six in the room," replied the clerk with obvious distaste, and grimaced at me as the Russian turned away.

Communist diplomats covered up their own contempt for the Guineans with clumsy flattery. Rank-conscious Guineans who liked to be addressed as *"Excellence"* or *"Monsieur le Directeur"* bristled at being called *"camarade"* and having their backs slapped. They were bored at the cheerless Soviet bloc receptions, where guests sat around in clusters on hard chairs, and put off by their hosts' grimly diligent efforts to be ingratiating. Even the Communist propaganda films would backfire—the sell was always too hard. One of my more radical Guinean friends told me he'd walked out on a Czech film about race relations in America because it was "insulting" to black people. "All they showed," he said, "were Negroes being oppressed and beaten and not fighting back."

The bloc diplomats were equally bored and irritated by the Africans and, as the tide turned against them, began voicing their exasperation—often indiscreetly. I recall the Hungarian Ambassador, who liked his Scotch, telling our British colleague within earshot of Africans that the Guineans had fooled the "socialist" countries in 1959 and 1960 by assuring them they were loyal Marxists at heart and not to worry about their ties to the West. "It took me only two months," he declared, "to realize these people could never be Marxists and that we had been deceived." At another party, the Radio Moscow correspondent told our USIS officer, again with Africans listening in, that the Russians had been made to look ridiculous in Guinea: "We gave them what they wanted and they didn't know what to do with it."

Yet they were under orders to be outwardly patient even when they were kept waiting for hours outside government offices and then scolded by Guinean ministers for importing allegedly shoddy equipment or giving passing grades to poor (but ideologically promising) students. They earned no respect for this—on the contary. We found it was better psychology, because more natural, to show indifference or even annoyance, and let the Guineans apologize later for the broken appointments.

The effect of Communist mistakes and miscalculations was of course compounded by Guinean inefficiency. It is hard enough to make "scientific socialism" work efficiently, even in countries with a tradition of self-government and centuries of administrative and technical experience; I saw that in Eastern Europe. But trying to put Marx's theories into practice in Africa is like making bricks out of quicksilver. The colonial authorities had concentrated on giving a classical French education to a handful of Africans in the expectation that these black Frenchmen would then keep the tricolor flying with the help of French advisers and civil servants. But when the latter pulled out, as they did so quickly and completely in Guinea, the thin layer of competent Africans was overwhelmed by the problems of administering a country, let alone running it as a "socialist" experiment. Lacking even stenographers and file clerks, cabinet ministers often had to answer phones, sort papers and type and mail official correspondence themselves. (Air France flights were suddenly banned one day because the company had not replied to a letter proposing reciprocal landing rights; the Guineans later discovered the letter had never been sent.) Some ministers worked long hours; others used their positions to feather their nests with petty graft (Guinea was too poor for big-time venality). When one minister built himself an eleven-room villa with public funds, Touré did fire him. But in other cases he couldn't do more than exhort and threaten. "I know he's crooked," he once said to me of a cabinet minister, "but I don't have anybody to replace him with."

Other ministers were honest but incompetent. Unenforceable decrees were often issued and then rescinded, such as an across-the-board price cut for consumer goods, which only caused scarce commodities to disappear into the black market. The Texaco representative was once called into the Foreign Ministry because gasoline stocks had run dry in the provincial capital of Kankan. He explained to a senior official that the reason was that fuel shipped there had been distributed to other towns in the region. The official looked bewildered, so he illustrated his point by saying that if you pour water in a dry hole it spreads out and disappears. The minister was indignant: "You mean you are pouring our precious gasoline on the ground?" (This was the same man who, when I delivered an *aide-mémoire* to him, would read on past the original into the carbon.)

Most officials in the Foreign Ministry also needed considerable coaching on world affairs. When the Chinese attacked India in 1962, I found myself explaining to one that the Indians were not American Indians, and that the invading Chinese were not Nationalists from Formosa but Communists from Peking.

At the lowest echelons the confusion and inefficiency were monumental. I once saw trucks lined up for two hours at the entrance to the port because the man in charge of raising the barrier was having a nap. In the post office, chaos normally prevailed. The French had naturally introduced their baroque administrative system into Guinea, and if you've ever sent a telegram in a rural French post office you know what I mean by baroque: Old ladies who know the routine—and in fact owe their jobs to it— perform complicated rites with rubber stamps, purple ink, scissors, dusty ledgers and glue. In Guinea the harassed African clerks who took over their jobs after independence regarded the ritual as sacrosanct; thus, when the ink pad went dry or a ledger was misplaced, telegrams piled up, fell on the floor and blew away. Incoming telegrams also went astray, since many messengers were illiterate. We once received a coded message from the Soviet Embassy with the explanation that it must be ours since they couldn't decipher it; and so it was. And every month our embassy, for some mysterious reason, would receive a North Korean bulletin in English, mailed in Tokyo and addressed to *Guinée-Matin* (a French paper that had closed down in 1958) in French *Guiana*.

I could go on for pages citing examples of incompetence: the prefab houses that melted in the sun because no one had read the labels; the gasoline truck that blew up when Guinean mechanics tried repairing it with a blowtorch; the bank clerk who added three ciphers—and 24,975,000 francs—to a Frenchman's balance and insisted that "the National Bank never makes mistakes"; the police sergeant who carefully studied a map of the world Sim gave him, turned it over and asked, "Who lives on the other side?" But I think you've got an idea of what everyone working in Guinea was up against, day after day. Luckily we could laugh it off. "It was a misunderstanding," we'd tell the Africans when something went haywire. *"C'est ça, c'est ça,"* they would reply gratefully. But the

Communists couldn't relax; their prestige was at stake and their superiors demanded results. So they fretted and fumed—and only succeeded in irritating the easygoing but prickly-proud Africans whom they were supposed to be guiding down the rocky road to "socialism."

We wanted results too, but our aims accorded with Guinea's own real interests and Touré's stated goals of economic development and nonalignment. Our operating procedure was also different. We were not interested in imposing any ideology on Guinea or in making it an American satellite. We did point out to the Guineans that economic cooperation with the West was the most effective way of obtaining capital for economic development without endangering their own independence. And they had FRIA as an example; in the past three years this plant was the only sector of the economy to show an increase in production.

In our aid programs we emphasized the kind of projects and training that Guinea needed, but did not try to push them; as I would tell Touré, we could always use the money elsewhere. This approach, so different from what they'd been hearing from the Communists, made a good impression. Diop, the new U.S. aid coordinator, did his homework, mastered our bureaucratic procedures and became convinced that our intentions were honorable and our proposals practical. As Touré told me himself, "We don't need anything grandiose; we just need small things fast." He signed a PL 480 agreement with us, early in 1962, to alleviate Guinea's growing rice shortage, and two agricultural experts arrived from Washington soon after to see what could be done to increase Guinea's production of subsistence crops like rice and corn. Another contract was signed setting up a school for training Guinean mechanics.

The effect on Guinea's leadership of what we were doing and saying in a quiet way became gradually evident. In the spring of 1962 the government promulgated a new investment law that explicitly encouraged private capital, declared its intention of joining the International Monetary Fund and signed an Investment Guarantee Agreement with the United States. Each of these steps was taken over the objection of the Communist advisers who still occupied desks in government ministries; that they *were* taken was evidence that the advisers weren't actually in charge, as we once suspected.

We were treated to a startling example of the official change in attitude during a visit to FRIA with Soapy Williams in April. The local provincial governor, who had always been hostile to private enterprise, made a speech of welcome in which he not only praised FRIA but appealed for more capital investment by American companies. "We know there are certain elements of the international press who are opposed to having private investment come to Guinea," he declared. "We know who these people are. They are the same reactionary circles who have always opposed the Guinean revolution." He managed to transmute the anticapitalist Soviets into wicked French reactionaries without the slightest difficulty, and also to refer to the enemies of the Guinean revolution in terms vague enough to conform to the rules of nonalignment.

Whenever we ran into real bureaucratic snags (at the Guinean end), I would go straight to the palace; there was no point in arguing with people who were either not authorized or temperamentally unable to make decisions. (Touré once told me the worst legacy of colonialism was that Africans lost the habit of making decisions.) Getting an appointment with Touré wasn't hard, but he was sometimes unpredictable about keeping them. One day he canceled an important date with me and the president of Olin Mathieson because of urgent business. We later learned he had spent the afternoon chatting with an American student who was doing a thesis on Guinea; Touré had taken a liking to him and felt like talking. But if something came up that I had to get an answer to in a hurry, I could usually go over to the palace—sometimes in a sport shirt—and he'd find the time.

Africans appreciate a certain amount of formality at first; above all they want to be treated with "dignity." But once you are accepted as a friend you can be as informal as you like.

One useful by-product of the aid program was that it did give me access to the President each time we had wrinkles to iron out. Diplomats from countries that weren't doing anything in Guinea found it harder to get an audience. And seeing Touré, whatever the business at hand, always gave me a chance to talk about American policy, to dispel any of his current misconceptions and to find out what was going on from the boss himself.

The West Germans also became more active in 1962 after President Luebke's state visit. Krupp trucks and earth-moving machinery arrived on easy credit terms, with technicians to see they were properly taken care of. Not only did the Germans have a part interest in FRIA, but they foresaw the time when a developing Africa would become a potential customer for German goods and wanted to build some goodwill in advance with some free samples. They also agreed to send Guinea a five-man military mission to teach an engineer company how to build roads. (For some reason —perhaps to annoy the Russians and French—the Guineans insisted they come in uniform, and I'll never forget the expression on the faces of an East German cultural delegation when the *Wehrmacht* officers walked into the Hôtel de France dining room.)

Early in 1962 I wrote a magazine article summing up what had happened and why Soviet policy was failing in Africa, based on what I'd observed in Guinea. (Since government officials can't be paid for writing articles, I suggested the magazine use the money to buy medicines needed for Conakry's hospital; after filling the Guinean request, the editor wrote me that this was the first time he'd paid off a writer in vaginal suppositories.) In the article, I concluded that the Russians had made five major mistakes: (1) they underestimated African nationalism and political sophistication; (2) Soviet aid programs neglected basic needs in favor of politically motivated projects; (3) Soviet barter agreements took advantage of Africans and ended up by antagonizing them; (4) Soviet bloc diplomats and technicians were unused to dealing with Africans, and friction resulted; and (5) African students invited to study in Communist countries usually came back disenchanted and envious of their friends who went to the West.

In my judgment, these conclusions were still valid when I left Africa four years later.

VII

Into the Bush

•

There was no gas in Macenta, but the chief of police thought we might find some in Kissidougou, eighty miles on through the rain forest. He couldn't be sure, because his radio had conked out. We had enough left in our jerrycans for the jeep and the carryall to get there, but no farther. And Conakry was three hundred miles away.

There were seven of us: Sim and I and the children, Don Herdeck, the embassy Economic Officer, and his wife, and a Guinean driver. We had been on the road four days, and looked it.

We had no trouble finding the deputy governor's office in Kissidougou; it was the only two-story house in town. But he was no help. "I haven't had any gas for two days," he said. "You might ask the Lebanese at the Caravanserai."

Two Africans perched themselves on our hood and guided us there. The Caravanserai was a kind of hotel that had known much better days. It was pouring rain and the mud around the entrance was ankle-deep. In the bar the Lebanese proprietor was drinking warm East German beer with three Africans. They didn't seem surprised to see six Americans, including an ambassador in a soiled T-shirt. (No one ever seems surprised in Africa—curious, yes, but not surprised.) We ordered beer and inquired about gas.

"Not a drop," said the Lebanese. "Do you want to spend the night here? No? I don't blame you. Why don't you try the Protestant missionaries?"

Two other Africans volunteered to show us the way. The mission was five miles out of town. There was a row of bungalows, and in one we found five Americans drinking coffee. Yes, they could spare us twenty gallons. That would take us as far as Faranah, where there might be gas; anyway, a fellow missionary and his family had just moved into a house there and we could spend the night with them.

The road to Faranah was bad, all potholes and slippery washboard. Our headlights barely pierced the curtain of rain. There was no traffic, but we passed a broken-down bus; the passengers were squatting patiently in the downpour while the driver banged away at the motor with a hammer. Occasionally, baboons scampered across the road.

Faranah's one street light glowed like a beacon in the darkness. An African was standing under it. *"Américains?"* we asked. He pointed to a bungalow across the muddy square.

The missionary family made us welcome. Their children stared shyly at ours. Except for a Czech midwife who spoke neither French nor English, they were the only "Europeans" in town. We cooked some canned stew and dried off by the wood fire, while he went over to see the party secretary. He came back with good news. The party had gas and would be honored to fill our tanks. Meanwhile, we could sleep in the chapel after we'd swept it out and set up canvas cots.

We rigged up a chain-and-bucket cold-water shower and washed off a layer or two of dust. Later, as I crawled into a cot with Sim and switched off the Coleman lantern, I heard Herdeck chuckling across the room.

"I was just thinking," he said, "that in the two years I was in Rome I only saw the Ambassador once—in the elevator."

We traveled in Guinea because you can never know a country by staying in the capital. (I've seen the articles foreigners write about "America" after visiting New York and Washington.) In the city the politicians made speeches about Guinea; in the country you saw what Guinea was really like. Thinking back, I find that the trips we took into *la brousse,* as the French called it, are what I remember most vividly about our stay in Guinea—probably because they were the most fun.

All American ambassadors are expected to travel around their parishes, but my going to Dalaba was a far different sort of expedition than, say, a visit by Chip Bohlen to Bordeaux. Guinea was not for tourists—at least not the kind who like to know where they're going to spend the night and expect things like hot showers and sheets on their beds. The main cross-country highway, a broad red line on the map, was nearly two lanes wide and paved for just one hundred miles; after that it looked less like a road and more like a three-hundred-mile detour—the kind you would expect in a stagecoach.

There were five so-called hotels, two of which had sheets. One, near the Senegalese border, was advertised in an old French guide as a hunting lodge and "rendezvous of the international elite." It might have been once, but when we got there the electric lights were out, the one toilet wouldn't flush, the kitchen was closed, the swimming pool had become a community washtub and the international elite consisted of two Polish geologists drinking palm wine in the bar. A peeling Air France poster and dusty copies of 1958 French magazines added a period touch.

So we learned to take everything with us—canned food, bedding, drinking water, medicines and plenty of soap, along with extra gasoline, spare parts and inner tubes. The Lebanese merchants—there were hundreds scattered around Guinea—ran a fairly efficient black market but could not always be relied on. Once, our carryall blew its last inner tube in a forest fifty miles from Mamou. It was late in the day and we were planning to sleep in an American mission school beyond the town. Hoping to find a garage, I took the jeep with the wives and children into Mamou, leaving Herdeck and our driver to watch the carryall. Connie Herdeck, who'd been in Africa just a week, was worried. We'd bought some panther skins earlier in the day, and she was afraid Don would be attacked in the woods. "Don can't cope with panthers," she said.

I was more worried about inner tubes, especially when we found Mamou's one service station shut down. Luckily, several sympathetic Africans materialized in the darkness and one led us across the street to a shabby-looking store front. We knocked and a Lebanese girl opened the door. In back we found her parents and relatives listening to the radio in a well-furnished living room. I introduced myself and they looked at me with more than casual interest. It was obvious to them that this dirty white man in greasy

blue jeans was not an American ambassador, but their curiosity
was aroused. They offered me a beer. Inner tubes? Nothing doing.
Just then an African policeman in uniform walked in, and I remembered my official travel document from the Foreign Ministry.
He took it, read it and passed it around as if it were a sheet of gold
leaf. I was promptly promoted to *"Excellence,"* inner tubes suddenly emerged from a storeroom, along with Scotch whisky and a
request for a visa to America, and we were invited to spend the
night.

Instead, we returned to where Don was waiting, as his wife
feared, among the panthers. We did find him surrounded, not by
wild beasts but by half a dozen enterprising salesmen. Figuring
that somebody would be coming along to get this stranded "European," people from a nearby village were now squatting beside
neat piles of oranges and bananas, waiting for their midnight customers. And we didn't disappoint them; before shoving off to the
Mamou mission school, we bought out their entire stock.

There were beds, showers and American accents at the school,
which boarded children of Protestant missionaries from all over
West Africa. And no one was surprised to see us arrive in the
middle of the night. The hospitality of the missionaries—there
were about 150 in Guinea—was as generous as it was welcome.
Yet I never felt entirely comfortable with them, for they lived in a
world and talked a language of their own. (It took me a while to
learn that single girls were known as "unclaimed blessings.") Most
of the Americans belonged to evangelical fundamentalist sects,
whose mission was conversion rather than teaching or healing.
Dedicated they were; they lived a lonely austere existence, dili-
gently canvassing remote villages with their tape recordings of the
Bible in local languages. But Guinea was 90 percent Moslem, and
French Catholics had already converted the pagans. And neither
the Moslems, whose religion lacks anxiety, nor the Catholics, who
liked to drink, could be considered likely prospects. A missionary
in Labé, who had translated the Bible into Fulah, could claim just
one real convert in thirty-seven years. At one mission we visited,
some Moslems came to Protestant services for the music and
lemonade, but only so long as no cross was in evidence. All in all,
these indefatigable Americans were regarded by Guineans as
harmless but perplexing eccentrics.

The Russians, of course, regarded the missionaries as CIA

agents in disguise. I only wish they could have overheard some of our conversations. While pleased to have us drop in, the missionaries had little to tell us, even though some had lived most of their lives in Guinea. I remember one earnest young couple mentioning how happy they were that the people in their area were finally saying nice things about America and bad things about the Communists. To what factors, I asked, did they attribute this evolution in public opinion?

"Well, every Monday evening for two years we've prayed to the Lord to bring this about. And of course we knew our prayers would be answered."

There were actually a few Guinean Protestants along the coast, small Anglican colonies dating back to the nineteenth century, when the British occupied the offshore islands and maintained trading posts north of Conakry. One day Sim and I drove up to Boffa to call on the African Anglican pastor, a Mr. Benjamin, who had a son at Yale. He lived in an old wooden colonial house with his large family and ministered to eighty parishioners. Although he had never been out of Guinea, he spoke fluent, self-taught English. His hospitality was overwhelming. After a strange lunch of tea and marmalade, followed by scrambled eggs, canned peaches and fried fish (in that order), he presented us with a young goat. We didn't need a goat but couldn't refuse. Our car was across the river—the vehicular ferry was out of order—and the police chief's jeep had not come to get us, so we had to walk the two miles to the ferry landing. On the way, the goat fortuitously escaped. While two Benjamin boys pursued it, we managed to get to the ferry—a twenty-foot launch—just in time. But it was too overloaded to drift loose from the muddy shore. The police chief appeared and, by dint of kicking, shoving and screaming, persuaded some people to jump off. He got us wedged aboard and we finally pushed free, but not before one of the Benjamin boys ran down the pier and triumphantly tossed the goat into Sim's lap.

In addition to calling on our missionaries—and parents of Yale men—we managed to visit the seven or eight American teachers scattered around the country under African-American Institute contracts. Young and dedicated, they predated the Peace Corps and, with a couple of exceptions, helped correct the distorted image of America that Guinean students were getting from the more numerous Soviet bloc teachers. One of the exceptions, the kind of girl who today would be taking LSD and picketing the White House, greeted me with a chip on her shoulder. She didn't want the American Embassy telling her what to say. I just told her she should be thankful to be an American and therefore not under embassy orders, like her Russian colleagues.

She was indignant. Was I suggesting that her Russian friends were anything more than teachers? I didn't try to argue. Some people have to learn the hard way how the Communists operate; some, I guess, never do.

Most of the time, when traveling upcountry, we would check in with the provincial governor or his deputy. Generally, if communications hadn't broken down, they were notified of our arrival in advance by the Foreign Ministry, and accommodations of sorts were laid on. In Labé we were offered Touré's own *case* (a circular hut with plumbing); in Kankan an empty villa with wall-to-wall roaches was put at our disposal; in Macenta we were ushered to the *Centre d'Accueil*—or guest house—where a single electric light bulb illuminated a dormitory of iron cots and the cooking was done in the courtyard.

A typical trip was one that Sim and I and our niece took with Gene Abrams and his French wife, Monique, and the Leo Sarkisians—an American couple who were in Guinea recording African music for a Hollywood record company. We took a jeep loaded with provisions, a light Rambler sedan and a Falcon station wagon. Our first overnight stop was Télimélé, a provincial capital on the route to northern Guinea, a region we'd never visited before. We left in the morning and lunched by the roadside, attracting, as usual, a shy but curious crowd. A couple of itinerant musicians entertained us with drumming, and we passed out rubber balls to the giggling, excited children. Later, pausing for a flat tire, we were surrounded by people who gazed longingly into the jeep at a box of illustrated *This Is America* pamphlets in French. The dozen or so we distributed were received as gratefully as if they'd been sets of encyclopedias.

We got to Télimélé late in the day and went straight to the governor's house on a hill overlooking the town. He was waiting with his two wives, the local party secretary and a Lebanese merchant; beds had been found for us and we were invited to an outdoor goat barbecue with various local officials. I told him the people along the road seemed extraordinarily friendly, waving and cheering as we passed by. "Very good," said the governor. "They didn't know who you were, but they saw a flag on your car. That shows they've had good political training."

We discussed local problems—they needed an irrigation system, schoolteachers and medical equipment. The only "European" in town was a Bulgarian midwife, and there was no doctor. Livestock was plentiful, but people refused to slaughter their herds for meat, since a man's worth was calculated by how many head of cattle he owned. So they died on the hoof, and Conakry was chronically short of meat. Télimélé's officials were also short of vehicles, but they doubted if any of the American jeeps being sent to Guinea would get up there. "They'll probably keep them all in Conakry," said the governor bitterly. I told him I'd look into it.

We needed our bug bombs that night. After breakfast, we exchanged gifts with our hosts—a sword and some wicker bags for books and a map of the United States. The Lebanese, who was in the essence-of-orange business, sold us some gas and we pushed on to Gaoual, the next provincial capital, a hundred miles to the north.

The narrow road twisted through sparsely settled hill country. We saw antelopes, baboons and wild boar and passed a few hunters with old muzzle-loading guns. (Once, near Macenta, we picked up a hunter whose musket had exploded in his hand and delivered him to an overworked Czech doctor—with whom we later had dinner.) At Gaoual we crossed the river on a new two-car West German ferry, one of twenty recently delivered to Guinea that had improved internal communications more than anything that had been done in years. The local officials were expecting us for lunch in the governor's red, yellow and green bungalow, so we had to eat it—chicken, rice, hot sauces and straight whisky (in cocktail glasses)—even though we'd just picnicked. Sipping the warm whisky was a painful but necessary ritual for us; Africans didn't drink themselves, but they had no doubt bought a bottle on the black market (for at least $20) just to be hospitable to Americans.

We spent the night in the ex-hunting lodge I have already described and do not want to think about again.

The next day, after waking early to the crowing of roosters and a radio blaring "Lady of Spain," we pushed on to Younkounkoun, an administrative center so far off the beaten track that not even Sékou Touré had visited it since independence. A broad, tree-lined main street led to a low-roofed house where several local officials, some in European dress and some in African costume, were milling around, along with various wives and innumerable children. The latter, wide-eyed and awe-stricken as we approached, melted at the sight of our rubber balls. Greetings were exchanged, warm orange pop was passed around, local problems were discussed and questions asked about America. (The police chief kept repeating *"Formidable!"* to everything I told him.) It was finally decided that we have a look at the Bassari tribe, one of the smallest and most primitive in Guinea, whose village was fifteen miles away, or at least an hour's drive on what passed for a road.

On the way, we stopped at a village market, where we shook hands with several lepers, admired some fresh lion skins and handed out candy to a squealing retinue of children. A village councilman told me that, according to local tribal custom, a prospective bride had to tell the council the names of all her previous lovers since each was obliged to donate a chicken to the council.

At a Bassari village, a dozen or so small huts made of loose stones, our escort introduced us to his withered aunt, who was sorting beans. I gave her a Polaroid snapshot of herself, but, never having seen herself in a mirror, she at first had no idea what it was. When the reality dawned on her, she screamed and dropped the print.

"She thinks it is magic," said her nephew scornfully. "Come back in three years and all this—" he gestured at the cluster of huts—"will be swept away and you will see a modern school in its place."

He was probably right. Africa is changing fast, and here, in this remote Bassari settlement, you could see the change in microcosm: the aunt, frightened, illiterate and naked except for a string of beads, and her nephew with his white shirt, Dacron trousers and dark glasses, talking French and listening to the Voice of America on his transistor radio.

On the way back our car stalled with condenser trouble—not

far, fortunately, from a French Catholic mission where two bearded priests, who were also mechanics, got us rolling again. We lunched with some PDG youth leaders in a newly built guest house in Koundara and headed back to Gaoual at dusk, scattering baboons and pausing only to commiserate with the drivers of two overloaded trucks and to pick up two hitchhikers who made us stop at sunset so they could say their prayers. Gaoual's governor was away, but his young wife, a Conakry girl obviously sulking in the sticks, had us over for dinner and asked about the latest capital gossip. Our lodgings, which had recently been vacated by the Bulgarian midwife, who was now in Télimélé, luckily included a cold-water shower as well as oil lamps, so we looked more presentable than usual.

It was cool in the morning, and we enjoyed exploring the town with our Guinean hosts, pathetically eager to show us some sign of progress. We saw a brick kiln and visited a new school, where the teacher acknowledged our gift of a few geography books and maps with an extravagant—and typically Guinean—speech about the brotherhood of man. At the local clinic we found a harassed male nurse and two midwives doing what they could for long lines of patients. They lacked even alcohol, and infections from inoculations were frequent. But all we had to give them were a couple of disposable needles and some bandages from our first-aid kit.

It was hard to break away from our hosts. (When Africans decide they like you, they want you to stay for days.) But we finally distributed the last of our Polaroid prints, accepted a panther skin and headed toward Boké, 120 miles away, over a road that we were told had not been used by a passenger car in three years. The village elders of Koumbia, ten miles down the road, who were lined up to greet us (the grapevine was working), said they *thought* the ferry near Boké was still operating, but couldn't be sure. We had enough gas to get that far, but not to drive back if the ferry was out. We decided to take the chance.

The road turned out to be a track that occasionally faded away in the high grass, and we averaged ten miles an hour. There were few villages and no traffic, and the heat was intense. We sucked on oranges, watched the gas gauge and wondered if the ferry was still working. It was. A raft was moored on the river bank, and two men poled us across—the first customers they'd had in a week.

Engine trouble held us up for an hour, so it was well after dark when we reached Boké.

No one expected us; the letter from the ministry had gone astray. We sat with the governor's three wives, who spoke no French, and drank fruit juice spiked with our own bourbon. We were dead tired and sweaty. A man came in and said there was an empty house available, but the man who had the key was out of town. So we went out and stopped at the first lighted building. It was a combination bar and brothel run by a Lebanese. He had an icebox and opened some beer while we explained our problem. A crowd of Africans had followed us in and a party got under way. They wouldn't leave until we promised to visit the town with them in the morning. Finally the Lebanese said Sim and I could take his room and he would clear out some others. We lay down with our clothes on; later in the night our niece joined us after finding spiders in her bed.

The final lap down to the coast was easy. The ferry at Boffa was working again, and at Kindia we met the paved road; it felt like velvet. There was a station restaurant there, too, where French banana planters came for Sunday dinners. Ahead were ice cubes, hot showers—and the sea. From Dakar, Conakry may have looked like a dump; to us, after one of these expeditions, it seemed like Palm Beach.

Our travels, grueling as they often were, served several purposes other than making us appreciate Conakry's modern conveniences. We met people who had never seen Americans before, and who would remember and tell others that we'd taken the trouble to come and see them and listen to their problems. (No other diplomats traveled as we did, and some never even left the city limits.) We developed outlets for USIS materials. We saw how the PDG was organized in the villages (there were 4,300 party branches in the country). We were able to verify that reports about hordes of Communist agents (five thousand Chinese, according to one news story) working upcountry were wildly exaggerated. On our last trip, the Bulgarian midwife in Télimélé and the two Polish geologists at the lodge—who had spent three weeks in the area looking for manganese—were the only Soviet bloc personnel we saw or even heard about; and in all our travels we found only four Chinese—on a tea plantation near the Liberian border. We could discuss Guinea's real needs with the ministers in Conakry, having seen for ourselves what they were. And last but by no means least, we always returned with our hearts warmed by the simple kindness and hospitality, primitive as it sometimes was, that we encountered everywhere we stopped; I sometimes wondered if a poor white society would welcome rich black strangers as we were welcomed by the people of Guinea.

Trips to neighboring countries would have been useful too, for the area was economically interdependent. But our travel budget was only $1,000 a year, and we had to use part of this to send people to the dentist in Dakar or Freetown (Conakry's one dentist, a Greek, was a sadist with a mechanical drill and no novocaine). So I seldom had a chance to get together with other American ambassadors. It is hard to conceive of any big private corporation not being able to afford to have its sales managers in, say, Ohio and Indiana, call on each other from time to time; but the State Department apparently couldn't find the money.

We did visit Mali for Christmas, at our own expense. From Bamako we drove through three hundred miles of West Texas landscape to Mopti, an old port and trading center on the broad Niger River; there we took an Air Mali DC-3 to Timbuktu, mostly to say we'd been there. It is one of those rare places in this world that is almost exactly what you expect it to be: sand and mosques and flat-roofed adobe houses, fierce-looking desert tribesmen wearing swords and bandoliers, camel caravans out of the *National Geographic* heading out across the Sahara in the red sunset. We rode camels and bought spears and slept in a neat little hotel run by—you guessed it—a Lebanese; and, of course, wrote postcards.

From Conakry, we occasionally drove down to Freetown in Sierra Leone, mostly for groceries and a change of scene—traffic cops in spiked helmets telling you in British accents to drive on the left, Brussels sprouts and porridge at the Paramount Hotel, the trooping of the colors and croquet at the Governor General's.

Yet it was always good to get back to the Gallic-African confusion of Conakry, where something unexpected was likely to happen every day and where diplomacy involved so much more than what they were used to at the Congress of Vienna.

VIII

Diplomacy Under the Palms

•

Popular stereotypes, like old soldiers, never seem to die or even fade away. They endure long after they have become obsolete. Any commercial artist will tell you that people expect all Frenchmen to wear berets and little mustaches, all Germans to have crew cuts, fat necks and dachshunds, all Englishmen to look like retired colonels with monocles and bowler hats—and all ambassadors to be bemedalled, white-tied aristocrats generally engaged in kissing somebody's hand under a chandelier.

If this book does nothing else than dent the ambassadorial stereotype, I'll be satisfied. I'm tired of being asked if I miss my silk hat and striped pants and having to reply that the only striped pants I ever wore were the rented ones I got married in.

What really distinguishes ambassadors from other people with jobs is just that they know more geography and work longer hours than anybody except politicians. Diplomacy is no nine-to-five profession, at least not in this century. In the past it may have been different. Prince Metternich defined an ambassador as a man sent abroad to lie for his country, but I don't ever recall having had to lie for mine. Napoleon urged his envoys to "pay attention to the ladies and serve good meals," and Talleyrand recommended, "above all, not too much zeal." Sir Harold Nicolson once described diplomacy as "juggling hot potatoes until they cool off," while Dean Rusk has been quoted as saying that a good diplomat is somebody who can keep four balls in the air at the same time without losing his own.

Diplomacy in Guinea was all this and much more. Our job was

a crazy quilt of public relations, problem-solving, economic counseling, strenuous socializing and political improvisation. With patience and detachment and a sense of humor you could avoid ulcers; if you enjoyed variety, you could also have fun.

As a rule, my working day started at seven, with the VOA news report. While we breakfasted on the terrace, Touré, the driver, polished the car. (I managed to exchange the Mercury for a more practical and less ostentatious Ford.) It was a ten-minute drive into town, past the hospital, the botanical gardens and the barracks of the Gendarmerie Nationale, where I always got a snappy salute from the sentries. (The Gendarmerie provided guards for the residence, and it was a popular assignment; after seeing one guard trying to read a volume of V. I. Lenin's essays, we provided them with picture magazines, comic books and an occasional Coke.)

At the office, I started the day by conferring with the DCM and going through my newly replenished in-box. Although the department constantly admonished us to save money by keeping our messages brief, the torrent of useless paper from Washington was so great that to read all of it carefully would have meant doing nothing else all day. I tried to reserve mornings for essential paperwork and meetings with embassy officers. Normally, I went home for lunch and a swim with the children and, usually, with the German and Israeli ambassadors as well. The Chinese Ambassador, with a retinue of ten or eleven, always appeared on the beach at the same time, but none of them ever acknowledged a greeting, not even from the kids.

Visitors trooped in and out of the embassy all afternoon—oil company representatives with foreign exchange problems, Guinean students going off to the States, hungover newspapermen in transit, American teachers who hadn't been paid by the Ministry of Education, people writing books about Africa, diplomatic colleagues checking out rumors, exiles from Portuguese Guinea looking for encouragement, staffers with customs or morale problems, new arrivals making courtesy calls—the procession was never-ending. I tried to get out myself during the afternoon. There was usually a minister or two to see about untangling a bureaucratic snarl or clearing up a "misunderstanding"; or I would look in at the AID and USIS offices, where some problem generally needed solving.

Once I found our new Public Affairs Officer, whose French was not quite fluent, putting up a "Negro in America" window display. He had incorrectly translated it as *Le Nègre en Amérique,* not realizing that to a French-speaking African *nègre* means "nigger."

Most days I got home by six for another quick swim and another change of shirt before the usual reception or dinner party—sometimes both. If we were lucky, we'd be home by eleven, waking up the night guard—who conscientiously slept on top of his rifle so that it wouldn't be stolen—and hoping the electric current was still on and the air-conditioner functioning. And before going to sleep, I'd jot down whatever tidbits of information I'd picked up during the evening's socializing.

Sim's days were full too. In addition to marketing—which took several hours—she had the children to look after, protocol calls to make and receive, first aid to dispense and three of the world's most amiably incompetent servants and a gardener—all illiterate—to supervise. And after visiting the maternity hospital's overcrowded and understaffed ward, she and Monique Abrams felt impelled to volunteer their services as nurses' aides three days a week. There were only forty beds in the ward for the whole city, and women often arrived at the hospital by taxi with the baby and placenta in a basin.

At first the Guineans, both the staff and the patients, were puzzled and even suspicious. They weren't used to "Europeans" soiling their hands at this kind of work, or to simple kindness from nonrelatives. A Czech doctor and a Bulgarian midwife assigned to the hospital were equally surprised; they told Sim that no ambassador's wife from a "socialist" country would dream of doing manual labor. But as time went on, the word spread around that Americans were "different," and Sim and Monique—and later Connie Herdeck—were not only accepted but sought after. We also raised more than $2,500 in donations from our home town in Connecticut to buy incubators and other equipment for the hospital; the gift, perhaps because it was so personal, got bigger news play in *Horoya* than any government-to-government aid offer.

When we finally left Guinea, the farewells at the hospital were tearful; the hospital director confided that nothing else would have convinced him Americans were "such good people and so free of racial prejudice." And Touré himself later told me, only half jokingly, that Sim's hospital work had done more to create goodwill for America than anything I or the U.S. Government had achieved.

What we did do, through AID, was accomplished because I had a staff with the energy and the will to battle the bureaucrats. While Guinea lacked people who knew what to do, Washington seemed to have too many; but the result at both ends was the same: action was held up by an excess of either inefficiency or red tape. For example, we almost lost the funds for Guinea's English-language training program—first because the Ministry of Education mislaid the necessary documents; then, with only five days to go before the end of the fiscal year, because Washington AID officials could not move fast enough to give us the authority to sign them. (They did, four hours before midnight on June 30, but only after a volley of telegrams from the embassy.) Our vocational training school was held up for months while the teachers waited for security clearances from the FBI. Messages from Conakry confirming or canceling appointments often reached the recipients too late to do any good. The man in charge of foreign trade at the National Bank, a former clerk for Texaco, did not know what a letter of credit was, so money that should have been paid wasn't—and everything would slide off the tracks again.

All this meant extra work for the embassy. At least, Conakry was informal enough so that we could deal with real people, whose inefficiency was somehow less frustrating than the indifference of a faceless and faraway bureaucracy. And you couldn't blame the Guineans for being confused by our procedures; we had trouble understanding some of them ourselves. Abrams finally drew up a chart with thirty-four boxes, each describing a different administrative action that had to be taken between the receipt of a request for assistance and its eventual—to use a popular bureaucratic term—implementation. The Guinean minister who memorized the chart confessed later that it dispelled his last suspicions about American intentions in Africa; any people who tied themselves up in knots the way we did could not be all that eager to muscle in.

I was patient with Washington—up to a point. One of the points occurred in the spring of 1962 when I read a Washington news story announcing the appointment of a new AID Director for

Guinea. He had been recruited under a new program called Operation Tycoon, the brain child of somebody—surely a PR man—who decided that filling key jobs in the field with available business executives would somehow restore public and Congressional confidence in the foreign aid program. The man picked for Guinea had never been to Africa and could not speak French; moreover, we didn't need him, and the announcement was made before my concurrence had been asked for.

I reminded Washington of this, adding that I had an extraordinarily competent acting director in Abrams and that this was no time to upset an effective operation by introducing a new and unfamiliar face at the top.

I couldn't sway them. But my concurrence was still required, and they still wanted that. So I took the bureaucratic tack and wired back that as head of the Country Team I was responsible for the efficiency of the whole mission and would therefore have to withhold my concurrence, and I cited the President's letter of May, 1961.

Considerable commotion resulted. Back in Washington—for a medical checkup at Bethesda—I found the AID bureaucracy up in arms. They didn't like ambassadors interfering with their right to send anybody they wanted, no matter how miscast, to the field. I finally said I would be forced to resign if my judgment was disregarded, and would have to inform the President of the reason. That clinched it; Abrams was left in charge, and Monique was able to continue working in the maternity ward and teaching the Twist to Guinean ministers.

For a city that lacked almost everything, Conakry attracted more than its share of American visitors, and all had to be looked after. Americans in Conakry invariably wound up at the embassy, if only to ask for pills after sampling the Hôtel de France cuisine. Whether the visitors were official or nonofficial, we were glad to see them. Most of them made a good impression on the Guineans and went home with a better idea of what Guinea was like and what we were trying to do. And we certainly needed understanding and support back home.

Soapy Williams and Senator Vance Hartke, being politicians, scored heavily with the Guineans. Watching Williams handshaking his way through a village, one of our escorting Guinean ministers turned to me and exclaimed with admiration, "There is a real politician!" Even with his halting French, Williams—like Shriver —got through to the Africans by talking about things they understood. One night at eleven, Touré came over alone to the guest house to see Williams (who was leaving at dawn) and kept him up until two with questions about how the Democratic party won elections in Michigan.

Hartke, too, performed in a way that surprised and delighted the Guineans, plunging into crowds to pat babies on the cheek, clap time for the dancers and bang the drums of the musicians. Neither the French nor the Russians did this kind of thing, and the people responded exuberantly to the sight of white men joining in their fun. Hartke also helped us, after visiting a country clinic where operations were performed by candlelight, by firing off a telegram to President Kennedy asking why the generators we had promised Guinea a year before had not yet been delivered.

Although we in the embassy were grounded by lack of travel money, there seemed to be plenty available in Washington. Officials from various government agencies and departments regularly drifted in, asked questions, snapped pictures and drifted out. There was nothing much we could tell them that they couldn't read in the files back home, but an annual trip to "the field" was part of the drill and did, I suppose, give them a better appreciation of our problems. Pentagon colonels and majors in civilian clothes regularly appeared on "area-familiarization" trips. They earnestly took notes about everything we told them, from which they would later write a report that nobody would read and that in any case contained nothing we hadn't already reported. One peripatetic colonel came to buy postcards of street scenes—to be filed away, no doubt, among thousands of others for contingency plans that would never materialize. Another visitor, funded by part of the Pentagon's $8 billion Research and Development budget, told us he wanted to gather material on native Guinean languages for possible leaflet use "if the balloon goes up." He finally went away after we told him that, since these languages were strictly oral, there was no material to gather, and not much point in preparing leaflets that nobody could read, wherever the balloon might be. I began to suspect the real reason for their journeys was a shortage of office space or an excess of brass in the Pentagon.

Aluminum industry executives were frequent callers, since the FRIA and Boké operations were under constant discussion with the Guinean Government. So were thesis-writing scholars and students. One of the latter unconsciously helped our public relations by accepting an invitation to stay with a Guinean family in Mamou; he became an instant celebrity as the first white man in town ever to be the house guest of an African.

Not all our visitors made such a hit as this student, but none did us any harm. "Ugly Americans" are much rarer than you have been led to believe. Our only problem American was a down-and-out Communist teacher who had come to Guinea from Mexico after jumping bail in California. He was kept on because he was a good teacher and willing to work for very little money, but he finally disappeared from the scene after we tipped off the Ministry of Education that he was distributing Soviet Embassy handouts to our AID English-language classes.

Entertainers touring Africa under State Department auspices were always a hit. They worked hard, made friends and seldom complained about late nights and dawn departures. The Africans, listening to Cozy Cole's drumming, were reminded of their own contribution to American jazz; they noticed our white and Negro musicians playing together, and they came away with a feeling that Americans were perhaps not so alien as some other "Europeans." Guinean officials welcomed these visits as symbols of their "non-alignment," and the Ministry of Youth, Sports and Culture invited the entire Diplomatic Corps to attend these "fruitful contributions to cultural cooperation with the United States." The Guineans we sent to the States for a few weeks under our cultural exchange program also invariably returned with glowing accounts of America's friendliness and hospitality; unfortunately we never had enough money to send more than five a year.

An ambassador also has to pay attention to his diplomatic colleagues, and the best thing about a small town like Conakry is that we diplomats could see each other with a minimum of protocol. Most of us lived in the same suburb; we swam together, played bridge together, complained together and suffered through interminable receptions together. A kind of kinship developed, even between those of us whose official relations were technically correct but cool.

The Russians always went out of their way to be pleasant, and I sensed they would have liked to be friendlier still. The baggy-trousered, unsmiling robots of the Stalin era were being replaced with younger, better-dressed and more sociable diplomats who weren't above cracking an occasional joke. One evening, I invited Ambassador Degtyar over to the house to see *Romanoff and Juliet,* a Peter Ustinov comedy about a mythical little country called Concordia that tried to avoid choosing sides in the cold war. Afterward, I gave Degtyar a Coke and asked him how he enjoyed the picture. Dead-pan, he replied, through an interpreter, that this film had been severely criticized in the Soviet Union for its lack of socialist realism. I remarked that, after all, it was a satire and wasn't meant to be taken literally.

"Ah, but you know why it is not realistic?" he persisted.

"Why?" I asked, playing the straight man now that I could detect a twinkle in his eyes.

"Because—" and now he laughed heartily—"because no small country ever refuses aid from both the Soviet Union and the United States!"

A few weeks later, I ran into Degtyar's deputy, a Mr. Kuretkin, under a palm tree at an evening garden party, and asked him in French how *he'd* liked the picture.

"What picture?" he replied curtly. "When? And what are you asking me for?"

I mentioned the title, and he became apologetic. "I didn't recognize you!" he exclaimed. "In the dark I thought you were somebody from the Czech Embassy. Please forgive me!"

The Russians had even less regard for their Chinese Communist cousins, whom they called "dogmatists." They liked to compare the Chinese and the West Germans: "The Germans are trying to get you to fight us, and the Chinese are trying to get us to fight you. But fortunately we are not so stupid." Once, when I told Marchuk that the Chinese didn't even nod to me when we swam together, he remarked with a shrug, "What do you expect? Those people aren't even human."

At parties the Russians usually congregated with the East Europeans and Mongolians; the Chinese formed another group with the

North Koreans, Cubans and North Vietnamese; and the West Europeans, a third. Topaloski, the Yugoslav Ambassador, and I generally circulated around with the Africans, avoiding only group two. Topaloski, like me, got only stony stares from the Chinese; he believed in the Yellow Peril and frequently protested to the Foreign Ministry about anti-Yugoslav items in the Chinese Embassy news bulletin. The Mongolians made a point of pumping my hand at receptions to prove they were in the Soviet and not the Chinese camp. I never could figure what they were doing in Guinea. On the Mongolian national holiday, the Ambassador would speak of the age-old cultural ties that united the Mongolian and Guinean peoples; his secretary, a homely but charming young lady with a one-way crush on the British Ambassador, would ask USIS for books by Kafka. I think they must have been homesick so far from the Siberian steppes.

The Chinese kept pretty much to themselves and their Guinean contacts. Their one aid project was a 1910-model match and cigarette factory that was still under construction when I left Guinea in 1963. They never ventured out of their compound except in pairs and shied away from casual contacts. Africans were generally ill at ease with them. Once, when the Chinese Ambassador's son was sick, the Guinean doctor called in the only pediatrician in town, the young wife of a Yugoslav Embassy officer. She treated the child but was neither greeted nor thanked by the Ambassador— presumably because of Tito's revisionism. Marchuk wasn't so far wrong; the Chinese may have been human, but they didn't act it. And the Africans who heard her story were shocked.

We had other members of the Diplomatic Corps who didn't speak to each other—the West Germans and the East Germans, the Israelis and the Arabs, the French and the Algerians, the British and the Saudis, the Cubans and us. This caused problems at parties, especially when the hosts didn't remember their politics. On New Year's Day, when the corps assembled at the palace to greet Touré, the Swiss Consul was snubbed by the North Korean (who thought he was American); the North Vietnamese dean of the corps had neglected to inform the French Ambassador, who arrived—late and furious—in a sport shirt; the Russian mistakenly introduced the new Lebanese Chargé as an Indonesian to the Dutch Consul, who began talking about West Irian; Topaloski and

I were seated next to the Chinese, and the Moroccan next to the Israeli. By the time Touré arrived, an hour late, no one was talking to anyone else.

This wasn't unusual. Hardly a week went by that didn't include a long evening of sitting on hard chairs next to the wrong people in the palace garden and watching Guinean dancers perform in honor of some visiting VIP. They danced well and the drumming was good, but not even *My Fair Lady* can hold your interest after the twenty-seventh time. They also started late, and the warm Scotch and orange pop wasn't served until the end. Later came ballroom dancing, mostly to Latin rhythms played by the all-girl Guinean Army orchestra; and no one could leave until Touré gave the signal, usually after 1 A.M., by leading the guests around the floor in a shuffling sort of procession called the High Life. The routine never varied, not even when the party was in honor of Conakry's new Catholic Archbishop and the guests included French priests and nuns; on stage, the sweating drummers pounded and yelled, the girls chanted and gyrated, the witch doctors bobbed and whirled in their fierce masks—and we all ended up doing the High Life.

Even more grueling were the performances of plays in local languages. Every town in Guinea had its own dance-and-drama group; national competitions were held and the best were shown in Conakry. The Diplomatic Corps got the front-row seats, so there was no escape except during intermission; but since I was usually seated next to the Chinese Ambassador, I had to stick it out as long as he did, which was all the way.

Embassy receptions for national holidays were all of a pattern: stilted expressions of mutual esteem were exchanged by the host and the ranking Guinean while the guests nursed their weak whiskies, avoided the canapés and counted ministers. The number of ministers who came to these affairs was supposed to indicate the state of the host country's relations with Guinea. At one of our July 4 parties—which we held on February 22 because of the rainy season—I remember being congratulated by my colleagues and thinking they were referring to the news that we had orbited our first spaceman. Not at all. Eight ministers and thirty lesser officials had come (as compared to two and seven the year before), and my fellow diplomats were properly impressed.

We always tried to liven up our parties with either a film or a band, and I suspect that's why most of them came. But it was nice to be congratulated anyway.

You wouldn't think anybody who didn't have to would want to crash Conakry's Diplomatic Corps, but one day an Iraqi Consul was added to the list and began turning up at all the receptions. A year went by before he was unmasked as a local Lebanese who just liked to go to parties—and be called *"Monsieur le Consul."* And he might never have been found out had he not gotten carried away and offered two Guineans scholarships to Baghdad University. (Everyone else was offering scholarships.) When the students got there, the Iraqis began asking questions, and their self-appointed consul moved into a Guinean jail.

Entertaining Africans at home could be a strain if you were the kind of host who liked to know how many guests were coming and at what time. Raised in communal homes where mealtimes were casual and round-the-clock, Africans came late or not at all, and sometimes—if they liked you—brought along friends and relatives. Phil Heller once invited the Ambassador of Mali to dinner. He was sick and couldn't come, but sent his wife, who spoke no French, and four children instead. African wives were always a problem; agonizingly shy and often illiterate, they would sit like statues, responding only to direct questions. ("Do you have children?" "Yes." "How many?" "Six.") One ambassador's wife from a former British colony spoke no French and only thirty-eight words of English—all nouns—and threw her chicken bones on the floor. So we served buffets and sat at bridge tables and didn't worry about who came and when.

For a while in 1962 we got a new American film from the Armed Services Motion Picture Service every two weeks, which we showed in the garden. They were good pictures; we all looked forward to them and they attracted Africans to the house. But when the State Department couldn't afford to pay the Pentagon for them, they stopped coming. If we'd had just one American in uniform on the staff, as our embassy in Bamako did, we would have received a picture every week. In the State Department you get used to being a second-class public servant, but it was impossible to explain this to our diplomatic colleagues and our African friends, who wondered why we had no more film showings.

Yet staff morale was never a problem. People got used to hardships. My secretary, who lived on the fifteenth floor of Conakry's only skyscraper, didn't even complain when her elevator stopped working; she just took care not to forget anything when she left the apartment. Bouts of fever and dysentery were too common to talk about. Everyone was too busy carrying workloads that three or four people would have shared at a European post. Nobody cracked up—like the Yugoslav psychiatrist who had to be sent home after working two months in the local hospital. We did have intramural squabbles brought on by tension and fatigue, but these usually got ironed out on Sunday, when most of us took to the water and headed for the offshore islands. Abrams and I had our own boats—seventeen-foot outboards—and one belonged to the embassy. Our destination was a strip of palm-lined beach on an island reputed to have been the site of Robert Louis Stevenson's *Treasure Island.* Jack Crawford, a pirate who preyed on the slave ships, operated in these waters, and you could see the ruins of a British fort on the island—which I noticed was shaped like the one on the map in the book.

Out there in the Atlantic, the surf was clean and cool and the big fish were usually biting. In the evenings we'd water-ski and then build fires and cook the day's catch—tuna, barracuda and mackerel—before falling asleep under the stars. Our conscience was clear; with the airport and post office closed on Sundays, there was no way of getting a message in or out of Conakry. On Treasure Island we were about as far away from it all as you could get without a space capsule.

There was an Anglican chapel on the nearby island of Tamara; it was the scene of our first embassy marriage. The groom was our junior economic officer, Bob Strand; his bride, Penny Packard, taught at the Conakry Girls High School. To get the wedding party out to the island, the captain of an Egyptian dredge digging out the harbor offered his launch. So we invited him and his officers to the reception at our house in the evening. Penny had asked all her fellow teachers—Czechs, Bulgarians, Israelis, Russians, Frenchmen, Haitians and even our Communist American—along with the staff of the Ministry of Education. We dug pits in the garden and barbecued six lambs; the fragrance attracted several more uninvited guests. Several cases of champagne and a four-piece Congolese band quickly turned the reception into the noisiest, longest and most successful party of the season. Egyptian dredgers twisted with Israeli teachers, Russians with Americans, Penny's father—a Harvard professor—with the wife of the Minister of Education. Some time after midnight, two unsteady Bulgarians led me down to the corner of the garden to reassure me that "none of us are Communists, not even the Russians." I told them it didn't matter. "But it does matter," they insisted, swaying in the moonlight. "We do not want you to think we are Communists."

"Let us have a toast," I suggested, and we went back and drank to President Kennedy.

Along about 2 A.M., our Budget and Fiscal Officer couldn't find his car; the Minister of Education promptly called the Minister of Internal Security and Defense (the phone was working for the first time in weeks) and reported the theft. Within minutes, the garden was full of armed Guinean soldiers and policemen. The captain in charge told me that roadblocks had been set up on the causeway.

"Rest assured, *Excellence,*" he said, eying the lambs, "the car will be recovered."

I invited him to join the party and drove some drunken Russian teachers back to their quarters. On the way back, two policemen, seeing an American car with diplomatic plates, flagged me down.

"Come with us," they said.

"Come with me," I suggested. "There has been a misunderstanding."

At my house, the captain was indignant.

"Imbeciles!" he cried. "Do you not see that the man you have arrested is *Son Excellence* himself?"

While they all disposed of the rest of the lambs and two Egyptians snored on the terrace, *Son Excellence* went off to bed with *Madame l'Ambassadrice.*

IX

To the White House and After

•

When the rains started in the summer of 1962, we took a month's leave with the children in Europe. One advantage of being at an African hardship post is that the government gives you a round trip, economy class, to Europe every two years for "rest and recuperation." The Pentagon naturally is more generous; when we got to Athens we found that American military personnel stationed there got two free trips a year to Western Europe, presumably to recover from too much rich food and sunshine.

We cruised along the Dalmatian coast and motored through Austria, Czechoslovakia, Germany and France, stopping from time to time at U.S. Army hotels and recreation centers, marveling at the luxurious low-cost facilities that Americans in uniform take for granted. From Paris, we sent the children home to boarding school. Tutoring them in Guinea hadn't worked out, and they were too often sick from parasites and debilitated by the climate. We returned to Conakry in late August, rested, recreated and ready for whatever was in store. There was, as usual, plenty.

Despite their political reverses, the Russians and their partners were very much in evidence. Work continued on their projects, though there were no new starts, and the flow of Guinean students to Communist countries did not slacken. At the new Patrice Lumumba University in Moscow, three thousand students from all over Africa were given scholarships and intensive indoctrination. Others who went to Paris were sedulously cultivated by the French Communist party. At the end of 1962 more than 1,200 Guinean students were studying abroad—580 in Communist countries, 190 in France, 146 in the United States, 62 in Western Europe and 223 in neutralist countries, including Yugoslavia. The Guinean Government accepted Soviet bloc scholarships partly because they were available and partly because to refuse them would violate their nonaligned posture.

The Soviet purpose was, of course, to train cadres of young Marxist Africans who would eventually replace the unsatisfactory "national bourgeois" and "neo-colonialist" leadership of independent Africa. (Touré had presumably been placed in this category since his reactionary behavior in December of 1961, for pro-Communist Guinean student groups in Paris were now attacking him for having betrayed the revolution.) Most of the African students who went to the East regretted it. They hated the cold dark winters, missed their families, resented the political indoctrination and police surveillance, complained about wasting a year learning a useless Slavic language, got into trouble over girls and accused their hosts of being racists. In Prague, during our vacation, I was told that at least three or four African students came to the American Embassy every week to ask about getting scholarships in the West.

It wasn't surprising that the Africans were made to feel unwanted in Communist countries. A Czech or East German student, short of money and living space and forbidden to travel, could hardly be expected to welcome a "savage" stranger with freedom of movement, pocket money and a taste for girls. Yet the Communist governments strained their resources and imposed their African visitors on their own universities because the Sovietization of Africa remained one of their priority political objectives. Even if nine hundred out of every thousand African students returned home disenchanted and embittered about Communism, the Soviets were interested in that other hundred who could be won over to their cause and relied upon to carry out orders. And in most African countries a handful of determined and disciplined young men, given the necessary support and hardware, can be a powerful political force.

In Guinea, the Communists continued to play it cool while the Guineans continued to make it plain they didn't trust them. On Guinea's Independence Day, October 2, Touré pointedly denounced "all the imperialisms"—which, in the neutralist vernacular, is the terminology used for attacking Communism. He also issued a memorandum to all cabinet ministers reminding them that "all Communist diplomats must be regarded as spies." In September a journalism school run by an East German and a French Communist was shut down and then reopened with a faculty recruited in Switzerland; some Guinean students came home in bandages after getting beaten up in Bulgaria; Touré's personal photographer, a Czech, managed to bring his wife to Guinea for a holiday—and promptly asked for and was granted political asylum; the distribution of propaganda bulletins from Communist embassies was strictly curtailed by the Foreign Ministry, and the radio news programs became so bland they were no longer fun to listen to.

The Soviets refrained from reacting to these pin pricks for fear of jeopardizing certain benefits they still hoped to derive from their Guinean investment. Conakry's Russian-built runway was completed in August, and the Russians now indicated they wanted to use it as a refueling stop on a proposed Aeroflot schedule of Tupolev-114 flights to Cuba and Brazil. Aeroflot already ran a weekly Ilyushin-18 flight down the coast to Accra and also wanted to refuel this plane in Conakry. At the time—this was in September—we didn't know about the missile sites they were building in Cuba, but the refueling request did present a ticklish problem; AID was supplying kerosene to Guinea for its domestic needs and we did not want any of it diverted to Aeroflot. Fortunately, the Guineans understood the facts of international life; despite some hesitation in Washington, I went ahead and told Ismael Touré that if even a gallon of our fuel was used to fly Russian planes instead of helping Guinea's economy, we would consider it a violation of our agreement. He said he appreciated our concern and agreed to storing our kerosene in separate tanks where its distribution could be supervised.

The Russian Ilyushins continued to stop in Conakry—sometimes with as few as four or five passengers—but were told by the Guineans that no fuel was available. And the inauguration of the Moscow-Havana flight was delayed while the Russians considered whether or not to bring in and store their own jet fuel at the airport.

About this time, the Russians also began pressing the Guineans to step up the repayment of the loans that had been extended during the past three years. You couldn't blame the Russians for wanting to recover whatever they could from a bad investment, but the Guineans didn't see it that way. Yet the country, because of its worthless currency, had become so dependent on imports from the Soviet bloc that it had little choice but to add some iron ore and bauxite to the tons of fruit and coffee that we'd see being loaded on Soviet freighters every time we drove our boat through the harbor.

This new economic squeeze, the chronic foreign exchange shortage and the absence of any visible improvement in living standards finally induced the Guineans to turn to us as the one country they could trust that was able and perhaps willing to bail them out. On September 6, Telli Diallo, who was now Guinea's Ambassador to the UN, came to the embassy to say that Touré would like to meet quietly with Kennedy before the end of the month to explain Guinea's desperate economic plight and ask for help. He said Touré could make the opening of the UN General Assembly a pretext for going to the States, and the meeting with Kennedy could be made to look like a courtesy call.

In reporting this to Washington, I urged a favorable response. Without committing ourselves in advance, we had nothing to lose and something to gain from listening to the Guineans; and an informal meeting between Kennedy and Touré would be an appropriate culmination of eighteen months of steadily improving relations. Washington finally agreed, and a date was set up for October 10. As it turned out, the meeting was well timed; the Cuban missile crisis flared up a week later, and the Russians had their eye on Conakry's jet runway.

I flew to Washington before Touré to brief the department on what he'd be asking for. (Our background airgram from Conakry managed to get lost and didn't arrive until after the visit.) Briefing papers had also been prepared for the President; as usual, these consisted of thick books with colored tabs that were full of irrelevant statistics about the country's economy, politics and tribal structure. The President couldn't have read all the material even if he'd wanted to and had nothing else to do all day. I therefore prepared a two-page paper that would let the President know what matters Touré might raise and what we should ask him. When I turned it in, Ball wondered aloud why State Department officials never seemed to be able to write anything under ten pages. One reason, I suppose, is that they never had the experience I did of writing news stories for a tabloid and captions for a picture magazine, where every word counts.

I met Touré at Idlewild Airport on behalf of the U.S. Government, and he went on to the United Nations with President Ben Bella of Algeria. He and Touré had both been invited by Castro to visit Cuba on their way home, but only Ben Bella accepted. One of his aides told me confidentially that Touré was more politically sophisticated than his own President. "He understands that you don't come to see Kennedy and then run off to Cuba—not if you want to make a good impression at the White House."

Touré happened to be the last chief of state Kennedy met at National Airport; thereafter they were taken to the White House lawn by helicopter. A Marine detachment did the honors and played the Guinean national anthem better than I'd ever heard it played in Conakry. We stood on a rostrum, and both Presidents made brief ad lib speeches. We then drove to the White House for formal talks in the Cabinet Room with simultaneous translations over earphones.

Touré spoke of his difficulties with the Soviet bloc, admitting that it had taken his government a couple of years to realize that Soviet aid programs included political agents disguised as technicians and that the Communist system was not what Guinea needed. He said that the experience of these years, while enlightening, had left his country bankrupt. Practical assistance, especially in agriculture, light industry and communications, was urgently needed. He remarked that, with palm nuts rotting on the ground, Guinea had to import soap and cooking oil; a small oil-extracting plant would save foreign exchange and provide employment. He mentioned the Konkouré dam and his desire to normalize Guinea's relations with France.

The President replied that the interests of the United States were best served by a free, stable, independent and unified Africa and that he was well aware of the reasons for Guinea's difficulties. He asked some questions and assured Touré of our willingness to be helpful.

We went upstairs for sherry and tomato juice, and the President took Touré down the hall and introduced him to Jackie and Caroline. Later, at lunch, toasts were exchanged, and Touré said, "Africa is independent today thanks to people like yourself." While they chatted (through an interpreter crouched between them), I mentioned a Drew Pearson column reporting a rumor that two thousand Guineans were taking military training in Cuba. Kennedy had read it too. Touré declared there were only twenty Guineans in Cuba—and not in military training; he said it reminded him of news reports about the six thousand Chinese in Guinea: "In both cases they added two zeros." (He was right.)

On the White House steps, after Touré had gone over to Blair House, the President asked me and an AID official about the palm nut plant. "That's something we ought to be able to do quickly," he said. I thought it made sense, but the AID man mentioned the difficulty of conducting feasibility surveys. "Well, get onto it," said the President, jabbing his forefinger at the man's chest, "and report to me in three weeks."

At Blair House, Touré held a press conference. "Don't judge us by what others say or even by what we say," he told the reporters, "but only by what we do." Rusk came over and promised Touré we would try to help with the French problem so that normal trade, at least, could be resumed. Touré also met Hodges and approved our holding a trade fair in Conakry in May. After meeting with some Guinean students at the embassy, we drove to the airport, with motorcycles and sirens clearing a path through the downtown traffic.

It had been a short day but a fruitful one. Touré was captivated by the Kennedy charm—a blend of attentiveness, humor, frankness and easy grace—and thereafter regarded him as a friend he could confide in. He wrote him frequently during the next year—long personal letters. After the assassination, Guinea was the first country in the world to issue a stamp honoring Kennedy's memory.

He also left three of his ministers behind in Washington with instructions to give us all the data we requested about Guinea's economy. In the past, the Guineans, secretive by habit and also embarrassed by the state of their finances, often withheld information that Washington needed to justify aid commitments. (In some cases, I suspect, they didn't have the figures and were reluctant to admit it.) The day after Touré left, his ministers met with our AID, Commerce and Agriculture people for a frank exchange that helped speed up several approved projects and cleared the track for some PL 480 rice imports. Among other things, we learned that the Soviet bloc was now taking 60 percent of Guinea's exports, none of which provided any foreign exchange.

Meanwhile, I touched the usual bases in Washington and found the seventh floor brass, except for Harriman, as inclined as ever to regard Africa as a European responsibility. At Georgetown parties, I found the talk—as always—intramural, the main topic being who was in or out of favor. Those who had sailed with Jack at Hyannis Port felt more secure than those who had merely swum with Bobby at Hickory Hill, and showed it. It was relaxing not to be involved; as a visitor from one of the New Frontier's remotest ramparts, I was no threat to anybody's position in the Washington pecking order; maybe that's why I was invited to the parties.

Before leaving, I went back to the White House for a private talk with the President about Africa in general and Guinea in particular. He said our balance-of-payments problem just now made it hard for us to do as much as we should, but that small-impact aid projects like the palm nut plant should not be sacrificed. He suggested I communicate directly with the White House if things got bogged down.

I remember our also talking about Cuba and agreeing that Castro was now more of a liability to his Russian backers than a threat to Latin America. He was about to become even more of a liability. But at the time—it was October 11—Kennedy didn't know for certain about the Soviet missile sites; nor could he know that the next two weeks would be the hardest and the most successful of his Presidency.

I was in Dakar, en route to Conakry, on October 22, when the President made his speech quarantining Cuba. Senator Ellender was in town, and an advance text of the speech came by telegram while we were having dinner with Phil Kaiser, our Ambassador to Senegal. Ellender wasn't worried; he'd been to the Soviet Union the year before and assured us the Russians were very nice people. The only thing that concerned him was that the United States was going broke; he couldn't understand why we were spending money in places like Korea and Formosa, let alone Africa. When I suggested that pulling out of these places would only encourage the Communists to be more aggressive, he retorted that I sounded just like General Lemnitzer. There was no point in arguing, so Phil and I let him lecture our wives about the virtues of Huey Long and the dangers of the European Common Market while we listened to the latest news on VOA.

When I got to Conakry the next day, I found messages indicating the Russians were planning a Moscow-Havana airlift via Conakry. I got an appointment at the Foreign Ministry for the next day. Meanwhile, the VOA announced that sixty-five Soviet ships, some with missiles, were now in the Atlantic on their way to Cuba.

On October 24 the Acting Foreign Minister, Alpha Diallo, confirmed to me that the Russians had requested landing rights in Conakry for long-range jets. But he told me not to worry; the government agreed with our stand on the missiles build-up, and Touré himself had made the decision to refuse the Soviet request. This left only Dakar as a possible refueling stop to Havana, but Senegal was unlikely to agree to what Guinea and Morocco had refused. It looked as if the Russians would be denied every access to Cuba by air that they counted on. I notified Washington by emergency telegram—which guaranteed immediate distribution—and was annoyed but not really surprised when we discovered the next day that the Conakry post office had forgotten to send it.

Ellender arrived on the twenty-fifth in a U.S. Air Force DC-3 and started right away inspecting the embassy for extravagance. We put him in the bedroom with the groceries and served him hamburgers. Cuba still didn't worry him. He used his movie camera, talked Cajun French to the Guineans and congratulated me for having turned down Pentagon suggestions that we have a military attaché assigned to Conakry. That evening we got a message that an Ilyushin-18 was heading for Conakry on a special flight going West. The Guineans knew nothing about it. More messages came in that night: What was the plane carrying? Who was aboard? Where was it going? When? In the morning the Ilyushin was parked on the apron next to our DC-3 when Diop, Sim and I went out to see Ellender off. Sim waited on the terrace of the terminal while the Minister and I walked with him to the runway. The Second Secretary of the Soviet Embassy was standing beside her. He smiled and said good morning.

"I wonder if you could tell me," he went on, "who that gentleman is and what your aircraft is doing here."

Sim explained that Senator Ellender was on a routine inspection trip of African posts in an attaché plane and was now on his way to Freetown and Monrovia.

"Thank you very much," said the Russian. "And now I will tell you something. Our Ilyushin is leaving for Recife tomorrow en route to Rio to pick up the body of the Soviet Ambassador—he was drowned last week while swimming. The plane is not going to Cuba. Your husband may be interested to know this." I was. Recife, sure enough, turned out to be the destination. At times like this we appreciated the informality of Conakry. It saved everybody a lot of trouble.

In the afternoon we got word that Senegal had also turned down a Soviet request for landing rights. This meant that Africa was now eliminated as a possible refueling stop to Cuba.

Khrushchev backed away from a showdown on October 28 and ordered the Russian missile ships to turn back. The crisis was over. Kennedy had called his bluff without driving him into a corner. And it had been a useful exercise; the Russians, having tested us, now understood that we would not allow the balance of nuclear power to be upset. Thereafter the cold war was defused, in the sense that there was less chance of dangerous miscalculations.

A few days later I called on Touré to deliver a letter from the President expressing his thanks for Guinea's cooperation during the crisis. I added that we hoped he would use his influence with Castro, who was holding up a final settlement by refusing to accept a UN presence in Cuba. Touré said he wanted us to understand that Guinea's role in the crisis had been guided entirely by its policy of positive neutrality.

"The reason we refused to help the Russians establish missile sites in Cuba," he said, "is that we are against all foreign military bases everywhere. For example, we agree with Castro that you should not have a base in Guantánamo. But we could not agree with him when he invited the Russians to come in with their missiles. That was a violation of nonalignment."

I couldn't help but reflect that this kind of nonalignment had served our purpose fairly well. I asked him about Castro, whom I had met in Cuba in 1959.

"I'm sorry for Castro," said Touré. "I think he is a nationalist and a neutralist at heart, whatever he sometimes says. But he had neither the intellectual training nor the ideological experience to understand the Communists. I did—in the trade union movement—so I know how they operate. But Castro is naïve and has allowed himself to be used by them. Even so, if you are flexible, I think he can be brought back to a neutralist position."

At a reception the same evening, I met the Hungarian Ambassador, hovering near the bar. He had been there quite a while. "Don't worry about that Castro," he told me after we'd clinked glasses. "Mikoyan is going to Cuba and he'll quiet him down." He smiled. "Mikoyan knows how to do that very well."

I was reminded, during the Cuba crisis, of Touré's remark at his Washington press conference: "Don't judge us by what we say but only by what we do." While he was turning down the Russians on the use of the airport, the Guinean representative at the Afro-Asian Jurists Conference in Conakry yielded to adroit pressure by Chinese and other pro-Communist delegates and voted for a resolution denouncing "American imperialism." Phil Heller, who covered the conference, was indignant, and I couldn't blame him. But while the resolution no doubt pleased Peking for its propaganda value, all it in fact accomplished was to annoy Touré—who said he wanted no more Chinese-sponsored conferences in Conakry—and to embarrass the Guinean delegates. Meeting one of them at a party, I remarked that the resolution he'd voted for certainly contradicted what Touré had told Kennedy two weeks earlier. He looked unhappy. "It was all a terrible mistake," he murmured. "We didn't know what to do. It won't happen again."

We also gained stature from the Cuban confrontation. Everybody respects a winner, and we had clearly won the round. In Guinea the crisis and its aftermath were accurately reported on the radio, and the people, who didn't care for the Russians anyway, seemed pleased with the outcome. The day after the Russian ships reversed course, the crowds lining the streets for Ivory Coast President Felix Houphouët-Boigny's state visit waved and shouted

"Vive l'Amérique!" when they saw my car in the mortorcade; later I found some schoolchildren erasing a "Cuba Shall Live" sign daubed on our front gate—presumably by our Chinese neighbors. And Soviet bloc diplomats remained as cordial as ever.

Early in November, Chet and Steb Bowles (he was now a Special Presidential Representative) stopped off in Conakry at the end of an African tour. We had dinner with Diop and his wife, who ran the maternity ward where Sim worked. During coffee, Steb looked up and said, "Who's that man at the door?"

"Why, that's the President," I replied.

Touré came in and sat down. He'd been driving his car around town, listening to the radio, and wanted to congratulate us on the Democratic victory in our Congressional elections. Bowles told him that he had come from Accra, where he found President Nkrumah constantly surrounded by bodyguards; it surprised him to see another chief of state apparently so unconcerned about his own safety. Touré smiled. "I'm not like Nkrumah," he said. "A man who has no confidence in his own people has no confidence in himself."

We talked about the fighting on the China-India border. The Guineans had been curiously uncritical of Chinese aggression—partly because their information came mostly from the Chinese Embassy (the Indians had no resident envoy in Conakry) and partly because they felt that nonalignment required them to take the Communist side now and then. Bowles, who knew India well, explained the situation to Touré, who listened with his customary intensity. They resumed their talk in the morning at the palace, when Bowles flattered Touré by asking his advice on how we should handle Castro. Touré thought we'd been right on the missile sites but cautioned us on pressing Castro too hard, since he was "salvageable." Bowles—one of the few Americans I knew who could outtalk Touré—also gave an eloquent exposition of American foreign policy, pointing out that never before in history had a wealthy country taken part in a world-wide revolution against social and economic injustice. It was the kind of thing that might have sounded corny to an American or European audience, but in Africa we couldn't reiterate this theme too often to overcome the deep-seated suspicion of the white and the rich by the black and the poor.

During Bowles's visit we also discussed our aid program with Diop. Bowles was complaining about a $4.5 million high school that AID was putting up in Liberia—at least fifteen smaller schools could and should have been built for the same price. But in Guinea our projects weren't showy, and they were becoming visible: the vocational training school teachers had arrived; so had an expert on corn production. (His Cuban passport—he was an exile —astonished the Guineans.) We were looking into the palm oil plant and were about to recommend setting up twenty hydraulic presses in the countryside instead of a factory in Conakry; they would cost less, employ more people and simplify transportation.

Meanwhile, Pan American representatives were in town negotiating landing rights in Conakry for their West Coast jet route. (The Soviet Chargé told me later, and somewhat wryly, "You should thank us for building the runway for you.") Some Alaska Airways executives were talking to Air Guinée about replacing their Ilyushins with DC-4's and training Guinean pilots in Seattle. A Peace Corps representative arrived in December and reached agreement on the number and kinds of volunteers Guinea would require in 1963.

On the political front, the year was also ending on a hopeful note. Touré was mending his relations with neighboring countries, where at one time Guineans were engaged in subversive activities, and the so-called radical Casablanca group of African states was falling apart.

A French delegation arrived in Conakry for trade and financial talks and was warmly and almost sentimentally received by the Guineans. (The French Ambassador told me the Guineans were ready to meet them more than halfway on the question of outstanding financial claims, and that De Gaulle's attitude had somewhat mellowed.) An Air France DC-8, on a test flight, became the first jet to land on Conakry's new runway.

Just before the annual PDG Congress on December 31, eight Lebanese were jailed in connection with a financial scandal involving 700 million Guinean francs and the diversion of four thousand tons of cement. Several high Guinean officials were also implicated. Touré opened the congress with an angry, emotional speech denouncing profiteers and announcing a cabinet shake-up that replaced old party hacks with more competent administrators. He appealed for hard work, integrity and dedication in tones that reminded me of Billy Graham in Madison Square Garden. He wanted this to be a "Congress of Truth."

And, in a sense, it was. For once, speakers refrained from blaming foreigners and "colonialists" for Guinea's problems. Instead, they criticized their own shortcomings. The old banners flaunting anti-Western slogans had been replaced with new ones hailing African unity. Between sessions, delegates seemed more interested in action than in ideology. Everyone sounded refreshingly practical.

Guinea had a long way to go, but on New Year's Eve of 1962 there was reason to believe that the worst was over. For all their inadequacies, Guinea's leaders were finally shedding their neuroses and talking in common-sense terms. And there was some satisfaction in knowing that we had helped speed up the process.

X

Missions Accomplished

•

We were all at the airport, all the Diplomatic Corps, to see some visiting chief of state off—I think it was President Senghor of Senegal—when the trouble started. A transit passenger on an Air France flight took some pictures of the Ilyushins parked on the runway, and a policeman demanded he turn over the film. The passenger, who was drunk, took out the film and threw it in the cop's face. He was taken in to the airport security office, and another policeman came out and tapped me on the shoulder. *"Excellence,"* he said, "we have just arrested an American."

I followed him back to the office. The American—sport shirt, loafers, dark glasses, swordfisher cap, cigar—was sulking in a chair. A security officer was filling out a form.

"Where are you from?" I asked.

"Windsor, Ontario," he said.

I told the officer to wait a minute. Out in the waiting room, I found the British Ambassador. Her Majesty's Government represented Canada in Guinea.

"Sorry, Donald," I said, "but he's your problem."

It was like that all during the spring of 1963, my last in Guinea. Problems arose, got solved or evaporated. Everything seemed to be moving on roller skates.

Politically, reason was replacing emotion. Guinea's policy of fomenting subversion in other West African states—which the Soviets, as in Cuba, had aided and abetted—was now officially jettisoned. Touré himself, in a New Year's talk to the Diplomatic

Corps, admitted that in 1961 Guinea's foreign policy had been guided "by the interests of people and not by the quality of relations with their governments"; he justified interference in the internal affairs of other countries because Guinea was politically more developed. Yet he now condemned such interference: "We respect the institutions of others, we respect their right to choose their own roads."

Beginning in mid-1962, African leaders he had denounced a year before as "colonialist puppets," like President Youlou of the Congo (Brazzaville), were now invited to Conakry and greeted with fraternal embraces. To the chiefs of state of Liberia, Senegal, Sierra Leone, Ivory Coast, Togo and Niger, he gave assurances of cooperation and, in some cases, disbanded exile political groups—like the Senegalese PAI—which plotted against neighboring countries from their Guinean sanctuary. Touré was not only seeking to erase his image as a Soviet-sponsored troublemaker, but was laying the groundwork for the formation of the Organization of African Unity, about which he had been in communication with Emperor Haile Selassie.

We welcomed these developments; the stability and viability we wanted for Africa could only come about through greater cooperation and unity under enlightened pragmatic leadership. But the Russians, whose African strategy was based on division and struggle between progressive (i.e., Communist) and neo-colonialist (i.e., nationalist) states, did not like Touré's new policy at all. The expensive political-action infrastructure they had erected in Guinea was no longer serving the purpose for which it was intended; one evening, listening to Conakry's Soviet-built transmitter broadcasting reports of Communist subversion in Venezuela and the Ivory Coast, I could—almost—sympathize with Ambassador Degtyar.

At home, Touré and his ministers were becoming more concerned about popular discontent. The assassination of President Sylvanus Olympio of Togo in January by army mutineers shook them. When several hundred Guineans who had been serving in the French Army were demobilized and sent home a few weeks later, they were turned away at the airport; Touré was taking no chances. When some hungry longshoremen broke open some crates marked "sardines" and found machine guns instead of lunch, troops hastily occupied the port area, and rumors spread through Conakry that the weapons were consigned to the Soviet Embassy. (It turned out they had been sent from Morocco to equip guerrillas in Portuguese Guinea.)

In March Touré suddenly announced the issuance of new currency, printed and minted in England, for which all Czech-made bills and coins had to be exchanged within seventy-two hours. Police and troops promptly sealed off Guinea's frontiers and airports and searched anyone coming in or out of the country. Even diplomatic pouches were impounded until after the currency exchange deadline, for the Czechs in particular were suspected of smuggling currency into Guinea for their embassy's use. Touré said the action was taken to put Guinea's finances in order before applying for membership in the International Monetary Fund. He all but admitted publicly that no one knew how many Guinean francs were in circulation.

The move had more of a political than an economic impact. While it helped the government exercise better control over its own finances, the new Guinea franc was still nonconvertible—and therefore worthless abroad—and Guinea's foreign exchange problem remained acute. Black marketeers, though hit hard, gradually resumed operations with the new currency. But the people liked the feel of the British-made money—the paper was sturdier and the coins heavier—and were delighted that Touré had caught the profiteers by surprise. Psychologically, he had scored some points; and from our point of view, any step that would bring Guinea into the enlightened community of nations that made up the IMF and the World Bank was a good thing.

Meanwhile, Guinean envoys fanned out to Germany, Italy, England, Switzerland and France in search of credits and capital investments. No further approaches were made to the Soviet bloc since Guinea was now trying to reduce the number of "Eastern" technicians and advisers in the country. Inefficient state trading and purchasing agencies, set up by these advisers, were dismantled or shuffled up. Some French supermarket executives were invited down to see what could be done about Conakry's nationalized (and bankrupt) department stores. In the Hôtel de France you could now find European businessmen, along with representatives of U.S. Steel, United Fruit and other American firms, mingling at the bar with the furtive and dispirited East European regulars, and the price of whisky soared to three dollars a shot.

In short, the Guineans were turning to people they felt had the know-how to repair their ruined economy. As Diop told me in April, "We have learned that we have a lot to learn. We are facing the fact that we will have to be apprentices for some time to come."

Austerity and hard work became the recurring themes at political rallies. The long French lunch break in government offices was abolished and a continuous eight-to-four workday instituted. Officials sent abroad now traveled economy class—like our own people. (I once told Touré he could forget about more U.S. aid to Guinea if some Congressman at Washington airport ever saw one of his ministers emerge from the first-class section while I stepped out of the economy exit.)

Negotiations with the French had already resulted in an agreement to furnish Guinea with more than one hundred badly needed teachers. The West German military mission was showing a Guinean Army company how to repair discarded Russian trucks, instead of replacing them, and to build roads. The Yugoslavs took over a nationwide hydroelectric survey from the Chinese. Ismael Touré told a Dutch reporter that Guinea's best friends had turned out to be the Germans, the Yugoslavs and the Americans "because they helped us when we were in trouble without interfering in our politics."

Our own aid program had been shaken up and revised and was now emerging from the bureaucratic underbrush. By February, 1963, we had committed more than $19 million in grants and loans, of which $10 million consisted of deliveries of surplus rice, flour, milk and edible oils for which Guinea paid us in local currency. About three-quarters of the proceeds were then plowed back into development. The second biggest item was a $3,430,000 loan for the purchase of American commodities, ranging from generators to sugar, that Guinea required but lacked foreign exchange to buy. Deliveries had just started.

Other components of the program included 150 scholarships in America geared to Guinea's manpower needs and specialized technical training for others in Europe; equipment and five advisers to

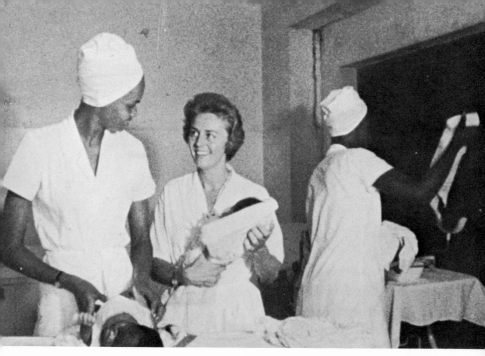

Mrs. Attwood and two nurses in Conakry Maternity Ward, Guinea. *(CBS News Photo)*

President Sékou Touré, of Guinea at May Day rally *(CBS News Photo)*

President and Mme. Touré and Mrs. Attwood watch Sargent Shriver demonstrate driver-training equipment at U.S. trade fair. *(Pan American Airways)*

Peter Attwood and friends kill a snake in Guinea. *(Look Photo)*

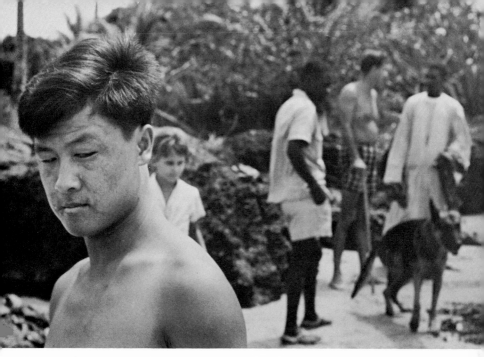

The Attwoods and the Red Chinese swam together daily but the Chinese never talked. *(Look Photo)*

Prime Minister Kenyatta meets the new U.S. Ambassador. Right, Mr. Joseph Murumbi, Minister of State. *(Kenya Information Services)*

The Attwoods and friend visit a Guinean home. (*Look Photo*)

President Johnson announces appointment of William Attwood as Ambassador to Kenya. (*White House Photo*)

Presenting books to children of Kenya. *(ABC News)*

The Attwoods on safari, outside Nairobi. *(John D'Souza, USIS)*

The author with Kamba drummers in Kenya. *(ABC News)*

The Attwood family with Masai students dressed for ceremonial dance.

Snow on the Equator,
Mr. Attwood on Mount Kenya.

Telli Diallo, Secretary-General of the Organization of African Unity;
Elihu Mathu, aid to Mr. Kenyatta; Prime Minister Kenyatta and Charles
Njonjo at Mr. Kenyatta's farm during Stanleyville talks with the author.
(Wide World Photo)

Oginga Odinga and Mr. Attwood. *(USIS Photo)*

East meets West. Attwood (U.S.A.) and Lavrov (U.S.S.R.) chat with Governor-General MacDonald of Kenya (center). *(USIS Photo)*

increase corn and rice production (on their way); rice land recla-
mation (an emergency contract was about to be signed); staff and
equipment for a national school of administration (surveyed and
about to start); a survey of Guinea's light industrial needs (a three-
man team had arrived and hydraulic palm oil presses for a pilot
project were en route); telecommunications engineering and instal-
lation (contracts for technicians were being negotiated with U.S.
firms); rural electrification (being surveyed); vocational training
for skilled workers (nine instructors had arrived and a building site
had been selected) and English-language training (regular classes
were being held with American teachers and equipment). Addi-
tionally, in response to a special request from Touré, we agreed to
train Guinean officials in commercial procedures, and an Ohio
State team was due to take on the project.

What pleased the Guineans was that, unlike the Russians, we
tried to keep American personnel down to the minimum necessary
to train Guineans to perform the work themselves. We always
made it plain we wanted to do our job and get out as soon as
possible. The appointment of Seydou Conté, Guinea's Ambassador
to Washington, as Minister of Education in January helped expe-
dite our program, since a good deal of our activity was in conjunc-
tion with this ministry; at the Washington end, Carl Kaysen of the
White House staff was good about prodding AID whenever their
administrative wheels stopped turning, as they so often seemed
to.

Our day-to-day working relationships with Guinean officials
also gave us a chance to help them clear up some of the mess
created by inexperience, incompetence and ideology. Reluctant at
first to furnish us with economic data that were, in Ismael Touré's
words, "humiliating," they gradually opened up when they discovered we didn't jeer at their mistakes and only wanted to give
them a hand. As a result we were able to locate an entire tire-
recapping plant in one warehouse that someone had ordered and
forgotten about. And when the Compagnie Minière de Conakry
had to curtail its mining of iron ore for want of spare parts, we
found an unused and overlooked $320,000 credit in the National
Bank with which to buy them.

The prospect of "commingling" was always a wheel-stopper
back home. This meant spending American money on a project in

which the Soviet bloc was also involved. The risk of commingling was that the Communists might conceivably get the credit for something we did, and that Congress would hear about it. This was a legitimate concern; I could understand, for example, our not wanting to put up a high school for which the Russians would then provide the faculty. But the reverse should have been acceptable. I would have liked to provide American books for the Soviet-built Polytechnic Institute, and I regretted having to turn down a request for jute bags needed to ship palm kernels to Russia, which would help get Guinea out of hock to the Soviet Union. But the commingling criteria were rigid. It was too bad, for when a Soviet-supported project clearly benefits a country's economy without giving Moscow a political foothold (which is rare enough) we gain nothing by being stand-offish; we just end up looking like fussy cold warriors.

Fortunately for our side, the Communists have a capacity for making mistakes—and making them with maximum publicity—that far exceeds our own. American bungles are mostly bureaucratic; theirs derive from their tyrannical and inflexible system. In February, thanks to a pretty girl who fell in love with the wrong man, the Russians in Guinea managed to lose whatever goodwill they had recovered (by being quiet and careful) since the 1961 plot.

Svetlana Ushakova was a young Russian teacher at the Conakry high school who looked much more like an Italian starlet than a Soviet pedagogue. She began going steady with one of her Haitian colleagues and ignored embassy orders to stop seeing him. (The Haitians, recruited under an African-American Institute program, were all regarded by the Russians—quite erroneously—as CIA agents.) Moscow ordered her home on the next Soviet plane going through Conakry. There was no time to get her an exit visa; besides, the Guinean Ministry of Education might start asking questions since she was under contract. Svetlana was given someone else's passport, properly stamped, and escorted to the airport by two Russians from the embassy. The Guinean security officer opened the passport and looked up at her.

"This is not your photograph, Mademoiselle," he said.

"It is not my passport," she replied. "These men are forcing me to leave. I want to stay in Guinea."

The Guinean Airport Commander, Commissaire Paul, was summoned. He told the Russians that Guinea was a sovereign country with its own regulations and that the girl could not leave without a proper document.

The Russians took her away. A few minutes later, Paul looked at the Russian crew walking out toward their plane—and noticed an extra stewardess. He stopped them and recognized Svetlana. Angrily, he posted guards on the plane and tried to call police headquarters in Conakry. The phone was dead, so he sent a message by motorcycle. Meanwhile Svetlana vanished again.

Just before the plane was due to leave, an ambulance drove up. A Russian got out, produced a passport and asked permission to drive out to the plane and put a patient aboard. Paul opened the ambulance. The patient's face was swathed in bandages, but he recognized Svetlana's figure. He had her taken out and placed in his custody. By now the Soviet Ambassador had arrived; he said this was a diplomatic matter and angrily demanded she be put on the plane. Paul knew he was acting without orders but didn't care; as he told me later, "My African blood began to boil."

A police jeep arrived from town and Svetlana was driven to headquarters. It was decided she would be temporarily put under the protection of the Ministry of Education. Meanwhile, since it was lunchtime, two Guinean detectives took her to a restaurant. The place began filling up with Russians, among whom one of the Guineans recognized her two airport escorts. Fearing a kidnaping, he phoned headquarters. A truckload of troops arrived, arrested two of the Russians and dispersed the others. Svetlana was taken to a villa and given a twenty-four-hour guard. She was safe at last.

The story was all over town the next day, with some racial embellishment. The Russians, it was being said, objected to her dating a Haitian because he was black. Conté told me Touré's first impulse was to declare the Soviet Ambassador *persona non grata,* but reflected that it was only just over a year since Solod had been expelled. "It might be overdoing it," he said. The Minister of Internal Security, Fodeba Keita, once known as a Communist sympathizer, was indignant when I saw him at a reception. "The Russians have their own methods," he said, "and we've seen what they are. But they forget they aren't at home, where they can do this kind of thing and get away with it."

By speaking up at the airport, Svetlana opened the eyes of a few more Africans to Communist reality. More important—to her— was that she had gambled and won a chance to lead her own life. When I met her at a party two months later, she was with the Haitian. They were about to be married and had asked Commissaire Paul to be best man.

Privately, other East Europeans deplored the way the Russians handled the Svetlana incident. "They shouldn't have made such a fuss," the Polish Ambassador told me. "It just irritated the Guineans, and now we have a precedent for political asylum, which is not good." The Radio Moscow correspondent tried to explain it all as a misunderstanding: the embassy had been told Svetlana's mother was sick in Moscow and wanted to get the girl home quickly without upsetting her with the bad news. But most of the Communists avoided mentioning Svetlana; they simply tightened surveillance on each other.

Soon after, the Russians tried a small gambit with us. As I left the house one morning, a white man darted out from behind my gate and tossed an envelope in the car. It contained a photograph of himself and a note saying he was a Russian and wished to see me alone at seven in the evening, when he'd be walking through my garden from the beach.

Two of us were waiting for him. He came right out and said he was an interpreter for the Soviet military mission and wanted to work in Moscow for "American Intelligence." We could detect no motive, personal or otherwise, for his wanting to defect, and he offered none. As a *provocateur,* he wasn't even convincing. We told him to get out, and he did.

But this was part of a game we all understood and didn't talk about any more than Degtyar and I would discuss Svetlana. Our personal relations were always friendly. When two Soviet cosmonauts visited Conakry, I went out of my way, as the representative of the only other space power, to leave the diplomatic enclosure at a reception in their honor and go up to the dais where they were sitting to congratulate them with a few words of Russian. They were delighted, and the Guineans pleasantly surprised. The more relaxed we are and the less we fight the cold war in public, the better we look to others.

We could make mistakes too. One of them, in April, gave the Russians a chuckle, probably the first they'd had in months.

For some time the Guineans had been looking for a way to phase the Russians and Czechs out of Air Guinée. The fleet of nine Ilyushins, for which Guinea had gone deeply in debt, was mostly idle and losing money. Planes averaged less than fifteen minutes' operation a day. The Guineans were also becoming embarrassed by having so many Russian planes and maintenance personnel around the airport. "Some of our state guests," I was told by Touré's protocol chief, "wonder on arrival if we are in fact non-aligned."

Pan American, which was about to schedule weekly flights into Conakry, would have been the logical airline for Air Guinée to deal with. But a small company, Alaska Airways, came up with a package offer that appealed to the Guineans more than an arrangement with Pan Am. A survey by Alaska showed that Air Guinée could convert its current monthly deficit of nine million Guinean francs into a four-million-franc profit by substituting two DC-4's and two Lockheed-60's for all its Ilyushins and concentrating on its domestic services. Alaska also would train Guinean pilots, navigators and mechanics in Seattle, something which the Russians and Czechs had neglected to do. (The few Guinean pilots sent to Prague were given military training with MIG's.)

A deal was made—Alaska's president even came over to close it—and Guinea then turned to us for a loan with which to buy the DC-4's. While we liked the idea of an American company easing out the Soviet bloc, we had doubts about Alaska's ability to do as good a job as Pan Am. But the combination of Guinean insistence on working with a smaller airline and pressure by Alaska in Washington finally got the loan approved. The four DC-4's arrived with fanfare on April 25. Two weeks later, on its second scheduled flight, one of them crash-landed when a defective strut in its landing gear gave way.

No one was hurt and the supicious Guineans at first assumed it was sabotage. (It wasn't.) But you couldn't blame the Russian and Czech onlookers for smiling as a Guinean fork-lift operator had to haul the plane away, carelessly crushing its nose in the process. The Ilyushin flights resumed the next day.

Eventually, Pan Am took over the Alaska contract, but only after this accident, and further difficulties with Alaska, had tarnished our reputation for efficiency.

We did better with bauxite. In 1961 a Canadian-American-French consortium of aluminum companies, headed by Alcan, wanted a U.S. Government guarantee and some additional financing before honoring their contractual agreement to build an alumina plant to process the vast bauxite reserves near Boké. When we refused, Alcan informed Guinea they were ceasing operations. The Guineans promptly took over the Boké concession and some mining facilities on Kassa Island operated by Alcan's French subsidiary. They gave Alcan several months to reconsider. Nothing happened—even when they offered to let Alcan mine the bauxite without building the plant—until a smaller American firm, Harvey Aluminum, appeared on the scene in 1962 with a proposition to form a joint Guinean-American company and take over the abandoned Boké operations. Capital to develop the area economically would also be provided by Harvey.

The Alcan group, which was mainly interested in Boké as a future source of bauxite, came to life. I won't go into details of the tough competitive bargaining that followed, nor the charges and countercharges of expropriation, favoritism, bad faith and worse that were flung around Washington and Conakry during the next few months. The embassy stayed impartial—not always easy since Harvey thought we should support their all-American offer—but we did urge the Guineans, in their own interest, to make a decision one way or the other. (In their dealings with FRIA, the Guineans had proved to be shrewd negotiators who figured, often correctly, that a few more drops of foreign exchange could always be squeezed out of a dry sponge.)

They chose Harvey in 1963. They figured Harvey would move faster since it needed bauxite more than Alcan. They also preferred dealing with Americans to dealing with Alcan's French representatives, of whom they had learned to be wary. And they liked the idea of forming a joint stock company with a single firm. "We feel more equal with Harvey," and the Minister of Mines. "The Alcan group is too big."

Harvey applied to Washington for an investment guarantee, which we finally granted despite intensive lobbying by the big aluminum companies, and operations got under way in 1965. Guinea's bauxite was now in good hands and would eventually be providing Guinea with urgently needed job opportunities, technical training and foreign exchange.

The month of May was my last in Guinea. It had been more than two years since we first touched down at Conakry airport, wondering what to expect. I had done all I could and was feeling restless; also, we didn't want to be separated from the children any longer. I'd already told Ball I was ready to leave Guinea but would be willing to stay in the Foreign Service if another interesting assignment were available. In April Bowles wrote me to say he'd proposed me to the White House as a replacement for George Kennan in Belgrade; the story broke in the *New York Times* a few days later. It turned out to be a White House leak, and the State Department, which had its own candidate for Yugoslavia, denied it. A telegram from Ralph Dungan in the White House arrived, suggesting I come home in June to talk about another "challenging" job. So I sent a letter of resignation to the President; announcing it, he said he was delighted I'd soon be accepting "an important new diplomatic assignment." I didn't know what it was (nor, it turned out, did anybody else), but we had too much to do in May to think about it.

The month started with May Day, my third in Guinea, and as hot as ever. But the parade featured tractors instead of Russian tanks, the slogans attacked nobody, and the Chinese Ambassador's sons, who sat next to me, wore cowboy hats and chewed gum. Touré talked of victory gardens and active leisure. The evening reception was mercifully free of speeches and films, and the band didn't even play the *"Internationale."* It was almost restful.

The opening of our trade fair was scheduled for May 4. A four-man team from the Department of Commerce had been supervising the erection of a geodesic dome which housed exhibits demonstrating the kind of tools and machinery that Guineans could understand and put to practical use. Students from our vocational training classes manned the exhibits and could answer questions in local languages. Among other things, we had a continuous film show, a gocart track, a space capsule, photo murals of life in America and an information booth with a push-button question-and-answer panel, staffed by Americans, both white and Negro, from our Department of Labor. All in all, it was a lively, informative and unpretentious contrast to the Chinese and Russian fairs of 1961 and 1962.

Sargent Shriver was to fly over and cut the ribbon with Touré on May 4. Two days before, the Guineans told us that we'd have to postpone it a day since they just remembered May 4 was a religious festival. The invitations had gone out, but that was all right; this being Guinea, they'd been misprinted and already read May 5.

Shriver came in on Pan American's inaugural flight to Conakry with a retinue of old friends, reporters and airline executives. He was promptly whisked off by a group of ministers for a tour of the countryside. Every village was a swirling, throbbing bedlam of dust, tom-toms and stampeding crowds. He'd been flying all night, but his politician's stamina carried him through, just as it had nearly three years before.

The whole Guinean Government turned up for the opening, the men mostly wearing African costume and their wives strikingly stately in their light billowing gowns and headdresses. Touré arrived and greeted Shriver like an old comrade while an army band played our anthems. After cutting the ribbon, we walked around the exhibits; the students demonstrated their metal and woodworking tools like veterans. Our Guinean guests were delighted.

Outside, I joined Shriver and Touré on the platform. In my remarks, I drew applause by praising the Guinean workers who had erected this fair on schedule. (Everyone remembered that the Chinese and Soviet exhibitions used imported labor.) Shriver spoke in French and said all the right things. And Touré let himself go, praising America in terms not often heard in neutralist Africa. "Every African leader with a conscience," he declared, "must now recognize the value of cooperation with the United States and that American assistance is, contrary to what we were told, the most disinterested, the most effective and the most responsive to our real needs."

The fair ran for two weeks and was visited by 103,000 people. On the last night, we invited the Diplomatic Corps for a private party under the dome. Conté, in a brief speech, singled out Gene Abrams for special praise as the kind of American all Africans could admire. (Ironically enough, I had just heard that AID planned to transfer him after my departure; the bureaucrats had never forgiven me for insisting that he run our program.) Later, while I was having a drink with Degtyar and his interpreter, he congratulated me on the fair. "But of course," he added, looking around, "the Guineans stop coming after the first few days. The same thing happened at ours."

The gates had been closed during our party, and there were about two thousand people waiting outside. I signaled to a guard to let them in. A moment later Degtyar was jostled aside by the throng that surged into the grounds.

Guinea's economic problems were still acute, and Touré spelled them out to Shriver at a meeting with his key ministers. There were shortages of almost everything, and unless people could see some tangible effects of Guinea's new policy of cooperation with the West, the pro-Communist faction in the party and government might be able to stage a comeback. He said Guinea needed $30 million now to get out of the woods. We were sympathetic but made no promises. The next morning Guinea's new Ambassador to Washington, Karim Bangoura, confirmed my hunch that Touré was unaware of the magnitude of our program, especially since the addition of PL 480 food shipments. (Economics was not Touré's strong suit.) But he emphasized that he needed to be able to give the people some good news before leaving for the OAU meeting in Addis Ababa May 20. And $30 million seemed to be his magic figure.

I told Bangoura it would be easier to get support in Washington if a few things were first done at this end. It was, I said, a matter of public relations rather than political conditions. The things I suggested were: (1) the assignment of another full-time man to our aid program, since Diop had taken over another ministry; (2) a reduction in the number of Soviet bloc technicians in Guinea, some of whom were in positions where they could sabotage our programs; (3) a phase-out of Soviet planes, which were wasting resources now that we were helping reorganize Guinea's civil aviation; (4) cancellation of the scheduled Communist World Federation of Trade Unions meeting in Guinea, which was a propaganda ploy to get anti-American speeches printed under a Conakry dateline; and (5) approval for Guinea trade union leaders (most of whom still harbored strong pro-Communist leanings) to visit the United States.

Bangoura lunched with Touré and came back to the embassy with his agreement on all points: A good man, Roger Soumah, was assigned to our program, the WFW conference would be canceled, the union leaders would go to the United States, Soviet bloc personnel were being gradually phased out and the Russians would be asked to take their planes back as soon as Air Guinée could replace them. I called Gene Abrams in, and we calculated that by putting together all U.S. aid commitments, both delivered and undelivered, to Guinea since 1960 and adding our as yet unsigned PL 480 agreements and tentatively approved future projects, we would have a grand total of just over $31 million.

On May 20 I called on Touré. He had been up all night and was wearing a *boubou* over his pajamas. I introduced Tom Cassily, my new DCM, who would be in charge after I left, and explained that my departure did not imply any change of policy. I handed him a friendly but noncommittal letter from the President in response to his aid request and then gave him a breakdown of our total aid compilation, pointing out that Guinea was getting more U.S. aid, per capita, than Nigeria. He thanked me and asked whether he could inform the cabinet about the $31 million figure. I said of course, since anybody could add up the total, as we had done. He said he now understood American policy, spoke feelingly about our two-year association and gave me a picture of himself inscribed to "our brother and friend, William Attwood."

The noon news broadcast opened with an announcement that Touré had just received a letter from President Kennedy promising Guinea $31 million in aid. I spent the afternoon setting the record straight for inquisitive newsmen and fellow diplomats. That evening we all went to the airport to see Touré off to Addis Ababa. I was sitting in the lounge with the other ambassadors when Touré called me up to the VIP room. He was grinning when I walked in.

"You gave me a hard time this afternoon," I said. "I had to explain to everybody that we hadn't given Guinea the kitchen sink."

"Good," he said, laughing. "That's your job as a diplomat, to correct wrong impressions. But I'm a politician, and I needed that figure for my own people and also at Addis. The French and the Russians may be upset, but why should you care? After all the Guinean people now regard America as their best friend. Kennedy will understand. He's a politician like me."

You couldn't fault him. I told him I'd just turned down a suggestion that I go to Indonesia (there'd been a news story to that effect) because I preferred dealing with politicians like him to dealing with people I didn't understand or respect, like Sukarno.

The official French news agency reported from Addis a few days later that the Guinean delegation had sponsored a resolution at the OAU meeting sharply criticizing President Kennedy for the racial violence in Birmingham. The Acting Foreign Minister was dumfounded when I told him I had another letter for Touré from Kennedy but would hold it until the story was checked out. Fodeba Keita, one of the ministers closest to Touré, said flatly that it was a French fabrication. "The French have put pro-Communist words in my mouth in the past," he said. "Now they are trying to sabotage our good relations with you. They think they can come back to Guinea and have things their own way as before. They're wrong. We are independent now and want good relations with everybody —especially with America and Germany."

Whatever the reasons for the French news story, Touré issued a statement in Addis a few days later fully supporting Kennedy's handling of racial strife "without any reservations."

It was certainly true that some French officials and businessmen regarded us and the Germans as interlopers in Guinea and sought to discredit us, often in petty ways, with their Guinean contacts. They sneered at entertainers like Cozy Cole as "American tom-tom players," referred to Harvey aluminum negotiators as "Wall Street sharks," knocked our fair—boycotting the opening ceremonies—and later spread a rumor that we had not asked them. (When I asked the French Counselor of Embassy for an explanation, he lamely explained that the invitations—which we had personally hand-delivered—were never received.) In Paris, French Foreign

Office officials, reflecting De Gaulle's personal pique, admitted privately they would prefer a Soviet Guinea to an "Americanized" Guinea.

In my farewell call on the French Ambassador, I congratulated him on the improvement in Franco-Guinean relations and emphasized that this had always been one of our principal policy objectives in Guinea. I doubt if he believed me. But I made it plain that we were fully aware of what some—by no means all—Frenchmen had been saying about us. I said I hoped that we could work together in the future since a stable, non-Communist Guinea was what we all wanted.

Although he changed the subject, my call had some effect; the Ambassador and all the top officials of the French Embassy came to the airport to see me off.

Farewell calls took up most of my last week in Conakry. Several of the Communist diplomats congratulated me on having done a good job, and Degtyar admitted they had made a lot of mistakes in Guinea: "We never should have sent them equipment without teaching them how to use it. You had more experience with Africans than we did."

With the Guineans, good-byes were hard. Africans have a half-embarrassed way of showing emotion that can quickly put a lump in your throat. Ismael Touré recalled our talk in July, 1961, when he defended Soviet policies in Africa, and added, "You must have thought I was pretty foolish. I've been wanting to tell you that I was."

Even Mamady Kaba, the trade union boss and the leading anti-American in the Guinean power structure, seemed to have mellowed. I called on him with Shriver during his visit to arrange for a special American film showing for union officials. He kept us waiting half an hour. When we finally walked in, Shriver had a handful of Communist pamphlets he'd been reading in the waiting room. At first, Kaba, who affected a Chinese tunic, seemed stiff and nervous. Finally Shriver switched to English. "You tell him," he said to me, "that the things I've been reading in his office about America are all a pack of Goddamn lies!" As usual, frankness broke the ice; Kaba and his staff laughed appreciatively, and we had a useful talk.

Before leaving, I gave a party for all the Conakry Americans. Our official and semiofficial family would no longer have fitted into Tony Ross's living room, where we first assembled in 1961. We now numbered more than a hundred, including AID contract employees. I told them this was a sign we'd been busy—and successful. For the new arrivals, I talked about how it felt to be an American in Guinea two years before, when the walls of hostility and suspicion seemed insurmountable. And I suggested that someday those of us who had labored here during this period might look back and, like Kilroy of World War II, be able to say with some pride, "I was there."

There were several reasons why we'd made headway in Guinea. First, and most important, the Communists overplayed their hand.

Second, Sékou Touré, for all his erratic idealism, was tough, honest and usually receptive to practical advice.

Third, as a noncareer ambassador who had nothing to lose, I could follow Robert Hutchins' dictum ("Behold the turtle—he makes progress only when he sticks his neck out") and fight the Washington bureaucracy for the tools we needed. Also, thanks to illness, Touré's visit and occasional emergencies, I was able to get back often enough to do battle in person.

Fourth, I had a staff any executive, in any business, would have been proud of. Tony Ross, Phil Heller, Don Herdeck, Hugh Mac-Dougall, Gerry Levesque, Gene Abrams—and I could go on—did their jobs with dedication, with enthusiasm, with patience, with humor, with professional skill. Those of us who worked together in Conakry will always be friends.

Fifth, we were carrying out policies that Africans could appreciate under the leadership of a President whom Africans admired. Having Jack Kennedy in the White House made the job of every ambassador easier; it was a wonderful time to be an American abroad.

On our last evening in Conakry, I invited the Soviet bloc teachers who had been using our garden path to stop by for a drink. They were painfully grateful for this small favor; I felt sorry for them. When they congratulated me on all that America had accomplished in Guinea, I thought how unusual it would be for Americans to say the same thing to a Communist ambassador.

Meeting people like this, you wonder how anybody can still believe that Communism is the wave of the future when its leaders can't even count on the loyalty of the people it sends abroad.

There was a big crowd to see us off at the airport; even the Catholic Archbishop, an African, showed up. The North Vietnamese Dean of the Corps, naturally didn't come but was courteous enough to send word he was sick. As I was about to board the plane, one of my Guinean friends from the Foreign Ministry shook my hand and said, "I hope you come back someday. There aren't very many people who understand us. You did." It was the nicest thing he could have said.

XI

The Glass Menagerie

•

The day after I got back to Washington I went to a cocktail party at Walter Lippmann's. Most of the guests were the kind of people who are "in" no matter who is President and who make it their business to know what's really going on. Circulating around, I was told confidentially and positively that my next assignment would be in Mexico, in Algeria, in Argentina, in Indonesia, at the Pentagon, at the White House. No one believed me when I said I hadn't a clue. I finally told one inquisitive columnist that I was assigned to Limbo—and she printed it.

Of course, the best way to get what you want in Washington is to plant your own rumors. My problem was that all I really wanted just then was to wind up my debriefings as quickly as possible and start my leave. But first I had to decide whether to stay on in the government. And that depended, in part, on what was available. A quiet ambassadorship didn't appeal to me; nor did a job in Washington—a frustrating, low-pay company town if you're working for the government. So I was noncommittal when George Ball suggested Panama, and I turned down offers to join the Defense Department as a special assistant to the Secretary and to join USIA as Director for Africa.

Soon after the Lippmanns' party, I ran into the President at Joe Alsop's. He didn't know I was back and suggested I come in for a talk. I remember that we sat in the garden talking about the Profumo case and reminiscing about our school days. Mary Meyer, a Washington artist who'd been my date at a prom twenty-eight years before, was between us, and Kennedy happily recalled having cut in on her on the dance floor. It was hard, at times like that, to realize he was President of the United States. And it was impossible to imagine that, inside of a year, both of them would be murdered, he in Dallas and she in Georgetown.

At the White House, two days later, I talked about Africa while he rocked in his chair. As to my own future plans, I told him that, without sounding corny, I could think of nothing more satisfying, at my age and at this time in history, than to be working for his administration. But I would only take another ambassadorship if it was challenging enough. "I'm not interested in the title," I said, "if it just means sitting on my ass with a flag on my car." He laughed and said he'd just asked Lodge to go to Saigon, so that was out. But he thought Latin America was where the big problems were and said Colombia would be available at the end of the year. Meanwhile, he agreed with my suggestion that I serve with the U.S. delegation at the United Nations during the fall. (I had already discussed this with Stevenson and Harlan Cleveland, the Assistant Secretary for International Organization Affairs, who wanted a special adviser with African experience for the General Assembly.)

So I wound up my Washington business. I put in long hours answering questions about Guinea for roomfuls of people at CIA (pipes, casual sport jackets and yellow pads) and State (cigarettes, dark suits and white notebooks). Short-handed as we were in the field, it always surprised me to discover how easy it is, in Washington, to assemble forty people for a conference at short notice. The tenor of the questions was skeptical; Guinea had been labeled as "lost" for so long that no one was quite prepared to believe there'd been a real change. Optimism, I've found, is always vaguely suspect in a bureaucracy; it's safer to predict the worst.

At USIA I pressed again and in vain for a film about African students in America; at AID, as usual, for speed and flexibility. I spent a couple of days on Capitol Hill, lobbying for Africa with Senators and Congressmen, and a couple of evenings doing the same with old friends at the National Press Club. I met with some French technical assistance officials who hoped we could "collaborate discreetly" in Guinea—discreetly because of De Gaulle. I was glad to learn that Jim Loeb, a newspaper publisher who'd been Ambassador to Peru, was going to replace me in Conakry.

(It was a White House choice; State wasn't keen on reappointing noncareer ambassadors.) Loeb would be brushing up his French during the summer, while I was brushing up my Spanish.

Home again in Connecticut, I was glad I'd decided to stay with the New Frontier. The occupations and preoccupations of my friends and neighbors did not now seem as meaningful as the problems we had been coping with. And it was depressing to note the doubt, anxiety, cynicism and indifference about our foreign policies that seemed to permeate the opinions of people who should have known better. It wasn't the ignorance that surprised us—we were used to questions about cannibals and our life in *New* Guinea; it was the widespread feeling that the Communists were making headway in the cold war, that Africa and Asia were as good as down the drain, that the UN was a failure, that foreign aid was a waste since everybody was anti-American. No one seemed to notice the repeated setbacks suffered by the now fragmented and frustrated Communist movement—in Berlin, in Cuba, in Laos, in India, in the Congo, in the Middle East—wherever its operatives had tried to muscle in. But foreign affairs is a topic about which everybody—no matter if he's never been abroad—considers himself an expert. While I'd hesitate to tell a good broker how to handle my securities, plenty of brokers would tell me with assurance how we should handle Khrushchev and De Gaulle or why we should cut out foreign aid. I found myself looking forward to getting away from the grandstand experts and back to where the action was—among the professionals who knew the real score and the name of the game, and back to working for a boss who understood what we were up against.

"We want to help make the world safe for diversity," said the President in a speech in June—coining a phrase that, like many other ambassadors, I'd be using often and to good effect in Africa. And he went on: "It makes little sense for us to assail, in speeches and resolutions, the horrors of Communism, to spend fifty billion dollars a year to prevent its military advance, and then to begrudge spending, largely on American products, less than one-tenth of that amount to help other nations strengthen their independence and cure the social chaos in which Communism has always thrived."

It made little sense, as the President said, but I got tired of arguing with my fellow citizens who didn't seem to have much.

Our experience in Africa had not only made Sim and me less tolerant of prattlers; it had done something else: it had made us color-blind. In America you can be free of racial prejudice, as we had always been, yet for some reason you remain color-conscious. When you have a Negro friend to dinner, you are aware that you are having a Negro friend to dinner. But in Guinea we lost that awareness, I think for good. We no more noticed the color of a man's skin than we did the color of his eyes or hair—perhaps because the Africans never appeared to notice ours, except as a sign that we were foreigners to be made welcome. So it distressed me as never before, here at home, to find so much time, energy, conversation and newsprint devoted to color; for nothing, let's face it, is more irrelevant to the real problems confronting mankind. Even the terms "Negro" and "white" had come to offend me, for I now understood that the crisis we are going through in America is not so much racial as it is human. I recommend a long visit to Africa to those, liberals included, to whom pigmentation is still an interesting subject.

Early in September, after a week of reading files in Washington, I reported to USUN—the United States Mission to the United Nations. The mission was organized and operated like any embassy abroad, except that Washington was on the phone several times a day and the Ambassador—Stevenson—was down there at least once a week.

For the annual General Assembly sessions, which last from September until Christmas, the permanent staff is reinforced by a couple of Congressmen, a few unemployed ambassadors like myself and some Foreign Service officers from the State Department who have recently served abroad and developed contacts with members of other delegations. There were a dozen of us with African experience at this session, since the agenda would be dominated by African questions—such as the Portuguese colonies, Rhodesia, *apartheid* and the status of Southwest Africa. Together, we managed to maintain regular contact with the thirty-two African delegations that comprised the biggest voting block in the General Assembly.

Each day started with a staff meeting in Stevenson's office, where we generally discussed what actions had to be taken to ensure that the spate of resolutions being debated and voted on would not weaken the UN and would not be too far out of line with our foreign policy. It didn't take us long to conclude that the UN—especially during a General Assembly—was very much like a permanent political convention where the caucusing, cajoling, horse-trading, arm-twisitng and passionate oratory were incessant—but where nobody ever got nominated.

I also began to appreciate Sir Harold Nicolson's observation that "the worst kind of diplomatists are missionaries, fanatics and lawyers." The permanent staff of USUN was top-heavy with lawyers (including Stevenson, a lawyer-politician), and many seemed more concerned with establishing legal precedents on which to build up cases for a nonexistent courtroom than in winning rounds in the propaganda contest for which the UN was the world's principal arena. For example, we abstained on a resolution supporting human rights after quibbling over some fuzzy wording, while the Russians—who naturally had no intention of carrying out the resolution—voted yes and got the credit for being champions of the oppressed. I suspect that our delegation would even have found good legal reasons for opposing a resolution commemorating and praising the Boston Tea Party.

Each day's proceedings were printed and circulated. A report on the 1259th meeting of the Third Committee will give you an idea of how time was consumed: "Draft International Covenants on Human Rights [48]. The Representative of Saudi Arabia introduced a sub-amendment (A/C. 3/L. 1169) to the sub-amendment proposed by Chile and the United Arab Republic (A/C. 3/L. 1168) which relates to the amendment of the United Kingdom (A/C. 3/L. 1167) concerning paragraph 3(b)."

The Foreign Service officers on the permanent staff were often so obsessed with rounding up votes for or against certain resolutions that they also failed to see the political forest for the legalistic trees. Ironically enough, Stevenson, who in 1954 had eloquently advocated mainland China's admission to the UN, now headed a mission that, year in and year out, used up most of its bargaining credit with other delegations to keep the Chinese blackballed, even though Peking had made it plain it no longer wanted to join the

UN. More at home with the UN's parliamentary-minded and mostly European charter members, the permanent USUN staff also seemed to resent the influx of new nations—thirty-one since 1956 —that had transformed a fairly sedate club into a crowded, swinging, go-go forum. They longed for the good old days of automatic pro-Western majorities, judged other nations (like Guinea) by individual delegates and muttered about the "teen-age" newcomers who needed to be slapped down. But as Sir Gladwyn Jebb once said, "The UN has become a mirror of the world, and if we don't like what we see, let's not blame the mirror."

And the emotional speeches and resolutions didn't really affect our vital interests or the central issue of peace as much as the UN veterans had come to believe.

"All these words," an Algerian delegate told me one day, "all these votes—all blah. The only thing that counts is relaxing tension between the Soviet Union and the United States."

The UN is by no means all blah. Useful, often unpublicized work is done behind its glass façade. The UN's various specialized agencies are quietly laying the foundation stones of that peaceful, integrated world order that will one day have to be built if mankind is to survive. And I hate to think what could have happened during the past twenty years without the UN there to damp down the brush-fire wars that might otherwise have blazed into nuclear bonfires.

The UN is also a place where nations can settle their quarrels without losing face; it's easier to give way to the world organization than to your opponents. And it's a great equalizer—it's where any country, no matter how small and poor and weak, can hold its own with the superpowers; it's where steam gets let off. Once, when one of my African acquaintances had delivered a diatribe against the United States for trading with South Africa, he came over to where I was sitting. "How did you like my speech?" he asked with a broad grin. "Terrible, wasn't it? But it made me feel better. Come and let me buy you a drink."

So the smaller, younger countries continue to support the UN against Soviet attempts to weaken it because it is a forum where they do not have to feel inferior. In this respect, our policy coincides with theirs. And the Africans, at first bewildered by some of the parliamentary procedures of the UN, have caught on fast. The chairman of the Fourth Committee, a young Guinean who had been a left-bank musician and dancer in Paris a few years before, ran the show as smoothly as Sam Rayburn did a Democratic convention.

The President spoke at the UN on September 20. It was a good speech that drew applause from every delegation except the Albanians. The speech made it plain that we opposed South Africa's policy of *apartheid*. And yet our delegation managed, later in the day, to make it appear that we didn't really mean what the President said.

The chief South African delegate was scheduled to speak, and the African bloc decided to stage a walkout when he did. It was an emotional and unorthodox gesture, and the Algerians softened it by suggesting instead that the General Assembly agree to a brief symbolic recess before his speech. It was approved, 68 to 17, as we knew it would be, but the United States still voted against it. This was a case of the lawyers on our delegation making a political decision. None of our mission's three ambassadors concerned with African affairs—Sid Yates, Mercer Cook or I—were even consulted about the vote.

A few weeks later, a resolution condemning South Africa came up for a vote in the General Assembly. Our instructions from Washington were to abstain. But we learned, just before the vote, that France and Britain were going to support it, leaving us as the only delegation—except for Portugal and South Africa—not voting in favor. Soviet propagandists were ready to make the most of it. Stevenson was away, so his deputy, Francis Plimpton, and I phoned Harlan Cleveland in Washington to get approval to change our vote. He said he'd have to consult Rusk, but unfortunately Rusk couldn't be found. I then put in a call to Williams, who was with Harriman, and they promised to do something. We requested and got a twenty-minute recess, and the authority to change our vote came through just in time.

I never understood why we never took the initiative with a resolution of our own that we could support without always appearing negative and reluctant.

While feelings about South Africa were intense, there was not much the UN could do. Economic sanctions, even if they could be justified under the Charter, were impractical. They would be almost impossible to enforce, even with a naval blockade, and South Africa was in any case self-sufficient enough to survive the squeeze. Yet morally and politically, we needed to do more than deplore *apartheid* in speeches that many Africans considered hypocritical in view of our massive investments in South Africa. In November I sent a memorandum to McGeorge Bundy—that was cleared by all the mission officers concerned with Africa—urging that we at least discourage further American investment in South Africa as a bad risk on the grounds that eventual political unrest and violence were inevitable. Such a step, along with a downgrading of our Pretoria Embassy to the chargé level, might at least cause the South African business community to have second thoughts about Verwoerd's policies; and would help convince the nonwhite majority in the UN that the United States was doing more than just deploring *apartheid*. We also recommended greater efforts to reassure enlightened South Africans about African intentions—the blacks wanted above all an end to humiliation—and to help re-establish communications between South Africa and the rest of the continent.

Bundy said the President was interested in our memo. But he got it only two weeks before he went to Dallas.

When a resolution on Southwest Africa came up in the Fourth Committee, I was sitting in for Sid Yates and recommended that for once we vote yes instead of retreating into lonely abstention. South Africa, which administered Southwest Africa as a League of Nations mandate, was accused of illegally introducing *apartheid* into the territory, and the sponsors wanted the Security Council to take up the charge. The department agreed on a yes vote only if we could get two changes made in the wording. (We didn't want the Security Council to act until the World Court had rendered a judgment on the issue.)

After some intensive lobbying, I persuaded the sponsors to make one change and suggested to Stevenson that we take care of the other by stating our reservation in a strong statement before the vote. The mission's legalists were opposed, but Stevenson backed me up and agreed we should go ahead and explain it to Washington later. The sponsors cooperated by amending the resolution, the Guinean chairman permitted me to explain our vote before I cast it, the Russians were surprised, the British switched from a "no" vote to abstention—and our African and Asian friends were delighted. Our vote cost us nothing—we supported a moral principle without committing ourselves to a course of action —and gained us considerable goodwill and publicity. But, as usual in government, it had taken effort and stubbornness to break an established policy pattern.

The USUN workday ended long after the lights had gone out in the midtown office buildings. With 113 countries holding receptions at the slightest pretext, there were at least three or four a night at which we had to be represented, both for protocol reasons and to find out what was going on or coming up. It was a rare evening that every mission officer didn't have at least one to attend. Stevenson did as much as his legs and liver could stand, and those of us with ambassadorial rank substituted for him whenever the load got too heavy even for him. During the day, we also spelled each other behind the "United States" sign in the main auditorium, where every country's chief delegate usually took full advantage of his right to speak as long as he pleased. Fortunately, there was an *espresso* machine in the Delegates' Lounge, to which we repaired from time to time when our eyelids began drooping, for you never knew when the television cameras would suddenly focus on your row of seats.

One of my duties, every Friday, was to talk to groups of out-of-town community leaders who visited the UN as the guests of the Foreign Policy Association. They were mostly businessmen and their wives from all over the country, and I came to regard these meetings as the most useful and rewarding part of my job at the mission. Many were uninformed and steeped in anti-UN and anti-State Department prejudice. But all were inquisitive and attentive, and their questions were searching. I think they went away with a better understanding of why we couldn't walk out of the UN just because we didn't always have our way, and a better appreciation of what USUN was doing.

I didn't try to argue with the Goldwaterites. I simply suggested that it made more sense to be practical and tough on issues where we could make progress than to strike futile and idealistic postures on issues like the freedom of Latvia, where we could make none.

And I may have convinced a few skeptics that foreign aid is a subsidy to American industry and agriculture as well as an instrument of diplomacy.

I was surprised to hear so many of these visitors tell me, after meeting our mission officers, how relieved they were to discover that people working in the State Department were "no different from any other Americans." (They probably expected to be greeted by stuffed shirts in frock coats.)

Although these meetings were sponsored by a private organization, I see no reason why the State Department couldn't set up a similar program in Washington. The word might eventually get around that Foggy Bottom is part of the United States.

Although my title was Special Adviser for African Affairs at USUN, I also found myself involved, during most of the fall, in a diplomatic exercise aimed at normalizing Cuban-American relations.

It began in September, when the Guinean Ambassador to Havana assured me that Castro, in contrast to his Communist "entourage," was unhappy about Cuba's satellite status and was looking for a way out. I also received information from other sources indicating that he wanted an accommodation with the United States and would make substantial concessions to this end; also that a rift was developing on this issue between Castro and his chief pro-Communist associate, Che Guevara, who considered him dangerously unreliable. The reports struck me as plausible; a long talk with Castro in 1959 had convinced me he was too emotional to be a disciplined Communist, though naïve enough to be swayed by Communist advisers. I therefore suggested to Stevenson and Averell Harriman that we establish discreet contact with the Cuban delegation at the UN and find out if in fact Castro did want to talk on our terms.

On September 19 Harriman told me he was "adventuresome" enough to favor the idea, but suggested I discuss it with Bob Kennedy because of its political implications. Stevenson, meanwhile, had mentioned it to the President, who approved my talking to Dr. Carlos Lechuga, the chief Cuban delegate, so long as I made it clear we were not soliciting discussions.

I casually met Lechuga at a party a few days later and recalled how I had enjoyed my talk with Castro, during which he spoke of wanting good relations with the United States. Lechuga replied that Castro still liked to talk, especially with someone he knew, and said there was a good chance he'd invite me to Cuba if I wished to resume the conversation. I said my status had changed —I was no longer a journalist—but that an exchange of views would be useful and I'd keep in touch.

In Washington I informed Bob Kennedy, who thought a meeting would be worthwhile if it could be held outside Cuba, perhaps in Mexico. He took a memo I'd prepared and would pass it on to Bundy. When I next saw Lechuga, I said I couldn't very well go to Cuba but that if Castro wanted to talk to us we were prepared to meet him or a personal emissary at some convenient place like the UN. He said he'd inform Havana; meanwhile, he warned me he would soon have to make a tough anti-American speech in the UN because of the Cuban blockade and exile raids.

He made the speech October 7. Replying, Stevenson suggested that if Castro wanted peace with his neighbors, he could have it if he stopped trying to subvert other nations, stopped taking orders from Moscow and started carrying out the original democratic pledges of his revolution.

Lechuga later told me Havana did not think sending a special emissary to New York "at this time" was possible, but hoped we could maintain contact. Meanwhile, Lisa Howard, a television correspondent who knew Castro well and had been briefed on my UN talks with Lechuga, had been in touch by phone with Castro's personal aide, Major René Vallejo. He told her Castro did want to talk personally to us about improving relations and was pleased to find out we were ready to listen. (Lechuga's message, which went through the Foreign Office, had apparently not reached Castro.) Vallejo said he could not leave Cuba just now, but promised to call her back.

On October 31 Vallejo told Miss Howard that Castro would like a U.S. official to come and see him alone. He appreciated the importance of discretion, and therefore offered to send a plane to fly the official to a private airport near Veradero, where no reporters would see him. She told him I was the official concerned and would communicate our reply.

I had kept Bundy informed. On November 5 I went to see him

at the White House. He said the President, more than the State Department, was interested in exploring this overture, but thought we should now find out just what Castro wanted to discuss before going into a meeting. He thought we should have a preliminary meeting with Vallejo and Lechuga at the UN to agree on an agenda.

Vallejo called Miss Howard again to say they would go along with any arrangements we wanted to ensure security. A Cuban plane could pick me up in Key West, or an American plane could land at one of several "secret airfields" near Havana. He stressed that only he and Castro would be present and that no one else—he specifically mentioned Guevara—would be involved.

Bundy called the next day and said this didn't affect the President's decision to hold a preliminary talk at the UN to find out, among other things, whether Castro was seriously interested in discussing the points made by Stevenson in his October 7 speech. He suggested I tell this to Vallejo.

I reached him by phone at a private number in Havana and confirmed that we were ready to listen to what Castro had in mind. Vallejo, who called me "sir," regretted he could not come to New York, but said Castro would instruct Lechuga to propose and discuss an agenda with me. I said I'd wait for Lechuga to contact me.

In the morning—it was November 19—I called Bundy, who said the President would want to see me and to call as soon as I'd met with Lechuga. The President, he said, would not be leaving Washington, except for a brief trip to Dallas.

I was lunching at Marietta Tree's with some UN delegates on November 22 when her daughter came in and said there was a report on the radio that the President had been shot. I took a cab back to the office and found the staff assembled in Stevenson's office, silently watching the television screen. When the news flash came that he was dead, I looked over at Stevenson. He covered his face with his hands; then he straightened up, quietly gave orders on what had to be done and reached for a pad to write the statement that had to be made.

A few minutes later we walked across the street to the UN auditorium. Crowds of delegates filled the lobby, waiting for us. I'll never forget the African hands pressing mine, their eyes full of tears, and my own voice, after the shock, finally choking up.

It was raining when we got to Washington in the morning. On the plane, I had started writing a reminiscence of Kennedy for *Look,* which was about to go to press. I wanted to thank him for all he had done to make me and some of my generation feel alive and exhilarated and proud to be Americans. And I concluded with these paragraphs:

Jack Kennedy was so much a part of everything we did in Washington that the day after his death, waiting at the State Department before going over to the White House, I still found it hard to believe, impossible, really, that the President would not be there to greet us in his office. He had been dead, after all, less than 24 hours. It wasn't until I walked into the darkened East Room and saw the flag-draped casket that I fully realized that we had lost him—and what an unexpectedly personal loss it was for someone like me, who had known him so fleetingly.

The Kennedy Administration was an exciting time to be alive, and a good time to be busy. I think the Johnson Administration will be, too, for the new President has the experience and the drive, and the nation now has the momentum. But my thoughts are still turned to the years just past, rather than to the years just ahead. All I know, as I end this memoir, is that I shall always be proud to have been involved with the history of this time—the New Frontier period, as the historians will surely call it—and that my children—the two old enough to have worn Kennedy campaign buttons and the one soon to be born—will also remember and be proud of what their father was doing in the early 1960's.

So I have that to thank Jack Kennedy for, too.

And now, with Christmas almost upon us, I find myself thinking of last Christmas and the present I brought back to my 11-year-old daughter from the White House. It was a note from the President in answer to a letter she had written him. She had it framed, and it has been on her bedside table ever since. The note is signed, "Your friend, John F. Kennedy."

She never met the President, but she always thought of him as her friend, and she was crying that terrible weekend because her friend was dead.

This Christmas, I think a lot of Americans, like my daughter, feel they have lost a friend. They have.

The Africans, I think, more than any other people, felt they had lost a friend too. (Although he had never been to Kenya, six thousand people packed the Cathedral in Nairobi for his memorial service.) Kennedy had said things, before he was even President, that Africans remembered because so few Americans were saying them. "Let us never assist Africa," he said in 1959, "merely because we are afraid of Russian assistance in Africa. Let us never convince the people of that continent that we are interested in them only as pawns in the cold war. Nor do we want them to regard us only as a military guardian, a giver of goods or a lender of cash." And he added that, like George Washington, he felt "irresistibly excited whenever in any country I see an oppressed people unfurl the banner of freedom."

Now we had a new President, whose qualities were relatively unknown abroad. At the UN there was speculation about whether American policy would change. When I saw Chet Bowles two days after the assassination, he thought that Johnson should address the General Assembly before it adjourned, to quiet the speculation; it was important for the departing delegates, who had heard Kennedy in September, to see the new President in person. I passed on Bowles's suggestion to Stevenson, who mentioned it to Johnson when he called on him with U Thant. ("This man," Johnson had said, pointing to Stevenson, "should have my job.") Stevenson said the President wanted him to prepare some appropriate remarks, and he asked me to work on a draft.

I called Ted Sorensen, whom Johnson had inherited as speechwriter. He knew nothing about a UN address, but phoned back to say he'd be working on the draft. (Later, Sorensen told me the State Department, fearing "overexposure," had advised the President against a UN appearance; after my call, Sorensen had gone in and talked him back into it.)

Meanwhile, while we were winding up our General Assembly, I met Lechuga again. He had received instructions from Castro on November 23 to enter into informal discussion with me. But he assumed the situation had changed. I said I didn't know. But I informed Bundy and later was told that the Cuban exercise would probably be put on ice for a while—which it was and where it has been ever since.

Stevenson had also been asked to write an introduction to a

collection of Johnson speeches. He called me to his office, where I found him normally harassed and fidgety behind his generally cluttered desk, to say that he had no free time in sight and would be grateful if I would try my hand at a few paragraphs for him to work on.

Not knowing how Stevenson felt about Johnson, I asked for some guidance. He pondered a moment and then said he had known Johnson for thirty years; he admired him both as a politician and as a liberal who cared deeply about the basic issues; and he knew Johnson would be the kind of President who would devote all his tremendous energy to making America a better and stronger country. With that much to go on, I managed to produce a few paragraphs that survived Stevenson's editing relatively intact.

The President came to the UN December 17. The USUN staff met him in Stevenson's suite. It was there that I noticed something that I had never thought about before. When Kennedy walked into a room, he brought with him a vibrancy and an almost electric sense of excitement that you could feel even at a distance. But when Johnson came in, I felt, as I had with Truman or Eisenhower, "Here is the President of the United States," and I was properly impressed; but the curious magnetism that Kennedy seemed to radiate was missing, and I have never sensed it again with any public figure. Don't misunderstand me. I don't care for the mythology about the Kennedy era that has blossomed since his death; the Camelot bit leaves me cold. Policies, programs and results are what matter to me, regardless of whether the accent is Texan or Bostonian. All I'm saying is that Jack Kennedy had a quality that made you feel that something exciting was about to happen every time he came into a room.

The President's speech to the General Assembly said all the things the world needed to hear from the man who had inherited the world's most powerful job:

We know what we want. The United States wants to see the cold war end, we want to see it end once and for all; the United States wants to prevent the dissemination of nuclear weapons to nations not now possessing them; the United States wants to press on with arms control and reduction; the United States wants to cooperate with all the members of this organization to conquer everywhere the ancient enemies of mankind—hunger and disease and ignorance; the United States wants sanity and security and peace for all, and above all.

And he concluded:

Man's age-old hopes remain our goal: that this world, under God, can be safe for diversity, and free from hostility, and a better place for our children and all generations in the years to come. And therefore, any man and any nation that seeks peace, and hates war, and is willing to fight the good fight against hunger and disease and ignorance and misery, will find the United States of America by their side, willing to walk with them, walk with them every step of the way.

The style, the delivery and the accent were different from the speech we had heard in September. But the message was the same. We were still on the right track, and I was glad, as I listened to the President, that I'd accepted another assignment and was going to work for him. This was no time, nor was there any reason, for anyone who believed in what the New Frontier stood for to quit— on the contrary.

XII

Back to Africa

•

When, soon after the assassination, the Director General of the Foreign Service offered me a choice of going either to Chile or to Kenya, it didn't take me long to make up my mind. I chose Kenya for a variety of reasons. First, here was a country about to undergo the birth pangs and growing pains of independence. There would be problems—the kind I enjoyed coping with. Second, the Soviets and the Chinese, who were already probing into East Africa, would no doubt be up to their usual mischief, and I now knew some of their tricks. Third, the Prime Minister, Jomo Kenyatta, was someone I'd read about and wanted to know better; the old Mau Mau chieftain excited my curiosity, just as Sékou Touré had three years earlier. So great was his prestige among other African leaders that he was bound to play an influential role in shaping the course of events, not only in Kenya but all over Africa. Fourth, I was interested in rounding out my African education by seeing how a former British colony in the East compared to a former French colony in the West. And finally, Kenya, because of its climate and school facilities, was a place we could take our children, including the new baby we were expecting. (The baby—we named her Susan—had already been responsible for our not going to South America in July. The State Department, whose lines of communication with the White House were often snarled, suddenly decided to send me to Bolivia, and the news even leaked out in the press. But the appointment was canceled when the Medical Division decided it might be unwise to send a pregnant woman to an altitude of 12,500 feet.)

Since November 22 there was yet another reason for my deciding to go to Kenya. Knowing how Kennedy's memory was revered in Africa, I felt that those of us whom the Africans identified with him and with the New Frontier had an obligation to go back and help reassure our friends that American policy was not going to change. This was no time to leave the scene. There weren't too many of us, and if our policy was in fact to stay on the right track, Soapy Williams and his able deputy, Wayne Fredericks, would need all the support we could give them, both from the field and in Washington. Although the new President had visited Senegal briefly in 1961, nobody except Harriman at the top policy-making level of our government—neither Rusk nor McNamara nor John McCone nor Ball nor Bundy nor Walt Rostow nor, later, Tom Mann—had ever set foot in Africa. Their knowledge of this vast continent was entirely secondhand.

The first Kenya officials I met were the members of the delegation that came to the UN after independence was proclaimed on December 12. They included the Minister of Home Affairs, Oginga Odinga; the Minister of State, Joseph Murumbi; the Minister of Health, Dr. Njoroge Mungai; and the Attorney General, Charles Njonjo. While they hadn't yet been told I was to be the first American Ambassador to Kenya, Murumbi called me aside at a reception to say that our Consul General, who had flown over with them, had violently criticized Mr. Odinga's UN speech (it was no worse than what we at USUN were used to) and had suggested they weren't welcome in America. So they were now thinking of cutting short their planned visit to Washington and Detroit. It seems our man had previously also threatened to cut off U.S. aid if they invited the Communist Chinese to their independence celebrations. I alerted Williams, who was to meet them in Washington, and concluded that I was inheriting a few additional public relations problems in my new assignment.

I went to Washington in January for my briefings, no longer the amateur I'd been three years before. I knew my way around the labyrinth and could call the key people by their first names. The Bureau of African Affairs had been strengthened but was still fighting for attention. Aid appropriations for all of Africa were down to $200 million—which may sound like a lot until you realize it's less than half the cost of a single nuclear-powered aircraft carrier. And with Kennedy gone, we couldn't be as sure of White House support on issues involving Portuguese colonialism, for the Bureau of European Affairs and the Pentagon—to whom the Azores counted for more than the goodwill of independent Africa—were a powerful coalition in the Washington power structure.

The pervasive excitement of 1961 was missing now, but this was only natural. Three years before, new people with new ideas were taking over command functions in every department and agency of government. Change was in the air. But today the Kennedy appointees had become old pros. They were still at their desks—in some cases at bigger ones—and none I met felt especially uncomfortable about having a new boss in the White House, for the goals of the Great Society were the same as those of the New Frontier. If what you cared about were policies and programs, the new Texas style and accent were irrelevant. I think that the only people who felt that an era had ended were the party-givers, whose guest lists had to be revised and who now wished they had spent more time cultivating Bill Moyers, Liz Carpenter and George Reedy.

Among some "in" people who were now "out," there was a tendency to disparage the President as being inexperienced in foreign affairs and consequently to view the future conduct of our foreign policy with gloom and apprehension. I had no such qualms. The world of the sixties was more than ever a political arena where a knowledge of traditional diplomatic practices was less important than political acumen. And I figured that anybody who had been as good a Senate Majority Leader as Lyndon Johnson could never be an amateur at modern diplomacy. Like Senators, the world's political leaders are motivated by pride, ambition and the demands of their constituents; a man like Johnson, who understood the value of persuasion, accommodation and compromise, could deal with them far more effectively than a general like Eisenhower or a corporation lawyer like Dulles. He would, for instance, understand Harriman's dictum that "You should never try to push a Russian through a closed door."

The riots in Panama were front-page news while I was in Washington; Congressmen were proclaiming in the finest jingo tradition that we would never yield an inch on renegotiating our canal rights. But the President fully understood that the world had changed since Teddy Roosevelt and that a big power didn't need to throw its weight around; so we quietly moved toward a solution that would satisfy Panamanian pride without sacrificing our real interests.

My Washington homework and briefings took longer than the last time, even though I now knew more of the ropes. For I was taking over a bigger operation than in Conakry. Our Consulate General in Kenya had been in business for a long time, and Nairobi, with a population of nearly 300,000, was a regional transportation and communications center for all of East Africa. In addition to a substantial AID mission, the new embassy included attachés for agriculture, civil aviation, commerce, labor and security who covered several countries. Thus I had more calls to make around the Washington bureaucratic circuit. Furthermore, I had to put in two weeks' attendance at a new interagency counter-insurgency school, the purpose of which I never quite understood. I suppose the lectures and simulated Country Team meetings were beneficial to people who had never served overseas, but I still believe you can learn more, faster, on the job than in a classroom.

At AID I found agreement on the need for us to be doing something, no matter how modest, wherever we had a diplomatic mission in Africa. At CIA I found that the new word this year was "phenomena." At the Pentagon I found myself again resisting demands for adding a military attaché section to the embassy; much as I would have liked to have an attaché plane at my disposal, I saw no advantage—and some disadvantages—in having personnel on my staff with no real function to perform. But the Pentagon people were always pleasant about it, and I liked going over there; unlike other, less affluent branches of the government, they could afford to send a car to pick me up.

I also spent a good part of every day reading about Kenya. I suppose that, for most readers, Kenya has some connotations: the Mau Mau, hard-drinking White Hunters, the lions of *Born Free*,

Ernest Hemingway and Kilimanjaro (which is actually in Tanzania). I would like to replace these with some basic data, just as we did back in Chapter II.

Kenya (don't call it "Keen-ya"—that's a British mispronunciation) is about the size of Texas. More than half its area is arid and looks like the worst of Nevada. The rest runs a gamut: the coast is hot, lush and tropical; the region just north of Nairobi and all around Mount Kenya is high (6,000 to 9,000 feet) and fertile, with lakes and forests and a temperature that ranges between 50 and 80 degrees. To the west, the land slopes down to Lake Victoria and up to the thickly populated hills near the Uganda border. In a two-day drive across Kenya, you can pass through country whose landscape reminds you of a dozen states as varied as Florida, Oregon and Oklahoma.

Kenya is an agricultural country. Its main cash crops are coffee, tea, sisal and pyrethrum (used for insecticides). Corn and wheat are the principal food crops. There are vast grazing lands and huge ranches where cattle and sheep are plentiful. Just about everything seems to grow and thrive in its equatorial but temperate climate— babies too. Half of Kenya's nine million people are sixteen or under.

The population is divided into a dozen major tribes and as many small ones, each with its own language. Most people also speak Swahili—a kind of lingua franca—and English is taught in the schools. The two biggest tribes, which account for 25 percent of the population, are the Kikuyus and the Luos. The former, tough, energetic and industrious, live mostly in the Central Highlands. The British settlers who came to Kenya after the railroad to Lake Victoria was built in the 1890's took over and developed some of their best land. The Mau Maus were Kikuyus who, in the fifties, wanted their land back.

The Mau Mau emergency has been highly fictionalized. Less than a hundred whites were killed, fifty-seven of them police officers; more than eleven thousand Africans died, either in tribal clashes or at the hands of the British security forces. Whether Jomo Kenyatta, who was jailed during the emergency, really masterminded the uprising is debatable. What is certain is that Kenyan independence was hastened by it; the British finally realized that the winds of change were blowing harder and faster than they thought and that an enclave of white settlers could not be maintained in East Africa indefinitely. In 1961 Kenyatta was released from detention, and two years later became the country's first Prime Minister.

Some 45,000 whites still lived in Kenya in 1964, along with 180,000 Indians and Pakistanis, the descendants of railroad workers who came with the British and stayed on as merchants and craftsmen. A majority were apprehensive about African rule, but hoped for the best; Kenya was the only home many of them had ever known. The new Kenyan Government, with British loans, was buying up the land of European farmers who wanted to leave; but in January Kenyatta personally reassured those who wanted to stay that they would be welcome in a multiracial Kenya.

The titular chief of state of the new nation was still the Governor General, Malcolm MacDonald, and the credentials I'd be presenting to him would be addressed to the Queen. But Kenyatta and his majority group, the Kenya African National Union (KANU), were now masters in their own country.

With independence, Russian, Chinese and Czech diplomatic missions lost no time setting up shop in Nairobi. The Poles and Bulgarians were to come later. The North Koreans turned up, too, but were outmaneuvered by the South Koreans and had to go home. Unlike Guinea, where the Soviet bloc moved into a vacuum and staked out a position of strength, Kenya must have looked to Communists like a long-range, uphill proposition. Most of the top leaders had been educated in England or America, and British officers in Kenyan uniforms ran the security forces. But East Africa was still a worthwhile target; it was a gateway to the riches of the Congo and Rhodesia and the natural base for eventual action against the even richer white-dominated lands to the south. Both the Chinese and Russians hoped to control the African "liberation" movements already headquartered in Dar es Salaam. They counted on anti-British sentiment, economic dislocation and political unrest to play into their hands and to win them acceptance as benevolent Big Brothers ever ready to help Africa defend itself against British and American imperialism.

Of course, by 1964 the Russians and Chinese were working at

cross purposes in Africa. Their only common objective was to reduce Western influence and undermine moderate governments; beyond that they were competing for African allegiance. The Russian interest in East Africa, in fact, was in part stimulated by Chinese activity in the area: Moscow didn't want Peking to take over the ideological leadership of the radical liberation movements to the south. But the Russians had learned to play their hand more discreetly than the Chinese since Mr. Solod's excess of zeal in Guinea.

The new Soviet strategy in the "uncommitted" world had been clearly outlined by Andrei Gromyko in a UN speech in September. Two paragraphs are worth quoting here:

We, the representatives of the world of socialism, have indeed waged and will go on waging an unremitting struggle for the triumph of the ideals of socialism and Communism. We shall accept no ideological compromise just as we are not demanding under threat of arms that our ideological opponents renounce their own ideology. What we are calling for is something else: it is not divisions of soldiers but legions of books, not nuclear bombs but the ability to produce more of the common benefits and to distribute them more equitably that must constitute the weapons in the fight between the two philosophies.

The Soviet people are imbued with the unshakable belief that the example provided by the Soviet Union and the other nations which are building socialism and Communism is convincing and will with growing strength continue to convince the people that it is this system that offers the maximum opportunities to develop man's ability and to assure the complete freedom of man from every kind of exploitation and oppression, from need and from fear for his future. We have given the start to a new relay race whose participants—the countries of socialism and the countries of capitalism—will compete on the roads of history.

These paragraphs should be required reading for Americans who want to cut foreign aid, withdraw from the global war against poverty and, in effect, let Mr. Gromyko win his relay race by default.

The Chinese had even fewer consumer and capital goods than the Russians to meet the needs of developing countries, and what they had was of even poorer quality. So Mr. Gromyko's strategy did not appeal to them. Propaganda, gun-running, indoctrination and subversion were the chief weapons in their arsenal. Some diplomats, like the Yugoslavs, thought their ultimate aim in Africa was colonization. Perhaps it was; certainly it did no harm to let the Africans think so.

East Africa hit the headlines in January when a revolt in the newly independent state of Zanzibar deposed the Sultan and triggered a massacre of thousands of Arabs and some Indians who had long ruled the island's African majority. A U.S. destroyer in Mombasa hurriedly borrowed a Swahili-speaking taxi driver and evacuated the Americans from our consulate and satellite tracking station. When the shooting died down, an African, Abeid Karume, was President, but power was in the hands of Abdul-rahman Mohammed Babu, an astute, hard-boiled, Marxist-trained correspondent for Chinese Communist publications. A Chinese Embassy opened up and offered Zanzibar $14 million in interest-free loans. Soviet bloc missions also mushroomed, with the East Germans out in front. Communist technicians poured in, as in Guinea, and took charge of key ministries. The British, who could easily have stopped the massacre (without backing the Sultan) by sending in a battalion of troops, did not even get around to recognizing the new government; they were busy with Cyprus, and we followed their lead. As a result, President Karume became convinced we were plotting to restore the Sultan and that the Communists were his only friends; Babu's hairy tales about the alleged activities of CIA agents disguised as newsmen fed his suspicions.

Within a month it was clear that the Chinese and the Soviet bloc had acquired a new and strategically placed foothold a few miles off the coast of East Africa. Zanzibar seemed ideally suited to their aims: It was small enough to be turned into a cut-rate propaganda showcase—an African Potemkin village to which impressionable leaders from all over the continent could be taken and shown what Communism could accomplish. Separated but still close to the mainland, it also provided a secure base for the training and indoctrination of guerrilla fighters from South Africa and the Portuguese colonies. And it was a convenient command post for planning and mounting subversive activities in Tanganika, Kenya and Uganda. All in all, the January coup gave the Communists an opportunity which they were quick to exploit.

Also in January, units of the Kenyan, Tanganyikan and Ugandan armies mutinied over pay and promotion grievances. British troops stepped in, at the request of the three governments, and quickly snuffed out the mutinies. But the military uprisings, coming on top of the Zanzibar revolution, shocked and alarmed the mainland leaders and made it seem to the world at large that independent East Africa was hell-bent for trouble and violence.

Some Washington officials were already fingering the panic button—not that there was much we could do without the British. (We did agree, in February, to establish diplomatic relations with the new Zanzibar Goverment and sent a first-rate young officer, Frank Carlucci, as chargé, with the difficult mission of disabusing Karume of what he'd been told by Babu and his Communist lieutenants.) But the American press had already pushed the button hard, and the Washington *Star* deplored the fact that we didn't even have an ambassador in Kenya while all this was going on. While I'd planned to go to Kenya with my family in April, after helping Sim pack up, the State Department suddenly decided I should leave as soon as I was sworn in. I agreed on condition I could come back three weeks later to wind up my personal affairs. It took some doing to find the money for the extra airline ticket— the African Bureau, as usual, was short of travel money—but we finally pried it out of the seventh floor. By the last week of February I had been confirmed by the Senate and booked on a flight.

Meanwhile, I had met two more top Kenyan officials in Washington—Bruce McKenzie, a white South African who had become a Kenyan citizen and was now Minister of Agriculture; and James Gichuru, the Minister of Finance. They didn't seem as worried as the Washington pundits about recent events. Nor was I, but I welcomed the chance to go over, look at the problems and return to Washington. I'd done it in Guinea, and it had paid off in terms of getting action on things we needed.

Before leaving town, I made certain that I had a line of communication to the White House, for I had learned how essential this was to an ambassador in the field. Bill Moyers, whom I'd met at the Peace Corps, had already called me over in connection with my writing an article for the the Democratic Convention Book. I went back later to discuss my new job with him. He was now sitting in Ted Sorensen's former office. We talked for half an hour, and I was impressed then, as I have been ever since, with his understanding of our foreign policy problems. His questions were incisive, and, as I discovered, he kept the President informed of what he learned. I found him more interested and receptive to new ideas than anyone in the old White House inner circle. Before I left, he told his secretary to add my name to the list of people whose letters and phone calls got through. It wasn't something to abuse, but it was useful to have in reserve.

On February 20 Mac Godley, our new Ambassador to the Congo (Leopoldville), and I called on the President, together with our new envoys to Venezuela and Jordan. We had only ten minutes—enough for pictures but not for any meaningful talk. But the President did get to the heart of Africa's major political problem with one remark to Godley. "What I'm worried about," he said, "is that the Congolese Army isn't going to be strong enough to keep order in the country after the UN leaves in June." It wasn't, and the consequences fully justified the President's anxiety.

Four days later, Mac and I were sworn in before Secretary Rusk, who observed that I was losing my amateur standing at State now that I'd accepted a third diplomatic assignment. Later, Sim and I and the children lunched with Soapy and Nancy Williams and Bob Kennedy. They were pleased that we'd decided to stay on and return to Africa. My daughter started talking about the 1960 campaign but changed the subject when, young as she was, she saw the hurt in Bob's eyes. In the evening we went to Art Buchwald's for a farewell party. Sim and I were wearing cardboard elephant heads and Art was reciting a mock oath, when the phone rang. It was Moyers, saying the President had signed a letter to Kenyatta and I'd just have time to pick it up before my plane. He also asked if I wanted to change my mind and come to work in the White House. I said no thanks; I had things to do in Kenya and was on my way.

From London, where I stopped to talk with Commonwealth Relations officials, it was an overnight flight to Nairobi, via Rome and Khartoum. The BOAC Comet started its descent in time for us to see the snowcapped peaks of Mount Kenya and the forested slopes of the Aberdares just north of Nairobi. Our Consul General, who was on his way home, met with me along with Kenya's protocol chief, some embassy officers and the press. I said the usual things about friendship and cooperation and drove into town.

We'll take a closer look at Nairobi later. My first impression was as dazzling as the sunshine: gleaming modern office buildings, broad streets landscaped with bougainvillaea and jacaranda trees, English country homes behind clipped hedges, golf courses and drive-in theaters and supermarkets. This was a different Africa from the one we'd known. So were the people, for Nairobi's population was about one-half African, two-fifths Asian and one-tenth European.

Our embassy occupied the three top floors of an office building in the center of town; from my window I could see the dim outlines of Mount Kilimanjaro across the wide Masai plains. Not far away were the AID headquarters, the USIS library and our Commercial Attaché's office and showroom.

After a nap, I called the Country Team together and told them I planned to learn as much as I could in three weeks and return to Washington with some recommendations. I said I wanted to keep our operation informal and internal protocol to a minimum; that instead of staying at a hotel (the residence was not yet available) I'd like to get acquainted with the staff and their families as quickly as possible by being a rotating boarder at their homes. In addition, I'd be sending out a confidential questionnaire, as I had in Guinea, to find out if anybody had any problems affecting his job. I told them that East Africa was in the spotlight, that we were going to be busy and that I wasn't going to put up with deadwood, muddy writing or red tape. From the way they reacted, I concluded we had a good team.

The big issues in Kenya, three months after independence, were unemployment, education and land. Nairobi had filled up with people from the former "native reserves" looking for the fruits of *uhuru* (the Swahili word for freedom) and finding none (I visited newly set-up unemployment registration centers with lines outside a mile long). Schools were overcrowded and short of teachers, even though public education wasn't free. (I learned that my gardener, who made $23 a month, spent $8 on school fees alone.) Landless Africans, who had not yet been absorbed into the new settlement schemes, were squatting on farmland and disturbing production. In some areas there had even been demonstrations against the government for neglecting its own people.

One step the government was contemplating—if it could find the money—was to establish a National Youth Service that would enlist young men for two-year periods on public works projects and help alleviate urban unemployment. We heard reports that both the Russians and the Chinese were prepared to finance this project in order to model it after their own Communist Youth Brigades, complete with indoctrination by hand-picked instructors. Some ministers wanted us to move first with an offer of equipment and thus be in a position to keep ideology out of the NYS camps. So I asked a member of the AID staff, who'd been with the CCC in the thirties, to work up a blueprint and cost estimate with the Kenyans.

I presented my credentials to Malcolm MacDonald at State House on March 2. We each made a small speech, sipped champagne and spoke of mutual friends. As Kenya's last British governor, MacDonald had persuaded London to support Kenyatta despite the protests of the Colonel Blimps among the white settlers, who, as late as 1961, talked openly of assassinating this "leader to darkness and death"—as one governor had called him. MacDonald was small but tough, loaded with charm, close to Kenyatta and popular with Kenyans—who sensed that he genuinely liked *them*. He'd be a good friend to confide in. Since Britain and the United States had a common interest in promoting East African stability, most of our policies and actions (for example, new aid commitments) were coordinated in advance.

I called on Kenyatta in his office a week later. On this first of many visits, he impressed me as sharp, engaging and tough. Although probably more than seventy—no written records were kept in the tribal village where he was born—he exuded vitality, swinging into the waiting room with a rolling swagger and greeting me with a wave of his fly whisk and a powerful handshake. I gave him letters from the President and Jackie Kennedy, and told him that our country wanted for Africa the things Africans wanted for themselves: full independence, rapid economic progress and political stability in freedom. We discussed events in Zanzibar and the dangers these posed to East Africa. He mentioned the urgent need for the National Youth Service camps, and I suggested he write the President in order to back up my fund-raising efforts in Washington; we agreed the camps should be administered by Africans without any ideological bias. I said I intended to be frank with him at all times and hoped he'd be the same with me. "Very good," he said, thumping his heavy cane on the floor, "that is the African way."

I also called on as many cabinet ministers as were available. Five of them had received their higher education in the United States, so conversation was easier than during my protocol calls in Guinea. Appointments were generally confirmed—the crisply efficient British and Asian secretaries saw to that—and when you walked into a ministry, you didn't feel, as in Conakry, that you had entered a rather disreputable boardinghouse by mistake. On these calls, I merely made the point that we Americans were here to help them with *uhuru* and reiterated my preference for frankness and informality in my dealings with them. (The quickest way to put an African politician at ease, when he's confronted with an ambassador, is to tell him you're not a professional diplomat.) These initial calls were essentially public relations exercises. I knew they had succeeded when one minister I hadn't yet called on drew me aside at a reception and confided, "We like you." The grapevine had been working.

I went to see Odinga with Wayne Fredericks, who was passing through town, and our departing Consul General. Odinga, who had refused to see anyone from the embassy since December, would not let the latter into his office. But he was all smiles with us. Although subsidized by the Chinese and Russians, he appeared anxious to keep on good terms with Americans and grateful we'd come to call. At fifty-three, Odinga was a paradoxical figure. A wealthy, emotional, unsophisticated businessman and tribal chieftain, he depended on Communist handouts to advance his own political ambitions. He was shrewd but also naïve, for he underestimated Kenyatta. I'll have a lot more to say about them both.

On March 7 Fredericks and I flew down to Dar for talks with some high-ranking British officials about Zanzibar. He had been attending a conference of the Economic Commission for Africa in Addis, and was deploring the fact that the realism and common sense displayed there by African economic ministers were getting less news play than a recent tribal killing in Rwanda. In Dar, which reminded me of West Africa, Carlucci joined us and reported the Communists were well entrenched on Zanzibar—the Chinese behind barbed wire, the East Germans behind steel gates. (The Russians, eager to get East Germany finally recognized by an African government, were channeling most of their aid through their German stooges.) A police state had come into being, and arms shipments were arriving regularly to supply the Communist-led militia. The British agreed with us that only the mainland governments could take the lead in cauterizing the Zanzibar infection; they would talk to Kenyatta and Nyerere about it.

I saw Kenyatta again on my return to Nairobi but didn't bring up Zanzibar. There was no point in our sounding excitable about Communists, as the Africans expected us to be. It was better to refer to Zanzibar as *their* problem, which it was. He gave me a letter to the President about the Youth Service, which we had estimated would cost us and the Kenyans about $2 million each; our contribution would be in trucks, equipment and uniforms. We also talked about a Kenya request for Peace Corps volunteers in education and agriculture; it had been made over the opposition of certain British civil servants, who underestimated the caliber of our volunteers. Kenya was also about to sign an Investment Guarantee Agreement with us, and Kenyatta said he hoped it would attract more capital and create the job opportunities that were so critically needed.

I flew home via London on March 20. AID officials, as I expected, could think of several reasons not to get involved with the National Youth Service; they were especially fearful (with Zanzibar in the news) of the Communists taking over our equipment. I felt the risk was less serious than turning down Kenyatta now and opening the way for the Soviets to step in and pose as friends in need. I knew from experience that when we don't toss out a life preserver to a deserving nation in distress, there'll be others tossed out that turn out to be nooses. Fortunately, Rusk felt the same way. So did Bob Kennedy, then chairing an Interagency Youth Committee. Most important, so did the President. His only comment, after I'd got his approval for the National Youth Service project, was: "Why doesn't Sarge Shriver start the same kind of thing here?"

My White House appointment, as usual, was set up informally, this time through Moyers. State still seemed administratively unable to arrange for an ambassador to see the President without several weeks' lead time. On this occasion, being alone, I at least had a chance to talk briefly about Kenya and to hand over Kenyatta's letter. We were interrupted by a muddy Presidential beagle —the one called Her—jumping into my lap while photographs were being taken. Thanks to Her getting into the picture, the news that I was now Ambassador to Kenya made front pages the next day and saved me sending out change-of-address cards.

When I left his office, the President said he hoped I'd find time to send Moyers some memos with speech ideas for the coming campaign. He wasn't worried about the outcome, but he wanted to win by the biggest possible margin; this was no time for the world to think America wasn't strongly behind the administration. I promised to keep in touch.

With the President's oral backing, and the support of State, I had no trouble getting AID to go along on the NYS. They even put a Priority tab on the folder.

After a couple of more days in Washington, I was ready to get my family, pack up and return to Kenya—really ready. In case anyone wonders how an ambassador on consultation spends a day in Washington, here's my schedule for March 31:

0830: CIA, for briefing and debriefing.
1045: Director of Public Safety, AID, to talk about police training for Kenya.
1115: Pan American vice president, to discuss investment guarantee for a Nairobi hotel.
1130: Television executives interested in a training program for the Voice of Kenya.
1200: Secretary of the Interior, to ask about sending some irrigation experts to Africa.
Lunch: Gene Abrams, now stationed in the Ivory Coast.
1430: Aid Director Bell, about Kenya program.
1500: Administrative officers at State about embassy personnel, housing and allowance problems.

1530: Visiting Kenyan member of Parliament.
1600: Pentagon, for talks on civic action programs and fleet visits.
1700: AID officials on NYS.
1745: Public relations executive looking for African clients.
1815: Meeting with Moyers at the White House.
Dinner: At the Deputy Assistant Secretary of State's, for shop talk.

Just before leaving, I spoke at the UN Correspondents Center in New York. Somebody asked me about Zanzibar. I said it was obvious the Communists, especially the Chinese, were trying to set up a non-African type of regime there and that the East Africans ought to be on their guard.

Karume used this speech as a pretext for demanding that we dismantle our tracking station on the island. (He'd been told it was a rocket base.) Actually, we were just as glad to move it elsewhere, and disarmed him later on by letting him have the generator as a gift. More important, my remarks got big play in the Nairobi papers. When I returned, my new African friends congratulated me. "You told us you were going to speak frankly," they said. "Now we can see you really mean it." Getting a reputation for frankness in Africa is sometimes worth giving up a tracking station site. It pays off in goodwill, and goodwill I would need in abundance before the year was out.

XIII

City in the Sun

●

That's what they call it in the travel brochures—City in the Sun. And it's not too far from the truth. Most mornings you can have breakfast on the terrace and watch the sunshine drying the dew on your rosebushes.

Around the time Jomo Kenyatta was born, Nairobi was a tent camp and supply depot for workers on the railroad that the British were pushing through the wilderness to Lake Victoria. In one man's lifetime it has become the commercial and industrial capital of East Africa, a city like no other in the world—a city where you can play golf every day on eight different courses, mingle with lions and rhinos five minutes from the jet airport, watch the latest American shows on television, buy elephant hair bracelets in the bazaars, dine on a one-dollar sirloin steak or a two-dollar *coq au vin* and sleep under blankets all year round. At the New Stanley Hotel you can sit on the terrace under the thorn tree and watch one of the world's most colorful sidewalk parades: turbaned Sikhs and prim Indian ladies in saris, British teen-agers with Beatle haircuts, dusty German tourists piling out of Volkswagen buses, Kikuyus carrying briefcases and Masai carrying spears, Americans slung with cameras, self-conscious Italian starlets and bearded Arabs from the coast. And no mosquitoes or flies to swat while you are watching.

The equator is only two hours away by car, but Nairobi, at 5,800 feet, is never too hot or too cold, and it gets just enough rainfall to keep everything green and fresh, like a perennial spring. No wonder the British kept getting off the train at Nairobi for sixty years—nor that 25,000 were still living here after *uhuru,* hoping that the man they once described as the "cunning, evil-eyed leader of the Mau Mau" would let them stay.

Kenya's white settlers had some reason to expect the worst. They had taken over a primitive land without roads or cities and made it a part of the modern world. But although missionaries did teach the Africans to read and write, the transformation wrought by the British had only a peripheral effect on how most of the natives lived. As late as 1946, Africans were referred to in the Kenya development plan merely as "units of labor." The British reserved the best land and cash crops for themselves; cotton or coffee planted by Africans was plowed under. Segregation was strictly enforced; unlike the French, who drew the line at education rather than color, the British excluded even African college graduates from their clubs. A Kenya minister told me that before *uhuru* he could not even exhibit his paintings in a Kenya art show—in his own country—because he was black.

These are the wrongs that people remember; humiliation is the hardest thing to forgive. Sensing this, and fearing revenge, thousands of white settlers, South Africans especially, packed up and left Kenya before *uhuru.* Fortunately for those who remained, and for the future of Kenya, Kenyatta was a bigger and wiser man than most British suspected. Soon after independence, he spoke these words to some apprehensive white farmers:

"If I have done a mistake to you in the past, it is for you to forgive me. If you have done a mistake to me, it is for me to forgive you. The Africans cannot say the Europeans have done all the wrong and the Europeans cannot say the Africans have done all the wrong. The good thing is to be able to forget and forgive one another. You have something to forget, just as I have."

When he ended his speech with a cry of *"Harambee!"*—meaning, "Let's pull together!"—the settlers broke into cheers.

If ever a man has earned the right to be called *Mzee*—"the wise old one"—it is Jomo Kenyatta. The son of a Kikuyu herdsman, he grew up in a thatched hut near his present estate at Gatundu. His name was Kamau. At a Scottish mission school, he was given a Christian name—Johnstone. Later, working as a meter reader for the Nairobi water company, he took to wearing an ornamental belt, called a *kenyatta* in Kikuyu. On his rounds he would often stop and hand out candy to children. They began calling him "Kenyatta," and the name stuck. When he became involved in nationalist politics in 1922, he substituted Jomo, which means "burning spear," for Johnstone.

He lived in England for fifteen years, getting to know the British and even marrying one. He studied anthropology at the London School of Economics and published a thesis on the Kikuyu tribe called *Facing Mount Kenya*. Back in Kenya in 1946, he headed the militant Kenya African Union until he was convicted (some say framed) by the colonial authorities in 1952 and jailed as the mastermind of the Mau Mau. In a curious way, the British did Kenyatta and themselves a favor by making him a martyr. For he became a genuine national hero in a country divided by tribal jealousies. And so great was the prestige he acquired in detention that he did not have to prove his nationalism by attacking the British when he was let out. Only a Kenyatta, with his prison record, could have afforded to retain British officers in his security forces and to ask British troops to suppress his army mutinies without being denounced by African radicals as a neo-colonialist puppet. Kenyatta came to power as a leader who transcended tribal divisions, and who was all but immune to criticism. And in 1964 he needed all the prestige he could command to hold his new nation together and make *harambee* a reality.

We were back in Africa, but so much was so different: the lights didn't go out, and when we picked up the phone, it worked; we could call a cab or we could call New York. When the phone was out of order, somebody named Singh came and fixed it. We had a big Spanish-style house and even a little government money to modernize it. We built a terrace, cut down some trees and planted shrubs and flowers that sprouted, bloomed and flourished like things in a greenhouse. (One bombax sprig became a shade tree in a year.) We canceled plans for a guest house and put in a pool in its place. Americans and their families used it, and we managed to stretch our entertainment allowance and save the taxpayers money by having poolside hamburger cookouts for ambassadors instead of sit-down diplomatic dinners with two kinds of wine.

Nairobi is a sprawling collection of rural suburbs around an urban core. You can drive for hours, get lost in the woods and still be inside the city limits. We lived in Muthaiga, north of the main part of town. It was a winding, ten-minute drive to the office— twenty if you caught the rush-hour traffic—past the Aga Khan hospital, the Goanese Roman Catholic church and the garish villas of the wealthy Asians; and then down Uhuru (formerly Princess Elizabeth) Highway to Kenyatta (formerly Delamere) Avenue.

The contrasts between Nairobi and Conakry were not only physical but human. We welcomed the well-stocked supermarkets but missed the tropical gaiety of West Africa—the women in bright colors, the nightly rhythm of tom-toms, the easy laughter. Here the men looked dour and the women drab; on Saturday nights they drank more but danced less. The combination of a cool climate, British discipline and urbanization had produced a different kind of African—not really unfriendly, but reserved in the presence of white strangers.

In government offices the number of competent Africans was far greater than in Guinea. The French colonialists tried to develop an elite of black Frenchmen; the British didn't bother—they concentrated on training competent clerks and civil servants. The result, as one of my fellow diplomats put it, is that in a former French colony the post office may be a shambles but the Minister of Communications is a delightful dinner guest, while in a former British colony the post office may be efficient but the minister is not likely to be such good company. I have heard "French" Africans speak of "British" Africans as uncultured—and the latter refer to the former as garrulous snobs.

Kenyan politicians were better versed in electioneering and parliamentary procedures than their Guinean counterparts but less sophisticated about world affairs. Except for a few, like Kenyatta, who had lived in Europe and associated with Communists, they had been largely insulated, in their colonial compound, from the political realities of the outside world. Thus it was hard to warn them about Soviet and Chinese intentions in Zanzibar without sounding like an alarmist; the only imperialism they had ever experienced was the relatively mild British brand.

The British attitude toward us was less hostile than that of the French in West Africa, yet a good many of the old Kenya hands still resented our "intrusion" into their East African preserve, blamed the Kennedy administration for having encouraged premature independence and tended to regard us as clumsy cold warriors with no understanding of Africans. British civil servants who had stayed on in the Kenya Government often opposed American initiatives in reforming bureaucratic procedures and adapting the rigidly traditional school curriculum to contemporary African needs; for example, our vocational agricultural courses were introduced into certain high schools over the strenuous objections of expatriate principals and education advisers. Other Britons, notably in the High Commission, welcomed us as partners with a common interest in keeping Kenya stable and progressive and were helpful in persuading their fellow countrymen that the bloody Yanks weren't such bad blokes after all. But I could see we had a public relations job ahead of us to dispel misunderstanding and minimize frictions with our British friends.

Americans comprised the fourth largest foreign community in Kenya after the Asians, the British and the Italians. (The Italians were mostly former prisoners of war who stayed on in Kenya as farmers and businessmen after 1945.) Of the nineteen hundred Americans in the country, fourteen hundred were missionaries and their families; the rest were mostly businessmen (twenty-one American firms had regional offices in Nairobi), U.S. Government personnel and a hundred-odd teachers recruited by AID. Our community was growing with Nairobi's increasing importance as the commercial and diplomatic capital of East Africa. Within two years the American population of Kenya would rise to 2,600 and the number of U.S. firms to 52.

The Diplomatic Corps was expanding too. Six months after independence, nearly forty countries had opened missions in Nairobi or promoted their consulates to embassies. One of my early protocol calls was on my Soviet colleague, Vladimir Lavrov. I had some trouble finding his residence in an outlying suburb; some Africans finally identified it to my driver as "the place where the people who don't speak English live."

Lavrov, who was about my age, spoke accented but fluent English. He had served in Washington and was a protégé of Gromyko's. While we sipped coffee served by a Russian maid (the Russians and the Chinese never employ local domestic servants), I mentioned Gromyko's speech about competitive coexistence as a challenge that could benefit us all without endangering world peace.

He agreed, pointing out that there was plenty to do for all of us who wanted to help Africa's economic development. "We must only be careful to obey their rules," he added, "and let them freely choose the system that is best for them." This was part of the new, reasonable Soviet line, just as the guards outside in their loafers, tapered pants and pullovers were part of the new stylish Soviet look. But the change was less than fundamental: before the year was out, we had positively identified one half of Mr. Lavrov's staff as KGB agents (the normal intelligence component in Soviet diplomatic missions is about 60 percent), and I knew that the KGB is not noted for its interest in economic development or free choice.

The presence of other sizable Soviet bloc missions in Nairobi was hard to justify on diplomatic or commercial grounds. Trade was minimal and there was no resident East European community to take care of. Yet the Czechs, whose only overt activity was supplying equipment and technicians to the Ministry of Information, bought an $80,000 residence across the street from ours, where they swam, played volley ball and somehow kept busy. (Their nine diplomatic officers included five intelligence agents, roughly the same proportion as the Russians'.) The Czech Ambassador, like the Pole, the Hungarian and the Bulgarian Chargé, all received me with the same hearty but rather evasive cordiality that I'd become used to in Guinea.

One noticeable change in the Communist diplomatic camp was that the Soviet and Chinese representatives no longer bothered to disguise their mutual distaste. At one diplomatic function at the airport, I found myself standing in line between Lavrov and Ambassador Wang. The former pumped my hand vigorously, the latter nodded (we'd been introduced by the Pakistani), but they didn't greet each other. It was an open secret they were competing for control in Zanzibar; and in June Sino-Soviet differences erupted into headlines when the Chinese warned African states to beware of Soviet aid offers, whose purpose was always political control. *Pravda* retorted by accusing the Chinese of trading with South Africa and selling opium for dollars with which to sabotage African governments. Hsinhua, the official Chinese news agency, boiled over in an article distributed by the Chinese Embassy in Nairobi: "It is ludicrous for *Pravda* to try to raise its own status by smearing others with the spittle left over by imperialism. . . . By doing as you did, what difference is there left between you and Western imperialism?"

Many of the charges being flung back and forth were helpful to us in that they added confirmation to what USIS had been reporting for some time.

The Dean of the Diplomatic Corps, after the departure of the first British High Commissioner, was the Ghanaian High Commissioner, a pompous and conspiratorial ham actor named David Busumtwi-Sam, who, I believe, is now under house arrest in Accra. The Russians had managed to offend Sam soon after *uhuru*, by inviting him to a film and not having anyone at the door to show him to his seat when he arrived a half-hour late. At a party at my home he scolded Lavrov in front of our colleagues. "The only reason I am speaking to you at all," he said, "is that Attwood here says you are a nice fellow!" Poor Lavrov, probably under orders to be pleasant to any and all Africans, was properly abject. But later, at a monthly corps meeting, he and I joined forces against Sam and the Chinese in favor of inviting the UN Representative, an African named Dr. Bernard Chidzero, to attend our meetings.

Diplomatic functions, I soon found out, could be just as chaotic and exhausting as those in Conakry—and not as lively. At a reception for Emperor Haile Selassie, the place cards had been so arranged that the Israelis found themselves with—you guessed it—the Egyptians, the Chinese with the South Koreans and I with an East German journalist. In the game of musical chairs that followed, Wang ended up with nobody on either side of him while I squeezed in between the Yugoslav Ambassador and the Finnish Consul. The former had a new anti-Chinese joke ("When you invite Chou En-Lai to a banquet, all he does is chew and lie") and told it twice while a Kenya Army band played selections from Vincent Youmans. Finally the Emperor arrived, an hour late, and delivered a lengthy toast in Amharic, which was then inaudibly translated into East African English. I found myself missing Touré's Guinean dancers.

I finished my protocol calls in May, gradually getting on a first-name basis with several ministers. (This was easiest with those who had lived in the States, like Tom Mboya and Julius Kiano.)

Many had never heard our African policy explained in simple terms, so that these calls were often as useful as those I'd made when I first got to Guinea. My experience over there also came in handy, especially when I was asked about Soviet aid and the reasons for Mr. Solod's precipitous departure. Few Kenyans had ever visited the other side of their continent, and they wanted to know more about it. (One reason for the lack of contact between East and West Africa is that airline routes in Africa, like Manhattan's subway system, are all vertical; in 1964 there was only one weekly flight, on Ethiopian Airways, that crossed the continent horizontally.)

Although the caliber of cabinet ministers varied a good deal, I found that their approach to Kenya's problems was generally more pragmatic than ideological. Except for Odinga and the Minister of Information, Achieng Oneko, none exhibited resentment against the British. Like Kenyatta, they were more inclined to look ahead rather than to brood about the past or search for scapegoats.

In April the Kenyan Ambassador to Washington made a speech at the Massachusetts Institute of Technology that reflected what I'd been hearing in Nairobi:

Our constant preoccupation with "Western Imperialism" and Colonialism and Communism prevents us from seeing ourselves and our performance, our successes and our failures. Not only must we be bold in seeking our own best interests but we must be frank in admitting our own failures and difficulties. . . . So long as we have someone to blame we feel good, and I suggest this is dangerous and prevents us from thinking objectively about just what we are doing for and by ourselves.

In my own speeches—to the Rotary, the Lions, the United Kenya Club and at ceremonies connected with AID projects—I always refrained from mentioning Guinea and the dangers of Communist subversion (which is what my audience expected). Instead, I praised nonalignment, citing our own experience after independence, and emphasized how important it was for young countries to scrutinize *all* aid offers, ours included, "the way porcupines make love—which is very, very carefully." This always got a chuckle and underlined the point that no aid offers are entirely "disinterested." While we wanted stability in East Africa and were prepared to support Kenyatta's program for Kenya, others might have different motives.

Chinese and Soviet bloc aid offers were soon forthcoming. In May, Odinga and Murumbi returned from Moscow and Peking with a whole catalogue of promises and commitments. The Chinese gave Kenya nearly $3 million outright and offered about $20 million more in interest-free loans to buy Chinese products. Unlike the Russians, who didn't talk cold war politics, the Chinese continually lectured the Kenyan ministers on the evils of American imperialism.

The $15 million Soviet package included a hospital, a radio transmitter, a technical school, a couple of factories and an irrigation scheme. Both offers got big headlines, and one columnist predicted quick action by the Russians; but in fact no details had been agreed upon in Moscow. According to Murumbi, the Russians did not appear overeager to make definite commitments, and the Kenyans planned to take their own hard look at the terms. Apparently there'd be no repeat performance of the Guinean Follies of 1959.

We had the advantage of having an aid program in operation at the time of independence. Since 1953 we had committed about $30 million in loans and grants to Kenya in the fields of agriculture, education, public administration and community development. Among other things, we built, staffed and equipped fourteen secondary schools, established 4-K Clubs (like our 4-H Clubs), expanded Farmer Training Centers, provided advisers in livestock production and range management, sent 250 Kenyans to the States for specialized study and financed the Kenya Institute of Administration—where civil servants were being trained to replace expatriate officers. In 1961 emergency food shipments from America had helped avert a famine in drought-stricken areas of the country. Partly because our program was so varied and had developed over a long period of time in conjunction with the British, and partly because little effort had been made to publicize it, few Kenyans appreciated what we'd done. But after banner headlines had proclaimed what the "disinterested" Russians and the Chinese were going to do for independent Kenya, I decided to put out an illustrated pamphlet summing up what our contribution had been. In the foreword I wrote:

In the past few months, during which Kenya has received several well-publicized aid offers, I have been struck by how little is known of the U.S. Government's contribution to Kenya's economic progress. Perhaps this is because we have not sought publicity. Our purpose in Kenya is not to score propaganda points, but to help this country develop its human and natural resources. Still, it is always gratifying to have one's efforts better known and appreciated.

The point is often made in newly independent countries that foreign assistance must be "disinterested" and "without strings." Personally, I doubt if such aid is ever given by any country. American aid is certainly not "disinterested"; we are very much interested in seeing Kenya create conditions of political stability and economic progress that will build a strong nation and keep the cold war out of East Africa.

And our aid does have strings: we expect countries receiving our assistance to be serious about preserving their freedom and respecting the freedom of others; and we expect them to be serious about rational economic development so that the benefits of our aid are shared by the whole nation and not by just a favored few.

We are satisfied that in Kenya these conditions exist. We believe that under the leadership of Prime Minister Jomo Kenyatta, this country has a promising future. That is why we look forward to being able to help his government, in the years ahead, make that future a prosperous and satisfying one for all the people of Kenya.

As I expected, the phrase about "strings" got plenty of attention. The same headline, "U.S. Envoy Admits Strings," was on the front pages of all three Nairobi dailies, and boosted our pamphlet's readership. Ministers friendly to the West were pleased. Frankness, as usual, had paid off.

Apart from getting settled and acquainted and explaining our policies, I had plenty to do around the embassy during these first two months. It was a busy post; in 1964-1965 we ranked eighth among all American embassies in volume of telegraphic traffic, but only forty-seventh in the number of personnel to cope with the workload this entailed. And there are always personnel problems that fester and administrative procedures that go slack without an ambassador's active and continual supervision. Luckily I had inherited a capable staff, headed by Jim Ruchti, the DCM, who was youthful, experienced, efficient and seemingly tireless. I had also persuaded Phil Heller to come to Nairobi as Chief Political Officer, knowing how effective he could be in overcoming African suspicions and getting them to understand our policies.

We had a torrential stream of visitors, since nearly everyone who came to East Africa stopped in Nairobi. In March and April alone, we had Cy Sulzberger, Joe Alsop, Marguerite Higgins and Drew Pearson from the press to take care of in one way or another. Some of our visitors didn't understand that arranging quick appointments for VIP journalists was a lot harder here than in PR-conscious Europe. Other Americans who turned up at the embassy were often armed with letters from Senators and Congressmen and expected both a personal briefing and an invitation to the residence. We would always try to oblige, even though it meant going out of pocket on drinks. (Our modest representation allowance—$4,500 a year for the entire embassy staff—didn't cover any entertainment of Americans.)

I tried to reassure those of our visitors who had just arrived from South Africa (or talked to disgruntled *bwanas* in the New Stanley bar) that Kenya had a reasonably good chance of building a prosperous and racially harmonious society. Whether it would, of course, depended in part on winning the confidence of potential investors. Many of these, unfortunately, took the word of their business contacts in Johannesburg and Salisbury that Kenya was run by savages and going to the dogs. White South Africans and Southern Rhodesians promoted scare stories for a very good reason: a stable and racially peaceful Kenya would further discredit their case for *apartheid,* segregation and minority rule. So they refused to admit that the Kenyan experiment might succeed and denounced those of us who thought it would. Soon after my return to Nairobi in April, I was attacked in Salisbury as a "bloody bootlicker" for speaking out at a press conference in favor of Kenyatta's policy of forget-and-forgive.

Inexperienced American reporters were often taken in by un-reconstructed whites who had sold their farms and were pulling out of Kenya. The *Wall Street Journal,* in June, published a lead story from a transient young stringer under the headline, "Whites Fleeing Kenya in Fear of Black Rule Add to Problems." The subhead emphasized theft and murder, and the story painted the kind of picture that justified most of the dire predictions of white racists.

One advantage of being an ambassador with a background in journalism is that you can spot the tricks and the ploys of bad reporting. So I managed to get some diplomatic mileage out of the story by writing the editor a letter correcting its inaccuracies and conclusions, which the *Journal* printed in part and the Nairobi *Standard* printed in full. Whether the *Journal's* readers accepted my more optimistic appraisal or not, the Africans and the British who knew the truth appreciated the fact that the American Embassy had confidence in the nation's leadership and supported its efforts to solve Kenya's real problems. Metternich's definition of an ambassador as a professional liar had become doubly obsolete; our job today was to dispel lies and misconceptions, not only about our own country but about the country we were accredited to.

The best way to learn about these problems at firsthand was out in the country. This is why I instructed all embassy officers to make at least one trip a month outside of Nairobi. I'll be describing our own travels in another chapter. But in June we made one three-day excursion to Eldoret, two hundred miles northwest of Nairobi, that belongs in this introduction to Kenya. For Eldoret, a trading center for an area that had been thickly settled by European and South African farmers, was a good place to see Kenya's agricultural predicament in microcosm. It was a predicament that could become a crisis, for agriculture was the backbone of Kenya's economy and export trade.

Before independence, five million acres of Kenya's best land was owned by non-Africans—about 1.1 million in ranches and plantations and the rest in mixed farming. The government's policy was to leave the former alone and buy up the mixed farms for African settlement with a $50 million British grant. By 1964, 2,200 of the 3,300 European mixed farmers had sold their property and been replaced by about 19,000 Africans. Some of the 1.7 million acres thus purchased were sold to individual Africans; others were turned into settlement schemes where a supervisory staff, usually headed by the former British owner, gave the new farmers guidance and advice.

Production had declined due to the division of efficient large holdings into small family plots and to the technical inexperience of African farmers. In Eldoret we found an overworked British farm manager and three African assistants trying to teach 250 new

African farmers about cattle dipping and fertilizing and the rudi-
ments of modern mechanized farming methods. They needed help.
So did the 130 European farmers left in the area (out of 530),
who were plagued by squatters and cattle thefts; many we talked to
wanted to stay but didn't know if they could afford to. Eldoret's
merchants were also in difficulties. Several shops had already
closed with the departure of their European customers. At a civic
reception in our honor, the African mayor and the European,
Asian and African councilmen told us industry was urgently
needed to provide jobs and to keep the town alive.

Driving back through the pine forests, sheep ranches and wheat
fields of the old White Highlands, I began to realize what independent Kenya was up against. It was going to be a difficult transition. Looking ahead, you had to qualify every prediction with an
"if." And the biggest question of all, the "if" on which so much
depended, was whether Kenyatta's health, vigor and active leadership would endure long enough for the transition to succeed. With
Mzee at the helm during the next few critical years, Kenya might
make it, but there was no successor in sight equal to the task of
building a united nation and inspiring the confidence abroad that
Kenya's economic progress required. Kenyatta—talking sense,
waving his fly whisk and roaring *"Haram-bee!"*—was, in short,
indispensable.

It was easy to be pessimistic about Kenya in 1964, but it was
more exhilarating to be an optimist. At least we optimists kept
busy, and in Africa we'd so far been proved right more often than
wrong. I liked what a British settler, one of those who wasn't
pulling out, told Sulzberger in March:

"Things will get a lot worse before they get better. But they'll
straighten up in the end. I'm not too old for risks. And there's a
real chance to help. I won't leave my new country. I won't leave
till the Africans stop smiling at me. As long as I can drive my car
through Nairobi and stop at a zebra crossing while an African
smiles and nods as he walks across, why, things are okay."

It was going to be an interesting time for all of us who wanted to
help Kenyatta keep things okay.

XIV

Forging a Team

•

Once upon a time an ambassador could do a good job merely by making himself popular with the king to whose court he was sent. He didn't have to weld together a Country Team. He didn't have to pay attention to public opinion. He didn't have to answer ten telegrams a day. He may have had a spy or two on his payroll, but he wasn't a circus ringmaster with six different acts going on all at once, or a Ward Bond trying to keep a bedeviled wagon train on the move. But that's what I often felt like in Kenya: a walleyed ringmaster when things were moving well and Mr. Bond, axles broken and the Indians waiting at the pass, when they weren't.

As the President's personal representative, I gave first priority to winning Kenyatta's confidence and trust. In this respect, I was still doing the royal court bit. But a modern American ambassador, especially in Africa, must utilize all the assets at his command, and some that aren't. He must create an integrated team out of the diverse elements under his jurisdiction; and he must persuade non-official Americans, such as businessmen and missionaries, that they also have a part to play in helping advance U.S. objectives, and good reasons to do so.

In Kenya these objectives were quite clear. We wanted a strong, stable and prosperous Kenya that would be a model of rational development and racial harmony for other African countries. We wanted to keep the cold war and its practitioners out of the area. We wanted Kenya to create its own social and economic institutions without interference from the neo-imperialists. We wanted

cooperation—between Kenya and her neighbors and between ourselves and other like-minded nations, like Britain and West Germany. And we wanted to see increased trade, investment and tourism gradually take the place of foreign aid.

The more we orchestrated our activities in the American community, the better were our chances of achieving these objectives.
(Sometimes an ambassador must be a Leonard Bernstein as well
as a Ward Bond.) The situation in Kenya, though outwardly
promising, was fraught with a good many dangers. If popular discontent mounted, if Soviet and Chinese agents and money succeeded in mobilizing the discontented, if their base in Zanzibar
(now united with but not fully controlled by Tanzania) was further
strengthened, if development capital from the West was not forthcoming, if the British decided they could no longer bear the heavy
burden ($168 million over a four-year period) of bolstering
Kenya's economy, if Kenyatta died—then we would need all the
assets and resources we could muster. Now was the time to build
up a credit of goodwill for the United States that we might have to
draw on later.

Priority one was to get the various elements of the Country
Team working smoothly together, and step one was to set up a
series of regular meetings. Once a week Jim Ruchti and I met in
my office with the AID Director, the PAO (who ran USIS), the
Peace Corps representative, the Agricultural Attaché and the CIA
station chief to exchange information, coordinate actions and plan
ahead. We held another weekly conference with the No. 2 men of
each agency: the embassy administrative, economic and political
officers and the labor, civil aviation, commercial, security and cultural attachés. Here, each officer talked about his current operations, and we ironed out any administrative, personnel or housekeeping problems. Once a month I met, first, with the embassy's
clerical and secretarial staff and then with the AID staff to tell
them about current political and economic developments and to
answer questions; it was like being on a ship and asking the people
in the engine room to come up to the bridge and see where we
were going and how they were helping get us there. I also used
these meetings to remind them all, especially the newcomers, that
nobody in the mission had an eight-to-five, Monday-to-Friday job,
and that I expected them all, whether on or off duty, to get ac-

quainted with Kenya and make friends with its people. The hardest group to stir up was the AID staff; with certain exceptions, they tended to be plodding, status-conscious civil servants—usually conscientious about their own job but indifferent to extra-curricular efforts.

To get back to the Country Team meeting, I know that the presence of CIA representatives on U.S. embassy staffs is never officially acknowledged, but I think it is common knowledge by now that they are attached to many of our overseas missions. Their work consists mainly in learning about and frustrating the efforts of their counterparts from other embassies which, in Kennedy's phrase, "do not wish us well." I'll be writing more about CIA in a later chapter; for the moment, I just want to emphasize that CIA employees are neither supermen, jackasses nor spooks—as they are so often and variously depicted. They do require supervision to ensure coordination. But an ambassador who treats his CIA chief as an integral member of his Country Team will generally find him a useful and cooperative associate; I know I did.

Country Team meetings kept us thinking about our main objectives and prevented duplication and dissipation of our efforts, something we couldn't afford with a staff that was lean compared with other embassies with our responsibilities. At these meetings our PAO might get an idea for a news story from something AID was planning to do; our Agricultural Attaché might tell us about a Russian agricultural survey team he had run into on a trip upcountry—CIA would be interested in that; the Peace Corps man might report on his plans for staffing high schools and settlement schemes —both Agriculture and AID would have suggestions; CIA might have identified a Czech newsman as an intelligence agent—this would be useful for USIS to know; the embassy's quarterly political report might be due—and all would have something to contribute to that.

I said our staff was lean. In round numbers (because people were always coming and going), we had about forty Americans in the embassy (including attachés), fifty in AID (not including contract personnel), five in USIS and six staffers in the Peace Corps (plus, eventually, two hundred volunteers). The missions also employed some seventy local employees—British, Asian and African—in clerical and maintenance jobs. It looked like a sizable crew until you sorted them out. Only ten officers in the embassy got out and around or did substantive reporting; the rest of the staff were inside people—code clerks, Marine guards, secretaries, accountants and so on—and our administrative section had to be big to handle payroll and other budgeting functions for seven neighboring posts.

Moreover, paperwork, protocol and visitors often kept the ten of us cooped up and tied down. For instance, we spent many long and useless hours on composing, editing and rewriting voluminous documents that were supposed to govern our actions, plan for contingencies and guide all government agencies concerned with Kenya. Writing such papers about a fluid, developing African country was like trying to take a still picture of a horse race: by the time they were edited, revised, cleared and published, they were usually blurred and out of date. All we really needed was a concise statement of our objectives in Kenya and enough flexibility to act as we saw fit to achieve them.

Also, as a former editor, I couldn't resist taking the time to rewrite a lot of the prose that went out over my signature, cutting out words like "nodality" and phrases like "complementarity is a desideratum." (Unfortunately, I had no way of blue-penciling the stuff that flowed out of Washington. One quote from an unclassified airgram will give you an idea of what we had to cope with: "The methodology of the Task Force study is compatible with the FAPS-EROP review process. . . . The methodology is also designed to tie in with the MUST program. . . . It is therefore hoped that a development of managerial talent will be a part of the criteria of the MUST staff in determining each officer's foreseeable career ladder." This was a tough one to decipher even if you knew what FAPS, EROP and MUST meant—which I didn't.) And visitors from the States, welcome as most of them were, often took up time we should have spent with Kenyans. We had no one, as our European embassies do, assigned to meeting, greeting and taking care of official visitors; thus at least one embassy officer had to be detached from his regular duties on the average of once a week for escort service.

AID was even more desk-bound. Nearly one-half of their people performed purely administrative duties, and most of the others seemed perpetually engaged in preparing bulky reports and charts that headquarters required for its Congressional hearings. The annual CAP (Country Assistance Program) book alone consisted of 180 pages, most of which I doubt were ever read by anybody in Washington. AID also had to handle a steady stream of visitors and inspectors from the home office. (I often wished we could have applied all their travel money and per diem to building a school or equipping a clinic.) For example, two high-priced "evaluators" came over for four weeks and produced a carelessly worded report on the Kenya program which we later had to correct with a report of our own on the outside chance that someone back home might have read theirs. Yet AID's criteria were well defined: to be eligible for U.S. assistance, a country had to prove that it was doing all it could to help itself, that it had a rational plan for mobilizing its resources and that it was concerned with the welfare of *all* its people. Bill Wild, my AID Director, had been in the foreign aid business for twenty years and knew his job. He and I didn't need people coming over all the time, at government expense, to verify that these criteria were being met. The Washington bureaucracy often seemed to forget that we were just as interested as any other American taxpayers in making sure every dollar was put to good use.

Our USIS operation, though tighter, was also hamstrung by paperwork and an inadequate budget. More than four hundred Kenyans used the library in Nairobi every day, but we couldn't get a few thousand dollars to open a reading room in Kisumu, Odinga's home town, and a center of anti-American propaganda; nor to put up an American exhibit at the annual Nairobi Agricultural Show, where the dramatic success story of American agriculture would have been an eye-opener for the more than 200,000 visitors; nor to help the Kenyans produce an Independence Day film that was shown all over the country—the Russians finally did that. John Hogan, our able PAO, practically ran a one-man news service; one tabloid paper got the Associated Press wire, but the Kenya News Agency and the *Standard* had to depend on Reuter's and Tass for their foreign news, and John's material was invaluable. It was frustrating to see him always short-handed while surplus USIS talent cluttered up our European posts.

Now and then we'd rebel. Soon after Washington had cut out one of our most successful small projects—a summer leadership

course in the States for two promising young Kenyans each year—
we were told of plans for holding a conference in Nairobi of
twenty interagency "youth coordinators" to "exchange information
and ideas and identify program strengths and weaknesses." We
figured the conference would cost three times as much as our
canceled leadership courses and would result in nothing but another unread report. We told Washington so in no uncertain terms
—and heard no more about the conference.

At least I was lucky in having a team of executive deputies who
were action-minded professionals, devoted to their work, impatient
with routine and exhilarated by results. Ruchti, Hogan, Wild and I
understood each other and didn't have to argue over the policy
messages we sent to Washington. It was just too bad that the same
harmony and coordination didn't exist at the other end. One reason we couldn't get a decision or even a reply out of Washington
was that the State Department desk officer for Kenya didn't have
the authority I did over representatives of other agencies at his
level; there was no Country Team in Washington. Thus, when they
couldn't agree on how to answer our telegrams, we had to wait
until their conflicting views were bucked upstairs to be reviewed,
debated, perhaps watered down and finally incorporated into a
sometimes ambiguous reply.

Thus, even with an integrated Country Team, we were handicapped by paperwork, overwork and a lack of funds from doing all
that we should to build up goodwill and understanding for the
United States. We needed help from all other Americans who had a
stake in a stable and friendly Kenya.

On the Fourth of July we gave a party for all Americans in
Kenya in a park on the outskirts of Nairobi. Nearly seven hundred
people turned up, including missionary families who drove hundreds of miles. Actually, since the embassy had no money, we
didn't really give the party—we merely organized it, charging everybody five shillings for the music, pony rides, softball games,
relay races and movies, plus an oration by the Ambassador. They
bought their hot dogs, hamburgers and soft drinks.

On this kind of occasion the best thing an orator can do is to
crib from Stevenson's speech on patriotism to the 1952 American
Legion Convention—which I did. But I also added a few words of

my own. I congratulated my fellow expatriates on having a chance to work in Africa, and especially in Kenya, at this time in history. And I added:

Most of us here, whether we are in government or business or teaching or whatever, are in some way helping this country develop its economic and human resources and to strengthen its independence. Kenya is trying to do what Americans were doing 188 years ago, and it is fitting that we should help them. And no American in Kenya today should feel defensive about the policies and actions of his government —in Kenya, around the world or, during this hot violent summer, back home. So, if any of you have any questions or doubts or misgivings about what your government is trying to do, come and see us. It's *your* embassy.

Soon after, we encouraged Nairobi's growing American business community to organize an American Businessmen's Club and hold monthly luncheons. From time to time we also assembled for a sundowner (British for late-afternoon drinks) at someone's house, where other embassy officers and I would tell the members what we were doing and answer their questions. Most of them had to cope with nervous executives in the home office and welcomed any words of reassurance we could give them. Meeting touring American businessmen in Africa, I realized they were a different breed from those who built our railroads and opened up the West; they weren't interested in any investment that wasn't virtually risk-proof.

Sim, meanwhile, organized an American Women's Association that was soon actively raising money and donations of equipment for charitable causes, such as the Starehe Boys Centre, the Amani old people's home, the Flying Doctors and self-help community schools. Until then there had been all too little contact between official and nonofficial American wives, and even less between them and Kenyan women.

So the American community gradually began functioning with more purpose and cohesion; and the Kenyans, who, like the Guineans, were always watching the strangers in their midst, began to notice that Americans weren't just gardening and golfing and playing bridge and sitting around the country clubs like so many other Nairobi "Europeans." They decided Americans were different— they seemed to care.

We also followed up our AID brochure with another booklet called *Americans in Kenya—Who They Are, What They Do, How They Help*. We wrote it ourselves and scraped up a few hundred dollars to print copies to send to all Americans, all diplomatic missions and all government ministries in Kenya. Enough were left over to hand out to visitors who asked about the scope of American private investment or the AID program. This pamphlet further knit the American community together and gave some well-deserved publicity to the quiet and effective work of some of our private missions and foundations.

We needed all the favorable publicity we could get in the summer of 1964, the summer we first heard about "burn, baby, burn" and "white backlash." Every morning I'd pick up the paper and find a picture of racial violence in America; every evening there'd be more to watch on television. You couldn't blame the editors, for the pictures were news all over the world. But they were also under some pressure from the Ministry of Information to play up the trouble. What the Southern whites were doing was a propaganda windfall for Oneko—one of the few racists in the Kenya Government—and even more for his Czech and Russian advisers; you couldn't blame them either for wanting to make the most out of it.

All we could do was try to minimize the damage. In USIS bulletins, in private conversations and in reply to questions after speeches and news conferences, we would point out that the news of violence was front-paged because it was exceptional, because it *was* news. We quoted President Johnson and the Civil Rights Act so that people would realize that in America, unlike South Africa, the federal government was on the side of equal rights. (What most Africans could not understand was why the government could not enforce its own decisions on desegregation in certain Southern states, so we often had to explain how our federal system worked.)

Our efforts no doubt did some good, but I think the most effective counterattack was simply for us Kenya Americans, both white and Negro, to go about our business and let people see for themselves that we weren't racists. I have found that any nation is often judged abroad less by what is written about it than by what impression its citizens make on others.

We also benefited from the presence of more than a thousand Kenyan students in the United States. Now and then one of them would get involved in an incident with the police, usually in the South, but by and large they encountered more friendliness and hospitality than they'd expected—and they wrote home to say so. On the other hand, Kenyans and other Africans who went to the Soviet Union expecting to be welcomed with open arms were usually shocked to discover they were resented by the all-white population—and they not only wrote letters about it but came home and sounded off.

"What I learned in six months in the Soviet Union," wrote a young Kenyan, Nicholas Nyangira, in a widely syndicated article, "is what some Africans will never learn. They are taken to Russia's showplaces and never experience the race hatred that I suffered at the University of Baku. I also discovered it is easy to get into Russia but leaving can be a nightmare. As a student leader who refused to swallow the Communist line, I went in fear of my life."

We also had some useful visitors who helped us mitigate the news from home. A U.S. Navy squadron that visited Mombasa made an excellent impression. More than four thousand sailors swarmed over the city for four days without a single Shore Patrol incident. The admiral came to Nairobi to pay a courtesy call on Kenyatta, sports teams competed with the Kenyans and work crews painted and spruced up the city's playgrounds while local dignitaries were entertained on board. When the nuclear-powered carrier *Enterprise* later sailed past Mombasa, a plane was sent to Nairobi to pick up a group of ministers and government officials. We landed on the flight deck and, after lunch with the ships' officers, were treated to a display of aerial firepower that was both ear-splitting and breath-taking. So enthusiastic were the Kenyans that when another American admiral happened to come to Mombasa a few days later aboard his fifteen-hundred-ton flagship, I found myself with more Kenyan guests than we could accommodate in his plane. It turned out they were under the impression we were going to revisit the *Enterprise*. Luckily I was able to tip off the admiral in time so that he managed to get us all aboard a launch, along with a supply of gin and tonic (no liquor could be served aboard ship). After we'd cruised around the harbor for an hour or so, our guests no longer seemed to mind how big his ship was.

What impressed me—and the Kenyans—about these naval visits was the courtesy, tact and easy informality of our officers. They said all the right things, they didn't brag about our military might and they left our guests feeling that our navy's primary mission was not to wage war but to preserve peace. Down in Zanzibar, Babu regularly denounced these naval visits as imperialist provocations; that didn't bother me. I could see no harm and considerable gain in discreetly reminding East Africa's leaders—including Babu—that we did have an Indian Ocean fleet. For this wasn't old-fashioned gunboat diplomacy; we sought no empire and threatened nobody—we were merely deterring those who might. And I think the Kenyans fully understood this. In thanking the commander of the *Enterprise* for his hospitality, the ranking Kenyan minister remarked, "It is comforting to us to know that we have such powerful friends."

Inland, we had other welcome visitors. A group of Operation Crossroads volunteers arrived in Nairobi in July and fanned out all over East Africa for two months of work on rural projects. I visited one of the two Kenya contingents near Kisii, two hundred miles west of Nairobi, where they were helping African students put up a new school. They'd also been traveling around and staying with Africans who'd never met any Americans. Everywhere they'd found an insatiable hunger for more education and curiosity about America. Young people all hoped to go there to study, even though they thought Negroes were mistreated—or at least treated no better than *they* had been by the British. The Negro Crossroaders were asked what tribe they belonged to (they replied, "Pennsylvanians") and why they didn't return to Africa (they explained they were Americans as well as Pennsylvanians). And, remote as Kisii was, people were concerned about Goldwater; they thought of him as a racist.

It was useful having the right kind of Americans visiting Kenya because people were sometimes more inclined to believe private citizens than government officials like ourselves whose job, they knew, was to make America look good. (This is why it was important never to try and cover up our mistakes and shortcomings; we always surprised people and gained credibility by admitting that American society, as well as American foreign policy, was far short of perfect.)

We had one not-so-welcome American visitor during this period of racial violence at home. I ran into him one afternoon at the Nairobi race track—a place where Kenya's multiracial society gathered around the bookies in a weird kaleidoscope of shooting sticks, saris, hound's-tooth jackets, bare feet, binoculars, turbans, pink gins and tribal robes. Kenyatta and some of his cabinet were sitting in the former governor's box, and I noticed a white man in the group. Moving closer, I saw it was Malcolm X. (Most American Negroes don't look very black in Africa.) I asked Dr. Mungai what he was doing here. Mungai wasn't quite sure; he had been introduced around by Oneko as America's outstanding civil rights leader. When I explained who he really was, Mungai said we should have warned them. Unfortunately we didn't know he was coming.

It turned out Malcolm X was touring Africa to drum up support for bringing the American civil rights problem before the United Nations. That night, on Kenya television, he identified himself as "the leader of 22 million American Negroes," painted an exaggerated picture of their plight and predicted a Goldwater victory (since he would get the votes of America's white majority). The next morning, he came to see me at the embassy. When I told him I had no use for racists, whatever their color, he assured me he had changed his views and now believed in cooperation between the races. After he left, I alerted other posts of his arrival, suggesting they enlighten their African friends in advance.

Malcolm X, though an embarrassment, didn't cause us too much trouble. The people he influenced were likely to be emotionally anti-American anyway; others soon forgot about him. And his prediction about Goldwater—to those Africans who remembered —made the Johnson landslide in November all the more impressive.

An average day in Kenya was a good deal busier than an average day in Guinea; part of the reason was the number of people who appeared at the embassy and insisted on seeing me. Some could be screened out, but every morning I could anticipate seeing at least one visitor who wasn't on my calendar.

It might be a harassed American businessman who couldn't find the minister he'd flown from Chicago to meet. We'd generally be able to locate his man, and our visitor would leave with high praise for the State Department, usually admitting that he'd never had much regard for it before.

It might be someone like Ronald Ramsey or Albert René. Ramsey was a bearded beatnik from California who had held a press conference in Zanzibar attacking the United States. I persuaded him to go home, but he got off the plane in London, went to Algeria where he was arrested as a suspected CIA agent and, the last I heard, was making pro-Vietcong broadcasts in San Francisco and Prague. René, the leader of the Seychelles People's United Party, was usually looking for financial support, which he never got from us. The Seychelles Islands, a thousand miles out in the Indian Ocean, were the site of a U.S. tracking station, and René's party, which opposed our presence, was always ready to change its policy—for a price.

My visitor might be the bearded Arab patriarch from Mombasa who asked, always in vain, for help in restoring the Sultan to Zanzibar. Or he could be the confidence man from Zambia with a calling card saying he was a deputy foreign minister and an invitation to join him for dinner at the New Stanley—after a quick hundred-shilling touch. Or the Minister of Education might turn up, as he once did, with two charming American ladies who wanted to start a World University in Nairobi.

My unexpected visitors were often tourists (with letters from Congressmen or mutual friends) who wanted to be reassured about coming to this savage Mau Mau country; or reporters— always looking for a story about "Communist" penetration. (When I'd ask them what kind of Communist they meant—Chinese, Russian, Yugoslav, Cuban or home-grown—they were always stumped; all they could see was the scare headline, and they just needed some words to go under it.)

The long day done, I'd try to find time for a swim with the children before the evening duty. This might be a reception—at which I was now enough of a veteran to hold two glasses (to avoid getting trapped, you could say you were taking one to your wife); or a dinner—where I might find myself next to the Soviet Ambassador's wife (who was convinced I could speak Russian), a British dowager (who would tell me Goldwater's main handicap was being Jewish), a fiery African radical (who would try to bait me with the old line about Americans being very nice people with a bad government) or a businessman from down south (who would contend, pompously but defensively, that Verwoerd was, after all, anti-Communist). Then again, I might be going to present a cup at the Uganda-Kenya basketball game (Americans coached both teams), or to shake hands with the participants at a Kenya-U.S. boxing tournament, or to answer questions about Vietnam and Cuba and Birmingham at the Kenya Institute of Administration.

It was always a long day. Sometimes I felt that being an ambassador was like running for office in a district where your name wasn't even on the ballot.

It was always a long day for Sim, too. For she not only had a house to run and protocol calls to make and the American Women's Association to organize, but she managed to discover things to do around the countryside that in their own way, as in Guinea, created more ripples of gratitude and goodwill than an AID loan. Thanks to her, we raised enough money from our friends back home to buy a generator for a hospital in Maseno, a television set for a leper hospital in Alupe and braille books and mattresses for a home for blind children near Meru.

These were things that people in Kenya remembered when those who did not wish us well tried to stir up anti-Americanism—as they did with a vengeance in the fall of 1964.

XV

The Road to Stanleyville

•

The President had been right, back in February, to be concerned about the Congo. The failure of the Belgians, the United Nations and the Congolese themselves to create a disciplined and dependable military force to maintain order after the UN forces left in June resulted in the massacre of many thousands of Africans and more than two hundred whites and risked turning the heart of Africa into another Vietnam.

This book is not about the Congo. However, what happened there in 1964 stirred up such emotion and so directly affected the course of events in Kenya—and indeed in all of Africa—that I must start this chapter with a little background information.

The Congo is the second largest country in Africa, about the size of the United States east of the Mississippi, and the richest in natural resources. It was also one of the least prepared to cope with independence in 1960. It was split into dozens of quarreling tribes and divided by nearly a thousand languages and dialects. The Belgians, who had exploited its wealth for eighty years, had neglected to train its people for self-government. They had run this vast area with ten thousand colonial administrators and educated the Congolese just enough to perform subordinate jobs. There were just thirteen African college graduates in the Congo in 1960, or one out of a million.

The Congo's first Prime Minister was Patrice Lumumba, a fiery, erratic, hard-drinking demagogue. But he did believe in holding the Congo together under a central administration, and he spoke the language of an authentic radical African nationalist. When Lumumba was mysteriously murdered in 1961—probably with the collusion of other Congolese politicians who were alarmed by his ambition—he promptly became a martyr, a legend and a symbol of resistance to "neo-colonialism." Although he was not a Communist, the Russians managed to cash in on his posthumous popularity by naming a university after him, and dozens of lesser Congolese politicians proclaimed themselves his spiritual heirs.

Meanwhile, the Congo began falling apart. The biggest secession was that of Katanga, where Moïse Tshombé, backed by Belgian mining interests, declared his independence of Leopoldville. The United Nations, with substantial U.S. support, finally restored the central government's fragile authority in Katanga. But in the spring of 1964 other rebellions were flaring up. Pierre Mulele, a Chinese-trained bandit, controlled parts of the western Congo; in the east, roving gangs of terrorists gradually took over the countryside. Kasavubu decided that only Tshombé had the energy and organizational ability to keep the Congo from disintegrating. In July he called him back from exile in Europe and made him Prime Minister.

Tshombé was tough, able and unscrupulous; he was also Africa's most unpopular African. His Katanga secession had branded him as a Belgian stooge, and he was widely regarded as the man who had Lumumba killed. Tshombé was also hated by Africans for employing white mercenaries, many of them South Africans, and for admitting that he did it because his troops wouldn't fight without white officers. Just as Lumumba was a symbol of patriotism to African nationalists, Tshombé was a symbol of treason. Yet for all his faults, he was a realist who wanted to restore civil order and who faced facts—no matter how damaging they were to African myths—and, now that he was Prime Minister, wanted to unite the Congo and make it a viable, independent nation.

On August 4 Stanleyville was captured by a ragtag mob of rebels consisting largely of teen-age "Simbas" (Swahili for lions) who believed that *dawa*—the magic of their witch doctors—would protect them against bullets. The dispirited Congolese Army garrison melted away. Michael Hoyt, our Consul in Stanleyville, and his four-man staff were suddenly trapped. For nearly four months they and hundreds of other innocent Europeans in rebel-controlled areas were held as hostages by an eccentric and disorganized mafia

that savagely murdered thousands of educated Congolese suspected of having worked with the central government. (For a full
account of their ordeal, the book to read is David Reed's *111 Days
in Stanleyville.*)

The "President" of what passed for a government in Stanleyville
was a cowardly second-rate political operator named Christophe
Gbenye, who had been a minister in the Leopoldville government.
But the Simbas were mostly controlled by a self-styled general,
Nicolas Olenga, and a barroom orator named Gaston Soumialot.
When Tshombé's Katangese soldiers and white mercenaries
stemmed the rebel advance in August and started moving back
toward Stanleyville, Gbenye and his associates began appealing for
outside assistance in the name of Lumumba and African nationalism against Tshombé, the all-African villain, and his American
imperialist masters. It was an appeal to which a good many international troublemakers were tempted to respond: Nkrumah,
Nasser, Ben Bella and, of course, those old cotton-pickers, the
Russians and Chinese.

With their Zanzibar offensive blunted by President Nyerere's
surprise move in uniting the island with Tanganyika, the latter saw
the spreading chaos in the Congo as a chance to leapfrog into the
heart of Africa as the champions of black nationalism against
Western neo-colonialism. If they could install a people's republic
in Leopoldville, they could hope to eliminate Western influence
from a valuable and strategic piece of real estate. They weren't too
worried about a strong U.S. reaction since they rightly assumed
Washington didn't want another Vietnam. Moreover, by staying
well in the background, the Russians and Chinese could make us
look like the intruders; and the more we or the Belgians intervened
on Tshombé's behalf, the easier it would be to turn *all* the Africans
against us. From their point of view, a Congo gambit looked very
promising indeed.

Kenya's leaders knew or cared very little about the Congo in the
summer of 1964. But to the various outside forces with a stake in
keeping the rebellion going, Kenya and Kenyatta were important
elements in a developing strategy. The most convenient supply
route for arms shipments to the eastern Congo was by way of East
Africa, especially through Kenya and Uganda; and Kenyatta, with
his tremendous prestige, would be a valuable recruit to the anti-

Tshombé cause. His domestic political rivals, Odinga and Oneko, also saw a double-barreled opportunity shaping up for them. If Kenyatta could somehow be involved in the Congo bedlam as a mediator, he might either become emotionally aroused against the West (in particular the U.S.), and thus draw closer to them, or, should he resist radical pressure, he could be portrayed as an imperialist stooge and discredited as Kenya's grand old man. In any case, he would be diverted from Kenyan politics, which he understood, and thrust into a situation where he would be out of his depth and susceptible to manipulation.

Meanwhile, ever since Tshombé's return to the Congo in July, all the various Communist and radical African propaganda media had singled out the United States as the sinister and hypocritical colossus that was using him as a front man to stake out a new empire in the heart of Africa. In July the arrival in Leopoldville of four American C-130 transport planes (with crews and guards), to help the central government maintain internal communications and logistics, provided the propagandists with all the evidence they needed to proclaim that the rebels were clearly freedom fighters in a war of independence against American aggression. The planes were pictured as bombers and the handful of noncombatant American military personnel in the Congo—never more than two hundred—as an army of rampaging, trigger-happy paratroopers.

The facts could never catch up with the fiction, especially when the fiction was more plausible to Africans conditioned by experience to be suspicious. Normally reasonable Kenyans were disposed to believe that our interest in the Congo must have some ulterior motives, economic or strategic, such as protecting mysterious investments or keeping control of the Congo's uranium deposits. The facts were that direct U.S. investments in the Congo came to about $25 million, or less than one percent of the total foreign investment, and that no uranium (which we didn't need anyway) had been shipped out of the Congo since 1960. But it was hard to convince people that we had provided the Congo with $420 million in aid since independence just to prevent chaos; they couldn't believe any country could be that altruistic.

It was also assumed that our aid was largely military, since most of the news out of the Congo was about the fighting. Yet the facts were that only $7 million of the $420 million were for direct military assistance. Nearly $250 million were in technical and economic aid (a third of it in foodstuffs), and about $160 million were in support of the UN peace-keeping force. It did little good to point out that we would hardly have contributed $160 million to help suppress the Katanga secession if Tshombé was really our stooge; the usual reply would be: "That was under Kennedy—now your policy has changed under Johnson."

Of course it had not. Our Congo policy since independence was consistently to support the legitimate central government headed by President Kasavubu, regardless of whether Lumumba, Ileo, Adoula or Tshombé was the Prime Minister. But in Kenya, as in most of Africa, logic and facts were no match for emotion in the late summer and fall of 1964.

The operation to involve Kenya—and Kenyatta—in the Congo crisis got under way early in September with the arrival in Nairobi of Thomas Kanza, an itinerant and usually unemployed Congolese politician I had first met in 1961 through Telli Diallo, then Guinean Ambassador to the UN. Kanza, one of the Congo's thirteen college graduates, was an interesting person—suave, ambitious, charming, deceptively ingenuous and smoothly bilingual in French and English, a confidence man in the great tradition of Mississippi river-boat gamblers, with the extra advantage of having a degree in psychology. Unfortunately for his career, his father had been a bitter political rival of President Kasavubu. As a result, his considerable talents were not employed, while lesser politicians got the good jobs. Adoula did send him to London as Ambassador; and when Tshombé, who recognized his ability, was in exile in Europe, they made a deal. Kanza returned to Leopoldville under the impression that he would be Tshombé's Foreign Minister. When Kasavubu blocked the appointment, Kanza decided his best chance for a big job was to use the rebellion to his own advantage and become the middleman between the rebels and the government; out of the ensuing confusion he might wind up on top. So he began soliciting support among African leaders for a round-table Congolese "peace conference"—and naturally turned up in Nairobi.

Kanza came to see me September 4, hoping we'd use our influence in Leopoldville to get Tshombé to agree to such a conference. I told him it was unlikely that Tshombé, who was now gaining the upper hand, would want to sit down with the gang of disreputable adventurers who controlled Stanleyville. But when I later saw Murumbi (who, as Minister of State in the President's office, handled foreign affairs for Kenyatta), I found that Kanza had sold him on the idea of Kenyatta's chairing such a conference. It was easy to see how Murumbi would be impressed by Kanza. A bibliophile and art collector, Murumbi was a half-Goan, half-Masai Kenyan who had, like Kanza, spent some time in London's intellectual and left-wing political circles (his wife was English) and who also saw a Nairobi conference on the Congo as a means of enhancing his own as well as Kenyatta's prestige.

When Murumbi asked me about American financial interests in the Congo—Kanza had been briefing him—I could tell he was skeptical about the figures I gave him. I assured him we were ready to cooperate with the OAU or anyone who really wanted peace and unity in the Congo. And I reminded him there was a legal Congolese government and that it was up to the rebels to seek a reconciliation. But it was clear that Kanza had become Kenya's unofficial expert and adviser on Congolese affairs and that he enjoyed more credibility than a white non-African like myself.

The OAU in September decided to appoint an Ad Hoc Commission on the Congo, with Kenyatta as chairman. The sponsors of the move got plenty of help from my old friend Telli Diallo, who was now the OAU's Secretary General. Telli, who liked his job, saw the Congo as an arena where the OAU and he could play an important role; with Tshombé so universally disliked, he figured the OAU's usually disunited members could at least be mobilized behind a campaign to get rid of him. Besides, he had always wanted to see Kanza, an old friend and protégé, become a power in the Congo.

The seven-nation commission assembled in Nairobi on September 18. Both Tshombé and representatives of the rebel regime turned up, the former with a large retinue of Belgian secretaries. Soon after, our Ambassador to Ethiopia, Ed Korry, arrived in a U.S. Air Force plane on his way to Mombasa for a holiday. The coincidence was unfortunate; within hours, the story was all over town that Korry, who knew Tshombé, had really come to advise him. This fitted in with the radical line that Tshombé was an American puppet.

The next day I found myself in a similar dilemma. While I had stayed clear of the delegates in order to avoid any accusations of meddling, Tshombé unexpectedly asked me to come over to his hotel suite after lunch. I couldn't very well refuse. For twenty minutes, he bragged about his success in winning over Kenyatta and other delegates to his point of view, and said he saw no reason to stay in Nairobi any longer. My only comment was that if he was doing so well—which I had reason to doubt—he shouldn't offend Kenyatta now by walking out; also, he would be leaving the field to Kanza and the rebels. But Tshombé said he had too much to do in the Congo.

At a reception at State House that night, Kenyatta's private secretary, George Githii, called me aside to ask if there was any truth to the rumors that I'd gone to see Tshombé to tell him to leave. He said Kenyatta was upset by his decision not to remain, and a lot of people believed it was my doing. I told George what had actually happened. "Well," he said, "now you see what you're up against." I did indeed, and I knew who were spreading the rumors.

Tshombé was nevertheless the star attraction of the reception, and he acted the part. (While he posed with Kenyatta for pictures, Telli kissed me on both cheeks, French fashion, to the Kenyans' astonishment.) But Tshombé had failed diplomatically. By not showing proper deference to *Mzee* ("He acted like a sultan," Kenyatta told me later), by chiding him about his own British "mercenaries" and by walking out on his conference, Tshombé antagonized the one man who could have checked the radical offensive.

On September 20 I saw Kenyatta, who told me he had reports of American planes bombing Congolese towns and said this made it hard to arrange a cease-fire. The reports were false (they emanated from Burundi, where the Chinese were then entrenched and from where they supplied weapons and advisers to the rebels); I told him so. I also explained that U.S. planes in the Congo—which now included four B-26's and twelve T-28's with Cuban pilots—were under Congolese command, just as his own British-piloted planes were under Kenyan command; and that we did not control Tshombé. Ruchti said the same thing to Murumbi, warning him about relying on rebel fabrications.

But I could sense we were dealing with people who had become convinced that a genuine nationalist movement in the Congo was being brutally suppressed by an African Quisling with the help of white mercenaries and American planes, and that he would collapse without our support. Kanza had done his work well; he'd fictionalized and simplified a complicated problem, and anything we now said sounded legalistic and hypocritical.

Tshombé left on the twenty-first, having refused to talk to the rebels. Telli came over and said the rebels would agree to a cease-fire (which is what Kenyatta wanted) only if we pulled our planes out. Later in the day I saw Kenyatta again, with Murumbi, to give him our official refutation of the bombing reports. Murumbi broke in with an emotional attack on American policy, which he said was dictated by our financial interests in the Congo. Kenyatta cut him off and told me he opposed *all* foreign interference in the Congo, and that the Africans would take care of the Chinese; but he did need our cooperation on grounding our planes and hoped we could work together to stop the killing. As I walked out, Ambassador Lavrov was waiting to come in: the campaign to confuse and capture Kenyatta was really in high gear.

The OAU commission wound up its meeting on the twenty-third. Murumbi phoned me at the end of the day to say it had been decided to send a mission to Washington immediately to see the President about stopping military aid to the Congo. After I'd alerted Washington by phone, Murumbi came to the office, where Ruchti, Heller and I were waiting, to explain jovially that the decision was made after some "very reasonable" testimony by Kanza. He "wasn't sure" whose idea it had been. We told him it sounded like an ultimatum and that it would have been wiser to consult us first. He admitted the atmosphere at the meeting had been "rather emotional." He said he'd be heading the mission, which would include representatives of four other African countries.

That evening I showed a film of the 1960 campaign at my house for some ministers and diplomats. All, except Oneko, were amazed that we had not been consulted in advance about the Washington mission. I was less surprised, for I knew how carefully Kanza had prepared the ground and how skilled he was at manipulating emotion. And the move was a clever one: if we received the OAU mission, this would drive a wedge between us and the Congolese Government; if we refused, it would justify all the suspicions that we cared more for Tshombé (and our mythical investments) than for African opinion as expressed by the OAU. Hostile propagandists would have a field day.

During the film, Telli called to say he wanted to see me right away. We met at the New Stanley. He urged me to help make the mission a success, stressing that it was a "friendly" trip and offering to issue a statement praising Johnson as a great leader and man of peace. He also hinted that, with an election campaign on, Johnson should appreciate the value of not antagonizing Africa. (I suspected that Telli, who'd spent some years in the States, had assured the OAU delegates that, for political reasons, the administration wouldn't dare rebuff the mission.)

I replied that he and the OAU were now out on a limb; while I did not yet know Washington's reaction, I could tell him that his political interpretation was way off the mark. If it came to a choice between showing weakness or resolution on the Congo during the campaign against Goldwater, there was no doubt in my mind what the President would do, whatever the emotional backlash in Africa. Telli seemed somewhat shaken but reiterated his hope that we'd cooperate to stop the bloodshed. He showed me a telegram from Burundi reporting that American bombers had just killed hundreds of civilians in the Congolese town of Uvira. I told him this report, like so many others, was a lie.

Telli smiled—an occasional burst of candor was his most redeeming feature. "I know these reports are lies," he said, "but the thing is, Kenyatta now believes them."

In the morning I was instructed to inform Kenyatta that neither the President nor the State Department could receive a mission to discuss stopping our assistance to the Congo in the absence of Congolese representatives. It was a perfectly proper position, but I sent a message suggesting that we find a way to receive the mission—if only as a courtesy call to allow us to explain our position—in order to avoid humiliating Kenyatta and giving extra ammunition to Kanza and company. This was a time to show some flexibility without yielding on principle. Meanwhile, I transmitted State's reply to Kenyatta and Murumbi; the latter stiffened when I explained why we couldn't receive him. Kenyatta offered to clarify the purpose of the mission, which was "friendly," and pointed out they weren't sending one to Peking only because he knew the Chinese, who were also involved in the Congo, would not cooperate with the OAU. I said I was waiting for another message from Washington and suggested that they make no move or public statement until I got it.

Later I told a group of inquisitive American reporters that some solution would probably be found. (I didn't know what it could be, but this was no time for news stories that might further inflame emotions on all sides.) The main thing now was to keep Murumbi from leaving until a face-saving compromise could be worked out. I knew that the idea of the mission appealed to Kenyatta: it was in the African tradition to solve difficult problems by getting all the chiefs together under a big tree to talk things out, and he instinctively liked the idea of getting through to President Johnson. Our objections, I knew, struck him as legalistic and irrelevant quibbling. He saw his job as restoring peace in the Congo and Johnson as the man who could help him do it.

That night we got word that Murumbi had suddenly left for Washington. (We had reports from other African capitals that several members of the proposed mission—notably Nigeria, but even Guinea—were having second thoughts about the trip; Murumbi no doubt figured that if he didn't move fast the mission might never get off the ground.) I met Ruchti and a code clerk in the office at 2 A.M. and, while Sim made coffee, we got some messages out to Washington. Jim suggested that, since Murumbi could probably no longer be stopped, we might be able to receive him as Kenyatta's personal representative rather than an OAU emissary. This would avoid the kind of rebuff the radicals were hoping to exploit as an insult to the OAU. We suggested this to Washington, requesting an immediate reply so that we could propose it to Kenyatta in the morning.

At nine, after an hour's sleep, I went straight to Kenyatta's office with Phil Heller. No reply had come from Washington, but Murumbi was due to board a flight to New York from London at one, and we had no time to lose. Oneko had also issued a statement declaring that the OAU would not be "intimidated" by Tshombé from undertaking the mission, and he was staying close to Kenyatta, whose private secretary and fellow prisoner he had once been.

Kenyatta seemed surprised that Murumbi had left without notifying us. I said this would make it harder for us to cooperate with him; we had acted in good faith and didn't like being pushed into a corner. Couldn't he recall Murumbi? He shook his head and repeated that the mission was friendly and that he knew Johnson was a man of peace who would understand this.

We were getting nowhere. Also, Odinga burst into the room during our conversation and told Kenyatta he wanted to see him urgently. (Outside, Odinga had been belaboring Heller with wild charges about how Korry and I had been masterminding Tshombé in order to wreck the OAU.) Kenyatta sent him out, but I could tell he had nothing more to say. So, on my own, I proposed the personal-representative formula to him, suggesting he send instructions to Murumbi to that effect. After a moment's hesitation, he agreed and called in the cabinet secretary, Duncan Ndegwa, to draft a telegram to Murumbi in London. Murumbi's new instructions were to say nothing to the press on arrival in New York except that he was there as the Prime Minister's envoy to have exploratory talks in Washington about the OAU mission.

We sent the instructions to our London Embassy by flash telegram for transmittal to the Kenya High Commission and Murumbi at London airport.

In the afternoon Kenyatta sent us a message for Johnson that seemed to contradict the instructions. We also got a telegram from Washington saying Rusk would see Murumbi in his new capacity but that a public statement should be made that he was just a special envoy. Murumbi, meanwhile, had received the instructions in London and postponed his departure to Washington. I managed to get through to Kenyatta, who told me to come out to his farm at Gatundu in the evening.

He was alone with one of his ministers, Mbiyu Koinange. When I said we might be able to save the situation—and his own personal prestige—if Murumbi just followed instructions, they both seemed relieved. (We'd been hearing that some of his Kikuyu colleagues, like Koinange, were beginning to worry about Odinga's and Oneko's motives in pressing him so hard on the Congo.) He made some revisions in his letter to the President and suggested we issue the public statement in Washington. When he saw me to the door, a light rain was falling. "That is good," he said. "For Kikuyus, rain is a good omen."

It was after midnight when we finished sending this and some other information to Washington, along with a draft of a press release. With all of eleven hours' sleep out of the last eighty-four, Jim and I were ready for bed. It looked as if the worst had been averted.

Except for one headline ("U.S. No, But Team Will Go"), there was a virtual news blackout the next morning. Williams had spoken to Murumbi on the phone and agreed to see him informally in Washington, though Murumbi refused to say he didn't represent the OAU. (The other four members of his mission hadn't yet boarded any planes.) Late in the day, Telli Diallo appeared at my office. He had been in Dar and wanted to know "how the OAU mission was doing." He had just seen Kenyatta, who told him everything was going to be all right and that the other members of the mission had been told to proceed to Washington.

I decided to play it tough. I said there was no mission, only Murumbi, and the only question now was, were we willing to save Telli's face? We might or we might not, depending on what happened next. I added that even Sékou Touré had said in Conakry that the sudden OAU decision to call on Johnson was ill-advised.

Telli, who was smart enough to know our cooperation was essential, suddenly became agitated.

"The old man is gaga!" he cried in French. "These British Africans don't understand anything about diplomacy!" He tried to call Kenyatta on my phone but couldn't get through, nor would Kenyatta receive him. He urged me to try, but I declined.

In Washington, Murumbi was proving to be stubborn, while in Nairobi the radicals redoubled their efforts to hold Kenyatta to a hard line. Under pressure from Oneko, the September 26 *Sunday Post* ran a headline—"Anger Grows at U.S. Refusal"—and the next day a gang of fifteen demonstrators, brandishing homemade anti-American signs, appeared at the embassy, accompanied by twice as many reporters and photographers. (The Soviet and Chinese press were well represented and, by bunching the demonstrators together around the embassy shield, managed to get some nice pictures.) The demonstrators, who claimed to represent KANU, had actually been hired by the Ghanaian High Commission. I agreed to see four of them. After listening to their invective I escorted them out, which gave me a chance to say a few things about our Congo policy to the assembled reporters. Another bonus for us was that one of the signs—"Hang Johnson"—was so offensive to Kenyatta that he had KANU issue a statement repudiating and denouncing the demonstrators.

His more reasonable advisers, with whom we'd been in touch, were also talking sense to him, pointing out that Kenya was more important than the Congo and that he was risking failure and humiliation by not meeting us halfway and by allowing Odinga to entice him out into left field. This made an impression, for Kenyatta was above all a politician, to whom Odinga was more of a threat than Tshombé. "He now wishes he'd never gotten into this OAU thing," one minister told me.

The break in the deadlock finally came on October 1, after Kenyatta told Murumbi to work something out. The OAU mission was invited to lunch by Rusk after everyone had agreed on a carefully phrased joint communiqué that saved all faces. We agreed to use our good offices to persuade the Congolese not to use planes if and when a cease-fire was arranged (something that we had agreed to do two weeks earlier, but not in a communiqué), and the OAU didn't insist on an American repudiation of its commitment to the Congo. When Murumbi returned to Nairobi the next day, he was all smiles, and the *Sunday Post* headlined the communiqué: "A Triumph of Good Will."

We were all out of the woods—for the moment—but in Stanleyville the situation was grimmer than ever. A Red Cross plane with Swiss doctors was allowed to fly in on September 29 to deliver medicines, but Gbenye refused to let them stay or fly anybody out. He didn't want the outside world to know what was going on in his capital, and he needed hostages as pawns to bargain with now that the Tshombé forces were on the offensive. A Red Cross official who came back said that even Gbenye's authority in the city was shaky and that the thirteen hundred foreigners trapped there, a majority of them women and children, might be murdered if Stanleyville were attacked. Tshombé wrote Kenyatta that there would be no air attacks on Stanleyville and asked his help in getting the Red Cross plane back in to evacuate innocent civilians. The Swiss made repeated but futile efforts all during October to see Kenyatta, and appealed to Gbenye to allow the plane to return. Not only were these appeals rejected, but the Stanleyville radio denounced the Red Cross as a Western espionage agency.

And no wonder. The rebels and their Communist and radical African supporters were now playing for time—time to mount an airlift of weapons and "advisers" into the northeastern Congo that might turn the tide before Tshombé's advancing columns reached Stanleyville. And a key element of their strategy was to slow the advance by threatening to kill the hostages.

The airlift got under way in late October, with Algerian planes flying Soviet weapons and Egyptian officers to the Sudan and northern Uganda. But it involved considerable spadework and liaison. Murumbi and Kanza, among others, were in and out of airports a good part of the month. They appeared in Cairo, Khartoum, Burundi and Uganda, sometimes traveling on nonscheduled flights, but never really able to conceal their movements. (In Africa it always pays to have a good man around the airports; that's where you really find out what's going on—or what's about to happen.)

On October 18 I ran into Kanza, cordial but nervous, in the Nairobi VIP lounge with Tom Mboya. He was booked to Dar, but suddenly changed plans when Prime Minister Obote of Uganda turned up, and flew off with him. Four days later, Murumbi and Telli also surfaced in Uganda; on his return, Diallo called me to say Murumbi was "not to be trusted so far as Kanza was concerned." I could only infer that the plotters were beginning to sicken.

In Stanleyville threats against the Americans and Belgians were increasingly strident. Washington decided it was worth ascertaining whether Kanza, whom Gbenye had just appointed "foreign minister," would or could arrange their release. Wayne Fredericks, who also knew him, was passing through Nairobi and we were to sound him out.

I happened to meet Kanza on a plane to Mombasa on October 27. He'd heard Fredericks was in town and asked to see us the next day. He came to my office in the afternoon and we talked for a couple of hours. Affable as always, Kanza said he had not accepted Gbenye's "appointment" since he wanted to retain his "political flexibility." But he was firm on the hostages: they could not be released until Tshombé's planes were grounded. That was the deal. "If you persist in helping Tshombé," he said, "the Algerians, the Egyptians and others will soon be in the Congo and you will regret it."

Kanza admitted he'd tried to get a job with Tshombé in July but then changed his mind. He was now writing a book proving that Tshombé's return to the Congo was engineered by our Ambassador in Madrid. Fredericks told him that was a lie. "Perhaps it is," said Kanza with a broad smile, "but it makes a better book."

We kept talking but could make no headway on the hostages. "Gbenye needs them as protection against Stanleyville being bombed," he said. "They are safe as long as nothing happens."

After our meeting broke up, I regretted not being authorized to say the one thing people like Kanza and Gbenye might have understood—that if a single American were killed in Stanleyville we would hold them both personally responsible, the way the Israelis did Eichmann. Knowing Kanza, I think this would have worked. But the more we appeared susceptible to blackmail, the more they figured they could get away with it, and the more they tried.

XVI

Dragon Rouge

•

Early in November, I began feeling like a passenger in a car that has suddenly gone into a slow but uncontrollable skid; we were headed for some kind of collision, and the only question was: How bad was it going to be? We were stuck with Tshombé, the mercenary-led columns were on the move, the Soviet-Arab arms airlift was under way, the hostages were trapped, the Red Cross was immobilized and emotions were heating up. A tragedy was in the making, and the best we could hope for was that not too many people would die. Those of us who cared about Africa and Africans hoped, too, that the onrushing tragedy would not also destroy the fragile bridges of understanding we had worked so hard to build.

It was easy, especially on wakeful nights, to mull over the series of actions and inactions that had steered us into this dangerous skid. Did we have to provide planes and Cuban pilots to Tshombé's army? Wasn't the spreading chaos in the Congo a Belgian and *African,* rather than an American, responsibility? Why hadn't we evacuated our consular staff from Stanleyville before the rebels took the city? Couldn't we have persuaded Gbenye, back in August, to let them—and the few missionaries in the area—quietly pack up and leave? Did we get involved to the extent we did because the collapse of the Leopoldville government might have handed Goldwater a campaign issue? Was a Communist takeover of this vast, chaotic morass of a country in fact a serious practical and logistical possibility?

These are the kinds of questions that sometimes kept me awake at a time when I needed more sleep than I got. But in a time of crisis there is neither sense nor value in brooding about what might have been done differently. (I can, on occasion, keep myself awake today with a similar series of questions about our involvement in Vietnam. I happen to think we should never have gone into Vietnam, but I also believe we now have no choice but to do what we are doing.) In a crisis you have to forget the past and act in the present to make the best of the future. And the important thing, the one thing to concentrate on, in November, 1964, was to prevent a massacre in Stanleyville.

On November 5 Gbenye arrested 280 Belgians and 16 American civilians in Stanleyville as "prisoners of war." He had admitted to the Red Cross in September that he couldn't control his own forces, and the rebels had to do something to keep the excitable and undisciplined Simbas in line and their chaotic regime from collapse. In desperation, they accused us of dropping an atom bomb on the Congo, declared war on the United States and proclaimed themselves a Communist people's republic—hoping thus to get more outside help.

Meanwhile, the mercenary-led column captured Kindu, 300 miles south, just in time to prevent the mass murder of twenty-four Europeans. (Hundreds of Congolese "intellectuals" had already been burned alive there by the Simbas.) It was clear that the more they were pushed back, the more likely the rebels were to take revenge on their white hostages.

Washington and Brussels still hoped to find a way to evacuate the Stanleyville "prisoners" with the help of the OAU and the Red Cross. But just as a precaution, it was decided on November 9 to move a battalion of Belgian paratroopers in American planes to a position where they could step in, if necessary, to prevent a massacre. Repeated efforts by the International Red Cross were stymied. They kept their plane in Burundi, ready to fly to Stanleyville at an hour's notice, but Gbenye did not know about the Geneva Convention, and refused to let them in. Swiss representatives of the IRC could still not even get in to see Kenyatta in Nairobi. A special envoy from the Canadian Government was also given the runaround.

One man with easy access to Kenyatta was Kanza. Murumbi, who trusted him completely, saw to that. And Kanza's line was carefully calculated to appeal to Kenyatta: the mercenaries were butchering Africans (he did have a point there, but ignored the fact that the rebels were butchering—often literally—many more); the Western powers cared about the hostages only because they were white, and beside they hadn't been harmed (not true—dozens of Europeans had been murdered as the Simbas retreated); the nationalists (rebels) were a disciplined force with a functioning administration (so false that Kanza, after visiting Stanleyville once in October, never dared return); the International Red Cross was a Western espionage agency (he managed to put that one over too); and the OAU should concentrate on obtaining a cease-fire if it really wanted to save lives (which would give the rebels time to get the Soviet-Arab airlift into operation).

Kanza had also been busy stirring up emotions in Dar, where he passed out crudely forged documents purporting to reveal plans for a U.S.-supported Portuguese attack on Tanzania. The forgeries were played up in the papers on November 11, and the Tanzanian Foreign Minister violently attacked us. But when Odinga tried to get Kenya to join the clamor, Kenyatta silenced him at a cabinet meeting. "The Americans may be dangerous," he said, "but they are not that stupid."

On November 14 Stanleyville radio announced that Paul Carlson, an American medical missionary, had been sentenced to death as a military spy. The same day, Gbenye published a statement saying the security of the Americans and Belgians "we hold in our claws" would depend on the "retreat" of the forces advancing on his capital. He concluded: "We shall make fetishes with the hearts of the Americans and the Belgians, and we shall dress ourselves in the skins of the Belgians and Americans."

On the sixteenth Rusk sent a message to Kenyatta stating "unequivocally" that Carlson was innocent and urging him to use his influence to get OAU or IRC planes into Stanleyville to bring out the hostages. The message was released to the press. When I called on Kenyatta, he said he had already acted on it: he had telegraphed Gbenye to spare Carlson's life "on humanitarian grounds." I told him we were worried about a possible massacre, and pointed out what it would do to Africa's reputation in the world. Kenyatta assured me the hostages were safe and that the first thing was to arrange a cease-fire; it would be "dangerous" for an OAU mission to go in otherwise.

Yet we kept trying. The next day I met with fifteen ambassadors from countries with nationals in Stanleyville, and we drew up a joint appeal to Kenyatta to be delivered personally by the Indian High Commissioner. But he was unable to get an appointment—Kenyatta, said an aide, was busy.

Gbenye, meanwhile, replied to Kenyatta's appeal by saying he would postpone Carlson's execution until November 23 if we agreed to enter into "negotiations" with his regime. This was black-mail, but the life of Carlson, as well as the lives of other Americans in rebel hands, hung in the balance. Washington instructed our embassy in Leopoldville to radio Gbenye that we stood ready "for discussions to insure the safety of United States nationals now in the Stanleyville area."

Gbenye wanted the talks to take place in Nairobi, and designated Kanza, Kenyatta and Telli Diallo to represent him. He also let Hoyt out of jail long enough to make him sign a message to Leopoldville begging for a cease-fire during the "negotiations" and concluding: "In case of delay I say for myself and my compatriots good-bye."

I remember how I felt when I read this message coming over the ticker in our code room. It was November 20, and I had just received another instructing me to open discussions with Kanza as soon as possible. Now I wished I'd spoken to him as I had wanted to back in October. For I had no illusions that he or Gbenye cared about saving any lives but their own. Of course, we had to make this last attempt—just in case. But I was glad to get still another message saying the Belgian paratroopers had been moved to Ascension Island in the South Atlantic.

The message had come in the evening. Earlier in the day, I had called on Murumbi, who was about to go to the UN. It was "Joe" and "Bill" and all smiles, as usual. We talked of UN issues, and he told me the newly imposed travel restrictions on diplomats applied only to the Russians and Chinese, not to us. Telli, who was in the waiting room, kissed me, complained about his high blood pressure and said there'd be another OAU commission meeting soon. Nobody mentioned Stanleyville.

After the messages arrived, I called Murumbi and asked him to tell Kenyatta about the Kanza meeting and the paratroopers. Ruchti and I met him at the airport at midnight. He said Kanza was being contacted in Uganda and I was to meet him at Gatundu at eleven in the morning. He added that Kenyatta agreed that the evacuation of the hostages had priority over a cease-fire; we wrote this down, and he approved it as Kenyan policy. Lavrov, who was also at the airport, barely acknowledged my greeting.

Back at the office, we found a message quoting the Stanleyville radio: The "Lumumbist Youth" were now threatening to "burn and devour" the hostages.

In the morning I drove out to Gatundu, where I found Kenyatta, Telli, Charles Njonjo, Eliud Mathu (one of the few Kenyan officials who had spent any time in the Congo) and a crowd of newsmen. Kanza did not appear. (It turned out he was in northwest Uganda supervising the transit of arms to the Congo.) But Kenyatta said he was on his way. Since the rest of us were there, I verified that Kenyatta now favored getting the hostages out first and then outlined our position. I said the paratroopers were now in Ascension Island. "Is that a British island?" Kenyatta asked. I said it was.

"Well," he said, "I hope the talks with Mr. Kanza will prevent their being used."

I agreed, saying the troops were a last resort. I added that history would judge all of us involved in these discussions if a massacre took place. I also emphasized I would be talking only to Kanza and said I assumed Kenyatta and Telli would be present only as OAU observers.

Telli then told Kenyatta he wanted to disassociate himself from any meeting with Kanza. As the OAU's Secretary General, he could advise Kenyatta, but no more. (He spoke in English, calling Kenyatta *"baba"*— the Swahili word for "father.") But if *"baba"* wanted to participate, that was all right.

Mathu and I then wrote out a statement for the press that said the purposes of the talks were "to explore all possible means to save the lives of the civilian population, including all foreigners in Stanleyville, and to avoid any actions which might prejudice our efforts."

Telli then asked if he could speak to Kenyatta alone, and I left the room. When they came out and we faced the press, a paragraph had been added calling on "all parties involved in the Congo to cease hostilities." I made it clear to the press that this was Kenyatta's statement, not mine.

When we broke up, Telli came over to my car and said in French, "The old one doesn't know what he's doing, getting involved with Kanza this way. I'm not making that mistake."

In the afternoon the Ethiopian Ambassador called me to ask, as a personal favor, that Telli be given a lift back to Addis on an American military attaché plane that was then refueling in Nairobi. (There were no commercial flights for the next two days.) I said I had no objection if the pilot had space.

That evening Tshombé appealed to the people of Stanleyville to liberate the hostages and arrest Gbenye before the *Armée Nationale Congolaise* (ANC) column reached the city.

The next day, Sunday, the twenty-second, Kanza arrived about noon and went right out to see Kenyatta. (Telli got away on the plane just before he arrived. When Kenyatta sent a police car to pick him up at the hotel, he had already checked out. Bernard Hinga, the Police Commissioner, told me later that Kenyatta "couldn't understand how I'd managed to lose the Secretary General of the OAU.") I was not informed of Kanza's arrival until 7 P.M., when Mathu called to say we'd be meeting at eleven in the morning. I immediately notified Washington and Brussels by flash telegram. (The Belgian paratroopers, who had been moved to Kamina, in the Congo, were planning to launch their rescue mission that night, since Kanza had not turned up at Gatundu the day before. As a result of my telegram, the operation—whose code name was Dragon Rouge—was deferred.)

That evening I was host at a downtown premiere, for the Diplomatic Corps, of *Years of Lightning, Day of Drums,* the USIS film about President Kennedy. All the Communist envoys except the Yugoslav walked out in the middle, but the rest of us enjoyed it; I'd been worrying all week about what might happen to Mike Hoyt, Paul Carlson and the others and welcomed the break afforded by the film.

After the show, I found a pile of messages at the embassy. In New York, Stevenson and the Belgian envoy had formally apprised the UN Secretary General of the situation in Stanleyville.

Hoyt had reported the hostages were still unharmed, but the Stanleyville radio sounded more hysterical than ever, charging that "American, Belgian, Italian and German planes" were now bombing rebel territory and calling on the people to "get their machetes and cut the foreigners to pieces."

The ANC column was less than two hundred miles from the city, and the 545 paratroopers of Dragon Rouge were ready to go. Whether they would or not depended on what Kanza had to say.

My instructions were simple and brief. I was to ask Kanza if the rebels were willing to release the hostages immediately and evacuate the city to avoid bloodshed before the arrival of the ANC. I was then to report his reply to Washington, but not to break off the talks until told to do so.

Before going home, I asked Washington if these instructions still stood. And I added that it was my personal opinion that any assurance Kanza might give would be worthless.

When I got to Gatundu in the morning, Koinange came out and asked me to wait on the veranda a few moments and have a cup of coffee. I could hear the sound of a recorded voice through the window. (I found out later that Kanza was playing a tape on which Olenga purportedly described how his wife and children had been killed by American bombs. This was Kanza's way of "preparing" Kenyatta for the meeting.)

After a few minutes the recording was turned off, the machine was removed and I was ushered into the cramped living room. Kenyatta was flanked by Mathu and an OAU representative. Kanza, smiling as usual, was on the other side of a zebra-skin coffee table. We shook hands and I sat down opposite him.

Kenyatta said he was glad we were finally gathered together. I quickly reminded him that my discussion was only with Kanza and not with the OAU. I then turned to Kanza and explained that I was here to talk about the safety of the innocent hostages who were being illegally held in Stanleyville and were now in great danger. I cited Carlson's death sentence and the Stanleyville radio broadcasts.

Kanza replied that the "prisoners of war" were quite safe and that the broadcasts were "American propaganda."

I said we had little time since the ANC column would probably reach Stanleyville in two days at the rate it was moving. Therefore I wanted to know if the rebels were prepared to free the hostages immediately.

Kanza said he was here to discuss the Congo as a whole and not merely the fate of the "prisoners of war." He said the ANC advance had to be stopped and a cease-fire put into effect before we could talk about the hostages.

Kenyatta interrupted to say this seemed reasonable since nothing could be done while shooting was going on. Kanza had evidently succeeded, on Sunday, in talking him out of his previous opinion that evacuating the hostages had priority over a cease-fire.

"I'm not authorized to discuss military operations," I said, "only the safety of the hostages."

We talked back and forth for a few minutes more. But Kanza was adamant about the cease-fire. I doubt if he or Kenyatta realized that nothing now could have stopped the gung-ho mercenary-led column from taking Stanleyville—not even Tshombé himself standing in the road and waving his arms.

Finally I said: "Since we seem to have different instructions about the discussions, I suggest I report back to my government and find out what they want me to do on the basis of what you've told me."

Kanza agreed. Kenyatta said he hoped I would get a quick answer so we could resume as soon as possible.

I then asked if he could guarantee that the hostages, including Carlson, would not be harmed while we waited for a reply. He nodded. I then wrote out a statement for the press saying that we'd had a useful talk, that I was reporting back to Washington before meeting Kanza again and that Kanza had meanwhile guaranteed the safety of the hostages. When I read it to him, he asked that the part about the hostages be deleted.

"If the mercenaries attack Stanleyville," he said, "we cannot guarantee the prisoners will be safe. Some might be killed in the fighting."

I then asked Kenyatta if I could have a few words with him alone. He agreed, and Kanza and the OAU man left the room. I explained that in our meeting this morning I had been a special U.S. representative and he had been chairman of the OAU commission. Now I was talking to him, as Prime Minister, in my normal role as Ambassador to Kenya. In this capacity, I wanted him to know that the paratroopers *might* have to mount a humanitarian rescue operation as a last resort; if so, I hoped he would understand the reasons for it. I also read him a personal message from Averell Harriman expressing the same hope.

He looked pained. "The paratroopers—that would be very bad," he said. "I hope it will not be necessary. Let us know as soon as you hear from Washington."

I went outside and read my brief statement for the press before television cameras. According to the *New York Times,* I was "grim-faced." A reporter asked me about Carlson. I went back in and asked Kanza, who was staying with Kenyatta, what I could tell them.

"Carlson is alive," he said, "and will not be executed while these negotiations are going on."

I wrote my report on the talks while driving back to the embassy. There was no doubt in my mind that Dragon Rouge would now get under way. But if Kanza knew it, and alerted Gbenye, the element of surprise would be lost and the hostages probably massacred. The rebels had to believe for a few more hours that their blackmail might work.

In the afternoon I attended a memorial service for President Kennedy at the Cathedral and later had tea with some of the priests. I felt dead tired and decided to go home and try to sleep. But I stopped at the office first. Kenyatta had just refused an invitation by Tshombé to come to Leopoldville, saying there had to be a cease-fire first. He had also sent me a personal letter urging us to use our influence on Tshombé to get rid of his mercenaries, stop the fighting and prevent an "invasion" of the Congo by Belgian paratroopers. As I was leaving, Mathu called to ask if we'd heard anything from Washington. I told him the eight-hour time difference between Nairobi and Washington made it unlikely we'd get a message until morning.

I had no word of Dragon Rouge. I assumed the jump would be at dawn. The time difference between Kenya and the Congo was one hour, so I told the duty officer to wake me up at seven.

Greg Kryza, the duty officer, came to the house at seven sharp with two telegrams that had arrived during the night. The first instructed me to tell Kenyatta we were breaking off the talks with Kanza since his terms were unacceptable and constituted "outrageous blackmail." The second telegram said the drop on Stanleyville would take place at 0400 GMT—or 7 A.M. Nairobi time.

I tried to reach Kenyatta by phone and through the police. He had left the farm but was not yet in his office. Finally, at nine, I got through to Koinange and Githii, gave them the message about Kanza and asked to see Kenyatta.

He received me at 10:30 in his office. (I learned later that Oneko had tried to block the appointment.) Njonjo was with him. They both looked solemn, and I could see the anger in Kenyatta's eyes. I knew that he felt I'd deceived him and that we'd pulled a Pearl Harbor on the OAU. But he kept his anger under control. He asked about the paratroopers, and I said I had no information yet that the drop had taken place. We reviewed everyone's efforts to save the hostages during the past two months, and I tried once more to unravel the web of lies that Kanza had woven so carefully. But it was no use. And this was no time to argue with him.

"Mr. Prime Minister," I said, as we got up, "I just want you to know that I've always been frank with you, and that I intend to be in the future. I hope we're still friends."

We shook hands. "We can be friends," he muttered, "only if you stop being friends with Tshombé."

From his office I went over to USIS, where we'd summoned the press at eleven. Knowing that Kanza and Oneko might be cooking up a phony statement about our talk at Gatundu, I decided to beat them to it and get the facts out and on public record. Hogan and I had prepared the following statement, which I read to a roomful of reporters and cameramen:

I have just informed Prime Minister Kenyatta that I received instructions from Washington during the night that proposals made yesterday by the Congolese rebel representative, Mr. Kanza, were totally unacceptable. His proposals constituted an outrageous threat on the lives of at least 1,000 innocent civilians held as hostages in violation of all traditional rules of international behavior in an effort to obtain an immediate cease-fire which the U.S. Government was obviously in no position to enforce.

I have so informed Mr. Kenyatta, at whose home the talks were held, and have asked him to inform Mr. Kanza. At this point, I would like to pay tribute to Mr. Kenyatta for his humanitarian efforts over the past few weeks to safeguard the lives of civilians in Stanleyville.

The talks with Mr. Kanza—and I want to emphasize that these talks were strictly with Mr. Kanza—were undertaken in good faith by us, for the sole purpose of securing the safety of innocent civilians from at least fifteen nations of Europe, Asia, Africa and the Americas. We regret that Mr. Kanza could not respond to this final effort except to try to use the lives of these people as blackmail to obtain military concessions.

Furthermore, the rebel representative refused to commit himself publicly that no harm would befall civilians in Stanleyville unless the military advance on the city was stopped.

It was for these reasons that it became necessary to terminate talks with the rebel representative.

The statement was never published or broadcast in Nairobi. Oneko was so furious that he persuaded Kenyatta to call in the editors of the *Standard* and *Nation* and request them not to print it.

When I got back to the office, we had the State Department's public announcement that the paratroopers had dropped on Stanleyville. As I was reading it, the phone rang. It was Koinange, asking if I would come over to his office, which was next to Kenyatta's, and if I had any objection to seeing Kanza there. I said I'd come over but had nothing more to say to Kanza.

Mathu was waiting in the hall. He started accusing me of deceiving Washington by misreporting what had been said at Gatundu. Before I could answer, Koinange and Kanza appeared in the doorway, and we walked in. I took the State Department announcement out of my pocket and read it to them. Kanza said he didn't believe me, that it must be propaganda. I passed it over to him. Koinange asked if he could show it to Kenyatta.

"Of course," I said. "You can keep it."

He and Mathu left the room.

"Well," I said to Kanza in French, "I've got nothing more to say to you."

"You've made a great mistake," he said. "I think you will regret it."

"We'll see," I replied. "Perhaps someday you'll decide you made a mistake getting involved with the rebels."

He smiled. "I'm sure we'll be seeing each other again," he said.

At the embassy we ordered sandwiches and gathered around the short-wave radio, waiting for news from Stanleyville. Arthur Bulens, the Belgian Ambassador, joined us. The first bulletin was that Hoyt and our consular staff were safe but that twenty-seven hostages had been gunned down by the Simbas a few seconds before the paratroopers could get to them. Twenty-five were Belgians—men, women and children—and two, including Carlson, were Americans. Bulens' eyes were filled with tears; then he went to the phone and called Koinange.

"You told me yesterday they were perfectly safe!" he cried. "Well, I want you to know it is a bloodbath—a bloodbath!" And he slammed down the receiver.

We were all feeling the strain. But later reports brought better news. The rescue operation was succeeding. Within hours, more than a thousand European, Asian and African civilians had been brought to the airport and were being flown out to Leopoldville. Some were wounded, but a massacre had been averted. The Simbas and their leaders had fled. And only one paratrooper was killed.

As I was about to go home, we got word that Kanza and Oneko were with Kenyatta and pressing him to issue a statement accusing me of double-dealing. I knew that Kenyatta felt let down and humiliated; in his present mood there was a chance he might be talked into it. If so, Kenyan-American relations—to say nothing of our personal relations—could be irreparably damaged.

After dinner I went to see MacDonald at State House. I filled him in on what had been going on, and told him of my concern that Kenyatta might say something he'd later regret. I knew that Kenyatta trusted him and that MacDonald might be able to caution him as an old friend. Malcolm promised nothing, but he thanked me for coming over.

I went to bed feeling relaxed for the first time in a week. Hoyt and the others were safe at last. Tomorrow we'd be getting the emotional backlash. It was going to be worse than most people in Washington expected. But we'd done the right thing. We'd done what we had to do.

XVII

After Stanleyville

•

If I may be permitted a cliché, there are few more useful qualities in life than to be able to put yourself in another person's shoes—whether in business, in politics, in marriage or in diplomacy.

We saw the Stanleyville rescue operation as a dramatic effort to save hundreds of helpless, innocent people. It was humanitarian, and it was necessary, since all other attempts to release them had failed. And the operation had to take place before the ANC column entered the city, for the panicky Simbas would probably have mowed down the hostages before fleeing from the mercenaries.

But if you could put yourself in the shoes of an average educated African, you got a quite different picture. When he looked at the Congo, he saw a black government in Stanleyville being attacked by a gang of hired South African thugs, and black people being killed by rockets fired from American planes. He did not know about the thousands of blacks who were tortured and murdered by the Simbas, but he did know that the mercenaries and their Katangan auxiliaries left a trail of African corpses in their wake. (The orgy of looting and killing that followed the capture of Stanleyville by the ANC was so bad that the Belgian paratroop commander was glad to pull his men out of the city for fear they'd start fighting the mercenaries.)

Even more galling to the educated African was the shattering of so many of his illusions—that Africans were now masters of their own continent, that the OAU was a force to be reckoned with, that a black man with a gun was the equal of a white man with a gun.

For in a matter of weeks, two hundred swaggering white mercenaries had driven through an area the size of France, scattered the Simbas and captured their capital; and in a matter of hours, 545 Belgians in American planes had defied the OAU, jumped into the heart of Africa and taken out nearly two thousand people—with the loss of one trooper.

The weakness and impotence of newly independent Africa had been harshly and dramatically revealed to the whole world, and the educated African felt deeply humiliated: the white man with a gun, the old plunderer who had enslaved his ancestors, was back again, doing what he pleased, when he pleased, where he pleased. And there wasn't a damn thing Africa could do about it, except yell rape.

The yelling started on November 25 and lasted for several weeks. Some of it was a natural and spontaneous reaction to humiliation; some was incited by those who had reasons for stirring up a wave of anti-Americanism and who saw the Stanleyville rescue operation as an opportunity to advance their own interests.

The inciters included Odinga and his supporters, the Congolese rebels and their radical African and Arab friends, and, of course, the Soviet bloc and the Chinese.

Odinga saw a chance to discredit Kenyatta's policy of multiracialism and cooperation with Britain and America. Although the British were not as directly involved as we were in the Congo, an anti-American wave was bound to splash them too. And Odinga, while emotionally anti-American, regarded the British presence in Kenya, particularly in the armed forces and police, as the principal obstacle to his political ambitions.

The Congolese rebels had not given up just because they had lost Stanleyville. They still controlled—if that was the word—all the territory adjoining the Uganda border. If Soviet weapons kept coming in and if the East African countries could be drawn in and actively involved on the "nationalist" (i.e., rebel) side, they might be able to mount a successful counterattack. The mercenaries were tough but spread thin, and the regular Congolese troops poorly trained. The rebels' best hope was to make Stanleyville the emotional rallying cry for an all-African, anti-Tshombé crusade.

As for the Communist powers, they had been handed a made-to-order propaganda issue. The single, indisputable fact that Belgian troops had come back to the Congo in American planes was all they needed to confirm their charges that the "Western imperialists" were still lusting after Africa. The reasons for the operation and the prompt withdrawal of the paratroopers were never mentioned; in Peking and Moscow radio broadcasts, the Belgians often became Americans (we were always target No. 1), and the drop was portrayed as a part of a coordinated military offensive to restore "neo-colonialism" in Africa. The paratroopers were even blamed for the deaths of the "prisoners of war."

In Nairobi I became the immediate target of the Odinga-rebel-Communist barrage, as the man who had deceived and humiliated Kenyatta. It had been a mistake not to appoint a special envoy as U.S. representative at the meeting with Kanza. As Ambassador to Kenya, an important part of my job was to establish warm personal relations with Kenyatta, and by the end of the summer he and I were on good terms. But as soon as he became chairman of the OAU commission and I became the spokesman for our Congo policy, we were wearing different hats and talking a different language. (For example, my instructions for the Kanza meeting were necessarily and rigidly explicit and could not take Kenyatta's feelings into account.) So our personal relations were bound to be affected. It was hard for Kenyatta and the Kenyans to separate the frank and friendly Nairobi Ambassador from the two-faced OAU "negotiator" when they were both named Attwood.

On the twenty-fifth, the day after the drop, Dick Catling, Kenya's Inspector General of Police, came to my office to tell us the government had authorized a demonstration by KANU's Nairobi branch outside the embassy the next day. He said plenty of police would be on hand, but suggested we move our cars out of the area. Meanwhile we heard that Odinga and his supporters in Parliament were pressing Kenyatta to declare me *persona non grata* and to break relations with the United States. Still, I was somewhat encouraged by Kenyatta's public reaction to the drop. He said he was "appalled," but this was milder than President Nyerere's angry accusation of "another Pearl Harbor" or Nkrumah's blast at "this flagrant act of aggression against Africa."

We also heard that Kanza was trying to persuade Kenyatta to associate himself with a statement charging me with duplicity. To forestall this, Ruchti and I prepared a telegram asking the department to let us release part of the text of my message about the Gatundu talks in which I had reported that Kenyatta voiced support of Kanza's stand on the hostages. Jim showed Ndegwa a copy, knowing he'd inform Kenyatta. This was playing it rough, but in Kanza we were dealing with a very rough customer. And we wanted to prevent Kenyatta just now from making a rash move that he'd regret later.

Kenyatta was annoyed, but the ploy worked. Kanza did issue a statement the next day asserting that "the U.S. Government was totally and intentionally misinformed about the nationalists' point of view," but it was issued only in his own name. And he even absolved me: "I forgive Ambassador Attwood for just doing his job".

November 26 was Thanksgiving Day. While I was reading the President's Proclamation at the church service for the American community, Odinga, at a cabinet meeting, was demanding my expulsion, claiming that he had proof I had personally telephoned Rusk and the Belgian Prime Minister to order the parachute drop. Several members of Parliament backed up his demand at a press conference and called for a break in relations with the United States, Belgium and Britain unless they stopped their "aggression in the Congo."

After the service, Ruchti and I drove back to the embassy. Just as we pulled up to the entrance, a mob of screaming demonstrators surged around the corner. A British police officer, shouting through a bullhorn, held them back while we U-turned and drove around to the back entrance. The building was full of police, blocking the entrance. We went upstairs and watched the street fill up with people, many brandishing anti-American and anti-Belgian signs. A Chinese Embassy car was parked across the way, and now and then one of the demonstrators darted over to confer with the occupants.

A four-man delegation asked to see me and was ushered to the office by one of our Marine guards. (Refusing to see them would have played into their hands.) They filed in nervously and sat down. One of them handed me a letter for President Johnson. Another, trembling with excitement, declared that Africa had powerful friends like the Soviet Union who would come and help drive us out of the Congo. "Let it be World War Three!" he cried. "We don't care!"

Ruchti, Heller and I listened quietly while a USIS man taped their diatribes. When they left, a group of reporters came in. We looked out the window. Down below, two parked cars suddenly burst into flames. A truckload of riot police swung out of a side street, scattered the crowd and began putting out the fires. (The cars belonged to the Swedish Embassy and the British High Commission.) One of the reporters asked me how I felt.

"Sad," I said. "I guess that's the mildest word I can use."

I gave them the news about a second paratroop drop—on Paulis. The Belgians had rescued 355 hostages and departed, leaving the town in rebel hands. Then I called Sim to say I'd be late for lunch since I couldn't get out of the embassy.

The demonstrators moved around the corner to the Belgian Embassy. Seeing another car with diplomatic plates, one of them tossed a petrol bomb through the window. Luckily it didn't explode; the car belonged to the Indian High Commissioner, and his son was sitting in the front seat.

The crowd finally dispersed and a police car escorted me home for some warmed-over turkey. Catling called to say not to worry but that he was assigning police guards to our residence until the storm blew over. There was a ceremony at the Princess Elizabeth Hospital in the afternoon to which the Diplomatic Corps was invited. Sim and I decided to go, and fly the flag on the car. This was no time to appear nervous or guilty; our best posture was to look unconcerned.

My fellow diplomats were surprised to see us. Mungai was there, representing the government, and I took him aside.

"All this emotion isn't doing any of us any good," I said. "It's building up on our side too. I hope the old man realizes that. The main thing is for all of us to keep cool and not say anything rash."

"I know," he said. "We're having a hard time in the cabinet, but I think it will be all right."

Sim and I went on to a Japanese reception. Everyone stared at us. I shook hands with my colleagues but didn't seek out the Kenyans. They nodded but kept their distance. Raja Tandon, the Indian High Commissioner, was seething over his son's narrow escape. When Odinga arrived, he headed straight for him; I was out of earshot, but I could see from Odinga's expression that he was having a hard time.

The embassies who had helped pay for and stage-manage the riot (and other demonstrations all over Africa) got their money's worth of propaganda pictures; for their purpose was to make the world think that all Africa was up in arms against us and to get Americans to say to hell with Africa.

But locally the morning's rioting was working in our favor. The government hadn't expected it to get out of hand, and Kenyatta was shocked by the fires. He later asked one of his ministers how the people had learned to make petrol bombs. The minister said he didn't know but they were called Molotov cocktails. "That's interesting," said Kenyatta.

And the long day ended with a whimsical postscript, as so many African days do. Our USIS man found that his tape of the demonstrators who came to my office was defective, and sent a local employee to find them in a nearby bar. All four were delighted to come back to the USIS library and retape their anti-American remarks. Afterward they asked if they could borrow some books about Lincoln and Kennedy—and invited our man to come out and have a beer.

The OAU commission convened in Nairobi on the twenty-seventh. I had already seen Telli and warned him that the facts about Simba atrocities were coming to light (some grisly documents were found in Stanleyville) and that he ought to think twice before embracing the rebels too closely. Now, with Kenyatta about to make the opening speech, I was worried about how far he might go in denouncing our "aggression."

I had a personal message from Rusk to deliver to Kenyatta. It expressed the hope that the meeting would be "constructive," pointing out that the drop would not have been necessary had the OAU come to grips with the problem earlier, and promised our cooperation if it were. It was a good message, and I passed it to one of Kenyatta's aides just before the meeting. Then I sat in the diplomatic gallery conveniently next to the aisle, in case Kenyatta's speech would be so rough I'd have to walk out. The Belgian Ambassador and the Acting British High Commissioner joined me.

Kenyatta reviewed the events of the past two months soberly and without emotion. He referred to Dr. Carlson as a medical missionary and to the hostages as hostages, not "prisoners of war." When he came to our last meeting at Gatundu, he said: "Mr. Attwood told me that his idea of the quickest and most humanitarian way was using force. In this I disagreed with him."

There was no implication of duplicity and no mention of aggression. I sat back and relaxed. I wouldn't have to walk out. When the Ethiopian Ambassador later referred to us as "international bandits," I shrugged it off; he was just hitching a ride on the emotional bandwagon. But the key man, Kenyatta, seemed to be putting on the brakes.

At the next day's session, the final resolution was sharply critical of our actions but referred the Congo issue back to the main body of the OAU. A Nigerian delegate told me later: "Don't let the words bother you. We just wanted to get the whole thing out of Nairobi." In his closing remarks, Kenyatta never mentioned us and spoke only of Africa's need for peace and economic development.

I saw Odinga afterward at a reception for the delegates. He greeted me like an old and dear friend, and drew me aside. "What you Americans must understand," he said, holding my hand, "is that we do not like Mr. Tshombé." I assured him that this had not escaped our attention. Other Kenyans began talking to me again. They hoped I hadn't been upset by the demonstration. Again I played it cool, remarking that in the long run these things hurt Africa more than they hurt us. Cornered by one enraged African from the Kenya News Agency, I merely listened and smiled, while the Tass correspondent—who was also a KGB agent—took notes. When I finally broke away, the Russian followed me to the door.

"You see what you'd be hearing," I said, "if the hostages in Stanleyville had been Russians."

He glanced around and then leaned close. "You're right," he said. "And we would have done the same as you to save them."

Red Duggan, of State's Policy Planning staff, happened to be passing through Nairobi after the OAU commission broke up, so we had a chance to talk about the Stanleyville backlash and how we should respond to it. We both agreed that our best posture should be one of indifference or, as he put it, "masterly inactivity." African emotion had to run its course, and the less we responded, the more quickly it would subside. We should not overreact but should keep them guessing about our future intentions. Would we continue aid programs to nations whose leaders called us murderers? Let them wonder, and let them conclude that perhaps Africa needed us more than we needed Africa.

We also agreed that we should try to disengage from the Congo —and especially Tshombé—now that the central government had the upper hand and our people were safe. Belgium had the major investments in the Congo, and there was no reason why we should continue to take the rap for appearing to protect them. Duggan had been and would be talking to other American ambassadors in Africa before returning to Washington; he thought we could get a consensus on these points and that an early chiefs of mission meeting would be useful both to develop a common posture and to review our African policy in the wake of Stanleyville.

Even though Kenyatta seemed to be resisting anti-American pressure from the Odinga forces, they were still pushing hard. Oneko made sure that wild claims and fiery statements by Kanza and Gbenye got good play on the radio and in the press, while President Johnson's comments on the Congo were suppressed. So was the news that the Belgian paratroopers were pulled out of the Congo. (Gbenye, early in December, asserted that the rebels had killed five hundred *American* paratroopers in Stanleyville and shot down ten planes.)

A concert by Paul Taubman's All-American Big Brass Band in Mombasa was canceled on November 29 by the mayor—an Odinga sympathizer—and Oneko's Kenya News Agency then "reported" that the Americans had been "afraid" to go. Telli Diallo was still publicly claiming that no hostages would have been killed if the drop hadn't taken place. When he tried this line on me in the lobby of the New Stanley, I told him, in plain French, to go to hell. In Washington, Murumbi "informally" suggested to Rusk that I be recalled along with two other embassy officers; the suggestion was rejected. A special Congolese envoy from Leopoldville was cold-shouldered by the government; no one would talk to him. And another "mammoth" demonstration against our embassy by KANU Youth Wingers was announced for December 1.

I decided to skip this one. I'd heard all the invective I cared to put up with. And Sim and I had a good excuse to drive up to the Alupe leprosarium, near the Uganda border, to deliver a television set, which had just arrived from the States.

It was good to get away from the political tension of Nairobi and out in the relaxed countryside where the Congo seemed a world away. At Alupe the Regional Government Agent and his staff were delighted to see us, and the ceremony at the hospital was heart-warming. On the way home, we stopped at Eldoret and I phoned Ruchti for news of the demonstration. The news was good. The government had refused to give the organizers a police permit. Instead of more pictures of anti-American placards, the morning paper had a story about our gift to the lepers.

We were over another hump. And we had reports that Kenyatta's political lieutenants, most of them Kikuyus, were once again focusing on the home front—where Odinga, the Luo chief, and not Tshombé, the American stooge, was the man they worried about. I was privately assured that the campaign to get me expelled was dead; Kenyatta's inner circle of advisers was more concerned about whether *our* emotions had been stirred up to the point that we had lost interest in helping Kenya's development.

On December 2 I signed a pending agreement with Gichuru for the delivery of surplus American flour to Kenya. I did not make the usual speech about cooperation, nor did we put out the usual USIS news release, but Gichuru himself had invited the press to cover it. Afterward, I called Hogan and suggested we could afford to take a break; the heat was off, and we were all bone-tired. So we chartered a plane and took our families for a long weekend at a fishing camp on the shores of Lake Rudolf, a jade-green, hundred-mile-long inland sea in the northern desert. It was just what we needed, although our pilot was the only one who caught a fish.

The heat was off in Nairobi, but I reminded the embassy and AID staffs, at our monthly meeting in December, that it would still be a hard winter for those of us who had fought for aid to Africa. Emotions had been aroused on both sides. It was a time for us all to remain cool and quiet and to assume that we were being watched and our phones tapped. Any indiscreet or angry remark by a member of the staff could provide ammunition for the Odinga forces.

And the heat was by no means off in New York, where the UN Security Council met in December to hear African complaints about the Stanleyville rescue operation. Speaker after speaker bitterly and angrily echoed the charge made by the Congo (Brazzaville) delegate that it was "the most ruthless and scandalous aggression of our era." Joe Murumbi, not to be outdone by anybody, declared that "Belgian and American aggressors were wholly and directly responsible for all the excesses that were committed in the Congo." He blandly claimed that Kenyatta was arranging for the International Red Cross to go to Stanleyville, ridiculed the "humanitarian" motives of a country "where Negroes are brutally done to death in Mississippi and elsewhere" and charged that U.S. offers to cooperate with the OAU were "only a ruse to further its domination of the Congo and its carefully prepared military objectives."

Stevenson was appalled by the violence of the African oratory. "Never before," he told the Council, "have I heard such irrational, irresponsible, insulting and repugnant language in these chambers; and language used, if you please, to contemptuously impugn and slander a gallant and successful attempt to save human lives of many nationalities and colors."

The diatribes were not so surprising to those of us who served in Africa and could understand them as the expression of an explosive sense of racial humiliation and frustration that had no other outlet. But speeches at the UN got more attention in the American press than anything said in Africa, and the violence of the African spokesmen did real damage to Africa's image in the United States. Serious commentators predicted that the damage could never be repaired. The *Christian Science Monitor* correspondent at the UN said Stanleyville would have the same consequences as the Boxer Rebellion in China. "There is serious concern here," he wrote, "that African-Western relations will be substantially worsened over the long term."

In a column called "The End of Africa," Murray Kempton voiced the feelings of other American liberals: "Africa hollers rape against us and does not even know that we no longer even care, let alone lust, and that our only reaction is to say, well, that's that and who's got a job for Soapy Williams?"

Many Africans, in their desire to vent their feelings, didn't realize that a public attack on the United States could be more harmful to them than an attack on the Soviet Union or China. For the latter would not be printed in the Communist press, and public opinion would be unaffected. But in a democracy like ours, where public opinion influences policy, the Africans risked losing support for the aid programs they would still need after their UN binge. (Soon after the Security Council session, Operation Crossroads Africa directors told me that private contributions from Americans dropped so sharply they had to curtail the 1965 program.) And the people who would be most hurt by American disenchantment with Africa would not be Africa's UN orators but Africa's impoverished masses—who bore us no ill-will at all.

Like Stevenson, many high State Department officials who were unfamiliar with African psychology reacted with alarm to the UN speeches. I was asked to see Kenyatta and talk to him "constructively" about the Congo, but I declined. This was no time to rekindle any emotional embers. I did see Kenyatta once, on December 14, when the Diplomatic Corps went to State House to congratulate him on becoming President of the newly proclaimed Republic of Kenya. (He was now officially chief of state, and MacDonald moved out of State House to become British High Commissioner.) When I was ushered into the room where he received us individually, Kenyatta was standing under television lights with his wife, Odinga and Murumbi. I had not spoken with him since the morning the paratroopers landed. After extending my best wishes, I handed him letters from President Johnson and Secretary Udall and a USIS book on farming. "I'm giving you this book, Mr. President," I said, "so that the next time I come to Gatundu we'll remember to talk about important things like farming, instead of the Congo."

He laughed. "Very good," he said, "let us do that. No more Congo, only Kenya."

Although the Soviets, Chinese and others had sent special delegations, bearing elaborate gifts for Kenyatta, to the Jamhuri (Republic) Day celebrations, the only picture to make the next day's papers showed me handing him my book.

Speaking after a military parade the next day, Kenyatta made no reference to the Congo, even obliquely. He was back on a Kenyan wave length, warning his audience against subversion and taking bribes from foreigners. Odinga, who had become Vice President under the new republican constitution, looked surly. But he greeted me cordially, as did Oneko and Murumbi—now Minister of External Affairs. This was one thing I liked about African politicians: no matter how hard some of them might work to undermine us, they never showed me any personal animosity or discourtesy. In a way they reminded me of professional politicians back home, who can accuse each other all day long of betraying the Republic and get together for a drink in the evening.

The Congolese rebels were still trying to muster support in January, but the wave of emotion they'd been riding was beginning to recede. Also, the Simbas were disintegrating as a fighting force. When Tshombé's troops captured Watsa, northeast of Stanleyville, they found twenty thousand gallons of fuel and sufficient stocks of Russian weapons and vehicles to keep going without waiting to be resupplied. The Soviet airlift, ironically, was now helping the mercenaries mop up the area ahead of schedule. Gbenye and his associates had managed to escape with enough gold and ivory to finance a peripatetic propaganda campaign, but their claims were getting too extravagant for most African leaders. In Dar he asserted the Belgian paratroopers had shot the hostages and that the rebels had received only food and medicines from abroad—even though Nasser was bragging about his arms shipments. On January 14 he met Obote, Nyerere and Kenyatta in Uganda and managed to get assurances of support. Obote went so far as to declare that *American* paratroopers were still in the Congo "exterminating" the population. But Kenyatta returned from the meeting disillusioned with the rebel leadership; Gbenye had admitted he wouldn't stand a chance in a free election against Tshombé, and rebel defectors had been trickling into Nairobi, denouncing their leaders for making off with the loot and trying to persuade us and the Belgian Embassy to intercede with Tshombé on their behalf.

There was a brief flare-up of anti-Americanism in Tanzania when two of our embassy officers were expelled for allegedly plotting to overthrow Karume in Zanzibar. The "evidence" was a tapped phone conversation in which they spoke about having the "ammunition" they needed to get a message from the State Department congratulating Karume on the anniversary of the revolution. The charge was so fantastic that some of our Kenyan friends wondered why we bothered to reply. But you have to blend patience with toughness. It was better to let Nyerere find out the truth for himself, as he would in time. Meanwhile, our Ambassador, Bill Leonhart, gave him the plain, unvarnished facts; when Nyerere said he could still not reverse the expulsion orders (which would be a public admission he'd been deceived), Washington quietly brought Bill home for consultation and asked for the recall of Tanzania's Ambassador to the U.S.

This was the way to cope with African emotion—with reason and with firmness but without unnecessary provocation.

Kenya, of course, was coming down to earth faster than its neighbors. I had suggested to Williams in December that I be called home in a few weeks to review our future posture and policy and that I use the trip as an excuse to have a talk with Kenyatta. He agreed and suggested I time my return so as to be in Washington at the same time as Leonhart and Olcott Deming, our Ambassador to Uganda. Since we were not going to have an African chiefs of mission meeting, this was the next best thing; it would provoke speculation about whether we were indeed going to change our policy, and might give pause to those who were still emotionally committed to aiding the rebels.

When I called on Murumbi to tell him I was leaving and to request an appointment with Kenyatta, he said he hoped we weren't planning to "withdraw" from Africa. He seemed genuinely concerned. I showed him Kempton's column and said I really didn't know what the current mood was back home; I was going back to find out.

This was a diplomatic variation on an exchange I had had with a group of excitable Odinga supporters at a reception a few nights before. "Why do you keep sticking your nose in the Congo where you don't belong?" one had demanded. "Go back to your own country! Africa for the Africans!"

"That's a good idea," I said. "We might just do that."

"What do you mean? How can you leave Africa?"

"Well," I said, "in Kenya it would take us about a week to close down our offices here and send all our people home. And we'd save quite a few millions a year in aid. We could liquidate our investments and buy our sisal and pyrethrum elsewhere. It wouldn't hurt us."

"You can't do that! Africa is too important to you!"

And the conversation-stopper was: "What makes you think so?"

I also talked bluntly to our friends, pointing out that tourism, which was providing Kenya with nearly $20 million in foreign exchange each year, would be hurt by wild charges and expulsions, as it already had been by the Thanksgiving demonstration. Oneko himself, whose ministry also handled tourism, asked if he could quote me as saying American tourists (nearly fifteen thousand visited Kenya in 1964) had no reason to be alarmed. He had just deported a *Time* correspondent, so first I requested and got written assurance from him that tourists were not the same as reporters.

On January 28 I formally handed my credentials to Kenyatta in his new capacity as President of Kenya. The protocol office, in a circular note, had asked each ambassador to confine the formalities to two minutes ("Good morning, nice weather we are having etc."). I skipped the weather and said I'd like to see him before reporting to Washington.

"Very good," he said, "I haven't seen you in a long time."

We met on February 2 at State House with Gichuru and Mungai. Kenyatta went on at some length about Tshombé, as if he wanted to get the Congo business out of the way, once and for all. Then we discussed Kenya, for the first time in months. He was pleased about our deliveries of PL 480 foodstuffs and our affirmative response to Kenya's request, back in July, to strengthen its police Air Wing. He also thanked me for our assistance to the National Youth Service, and said he hoped we could send Kenya more Peace Corps teachers.

I asked him how he explained President Nyerere's intemperate and impulsive action in expelling our diplomats.

"Well," said Kenyatta, "I think he has too many foreigners and other people around, all spreading stories and causing trouble. But Julius himself is all right."

I said I'd be talking about our policy in East Africa while in Washington and would call on him when I got back.

Just before leaving, I saw Murumbi again. He said the OAU planned to send a delegation to Leopoldville before the meeting of the Ad Hoc Commission early in March. I told him it was about time the OAU had a firsthand look at the Congo.

He lectured me genially ("It's better to be frank") about our "obsession with Communism" and acted as if he had never slandered us in the UN. But his charm, though agreeable, was deceptive. The same evening he was declaring in a television interview that he knew the drop on Stanleyville had been planned six months in advance to further America's colonialist designs on the Congo. You could never anticipate what Joe would say next; anyway he was no longer a member of Kenyatta's inner circle of advisers.

I got to New York February 7. At USUN I found Stevenson and his staff still indignant about the African speeches in December and uninformed about the brutality of the mercenaries and ANC. (It was easier to be righteous at the UN than in Africa; people I'd talked to with firsthand experience in the Congo said it was hard, once you'd excluded the wretched rebel leadership, to sort out the good guys from the bad guys.)

In Washington, when I asked my State Department associates how our African policy was shaping up, most of them would smile and say, "If you find out, let us know." There seemed to be a division of opinion in the Department between those who thought Africa was important and those who did not, and, in the first group, as to whether we should disengage or get more deeply involved in the Congo. The Pentagon was certainly not in favor of committing any American forces to an area that might turn into another Vietnam. Leonhart, Deming and I appeared before several interagency and intradepartmental policy-making committees and fortunately spoke on the same wave length. We counseled patience, firmness and a certain amount of indifference until the emotional storm blew over. We suggested that things weren't so bad from our point of view as they looked or sounded from a distance, and that the Chinese and Russian cold warriors had still not scored any permanent points. We also thought that we should remain responsive to and ready to cooperate with *constructive* African proposals on the Congo, and also use what small leverage we had on Tshombé to induce him to attend the OAU commission meeting early in March and convince some of his fellow Africans that he was not the arrogant puppet they imagined him to be.

Along with Fredericks and Bob Komer (of the White House staff), we also drew up a Congo policy paper that we thought would appeal to a majority of the OAU; it included, among other things, a cease-fire as soon as outside support of the rebels was halted, OAU border patrols to prevent arms going into the Congo, OAU observers at the Congolese elections, amnesty for rebels who laid down their arms and an invitation to them to participate in the elections. Whether or not Tshombé and his adversaries would accept these points, we would at least show the Africans that we were interested in helping stop the bloodshed, and the onus for continuing and promoting disorder would be on those who supported the rebels.

Our recommendation satisfied most of the individuals and agencies concerned with Africa, and we now had a consensus to talk from when we got back to our posts. By mid-February, we were ready to go. But we were still waiting for an appointment with the President. (If we could not tell Kenyatta, Obote and Nyerere that we had talked with the President about East Africa, much of the effect of our sudden Washington consulation would be vitiated.) The State Department had been unable to set up an appointment by noon on the nineteenth, and two of us were leaving that night. At this point, we were ready to settle for a picture of us with the President for the East African papers.

So I called Moyers' office and got word to Jack Valenti that we had to have at least a picture taken at the White House that afternoon. He promptly set it up for five, in between other appointments. (If you're wondering why someone upstairs at State couldn't have phoned Valenti, my only explanation is that the system isn't geared for this sort of initiative.)

We went over armed with brief summaries of the situation in our countries for the President to stick in his pocket after the flash bulbs went off. But after the picture-taking the President read our memos, sitting on the edge of a table, and we ended up talking with him for about twenty minutes. He was bothered about the violent reaction to Stanleyville. "We had thirty-one Americans there. What did they expect me to do—let them die?" We tried to explain the reasons for the emotional reaction and predicted it would die down. It seemed to reassure him.

All in all, it was a useful meeting. But if I hadn't been a non-career ambassador, with telephone access to the White House, it wouldn't have taken place.

While we were in Washington, the rebels and their supporters made one last frantic effort to involve East Africa in the Congo fighting on the eve of the OAU meeting. With the mercenary-led columns pushing north to seal off the rebel supply routes, hundreds of Simbas fled across the border into Uganda. Using some of their Congolese loot, Gbenye and others managed to persuade certain Uganda Army units to join them in raids across the border. Tshombé's planes reacted by blowing up two border-crossing points with rockets. This was the signal for a new propaganda offensive: "American" planes were now "bombing" Uganda towns and "murdering" innocent women and children. The border area was sealed off to visitors, crowds tore down our embassy flag in Kampala, and Obote (who a year later admitted his troops *had* gone into the Congo) denounced this wicked and unprovoked attack.

In Nairobi the Youth Wingers and their sponsors once again went on the warpath. When I got to London, I found a message from Ruchti suggesting I delay my Nairobi flight; a demonstration, which might get ugly, was being planned for my arrival at the airport. But I was in no mood to change my plans. Moreover, I felt that another anti-American demonstration was the Kenya Government's problem, not mine. So I went ahead.

Nairobi's air terminal looked very quiet for a Saturday morning when we taxied in from the runway. And so it was. Bernard Hinga, who had succeeded Catling as head of the police, had neatly taken care of the demonstration by closing the airport to all visitors. There were just two police cars parked next to mine, waiting to escort me home.

The next day, Daniel arap Moi, the new Minister of Home Affairs, asked me to come around to his office.

Soft-spoken but tough, Moi had no use for Odinga, and vice versa. He came right to the point.

"I thought you might be feeling badly about yesterday," he said. "So I wanted to tell you personally that you have many friends— America has many friends—both in and out of the government.

The demonstrators mean nothing. I hope you understand that."

I said I did, and thanked him. I was just sorry that people back home, reading the papers, would only know about the near-demonstration and not what people like Moi were saying. Nor would they hear what a group of American missionaries from all parts of Kenya told me a few hours later—that, except in Nairobi, they had not detected any anti-American sentiment among their Kenyan friends and students during this long stormy winter.

The OAU met in Nairobi early in March after a month of wrangling over whether to send a delegation to Leopoldville. Kenyatta was anxious to wind up his mandate as chairman of the Ad Hoc Commission. He resisted pressure from the radicals to send Kenyan troops to Uganda as a gesture of solidarity against U.S. "aggression." He had too many pressing domestic problems to be able to afford prolonging the Congo diversion.

I went to see him after my return and outlined our views on the Congo as I'd gleaned them in Washington: in short, how we'd be willing to cooperate if the OAU was realistic. He seemed to be really listening for the first time in months; Mathu took notes on what I said, and sent me a copy later—which I revised for the record. We were re-establishing communication.

Tshombé came to the meeting and handled himself well; he acted firmly but reasonably. He called on Kenyatta at Gatundu, and they talked for two hours in Swahili. Later Kenyatta told me he'd been impressed. "I still think he's a scoundrel," he said, "but he's a man you can do business with—if he means what he says." Kenyatta, a tough politician himself, recognized a fellow professional.

Tshombé's delegation refused to meet the rebels, but he was now dealing from strength, and most of the delegates accepted the fact. The turning point of the meeting came on March 6 when only thirteen out of thirty-four nations voted in favor of seating the rebel representatives. Tshombé had won acceptance as the legitimate, if still unloved, spokesman for the Congo. And the final communiqué was a Kenyan-Ethiopian compromise that left the Congo alone and deftly papered over the split between the OAU's moderate and radical states.

So the carefully planned campaign to use the Congo and

Tshombé to turn Africa against the West finally fizzled out after seven months of behind-the-scenes intrigue and on-stage histrionics. And the only losers were the OAU, which emerged with its membership split and its prestige dimmed; the mischief-makers—Communist, Arab and African—whose strategy was based on wishul thinking and whose arms airlift was mounted too late; and the plain people of Africa, so deserving of understanding and help, who were now tarred in the eyes of the world by the actions of a handful of irresponsible adventurers in Stanleyville.

And we Americans, the chief target of the campaign, came out of it all relatively unscathed. The storm did pass. I enjoyed listening to Joe Murumbi opening a U.S. trade fair in Nairobi on March 7 with a warm speech praising our constructive contribution to Africa's economic development. I enjoyed receiving Kanza at my house, a few months later, and listening to his assurances that he and Gbenye were really pro-American—and would we put in a good word for them in Leopoldville? I enjoyed the irony of Kanza's eventual expulsion from Kenya, with Murumbi, on Kenyatta's instructions, issuing the deportation order.

But what I enjoyed most of all were a few casually spoken words in Kenyatta's office just five months after Stanleyville. I had been talking to him and some of his ministers about ways of alleviating the food shortage caused by a bad drought. As we were walking out, he called me back. He was standing by his desk and held out his hand.

"The Congo is finished," he said gruffly. "Now we are friends again."

XVIII

The Old Man and Double-O—
Round One

•

Oginga Odinga, Oginga Odinga,
In Kenya's black pie he is Mao's red finger.
Though his name leads me into this frivolous jingle,
Not one to laugh off is Ogingle Odingle.
I hope that Kenyatta, the lion of Kenya,
Will settle the hash of this mirthless hyenya

If Ogden Nash, who wrote this ditty for the *New Republic*
in 1965, had ever met Odinga, I'm sure he would have found a
better adjective than "mirthless." For Odinga had charm and
humor in abundance. I always enjoyed his company. Exasperating
he could be, but boring he was not.

Mr. Double-O, as the British nicknamed him, was a prosperous
Luo businessman from the Lake Victoria area who drifted into
politics during the fifties. He earned Kenyatta's gratitude for lending him money during the Emergency and demanding his release
from detention. He also helped Kenyatta become Prime Minister
by working hard for a KANU victory in the 1963 elections.
(KANU, backed by the dominant Kikuyus and Luos, favored a
strong central government; the opposition Kenya African Democratic Union—KADU—represented the smaller tribes and therefore advocated more regional autonomy.) Odinga became a Kenyatta intimate; like him, he carried a cane and fly whisk, and
Kenyatta took to wearing a beaded Luo cap.

But Odinga had ambitions of his own. Just past fifty and the leader of an important tribe, he saw himself as Kenyatta's logical successor. At public ceremonies, he took pains to be seen and photographed at Kenyatta's side, properly conspicuous in his distinctive Chinese-style pajama suit and waving his fly whisk like *Mzee*'s understudy. So convincingly did he play the role of No. 2 that the Russians and Chinese, looking ahead and figuring that Kenyatta was becoming senile, decided to make Odinga their man in Kenya. On trips to Moscow and Peking he was given the full VIP treatment and assurances of ample political funding. And his Communist hosts found him wonderfully susceptible to flattery and receptive to their sales pitch. He was the kind of African they knew how to handle—ardently nationalistic, but naïve about world affairs. The Chinese were especially successful, as they were with a good many impressionable Africans, in persuading him that the many marvels he was shown were the result of fifteen years of Communist "liberation" rather than five thousand years of Chinese civilization. And if China could do it, went the argument, so could Africa—just as soon as the Western imperialists were driven out.

However, both the Chinese and the Russians made some major miscalculations with respect to Odinga, Kenyatta and Kenya. Odinga may have been shrewd and crafty, but he was also emotional, which in big-league politics can be fatal. Also, Kenyatta was by no means senile, as they were led to believe; aside from being a national hero, he had the undivided loyalty of the disciplined and industrious Kikuyus, who scorned and distrusted the more indolent Luos. Thus, by supporting Odinga's ambitions, the Communists were bound to alienate not only *Mzee* himself but the most powerful tribe in Kenya. Finally, the Russians and Chinese suffered from their usual delusion that the Kenyans, like all colonized peoples, must hate their former British "oppressors" and—to use the Communist jargon—would gladly welcome new allies in their struggle to liquidate the last vestiges of Western neo-colonialism.

So they put their money on the colorful but erratic leader of the wrong tribe with the expectation that he would someday, somehow, come to power in an area where they wanted a foothold. Their support both incited and enabled Odinga to challenge Kenyatta's leadership, at first indirectly and finally openly. The story of this struggle for power, much of it conducted behind the scenes, is therefore worth relating in some detail.

The easy way to dramatize the Kenyatta-Odinga rivalry is to describe it solely in cold war terms—with "Mao's red finger" challenging the pro-Western "lion of Kenya." Not only Ogden Nash but a good many newspapermen pictured it this way. It's true that Odinga used Communist money to build his own political organization and that Kenyatta's government was strengthened by Western aid programs. But both men were essentially African nationalists who, like Sékou Touré, didn't consider themselves beholden to any foreign power. Odinga, though attracted by what he'd been shown of Communist achievements, didn't expect to be dictated to by Moscow and Peking if he came to power; as for Kenyatta, he welcomed cooperation with the West only so long as we supported what *he* wanted for Kenya.

It would therefore be more accurate to say that the struggle was between the Kenyatta "constructivists"—who wanted to make Kenya's existing social, political and economic institutions work better—and the Odinga "dislocators"—who advocated widespread nationalization and immediate Africanization without realizing what the consequences would be. There are several appropriate terms we can use to describe the protagonists: moderates vs. radicals, pragmatists vs. ideologists, modernizers vs. agitators, progressives vs. extremists. But we should try to avoid labeling them "pro-East" and "pro-West," for African leaders, with few exceptions, are simply pro-themselves.

Kenyatta's political assets were his own personal prestige, a competent team of loyal ministers and a reliable security apparatus. His priority objective was to minimize popular discontent by producing signs of economic and social progress. His problem was to keep Odinga under control without making him a martyr to 1,100,000 Luos.

Odinga's political assets were ample sources of funds, the loyalty of a majority of the Luos, control of immigration and (through Oneko) of the radio, and the services of a brilliant tactician named Pio de Gama Pinto. His priority objectives were to whittle down British influence, especially in the army and police, broaden his political base to other tribes and become the champion of landless peasants and the urban unemployed. His problem was to work toward these goals without separating himself from the ruling KANU party or appearing to be directly challenging *Mzee*'s leadership.

Personally, Odinga's strengths were his charm and a crowd-pleasing platform manner. His weaknesses were his emotionalism and a vast ignorance of the outside world. On different occasions he asked me why we did not "liberate" West Germany as the Russians had "liberated" East Germany, why we kept American Indians in "concentration camps" and why we had "attacked" North Korea in 1950; he swallowed the Malcolm X line on American race relations and was convinced the West was engaged in a "gold rush" for Africa. And he seemed immune to contradiction.

Kenyatta's associates were alert to the Odinga challenge from the beginning, as I discovered soon after my arrival in Kenya. Some were already urging him to break with Odinga and drive him out of the party and government before he could build up his own subversive apparatus inside KANU. They also feared that the longer Odinga was allowed to wave his whisk at Kenyatta's side, the better his chances of claiming the succession if something happened to the Old Man, for in the ensuing political free-for-all he would have the inside track so far as public opinion was concerned.

But Kenyatta's inclination was to sit back and give Odinga more rope. He opposed a showdown now that might split the party while KADU was still in the opposition. He wanted the anti-Odinga forces to be brought together into a multitribal coalition first; otherwise an open fight with Odinga would look like a Kikuyu-Luo feud. So he preferred to maintain a façade of harmony for the time being.

Meanwhile, Odinga kept busy. On a trip with Murumbi to Moscow and Peking in the spring of 1964, he arranged for Soviet financing of a Nairobi school for KANU party leaders. The school —predictably called the Lumumba Institute—was quietly constructed in the suburbs and suddenly unveiled seven months later with a faculty headed by two Russian professors (one of whom was a KGB agent). He also arranged for military training in China and Bulgaria for more than a hundred hand-picked "students"; as Minister of Home Affairs, he was well placed to get them discreetly out of Kenya and back again. And an unpublicized clause in the Soviet aid package he brought back from Moscow provided for Russian weapons to be sent to Kenya after the proclamation of the Republic and the departure of the British troops in December.

Of course, there was not much Odinga could do inside Kenya without Kenyatta knowing about it. The police and Special Branch (Kenya's FBI) under Catling and Hinga were directly responsible to the Prime Minister's office. Their orders were to keep an eye on Double-O, and they did.

The first indication I had from Kenyatta that he didn't trust "Jaramogi" (which was Odinga's Luo title) was in mid-June, when he called me over to discuss outside financing of Kenya's politicians. Before independence, Tom Mboya had been getting help from the AFL-CIO and other Western labor groups to build up Kenya's trade union movement. Kenyatta wanted to make certain such assistance had now stopped. I said I'd make inquiries and agreed with him that all aid to independent Kenya should go through the government. But what about Odinga's subsidies from the Chinese and Russians?

"I know about them," said Kenyatta. "I've already called in their ambassadors and told them to stop."

He and Murumbi, who was present, then asked if the United States could provide the police with some planes to increase its mobility in case of a "Zanzibar" kind of uprising. (Murumbi pointed out that Kisumu, Odinga's home base, was all of four hours by road from Nairobi.) I promised to forward the request to Washington.

Kenyatta's first public repudiation of Odinga came two weeks later when he announced that Murumbi would be Acting Prime Minister during his absence at the July Commonwealth Conference in London. Odinga, who had led his backers and supporters to believe he was No. 2 man in the Kenyan hierarchy, was so outraged that he refused to come to the airport to see Kenyatta off—a characteristic display of temper that did him no good. It not only called attention to the snub, but promptly started rumors among the Kikuyus that Odinga had been plotting to seize power in Kenyatta's absence.

Odinga came to my house for a stag dinner while Kenyatta was in London. He brought an aide and a bodyguard, and I invited Ruchti and Heller. He was delighted to hear me say I thought tribalism was one of Kenya's biggest problems, and the conversation then ranged far and wide. It was hard not to like him; like most Africans he enjoyed political give-and-take, and none of us minced words—though he deftly evaded our questions about the "plot" rumors. He seemed to welcome our suggestion that he come to the States for a longer visit and see for himself that we weren't the sinister imperialists he imagined us to be. He knew little about our aid program in Kenya and was surprised that we did not oppose "nonalignment." When I saw him to his car, he paid us a compliment which I am sure was genuine but which left me with absolutely nothing to say.

"I enjoyed myself," he said, holding my hand. "You Americans remind me of the Chinese. We can talk frankly together and we can laugh. But the Russians—well, they are different—they are too much like the British."

On his return from England, Kenyatta made a speech denouncing "politicians" who accepted bribes from foreigners and who wanted to expropriate European-owned farms. He didn't mention Odinga by name; he didn't have to.

Meanwhile Tom Mboya had been assigned to draft a new republican constitution. This was a key move in thwarting Odinga's ambitions. Since it would be hard to choose any other Vice President but Odinga without antagonizing the Luos, the best strategy was to cut down the powers of the Vice President and deny him the right of succession.

Mboya was a good choice for the job. Kenyatta did not fully trust him (he was, after all, another ambitious Luo), but he rightly figured that Mboya and Odinga could not work together. Temperamentally and ideologically, they were natural rivals. At thirty-four, Mboya was cool, reserved, modern-minded, pragmatic and hard-working. He scorned Odinga's histrionics and sloganeering, just as the latter despised Mboya's seeming intellectual arrogance.

The new Constitution was submitted to Parliament in October. Odinga's supporters could not oppose it publicly, as supposedly loyal members of KANU, but hoped to defeat it and call a new general election.

They failed. One reason was that Kenyatta and his lieutenants on November 9 persuaded KADU's leaders, Ronald Ngala and Daniel arap Moi, to dissolve their opposition party and join KANU. Kenya became officially a one-party state. But in fact KANU was still divided between its pro-Kenyatta and pro-Odinga factions. By absorbing KADU, most of whose members were anti-Odinga, Kenyatta substantially increased his parliamentary strength. This was the second key move in the developing strategy.

In the government reshuffle that followed, Odinga became Vice President, but found himself stripped of most of his powers; also, the Constitution decreed that Parliament would choose the new President in the event of Kenyatta's death. Moi got the Ministry of Home Affairs, Odinga's old job. Ngala remained in Parliament where there was work to do, since Odinga men still held some key committee posts. Kikuyus were assigned as junior ministers—and watchdogs—in Odinga's and Oneko's offices.

Meanwhile, Kenyatta asked London to assign a British officer, Brigadier John Hardy, as Commander in Chief of the Kenya Army. Other British officers were put in charge of the air force and navy. Hinga replaced Catling as head of the police, with a British inspector as his deputy and 250 British officers on the force. Few African leaders except Kenyatta could have afforded to take these precautions against a coup without being accused of selling out to "neo-colonialism."

And all this, mind you, was going on just before and just after Stanleyville, when anti-Western emotions, at least on the surface, were at fever pitch.

When Governor General Malcolm MacDonald left Kenya on December 12, along with the last contingent of British troops, he and Kenyatta made brief speeches of farewell at the airport. (The farewell was symbolic since MacDonald would soon be returning as British High Commissioner.) After Kenyatta referred to Mac-Donald's hobby of bird-watching, Malcolm replied that he had been especially happy in Kenya where there were so many varieties of birds to watch—"including the wisest old bird in Africa, *Mzee* Jomo Kenyatta."

The crowd roared appreciatively. But when Kenyatta escorted him to the plane, Odinga stayed behind with the other ministers.

The rift between Kenyatta and Odinga was common knowledge by the end of 1964. On November 29 the London *Sunday Telegraph* ran a story under a three-column headline ("Kenya Facing Threat of Red Takeover") reporting what the Kenya Special Branch already knew—that mysterious crates had recently arrived at Nairobi airport aboard a Czech plane and had been trucked away, without customs inspection, by one of Odinga's henchmen; the story also told of forty young Luos who returned from training in Communist countries and were exempted from immigration checks, on Odinga's instructions. Oneko promptly expelled the *Telegraph*'s Nairobi correspondent from Kenya—which only gave the story wider circulation. Copies of the paper were quickly sold out, but the grapevine spread the word, no doubt with embellishments. Stanleyville was remote; a threat to *Mzee* was close to home. "The Kikuyus," someone told me, "are beginning to sharpen their *pangas.*" And a *panga,* as you may have guessed, is very much like a machete.

No one was quite sure of Odinga's strength in Parliament, where, under the new Constitution, the next President would be chosen if Kenyatta did not live out his term. Out of 140 MP's and 41 Senators, Odinga could certainly count on 35 to 40 as being personally loyal to him. The big question was: how many others had been "bought"? For Odinga never seemed short of funds. (In 1966 Moi publicly declared that Odinga had personally received more than $1 million from Communist sources for political action.) What was obvious was that his supporters were well heeled, drove new cars and voted as a bloc.

In February half a dozen MP's who were anti-Communist, loyal to Kenyatta and fed up with Odinga's flagrant pay-offs organized an informal coalition called the "Kenya Group." Within a few weeks their numbers swelled to nineteen, then to thirty-five. They decided to vote together and support each other, whether or not *Mzee* openly gave them his blessing. (Kenyatta's strategy was to avoid getting publicly identified with any faction; he wanted Odinga to bear the responsibility for splitting KANU.)

Some of the Kenya Group members, like one MP who came to see me, had become convinced on their own of Communist deceit. On a visit to Peking, he had been told that Taiwan was "occupied" by American troops and that Americans had "colonized" the island. So he had gone there to see for himself, and now wanted to start a paper to expose Chinese Communist "lies." Others were alarmed by the way the Chinese and the Russians spent money, through Odinga, to corrupt their fellow MP's.

On February 24 Odinga's chief braintruster, Pio de Gama Pinto, was shot dead in the driveway of his home by two gunmen who escaped in a car. Pinto had been Odinga's principal liaison man with Communist embassies as well as his chief political adviser; Pinto's wife was also Oneko's private secretary. Although two men were later arrested and jailed for the murder, it was never really satisfactorily explained. Some said Pinto was killed because he was going to tell Kenyatta about a plot to overthrow him; others suspected that some activist Kikuyus—with or without Kenyatta's tacit approval—decided to deprive Odinga of his services. Two things are certain: Pinto knew too much, and a lot of politicians had reason to want him silenced; and Odinga sorely missed his guidance and counsel, as he demonstrated by committing blunder after blunder in the months that followed.

Pinto's death gave the Kenya Group an opportunity to test its strength when the KANU leadership nominated another Odinga man to fill his seat in Parliament. In a surprise move, the Kenya Group refused to go along with what was a gentleman's agreement, named its own candidate and elected him by a 71-to-34 margin. Odinga discovered that some of the people he had "bought" turned out to have been only rented.

The upset vote spotlighted the split in the party and government. The struggle going on in the wings now shifted to center stage. Mboya and Odinga, both Luos, began trading verbal blows in Parliament, while Kenyatta took on Bildad Kaggia, a disaffected Kikuyu who had joined forces with Odinga. Meanwhile, rumors multiplied that the extremists, now increasingly frustrated and isolated in Parliament, were preparing a coup against the government in mid-April. They may have been. But as it turned out, the spring of 1965 was a bleak one for the Soviet and Chinese Communists and their Kenyan clients, bleaker even than we had reason to expect.

On April 6 twenty-nine Kenyan students returned from the Soviet Union loudly complaining about the brutality and racial prejudice they had encountered.

On the seventh, *Revolution in Africa,* a Chinese pamphlet printed in Albania and circulated in East Africa, was banned by the government for advocating the overthrow of Kenya's present leadership.

On the night of the eighth, troops surrounded the building where Odinga had his office and impounded several dozen crates of small arms, including grenades and machine guns, stored in the basement. A second raid on another cache took place two days later.

On the eleventh one of the East European envoys, alarmed by the raids, informed the government that he also had several crates of weapons stored in his embassy and would like to get rid of them. The police quickly obliged.

On the thirteenth the government requested all embassies to report whether Kenya students in their countries were receiving military training. Murumbi told me that hundreds of young men had been secretly sent to Communist countries by Odinga and the whole matter was "under investigation."

On the fourteenth a Soviet freighter, the *Fizik Lebedev* appeared in Mombasa Harbor with a cargo of heavy weapons and tanks destined for Kenya. The shipment seemed to take the government by surprise. So did a Soviet military mission of seventeen technical "advisers" who suddenly arrived by plane two days later and moved into the Panafric Hotel at Kenya Government expense. Kenyatta refused to allow the ship to unload until its cargo was inspected. The Russians replied that no "white" officers could inspect the weapons, which were to be turned over to "Africans" only.

By now Kenyatta and his ministers were developing a slow burn; he concluded the Russians were trying to put something over on him (as indeed they were—the military mission was headed by a KGB general). He sent Brigadier Hardy, Bruce McKenzie and

Dr. Mungai, now Minister of Internal Security and Defense, to Mombasa to see what was aboard the ship. The military mission was then given twenty-four hours to get out of the country. On the basis of the Hardy-McKenzie-Mungai report, the government issued a statement (over Oneko's objections) saying the Soviet arms had been rejected as being "old and obsolete" and "of no use to a modern army" like Kenya's. The *Fizik Lebedev* sailed away, its hold still full of World War II tanks and howitzers, and Ambassador Lavrov, after a heated session at State House, became unavailable for comment. The Russians had blundered again in figuring they could infiltrate Kenya's armed forces with a gift of old weapons. Perhaps Professor Potekhin had been reading the accounts of nineteenth-century explorers and decided that African chiefs could still be flimflammed with the modern equivalent of cheap trinkets and colored beads.

There was more to come. On April 28 Parliament's Sessional Committee issued a paper entitled "African Socialism and Its Application to Planning in Kenya." The paper, which Kenyatta later referred to as Kenya's "economic bible," encouraged private investment and explicitly rejected Marxism and "scientific" socialism. ("The historical setting that inspired Marx has no counterpart in independent Kenya.") It was a flexible, pragmatic document that reflected Tom Mboya's practical thinking. Roscoe Drummond, who was visiting Kenya, described it in his column as standing "about midway between Lyndon Johnson's Great Society and the conservative wing of British Socialism."

It was hard for Odinga, as a member of the government, to oppose it publicly. But the students at the Lumumba Institute expressed his private views the next day in an angry, ill-timed manifesto criticizing the government's "alignment" with the West, defending "scientific" socialism and attacking the Peace Corps. One could easily detect the heavy Russian hand of the faculty's two Leningrad professors in the phrasing of the manifesto, and Kenyatta's reaction made it easy to predict the early demise of the Institute.

On May 4 diplomats were ordered to restrict their movements to within ten miles of Nairobi and to request permission for travel outside this limit two weeks in advance. But the order was aimed solely at the Chinese and Soviet bloc embassies and was not strictly enforced on the rest of us. (We complied to the extent of "notifying" the Foreign Ministry each time we took a trip out of town.)

On May 17 a convoy of forty trucks loaded with Chinese weapons was intercepted by Kenyan police after they crashed through a roadblock at night while in transit through Kenya from Tanzania to Uganda. The convoy and its cargo were impounded and the Uganda drivers taken into custody. Kenyatta was shocked that he had not been informed about the convoy or its cargo; he called it "an act of criminal folly" and refused to release the convoy or the drivers until Obote came to Nairobi to explain and apologize. The fact that the trucks were passing through Odinga's home area gave rise to rumors that this was their destination; actually, the arms had been shipped there for delivery to the now dispersed Congolese rebels—with the tacit cooperation of Tanzania and Uganda—on the assumption that the rebels would still be there to receive them and that the Kenya security forces would not present a problem. But the unforeseen events of April had put the Kenyan police force on the alert, especially in Luo land; the roadblock was no more anticipated in Peking than was Kenyatta's angry reaction.

Odinga, now deprived of Pinto's counsel, began lunging and floundering like a wounded bull in an unfamiliar arena. After the arms raid in his basement, he followed Kenyatta to a reception and posed with him before massed photographers; but no pictures appeared in the next day's papers. After the African socialism paper was endorsed by the government, he made a series of speeches asserting that Communism is "food," that America was "squeezing its nose" into Africa to grab its wealth and that only true socialism eliminated the waste and unproductivity of capitalism. In a calm but pointed rejoinder, the Kenya *Weekly News* declared: "A country can afford to reject Darwin without grave risk, but cannot reject Pasteur without a radical increase in the death rate. No country can reject capital without also rejecting economic development and being content with stagnation."

Odinga's bleak spring was not made any easier by his Chinese and Russian sponsors. Not only were the latter competing with each other (the Chinese were delighted with the *Fizik Lebedev* episode), but neither of them fully trusted Odinga now that Pinto wasn't around to serve as a kind of intellectual linchpin among them all. The Russians, more experienced in Africa, wisely decided to lie low and avoid antagonizing Kenyatta any further. They and the Czechs even cut down their subsidy of a local extremist magazine called *Pan Africa* to the point that its editor offered to sell out to us—for a price. (We weren't interested.) When the government decided to close down the Lumumba Institute, which had cost the Russians about $2 million, they took it as stoically as they had Mr. Solod's expulsion in Guinea. Neither Lavrov nor Wang bothered to attend the graduation ceremonies of the Institute's first and final class in June 19. I went and heard Odinga make a rather pathetic "nonaligned" appeal for funds from "East and West" to keep the place open for the cause of African nationalism, but the overtrained graduates let the cat out of the bag by shouting "Kenya and Communism!" as they received their certificates. This excess of revolutionary zeal was duly noted and reported to State House by the Special Branch observers in attendance.

The Chinese caused Odinga some more grief in May by throwing a party to which they apparently invited all the Kenyans with whom they had had any contact, directly or through Odinga. Again, police agents were interested in the number and identity of lesser politicians and KANU branch officials from faraway districts who turned up for the festivities. The Chinese got themselves deeper in the East African doghouse early in June when Chou Enlai, on a visit to Tanzania, declared that Africa was now "ripe for revolution." African leaders were so indignant ("Revolution against whom?") that Chou found himself with no place to visit after Tanzania. Kenyatta let him know in no uncertain terms that he was not welcome in Nairobi, and the Chinese Embassy was put under closer surveillance.

While the Communist powers played cold war games, we quietly went about our business of helping the government cope with its problems, both economic and political. The first shipload of American corn arrived just as stocks were running out in drought-stricken areas; five U.S. Cessnas and a C-47 had been ordered for the Police Air Wing; more than one hundred Peace Corps volunteers were now working in schools, cooperatives and settlement schemes; the National Youth Service was recruiting unemployed young men at the rate of four hundred a month and putting them to work with American trucks and shovels. And the government appreciated the leads we were able to furnish them on certain strangers in town. After investigating the activities of a New China News Agency correspondent (and just before expelling him from Kenya), one minister told me: "I see now we had a lot to learn at *uhuru*. All along, I thought these people were really *journalists*."

The Kenyans gradually satisfied themselves we weren't meddling in their politics. (I welcomed the fact we were being watched and our phones probably tapped, for there was little I would not have wanted the Kenyans to know about our activities.) And our personal relations became even more cordial. Of course, small gestures made a difference: if Kenyatta was dedicating a hospital on a Sunday afternoon, the diplomats who skipped their golf game or siesta to attend the ceremony were noticed and remembered. Often we'd be the only foreigners present at these functions except for the British, the Israelis and, occasionally, the Germans and Japanese.

Our national image was improving too. The Congo seemed long ago, and Vietnam far away. Racial violence in America had subsided, and President Johnson, in his speech on voting rights, struck a chord that brought him to life—I think for the first time—in the eyes of informed Africans:

"I want to be the President who helped to end hatred among his fellow men, and war among the brothers of this earth. . . . Their cause must be our cause too. It is not just Negroes, but all of us, who must overcome the crippling legacy of bigotry and injustice. And we shall overcome."

I sent copies of the speech to all members of the government. Many of them phoned and wrote me later. Kenyatta sent Johnson a personal letter about it.

It had been difficult to make Africans understand that we had a President who was carrying on where Kennedy left off. The Congo and the confusion about our apparent change of policy about Tshombé had made it more difficult. Now it was easier for Kenyans to accept what I told some of them in a speech in May, 1965:

Those of us who came into this government with Jack Kennedy because we believed in him and his programs are proud today to be serving under Lyndon Johnson, whether we are in Africa, Asia, Europe or back home. And I hope that people all over the world who revere the memory of President Kennedy realize this and understand that there has been no change in the purpose and direction of our policy since his death.

Kenya, in June of 1965, was internally oriented and alert to the dangers of subsidized subversion. Three months earlier, Odinga and his backers were still in a position to stage a coup. They had the weapons and enough people in key places, such as the radio station, to conceivably seize power in Nairobi in the event Kenyatta were assassinated. They might not have succeeded in the long run, but the potential was there. Odinga's blunders, and those of his Communist backers, opened the eyes of a good many hitherto complacent Kenyans and put the security forces on their guard. The task ahead was to forge a coalition that could be strong enough to keep Kenya on the steady, progressive course that had now been charted even after *Mzee* was no longer at the helm.

In a forceful and carefully phrased speech on June 5, Kenyatta told his people what he expected of them and made it plain, without mentioning Odinga by name or abandoning the principle of nonalignment, that there would be no compromise with those who wanted Kenya to change course:

Let me say it quite plainly today that Kenya shall not exchange one master for a new master. We intend to remain our own masters forever. Let every nation in the East or West take heed of this warning today.

We welcome genuine friendship, but we detest flattery. We welcome cooperation and assistance, but we shall not be bought or blackmailed. We may be underdeveloped, and our people may walk barefoot, but we are a proud people—proud of our heritage, our traditions and ancestry. What is more, we will not betray our children.

I must warn those in our country who seek to create confusion. It is true that we have passed through many years of Western imperialism. It is natural that we should detest Western colonialism, and associate the word imperialism with the West. But if we are truly nonaligned, we must not avoid making friends with those Western countries who extend an honest field of cooperation and trade.

It is naïve to think that there is no danger of imperialism from the East. In world power politics the East has as much designs upon us as the West and would like us to serve their own interests.

This is why we reject Communism. It is in fact the reason why we have chosen for ourselves the policy of nonalignment and African socialism. To us Communism is as bad as imperialism. What we want is *Kenya nationalism,* which helped us to win the struggle against imperialism. We do not want somebody else's nationalism. It is a sad mistake to think that we can get more food, more hospitals or schools by crying "Communism."

I speak plainly on this subject today because the time has come for us to do so in order to leave no room for confusion. I am also happy that we have our Constitution, a document on African socialism and a party manifesto. These three documents have been endorsed by our people and Parliament and must be a guide to our new society. It is now for the public to judge the actions of the government and the utterances of all our leaders according to what is laid down in these documents. The world is looking to see if we shall be able to live according to these policies and ideals. . . . There is no room here for the lazy and idle. There is no room for those who wait for things to be given for nothing. There is no place for leaders who hope to build a nation of slogans.

Round one was clearly Kenyatta's. Odinga had been hurt and was now on the defensive. But he was still on his feet, still in the ring and still swinging. The second round could not be taken for granted.

XIX

The Old Man and Double-O— Round Two

•

The trend of events in Kenya, and elsewhere on the continent, since Stanleyville should have caused the Russians and Chinese to conduct what John Foster Dulles would have called an agonizing reappraisal of their African policies. And yet, other than a tapering off in Russian diplomatic activity, there was no evidence that they had done so. On the other hand, we Americans, who were making out all right, undertook a review of our own policy at two chiefs of mission meetings in the late spring of 1965.

The first meeting, at Addis Ababa, included our envoys in eastern Africa all the way from the Mediterranean to Cape Town. The second, at Abidjan, was attended by our West African ambassadors. (Mac Godley, who was in the Congo, went to both.) Averell Harriman, Soapy Williams, Wayne Fredericks and a retinue of Washington Africanists from various government agencies took part in all the sessions.

Before we converged on Addis, Washington had solicited our views about promoting "A New Program for Africa." In my reply, I urged that we be careful about creating the impression that we were embarking on a new course (unless we were) or raising expectations that more aid money would be available (unless it was).

I was glad to discover, in Addis, that my colleagues also felt the same way. We all agreed that our basic policies were sound and had proved successful over the past two years. So it was agreed that the title of the paper to emerge from our deliberations would be changed to "A *Strengthened* Program for Africa."

Our sessions, which lasted five full days and part of each evening, were more profitable than our 1961 conclave at Lagos. I had now mastered the jargon ("We're hearing static on the grapevine." . . . "The Chicoms are getting their trunk under the tent." . . . "We ought to hold his feet to the fire"), and most of us were now personal friends as well as diplomatic colleagues. So there were fewer speeches and more informal discussion. And the discussion was practical, based for the most part on experience rather than theory. We had all learned a good deal about Africa in the past four years, and it showed in the way a consensus quickly developed.

We agreed that any change in our African policy should be in the direction of a firmer stand against white minority rule in the southern part of the continent. Most of us favored short-term rather than long-term economic aid projects—projects that would assist progressive governments satisfy the immediate needs of their people. We concluded that military aid to African countries, generally speaking, was both wasteful and potentially dangerous. We asked for greater flexibility in using available aid funds in countries where self-help was a part of economic planning. We agreed that poverty, ignorance and disease, not "Communism," should be our principal targets; and that the less we talked about the Communists, the more the Africans themselves would take note of what they were up to. And we suggested that ambassadors be given more of a chance to tell their stories in Washington to the Senators and Congressmen whose votes and opinions not only influenced our foreign policy but directly affected our capacity to carry it out effectively.

We returned to our parishes after a final admonition by Harriman to make sure strong delegations were sent to the forthcoming Afro-Asian conference in Algiers—delegations, he meant, which would oppose anti-American resolutions on Vietnam. This was one of the few times I (and most of my colleagues) disagreed with Harriman's judgment. It was clear that the conference would be merely an expensive and meaningless propaganda exercise under pro-Communist auspices, and our best tactic was to label it as such and shrug it off. But Harriman seemed to be reflecting the attitude of a gung-ho element in Washington who believed we should try to play every hand and win every pot, no matter how small, even when the cards were stacked against us.

As it happened, the admonition, and the flood of follow-up telegrams from Washington, turned out to be unnecessary. Ben Bella was overthrown three weeks later by his own army, and the Algiers conference, suddenly deprived of its host, was indefinitely postponed.

Meanwhile, back in Nairobi, Kenyatta's lieutenants pursued their quiet but carefully synchronized campaign to isolate and neutralize Odinga in Parliament. We must remember that Kenya is a parliamentary democracy. (You had only to sit in the gallery and watch the Speaker, Sir Humphrey Slade, presiding over the heated but disciplined debates, to appreciate its vigor.) Therefore Parliament had to be made secure against manipulation by the Odinga forces. On June 25 Odinga was removed as chairman of the powerful backbenchers group by a 44-16 vote, and replaced by Ronald Ngala, the former KADU leader. Soon after, Odinga men were ousted as chief and assistant whips, and the Sessional Committee (similar to our own Rules Committee) was taken over by Kenyatta supporters. Thanks to the KANU-KADU merger and the formation of the Kenya Group, the moderates now had the organization, the confidence and the leadership to assert themeslves in Parliament. And control of the Parliament was essential, for it was here that Kenyatta's successor might one day have to be elected.

Kenyatta himself remained aloof from the parliamentary maneuvers; but when I called on him at Gatundu on June 26 with a visiting American television crew, he was clearly elated, even though neither of us mentioned Odinga or the vote.

With Parliament taken care of, the Kenyatta team directed its attention in July to the labor movement. Several unions, led by Odinga sympathizers, had recently broken with the Kenyan Federation of Labor and formed a rival federation covertly subsidized by Communist funds. One of the breakaway unions was the Dockworkers, which in an emergency could tie up the port of Mombasa. Rather than try to crush the insurgent group, Kenyatta suddenly announced the dissolution of both federations and appointed a hand-picked commission to set up a new central organization that would include everybody. Odinga's people grumbled—they knew their subsidy would be cut off once they were absorbed—but they could not openly oppose what appeared to be an admirably impartial compromise. A few months later, when the new combined federation was unveiled, one of the two most important pro-Odinga union leaders got a title without any power, while the other eventually landed in jail.

The next move took place inside the KANU party organization. The party had forty-one branches, and new officials now had to be elected in former KADU districts. Also, Odinga men controlled or were contesting at least a dozen branches, and Odinga money was being liberally distributed in other districts. But hard work and superior organization managed to solidify Kenyatta's control over KANU in all the branch elections held in the fall of 1965.

Kenyatta's chief tacticians were Njonjo, McKenzie, Gichuru, Mungai, Mboya, Moi and Ngala. Of these, the first three, and sometimes Mungai and Mboya, comprised an inner circle of advisers who stayed close to Kenyatta and got together on an *ad hoc* basis to map out strategy. The group as a whole differed in age, temperament, tribal affiliation and even—in McKenzie's case— skin color; what they had in common were brains, energy and an aversion to Odinga and what he stood for.

Odinga had no such loyal braintrust. His followers, except for Kaggia and Oneko, were mostly ambitious amateurs. Murumbi, a close friend of Pinto's, sometimes seemed to be playing Odinga's game but was now trying to get back on the Kenyatta bandwagon. Thus, with Pinto gone, Odinga's strategy often appeared whimiscal and rudderless. In July, three weeks after graduating from the Lumumba Institute, a gang of KANU branch officials tried to seize the party's national headquarters in Nairobi, claiming to have elected a new Secretary General in place of Mboya. The police moved in quickly and arrested twenty-seven of them, including the Institute's vice president and the secretary of the Students' Union, for breach of the peace. Njonjo, as Attorney General, threw the book at them, and KANU branches got the message straight from Gatundu: all Lumumba Institute graduates—whom Odinga had selected and the Russians had so carefully groomed to take over the party—were now out. The hotheads who staged the abortive raid on party headquarters had clumsily played into Kenyatta's hands; by challenging Mboya they were also challenging the party leadership, and KANU's president was also Kenya's President, Jomo Kenyatta.

While Odinga's political power—in Parliament, in the trade unions and in the party—was being progressively sapped, the roots of his strength, grounded as they were in popular discontent, were still intact. *Uhuru* had not yet made much difference in the average Kenyan's standard of living. Jobs and land remained scarce. In June Kenyatta had announced that hospital outpatients would get free medical care, but public education was still not free. And the shortage of teachers, books and equipment was acute. Only about one-eighth of the 126,000 primary school students who passed their secondary school entrance examinations could hope to continue their education. In the villages parents built "self-help" schools with their own hands, only to learn that there were no teachers to staff them.

Thus, winning branch elections wouldn't matter in the long run, if the people became disenchanted and turned against KANU. Fortunately, there were a good many things we and other Western countries could do to help the government mitigate the discontent. In addition to our existing AID programs—which were concentrated in education, agriculture and community development—we sold Kenya on credit nearly $4 million worth of corn, wheat and other surplus foodstuffs in 1965; under the terms of our loan agreement the proceeds of the sale were to be invested in revenue-producing projects that would develop the economy and enable Kenya to repay the loan in twenty years. We were also helping set up teacher training courses at Kenyatta College, where the students had started conducting adult literacy classes on their own time. AID had also made available a $50,000 contingency fund, which I could use at my discretion to assist small self-help projects in rural areas. (A pump and a few hundred feet of pipe could make a big difference to a village that lacked water, and the people remembered where they came from.)

U.S. private firms also did their part. More than five thousand Kenyans were employed by American companies, with an annual payroll of $16 million, and three new firms were undertaking to build manufacturing plants in Kenya during 1966. Wages paid were higher than average; also, most companies set up training programs to qualify African employees for managerial jobs.

Tourism, already Kenya's No. 3 source of foreign exchange, was given new impetus with the scheduling of a weekly Pan American flight to New York; Pan Am also decided to build a hotel in Nairobi. (Kenya's First Lady, "Mama Ngina" Kenyatta, was a guest aboard the inaugural flight on October 1.) Tanzania had objected to granting Pan Am landing rights in East Africa since "nonalignment" decreed that a "Western" airline had to be balanced by an "Eastern" airline. But Kenya and Uganda went ahead anyway; they saw no economic advantage in having Aeroflot or Ghana Airways come in.

One of the Kenyan ministers explained it to me this way: "Nonalignment is all right as a principle so long as you don't make it an obsession. Naturally we don't want to get involved in the cold war. But we must always think of what's good for Kenya, of our own self-interest. And if economic cooperation with the West benefits us, then let's cooperate and not worry about whether we look aligned or not."

You could call this pragmatism or just plain common sense. At any rate, it had become the prevailing attitude at the top levels of the government.

The Russians had been keeping quiet—and out of trouble—ever since their weapons were sent away and the Lumumba Institute closed down. Construction of their hospital in Kisumu, which was a gift, did get under way in the fall of 1965, but the rest of their 1964 aid package began unraveling. They insisted on paying for local costs with imports of Russian consumer goods which the Kenyans didn't want. As a result, several projects were dropped and the government turned to the World Bank, the UN and four Western countries to join forces in financing the most important of them—a $45 million scheme to irrigate the vast Kano Plains bordering on Lake Victoria. By the spring of 1966 an American survey team had arrived to make a feasibility study of a pilot project in the area.

Lavrov went back to Moscow for consultations in the summer; when he returned, he invited me and Sim to lunch, along with the Polish and Nigerian envoys. The caviar was delicious and the conversation laboriously cordial. ("It is true what you say about the population explosion; however, in the Soviet Union we are developing new methods of food production which will solve the problem. And now we shall drink to peace.")

The Chinese, on the other hand, kept pushing and were now Odinga's principal source of financing, usually through their embassy in Dar. On September 2 Marshal Lin Piao laid down the hard line in a speech in Peking that received wide circulation and unfavorable comment in the Kenyan press: "In the final analysis, the whole cause of world revolution hinges on the revolutionary struggle of the Asian, African and Latin American peoples who make up the overwhelming majority of the world's population. . . . This area is the main battlefield against U.S. imperialism and its lackeys." Two weeks later, pamphlets reiterating these views and praising Odinga appeared in Nairobi; they had been mailed from Tanzania.

Some of Kenyatta's associates were urging him to break relations with China, since it was now obvious to all that the Chinese Embassy was encouraging subversion against his government. But Kenyatta sensibly preferred to keep the Chinese aboveground where they could be watched. Wang and his staff had just moved into a new building enclosed by a high wall, to which Kenyatta archly referred as Nairobi's newest tourist attraction. "We now have the Great Wall of China here in Africa," he told me when I called on him in September. "Our police will have to use helicopters to see what those people are doing behind it."

I noticed that Kenyatta was no longer wearing the beaded Luo cap that Odinga had given him after his release from detention; I had never seen him without it. Later, Njonjo told me that the President had decided it was inappropriate for him, as a national leader, to wear tribal headgear. Another reason, of course, was that it prevented Odinga, who continued to wear his cap, from looking like No. 2 when they appeared together in public. Kenyatta never wore the cap again.

I was called back to Washington in August. Stevenson had died in London (as he had always lived—at work); and Arthur Goldberg, who was recruiting a new team to serve at the UN, wanted to talk to me about joining the U.S. delegation. I explained that this was no time for me to leave Kenya, and he understood how I felt. Moyers told me later the President didn't really expect that I'd want to change jobs just then. At least the Goldberg talk gave me a chance to touch some bases in Washington, and convince the usual skeptics that good things were happening in Kenya. Mac Bundy agreed with me that having Communist Chinese embassies operating in Africa had been an educational experience for Africans. "The only problem," he said, "is having just enough Chinese around to inoculate them but not enough to infect them."

Kenya, by October, was pretty well inoculated. Odinga, increasingly frustrated, was also being provoked into losing his temper by deliberate slights. When President Kaunda arrived on a state visit, Odinga was not even asked to accompany Kenyatta to the plane; on UN Day, Mungai, who represented Kenyatta at the official ceremonies, did not bother to address the Vice President, who sat with him on the rostrum; after Odinga attended a party at the home of an East German correspondent, his host was summarily expelled from Kenya.

You couldn't help but feel sorry for Odinga. Badly advised, sensitive to pin pricks, pressed by his oriental sponsors, shadowed by the police, he was reported to have started drinking heavily and taking *bhang*—a kind of African marijuana. As the ranking Kenyan at the big Soviet party on November 7, his reply to Lavrov's toast was painfully incoherent. From time to time, he would burst into Kenyatta's office to denounce the colonialist machinations of MacDonald and me. (He always put us in that order.) To his own followers, he blamed all his reverses on our "subversion" of Kenyan politicians. There was a risk that some of his loyal Luos might get so fired up as to take direct action. We did hear of a "plot" to assassinate MacDonald and me in June, but the police were tipped off and put a young Luo away for three years.

In November I invited Odinga to my house for another meal. This time he came with an aide and two bodyguards—one of whom had to sit across the table from him—and a carload of Hinga's police, who appeared to be watching the bodyguards. So we had seven extra mouths to feed. I invited Bob Skiff, our new political officer, and Bev Carter, our new PAO. (Carter, a six-foot-seven Negro and a crack golfer, was already something of a local celebrity.)

Odinga, stiff at first, unbent as the lunch progressed. He asked why there were not more U.S. aid projects in his area. I said we already had a good many teachers in Luo country and would be glad to look at other worthwhile projects. But since he had recently called us dangerous imperialists, did he really want more Americans around?

"Yes, yes, to help us," he replied. "It is just that my people are worried, sometimes, that you will come with guns, as you do in Vietnam. And also, you Americans, you think all Luos are Communists." He leaned closer, framing his face in his hands. "Look at me! Do you see Communism in my face?"

"No, Jaramogi," I said, unbuttoning my jacket. "And do you see any hidden guns on me?"

He laughed delightedly. This was the kind of exchange he enjoyed. And the odd thing was that he was sincere. He didn't consider himself a Communist and was naïve enough to think that the people who bankrolled him would not expect a return on their investment.

There was no Congo crisis for Odinga to exploit this year. But a situation was developing in Rhodesia, whose racial overtones offered him an opportunity to stir up popular emotion against the British. And the British, because of their presence in Kenyatta's security forces, represented a greater and more visible obstacle to his political ambitions than did the Americans.

When Ian Smith, the Rhodesian Prime Minister, virtually declared his territory's independence from Britain in October, he was in fact telling London that Rhodesia's 225,000 whites were not going to make any concessions that might lead to equal rights or majority rule by Rhodesia's four million blacks. Considered from an African point of view, his action was one more arrogant assertion of white supremacy on a black continent: a handful of European immigrants—less than the population of Nairobi—were in effect thumbing their nose at African opinion, as the mercenaries had done a year before.

They were also directly challenging Britain's authority, and Africans waited to see how Prime Minister Wilson would react. A quick show of force at the outset would probably have squelched Smith's rebellion; but Wilson hesitated—his parliamentary majority was then paper-thin—and the white Rhodesians gradually concluded they could get away with their defiance in spite of financial and economic sanctions by Britain and her allies.

In Kenya there was a danger that the feelings aroused by the white rebellion might be turned against Kenya's own "Europeans." This would have suited Odinga's purposes. Fortunately, just before Smith's defiance, fourteen of Kenya's most prominent white residents—including men like Lord Delamere and Sir Humphrey Slade, who had become Kenya citizens—wrote a widely publicized open letter to Smith that left no doubt as to how they felt and where they stood:

We the undersigned are either Kenya citizens of British origin or British residents of Kenya. Most of us have held, or still hold, positions of some responsibility in the public, commercial or agricultural life of the country. We wish to express our feelings of deep shock and dismay at the declared intention of the Rhodesian Government to seize independence in the name of a White minority and in defiance of the British Government's persistent efforts to secure legally enforceable safeguards leading by stages to African majority rule. . . . Most of us had perfectly sincere reservations about the speed with which independence was granted to Kenya. Today, however, we must readily admit that a great many of our fears have so far proved totally unfounded. Like any other new country, Kenya has its fair share of intractable problems. The disruptive forces of tribalism are not yet stilled. The Cold War exerts its malign influence in East Africa as it does in most other parts of the world. Stock thefts continue to harass European and African farmers. Drought and famine have added to the difficulties of the settlement schemes in the Highlands. We desperately need more overseas investment to fight chronic unemployment.

Kenya, in fact, is no Shangri-la. But what country is? To weigh in the balance against the shortcomings just described we can honestly say that President Kenyatta's Government has kept its pledge to respect the rights of all races and the bitterness of the past has been largely forgotten in the spirit of Harambee. Racial prejudice is minimal. The rule of law has been preserved. Feedom of religion, speech and of the Press has generally been respected. Law and order has been maintained by a first-class police force under African command.

Above all, the Kenya Government has succeeded in the face of enormous difficulties in creating a genuine feeling of stability—an atmosphere in which every man, whatever the colour of his skin, feels free to get on with his job, to earn his living and bring up his family in peace. The European and the Asian are united, in fact, with the African in the urgent task of building a new nation. This is not a politician's platitude. It is a fact which any visitor to Kenya can see for himself.

Indeed, it is a pity that more of Rhodesia's (and South Africa's) leaders do not take the trouble to visit East Africa to learn at first hand what independence has achieved. At all events we hope it is not too late, even now, to add our voices to the British Prime Minister's and say to Mr. Ian Smith: Prime Minister, think again.

Kenya's leaders knew that the whites in their midst *had* changed, as I learned from talking to the latter. In fact, many who visited England came back indignant from arguing with their countrymen who believed Kenya was now run by thugs and savages and that Kenyatta was a bloodthirsty scoundrel. But realism was beginning to prevail over prejudice. In 1963, 4,700 more whites left Kenya than came in; in 1964 the figure was 4,200. But in the first nine months of 1965 the trend was suddenly reversed: the influx of whites *exceeded* the outflow by 133.

Unfortunately, the truth was concealed from the white Rhodesians. Those who came to Kenya were invariably astonished to discover that African majority rule, contrary to what they were told, was not the end of their world.

On December 7 the OAU, swept along on a wave of emotion, voted a resolution calling on its members to sever diplomatic relations with Britain because Wilson had not yet crushed the Smith rebellion. It was a hollow gesture that hurt the OAU more than Britain. Only nine nations, one of them Tanzania, complied with the resolution. The others realized this was no way to put pressure on London and might even be counterproductive. Kenyatta, in a firm but carefully worded statement, announced on December 10 that Kenya was willing to give London more time before taking any overt action. There was grumbling from the Odinga camp, but the Rhodesian issue had been put on ice for the time being.

Nor were the extremists able to make headway with the Vietnam issue. Not only were the Chinese suspect in government circles because of their subversive activities, but the persistent refusal of the North Vietnamese to stop fighting and start talking—as we kept suggesting—did not help their cause with the Africans. In July Kenyatta, in a speech to the Diplomatic Corps, had praised Johnson's initiative in bringing the Vietnam issue before the UN. (All present except the Chinese applauded his remarks.) But in October Joe Murumbi, who seemed to get carried away whenever he mounted the podium in the UN General Assembly, accused us of using Vietnam as "a testing ground for newly devised weapons of destruction," and of talking hypocritically of peace while engaged in aggressive military action. He described our actions then as "the greatest menace to international peace and security."

I promptly called on Mungai, who was Acting Foreign Minister, and asked for clarification of Kenya's position. He had not yet seen Murumbi's speech but assured me Kenya was *not* taking sides, as Joe implied. He suggested I talk to Kenyatta about it. A couple of days later I went over to State House, where Kenyatta told me the same thing, adding that Joe sometimes exceeded his instructions. (Later, Murumbi was instructed to call on Secretary Rusk and "clarify" Kenyan policy.)

Early in January, 1966, when Soapy Williams came to Kenya as part of our "peace offensive" during the thirty-seven-day bombing pause, Murumbi was on hand to greet him and fly with us to Mombasa, where Kenyatta was vacationing. The visit was well worthwhile, as indeed was the whole diplomatic exercise of sending personal emissaries to explain our position to world leaders. (Critics of the peace offensive seemed not to remember that our own Declaration of Independence was written out of "a decent respect to the opinions of mankind," and that respecting these opinions was even more important today.) Kenyatta listened attentively to Williams' exposition of our fourteen-point program to end the war. Then he said, "You are willing to stop all fighting today and start negotiating?"

"That's right," said Williams.

"But the others—the Communists—refuse?"

"So far, yes."

"Well," said Kenyatta, "your position seems to be correct."

He told us he would ask McKenzie and Mboya, who were going to Moscow, to see if the Russians might persuade Hanoi to be more reasonable. In a follow-up letter to Johnson, Kenyatta expressed his appreciation for the Williams visit, suggesting only that we consider including the Vietcong in the peace talks.

And that was that. Williams, who had seen the Emperor of Ethiopia that morning, flew on to Dar in the evening for an appointment with Nyerere. LBJ emissaries don't get any more sleep than LBJ White House staffers.

A month later, I reaffirmed our fourteen points in a speech to the United Kenya Club. For the important thing, in Africa, was to keep reminding people to whom Vietnam was both remote and perplexing that we were always ready for a *baraza*—Swahili for talking out problems—any time the other side wanted to meet us halfway.

Rhodesia and Vietnam were thus neutralized as exploitable political issues in the showdown now imminent between Kenyatta and Odinga. By mid-February, only five of forty-one KANU district branches were still factionally divided. The rest had elected officials loyal to Kenyatta and the multitribal coalition that had been systematically assembled and consolidated by Mboya and the former KADU leaders. One of the latter, Moi, had been entrusted with the police in December, while Odinga's already limited powers as Vice President were further whittled down to merely ceremonial functions. An Odinga ally in the cabinet, Paul Ngei, became the target of a press campaign accusing him, as Minister of Marketing, of diverting grain stocks for his own profit. The campaign was led by George Githii, formerly Kenyatta's private secretary and now the editor of the *Daily Nation*. (One of its by-products was to call attention to extravagance in high places; as a result, the Mayor of Nairobi, who had ordered an official Rolls Royce, was forced to send the car back when it arrived in Mombasa.)

In short, there were organization and orchestration in the Kenyatta camp, and confusion and anger in the other. On February 15 Mboya put Odinga on the spot in Parliament by moving a vote of confidence in Kenyatta's leadership. Sim and I were sitting at State House with the Kenyattas listening to a special concert by the De Paur Chorus when the motion was sprung, and I remember Oneko coming over during the intermission and vainly trying to persuade Kenyatta to disassociate himself from Mboya's action. He got brushed off, and Odinga angrily stalked out of Parliament, leaving his supporters no choice but to go along and make the confidence vote unanimous.

Odinga's growing isolation was part of a calculated plan. In

January the Kenya Group could count on sixty-five votes in Parliament against Odinga's thirty-five—with twenty-nine uncommitted. Motions like the confidence vote brought the latter around; they could see how the tide was running. But it was no time to take chances. Just before the vote, Moi called me to say he was going to ban *U.S. News & World Report* from Kenya. The magazine had just come out with an article saying Kenya's leaders were "primitives" and Odinga's people had got hold of it. Since Moi had recently banned a Chinese publication, he wanted to be able to silence any charge that he was playing favorites, especially with respect to an article guaranteed to arouse emotion. I told him I fully understood and would personally write the editors to explain the circumstances—and to correct some bad reporting.

On February 27 Mboya suddenly announced that a KANU reorganization conference would be held March 11. Surprise was essential; Odinga had the money to buy votes if given time. As it was, he tried hard. His political slush fund for the conference was estimated by Njonjo to be more than $150,000, much of it in green dollars provided by the Chinese Embassy in Dar, and converted to shillings in Mombasa. But he could sense he'd been outmaneuvered. Two days before the conference, he issued a bitter statement accusing State House of rigging the conference and implying that MacDonald and I were masterminding the operation. (A Czech working in the Ministry of Information helped draft it.)

Mboya, as secretary general of KANU, replied on behalf of Kenyatta. The next day, without warning, the Ministry of Home Affairs ordered six Communist diplomats and newsmen, including the first and second secretaries of the Soviet Embassy and a Chinese Embassy attaché, to get out of Kenya immediately. No public announcement was made nor explanation given, but the press was tipped off to be at the airport in the evening. All six happened to be intelligence agents with records of close association with Odinga and his lieutenants. The action, coming on the eve of the conference, put the delegates on notice that the police knew who the paymasters were, and with whom they were dealing.

The expulsions were headlined in the morning papers, along with a statement signed by Ngala and one hundred members of

Parliament, denouncing Odinga and his supporters as "agents of rapacious international Communism." These were the stories that delegates read on their way to the opening of the conference at Limuru, twenty miles north of Nairobi.

The outcome was now predictable. The delegates overwhelmingly approved a new party constitution abolishing Odinga's post of deputy president of the party and substituting eight provincial vice presidents, all loyal Kenyatta men and several of them cabinet ministers. Mboya was re-elected secretary general by a five-to-one majority. I was told later that at a closed session Kenyatta himself took care of the Odinga men who seemed to challenge his leadership. Pounding the speaker's table with his cane, he shouted, "Do you want me to tell this conference how you get your money and from what foreign embassies?"

Odinga didn't wait for the conference to end. He walked out in a rage, out of KANU and into Kenyatta's trap: KANU had not expelled *him; he* had rejected KANU.

The conference, by tying the party more closely to the government, had insulated it against infiltration. But Kenyatta's political victory would not be worth celebrating if KANU did not now stay close to the people and be responsive to their aspirations. I reminded two cabinet ministers who stopped by the house for a drink that the road from Limuru had taken them past the shantytowns of Banana Hill, where idle men and ragged children stared sullenly at the passing cars and called their own government leaders *"wabenzi"*—the Mercedes-Benz ones.

I had been on that road earlier in the day, taking my daughter back to her boarding school, and mentioned to my guests that I had seen Mr. Soliakov, the Tass correspondent, parked in the bushes not far from where the conference was in session; he had even waved to me. They smiled and said that he was also on his way out of Kenya for nonjournalistic activities. Sure enough, he and four more Soviet, Hungarian, Czech and Chinese newsmen and diplomats—again, all intelligence agents—were expelled a few days later. Kenyatta had told the police to be on the lookout for any foreigners trying to contact delegates.

The second batch of expulsions all but cut communications between Odinga's forces and their sponsors. (It also deprived the Czech Embassy volleyball team, which had recently crushed a

Peace Corps team, of one of its star players. To people who asked me if we'd had anything to do with the expulsions, I pointed out that obviously we wanted to win the return match. The truth is that the Kenyan police had asked us to verify their suspicions that certain people were not what they pretended to be, and we had obligingly checked their names against our files. Other friendly embassies had probably rendered the same service.)

Odinga now had to decide whether to leave the government as well as the party. As Vice President, he still had some prestige; he attended cabinet meetings and could pretend his title meant something. But he was too emotional a man to take any more humiliation at the hands of the Kenyatta coalition. When some of his supporters said in March they were going to form a new political party, he began looking around for financing. On April 12 he met secretly—or so he thought—with Babu and other extremists near the Tanzania border. (When he and Babu flatly denied press reports they had met, Moi made public the exact time, place and license numbers of their cars; it turned out that Nyerere had tipped off Kenyatta about the meetings.) Funding was apparently assured, and on April 14 Odinga formally resigned as Vice President of Kenya. He complained that he had been systematically humiliated and charged that Kenyatta and his associates were being "manipulated by an invisible government." (This was one way of taking a swipe at us, since a good many African politicians were familiar with a book called *The Invisible Government* that pretended to expose the CIA.) He also sent a wrathful letter of resignation to Kenyatta.

A few days later, Odinga accepted the presidency of a new opposition party, the Kenya People's Union. Twenty-nine Senators and members of Parliament—including Oneko, Kaggia and one assistant minister—quit KANU and rallied to his support. So did three top trade union leaders.

Kenyatta had waited a long time for Odinga and his friends to come out in the open. And now the old lion of Kenya pounced.

In a blistering statement, KANU denounced the new opposition leaders as corrupt, self-seeking and treasonable. The Attorney General registered the KPU, and Kenyatta immediately called Parliament into emergency session to approve a constitutional amendment requiring elected officials who changed parties to run again under their new label. (Sixteen of the twenty-nine defectors promptly tried to withdraw their resignations and rejoin KANU; they were turned down.) Kenyatta also called in the Soviet and Chinese ambassadors and warned them that if they continued to support what was now an opposition party, Kenya would consider this as cause to sever diplomatic relations. (I was told that Wang said nothing, but that Lavrov rather plaintively explained that he could not always control the "after-hours activities" of some members of his staff.)

Pravda clumsily managed to give Kenyatta an assist with an article praising Odinga and the KPU and accusing KANU of leading Kenya "back to capitalism." The Voice of Kenya, no longer under Oneko's control, played up the article in its newscasts as an example of "usual Communist jargon" and as proof of who'd been interfering in Kenya's internal affairs.

The *Pravda* article was also proof that the Russians had now written off the Kenyatta Government as hopeless from their point of view. Privately, Communist diplomats in Nairobi cynically blamed Odinga's defeat on the fact that the West had handed out more money to politicians than they had. While this was nonsense, it showed that they still underestimated the political sophistication of African leaders—and overestimated their purchasability.

Kenya again had a two-party system, this time the only one in Africa drawn on ideological rather than regional or tribal lines. And the evolution was achieved legally, democratically and without bloodshed. In June KANU ran candidates in special elections against the twenty-nine defectors to KPU and beat twenty of them. Only Odinga and a few other Luos held onto their seats. The danger that the KPU would become a broadly based party of the discontented was momentarily averted.

Odinga was now a political outcast without a coherent program to offer as an alternative to Kenyatta's African socialism. Good teamwork had given Kenya's constructivists a political victory. But if they did not now follow it up with a concerted effort to raise Kenya's living standards—with new land, new jobs and new schools —then Odinga might yet become the spokesman and champion of the discontented and his party a real threat to KANU in the 1968 elections.

Odinga had played his cards badly since *uhuru*. Had he loyally served Kenyatta and not tried to build up his own political apparatus, he might have established himself as *Mzee*'s logical successor. Another ambitious Luo, Tom Mboya, managed to overcome the suspicions of Kenyatta and a good many Kikuyus by his hard work on behalf of the government team. But Odinga was too emotional and in too much of a hurry to take a back seat. And the money he was offered by his Communist sponsors was too tempting to turn down.

I went out to Gatundu one weekend not long after Odinga resigned. Kenyatta and I sat and drank coffee and talked of Kenya's future in the living room where I had once faced Kanza across the zebra-skin table.

"I am not bitter about Odinga," he said. "I like Odinga. But he was very foolish. When I first met him, he was a successful businessman. Then I persuaded him to come into politics. That was a mistake. He does not understand politics." He smiled and rubbed his chin. "Now I think he should go back and be a businessman again. That would be good for him and good for Kenya."

XX

On Safari

•

Whenever I tell an American friend that I used to go on safari every few weeks in Kenya, the picture that flashes into his mind's eye is always sharp and clear: He sees me in a bush jacket trudging through the jungle, a pith helmet on my head, a White Hunter by my side and a file of native bearers strung along behind; or perhaps sitting by a campfire, a gun on my lap, the White Hunter spilling whisky into a canteen cup, my wife racked with malaria on a canvas cot, the war drums ominously silent.

"Tell me about it," says my friend, hoping I won't be able to find the color slides and vaguely disturbed to discover I am more eccentric than he thought ("A *safari,* for God's sake—what's Attwood trying to prove?").

"Safari" is the Swahili word for "journey." When a Kenyan goes on safari, he doesn't usually plan to shoot an animal, or even see one. His safari could be to visit his sick mother in Thika or to sell insurance to a client in Fort Hall. I recently received a letter from one of our embassy drivers. "I hope that you and Mrs. Attwood," he wrote, "had a good safari from Kenya to the United States."

Our safaris in Kenya were usually by car. There are three main highways out of Nairobi: south, across the plains and toward the coast; northeast, past Gatundu and through Kikuyu land to the slopes of Mount Kenya; and northwest, into the Rift Valley and then on to Lake Victoria or up to the old White Highlands. Most of our trips started on this last road. We drove through the cool green uplands to the edge of the great Rift escarpment, where, coming out of a pine forest, we looked across the wide, brown volcanic plain, 2,500 feet below, that stretches the length of Africa. The road curves and winds to the floor of the valley. If we were going south, we turned off the pavement onto a dirt road and away from the service stations and speeding traffic. And suddenly, still only thirty-five miles from the neon lights of Nairobi, we were in a world that had hardly changed in ten thousand years. Giraffes peered at us over the low brush and impalas and hartebeests bounded across the road; every few miles, a tall stately Masai herding cattle would pause, a spear in one hand, and wave at us as we went by.

If we stayed on the main highway, we might pause at the Lake Hotel at Naivasha to fish for bass and talapia along the lakeshore and listen to the hippos grunting in the reeds. Or we might go on to Nakuru, where hundreds of thousands of flamingos cover the lake water at twilight with a canopy of pink and white plumage. Or we might be in a hurry and drive on. In Kenya there was always a lot to see, and so much to do . . .

One night we were stuck outside Kakamega with a punctured radiator. The Catholic brothers at Mumias, twenty miles down the road, were expecting us for dinner but they had no phone. It was Sunday and all the service stations were closed. A carload of Africans, transistor radios blaring rock and roll, pulled up alongside. "Wapi PC?" I asked, which meant "Where is the provincial commissioner?" They spoke some English: "Come with us." I left John D'Souza, our USIS photographer, with the car and squeezed in with them. The driver told me he was the Singer Sewing Machine representative in Kakamega. A bottle of warm beer was passed around. We found the PC, Mr. Josiah, stretched out on a couch, reading the paper and also drinking beer. We had met before. His son was a student at Howard University and did broadcasts for the Voice of America. "Don't worry," he said, opening more beer, "we will get you to Mumias." Everybody was pleased that there was a problem to solve. Finally we went out and found the Sikh who owned the garage and he towed our car to his place. We also located Mr. Josiah's driver in a bar. He drove us to Mumias in the PC's sedan. When we reached the mission, it was after ten but the brothers were still waiting dinner. They were mostly from New England, so we sat up late, talking about home. In the morning the

African sisters served us breakfast and then I handed over some books and maps to the mission school. The students in their white shorts and shirts were lined up on the lawn under the eucalyptus trees. The president of the student council made a speech of thanks. We all shook hands and posed for pictures before driving back to Kakamega. The car had been fixed and we went to Mr. Josiah's office, where we met the local member of Parliament, Edward Khasakhala. With him, we visited some schools and passed out more books in classrooms crowded with wide-eyed children who stood up and chanted in unison, "Good morning, Mr. Ambassador from America." There were twenty people waiting at Khasakhala's house for lunch, local officials and their wives and a couple of missionaries. It was late in the afternoon when we broke away to start the 250-mile drive back to Nairobi. Everybody was pleased we took the trouble to come so far to see them. . . .

We were touring the Kitale area with the Assistant Minister of Lands and Settlement, Daniel Moss. We stopped for lunch at the Kitale Golf Club. The bar was full of white farmers and their wives. Moss had never been inside the club before. There were no other Africans around and he was ill at ease. The crowd around the bar gradually thinned out. Only three British farmers were left, drinking pink gins. Moss went up to them. "This is a nice club you have here," he says. "I think I would like to join it." The farmers made room for him. "It would be an honor to have you as a member, Mr. Minister," said one. Moss smiled, suddenly relaxed, and offered to stand a round. Two years before, he would have been thrown out if he'd tried to walk in the door. . . .

Astronaut Gordon Cooper was at the controls of our Cessna 205. Charles Conrad was beside him. We were flying over the Masai-Mara game reserve at forty feet, looking for buffalo. "This is great!" shouted Cooper as we skimmed over the thorn trees. "The last time we were over Kenya we were a hundred miles up. Couldn't see a thing." Conrad tugged at his sleeve. "Watch out for that hill, Gordo!" We swerved up and then down again. A big herd of buffalo was moving across the plain. We followed them and lost the road that we were navigating by. Kenyatta was waiting for us at Keekerok Lodge, and now we didn't know where we were. So we rose and circled around at a thousand feet. Finally we spotted another Cessna and followed it to the Keekerok airstrip. Sim and the astronauts' wives were waiting for us in the midst of a crowd of painted Masai warriors. When we joined them the Masai started chanting and leaping up and down in a dance of welcome. "My goodness," said Mrs. Cooper, "they don't have *anything* on under their robes!" At the lodge, Kenyatta gave the astronauts some Masai spears and we had tea. Then he took us out in a Land-Rover bus to look at some lions. We found three big prides within a mile of the camp. On the way back to Nairobi, Conrad was piloting the plane. "This is the way to travel," he said. "Up there where we've been, you don't get to see anything. . . ."

Sim and I were visiting a school for blind children near Embu. Our home town had raised nearly $2,500 to buy them mattresses and braille books and musical instruments. They were saying thank you by dancing and singing for us. They gave us a rug that they wove themselves, and a letter in braille for the people of New Canaan. None of them had ever slept on a mattress before. You could hardly tell they were blind until they groped for our hands when we had to leave. . . .

I was sitting on a platform somewhere in the Western Region. We were dedicating a school laboratory built with AID funds. The Minister of Education was making a speech. Hundreds of people were squatting on the ground all around us, the elders in front, the children in their blue and white school uniforms behind. The Minister was telling them that when he was a boy there was only one school in the district and now there were twenty. So they must work hard and not complain. They should be glad a big country like America had given them this wonderful laboratory. Everybody applauded. A student read a petition asking for school lunches; some of the children had to walk eight miles from their homes and they needed a hot meal at midday. The Minister promised to do something. The school principal, an Englishman, told me that fifteen years ago the children had to be coaxed to come to school. "Now we have to turn them away. We don't have enough teachers." When it was my turn to speak, I told them I had also brought them some textbooks from the people of America. I told them to work hard because the future of Kenya depended on them. I said they had many friends all over the world who wanted to help them get an education and this was international *harambee*. After the ceremonies, the drums and flutes started up and we made our way to the new building to cut the ribbon. The crowd pressed around us; there were dozens of hands to shake, dozens of voices all talking at once. *"Asante sana!"* they said again and again. *"Asante sana!*—Thank you! Thank you! . . ."

My two children were clearing the snow off a patch of flat ground so that we could pitch our tent before dark. I was heating some water over a wood fire and wishing I were nearer sea level. We were at 14,500 feet, with the white peaks of Mount Kenya towering just above us. My head was pounding and my back was sore from a long day's ride on horseback. We turned in early. In the night I was awakened by the screech of a rock hyrax, the only animal to live at this altitude, and it was too cold to get back to sleep. But next morning the sunshine was glistening on the glaciers as our horses and zebroids picked their way up the steep, stony trail. At 15,500 feet, Jan and I decided to look at the view while Peter and our other friends scrambled up the ice another 800 feet to Top Hut to sign their names in the book. Two days later we were back at the Silverbeck Hotel, glad to be sipping our bourbon next to an open fire even though a brass plate on the bar told us we were standing on the equator. . . .

We were looking for lions near Samburu with Rodney Elliot, the game warden. I was driving the jeep and he was telling me that if you meet a lion on foot there is no reason to be alarmed—as long as you don't act alarmed. But if you panic and run, the lion will either attack you out of fright or his instincts will take over and make him chase you. "The thing to do is to step very slowly backward until you are out of sight," he said. Just then we rounded a bend in the road and were face to face with an elephant and her calf. Their trunks went up and their ears started flapping. "Back up—fast!" said Elliot. I went into reverse as they charged, frightened and furious. Finally they stopped, a few yards short of the car, and watched us menacingly as we turned around and moved away. I asked Sim if she got the picture through the windshield. Somehow she had forgotten about the camera. We agreed not to try to set it up again. . . .

The young African Community Development Officer in West Pokot had problems. There was a new religious sect in the region that opposed labor, taxes, hospitals and schools with the argument that "God will do it." He showed us his report: "Since the government has allowed freedom of worship (and this disastrous religion is included), the only way is to educate people that nothing comes free and education is the key to development." But he had good news to report too: "Womenfolk now walk in fashionable frocks including brassieres and nylon handkerchiefs and shoes. The *hando,* which is the traditional dress, is out of date. The *hando* is just a bulky skirt with the look of bundles of sisal squeezed together. It is thick, heavy, untidy, unwashable and alarmingly short. . . ."

We were sitting in the shade after trudging up the path from the quarry, and we were listening to the spokesman of the Bomware Tabaka stonecarvers. We had just presented them with new tools and goggles and some roofing for a building where they could display and sell their carving. They had given us some samples of their work—lions and fish and other animals made of soapstone—and I had ordered an African chess set that would take two months to carve by hand. Their spokesman was laboriously reading a speech in English: "The proverb says that a friend in need is a friend indeed and so by your gesture you have proven to us that you are a real friend. It was because of your most generous gift that we were able to complete our building and thus we shall be able to commence our business in the very near future. This gesture of friendship we hope will mark the foundation of a lasting friendship between us the members of this factory and you and the people of the United States of America. We kindly ask you on your return to Nairobi to convey to the people of the United States our sincere greetings and heartfelt thanks for their generosity to us. . . ."

Susan was just one and she was watching her first elephant from the back seat of our station wagon. He was holding up traffic on the Mombasa-Nairobi highway. He lumbered off and the cars moved again. We stopped for the night at the Tasvo Inn. Susan was fascinated by the big rhinoceros beetles in the lobby. The inn had been recently opened by Oneko in his capacity as Minister of Information and Tourism. "Odd his being the one to come," said the British manager over our after-dinner brandy. "I hadn't seen him since prison camp in the fifties. I was the commander and he was our chief clerk. Nasty sort of chap he was then, but quite nice the other day." He raised his glass. "Well, cheers. Times do change, you know. . . ."

The livestock-dipping cooperative at South Kinangop was a bedlam of shouting Kikuyu farmers and protesting cattle as George Owen, a Peace Corps volunteer from Arkansas, came galloping up on horseback. He was wearing jeans, a sweatshirt and a cowboy hat. He dismounted, greeted us and started giving instructions in Swahili to the farmers milling around him. "Come on up and see how we do it." The cattle were moving reluctantly along a runway to the dipping shack. Owen hitched his horse to the pole that carried the power wires to the shack. The horse suddenly reared up and the pole came crashing down. We were all sprayed by the hose. The Africans got the pole back in place, and Owen shinnied up to fix the wires. "That was a dumb thing I did," he said. "I guess I was rattled, your being here and all." The cattle began moving again. "I majored in psychology at college," said Owen. "You'd be surprised, but it comes in handy over here." He had been in Kenya a year and loved his job. He had nine hundred farms to look after and was proud of the sheep dip he designed for the co-op. He lived alone with his dog in a little house nearby, the only "European" for miles around. In the evening African friends came by and listened to him play his guitar and sing folk songs. They all called him "Bwana America." They had never met anyone from the United States before. People had become quite pro-American in South Kinangop . . .

You can see more than a hundred miles from the terrace of Sir Michael Blundell's farmhouse. After lunch, he drove us into the Sabukia Valley. All the farms hereabout were big—fifteen hundred to three thousand acres—and most were still owned by Europeans. Some, like Blundell, had become Kenyan citizens. "We plan to stay," he said. "It's going to be all right. We'll just have more African neighbors now. They work hard, but they lack experience in marketing. We can lend them a hand." He showed us some acreage where he had started planting tea. On the way home, we stopped to look at a family of black and white colobus monkeys in the forest. We had tea in the garden. In the evening, we drove into Nakuru for a premiere of *My Fair Lady*. I hadn't seen so many Englishmen in dinner jackets since I was last in London. . . .

It was a big day for the African Farmers' and Traders' Association of Machakos. The seven AID brick-making machines had finally arrived. The machines were going to put the association into the brick business. There was plenty of clay in the area, but up to now bricks had been made by hand. (They made enough this way to build the Machakos High School.) I was the guest of honor at the celebration since I had managed to get the money for the machines out of AID. This meant shaking hands with all seventy-eight members of the association and then sampling some sugarcane beer at the local brewery. Mr. Mukeka, the KANU branch chairman, also had several groups of choir singers and traditional dancers at his house. So a good part of the afternoon was spent listening to young people singing Presbyterian hymns in the Kamba language and older people whirling and stomping to the rhythms of cowhide drums. Finally one of the machines was uncrated. Clay was pressed into the mold, I pushed the lever back and forth and Mukeka exhibited the first brick, ready for baking, to the cheering audience. There were speeches, and I was presented with gifts—a bow and arrow set for me, a carved cane for my father, a chief's snuffbox for President Johnson and a Kamba market basket for Jacqueline Kennedy. Mukeka explained that chiefs used the snuff to sneeze for silence during a *baraza;* the basket, he said, was for a widow to use when she went to market —the design on the strap meant she was not a prostitute and should be treated with respect. In my speech of thanks, I promised to deliver the gifts and explain what they were for. (I did, and Mrs. Kennedy later wrote them a nice note.) There were more speeches about the friendship of the Kamba and American people, and more dancing. At last Mukeka drove us to the Machakos Sports Club for a beer before we went home. "I was put in jail three times for walking in here before *uhuru*," he said proudly. "I knew it would help my political career." At the bar he introduced me to an Englishman as "one of the members who had me arrested." They argued about who would buy the beers. I settled it by putting a shilling in the slot machine and getting three bells. I bought the beers. . . .

Two male lions were walking beside our car on the Serengeti Plain. A procession of wildebeeste was crossing the road up ahead. We stopped and turned off the motor. As the lions approached, the frightened wildebeeste cavorted wildly in all directions. But the lions were already well fed and strolled indifferently through the herd. The procession gradually re-formed and continued on its way. We paused a moment longer in the silence of the vast plain before starting the car. . . .

We were visiting a National Youth Service camp in the Highlands. They were replanting windbreaks of gum trees that the African farmers cut down when the area became a high-density settlement scheme. All the young men in the GI fatigue uniforms were lined up in formation, and a visiting U.S. Congressman was passing out political postcards and having his picture taken. "General China," a former Mau Mau guerrilla fighter, was there too, wearing a NYS lieutenant's uniform. In the distance, the Aberdare Mountain Range rose into the clouds. I mentioned that I had never been up in those mountains. "He'll take you there if you want to go," said a British NYS adviser. "He knows all the trails. That's where he was hiding during the Emergency." The "General" smiled and agreed to show me the hills. We left the tree-planters outside their U.S. Army tents and started back to Nairobi. We stopped for coffee with a young Peace Corps couple living in a former British farmhouse. The husband had been coaching a basketball team in his spare time. Our Congressman was in a hurry to get back to his hotel; he had stayed up too late at the Equator Club the night before and looked pale when I told him we had one more stop to make—at the home of a Kikuyu friend near Limuru. When we got there, John Njenga proudly showed us around his place, which he bought from a South African who went home. He had planted coffee and maize and had bought an encyclopedia for his son, who was an honor student at the Duke of York School. Finally he offered us some refreshment. "All I have is whisky and beer," he said. The Congressman smiled for the first time in two hours. "Where I come from," he said, "we have a drink called a boilermaker. . . ."

Mrs. Crosskill was presiding at the bar of the Highlands Hotel at Molo. It felt good to stretch out in front of the fire with a drink after eighteen holes of golf at eight thousand feet. There were plaques on the wall listing the tournament winners back to 1931. Mr. Crosskill, who used to be Minister of Agriculture, and Mervyn Hill, the editor of the Kenya *Weekly News,* were telling me about the old days, back in the twenties, when the wagon trains took three days to make the 140 miles from Kitale to Nakuru. "There was a place called the Pioneer Bar in Eldoret," said Hill. "One night, during a party, somebody shot out all the oil lamps. The district officer came over, wearing his dinner jacket, and looked around at the mess. He ordered six bottles of champagne and lined them up on the veranda. Then he borrowed a pistol and shot out all the corks, one by one. 'If any of you chaps can shoot like that,' he said, 'you can carry a gun in Eldoret. I don't think you can, so you're all fined five pounds.' And then he stood a round of drinks." After dinner, we went out on the terrace. The air was thin and cold and smelled of wood smoke. There would be hot-water bottles in our beds and early tea at seven in the morning. . . .

Jesse Gachago and I were making our fifteenth stop of the day. Jesse was an Assistant Minister, and we were visiting self-help schools in his constituency, near Fort Hall. The men and women were gathered around, holding picks and shovels. They had almost finished building a school for their children but lacked roofing and windowpanes. There were speeches of welcome and I was introduced. I started with a Kikuyu greeting—*"Muri-ayga!"* They laughed and clapped their hands. Then I told them that yesterday was the Fourth of July, when we Americans celebrated our *uhuru.* "We were a poor country. But we worked hard and sent our children to school and now we are strong and prosperous." I paused while Gachago translated this into Kikuyu. "You must do the same in Kenya to build your nation and give your children an education. For education is the key that opens the door to a better life. And we want to help you help yourselves. That is what *Mzee* means by *harambee*—that we help each other. For the world is now a big village, and we are all neighbors. *Kwaheri na asante sana!"* The people crowded around the Land-Rover as we drove away. Jesse was pleased. It had been a good day.

Kwaheri means "good-bye" in Swahili, and in the spring of 1966 we were saying good-bye to Africa. It had been five years since we first landed in Conakry, and I had to decide whether to stay on in the Foreign Service or go back to journalism. Gardner Cowles, my former boss, visited Kenya in February and helped me make up my mind; the job he wanted me for had to be filled right away.

We were saying good-bye, but not farewell, to Kenya. Before knowing that we were leaving this soon, we had already picked out fifty acres of land to buy and to build a house on. Our land overlooks the Nairobi Game Park and the Ngong Hills. It is not far from Karen, the Nairobi suburb named after Karen Blixen, who lived there before she became well known as Isak Dinesen, the writer. In her book, *Out of Africa,* which tells you more about Africa than any book I know, she describes this place where we now have our land. She describes it better than I could ever hope to:

I had a farm in Africa, at the foot of the Ngong Hills. The Equator runs across these highlands, a hundred miles to the north, and the farm lay at an altitude of over six thousand feet. In the day-time you felt that you had got high up, near to the sun, but the early mornings and evenings were limpid and restful, and the nights were cold.

The geographical position, and the height of the land combined to create a landscape that had not its like in all the world. There was no fat on it and no luxuriance anywhere; it was Africa distilled up through six thousand feet, like the strong and refined essence of a continent. The colours were dry and burnt, like the colours of pottery. The trees had a light delicate foliage, the structure of which was different from that of the trees of Europe; it did not grow in bows or cupolas, but in horizontal layers, and the formation gave to the tall solitary trees a likeness to the palms, or a heroic and romantic air like fullrigged ships with their sails clewed up, and to the edge of a wood a strange appearance as if the whole wood were faintly vibrating. Upon the grass of the great plains the crooked bare old thorn-trees were scattered, and the grass was spiced like thyme and bog-myrtle; in some places the scent was so strong, that it smarted in the nostrils. All the flowers that you found on the plains, or upon the creepers and liana in the native forest, were diminutive like flowers of the downs,—only just in the beginning of the long rains a number of big, massive heavy-scented lilies sprang out on the plains. The views were immensely wide. Everything that you saw made for greatness and freedom, and un-equalled nobility.

The chief feature of the landscape, and of your life in it, was the air. Looking back on a sojourn in the African highlands, you are struck by your feeling of having lived for a time up in the air. The sky was rarely more than pale blue or violet, with a profusion of mighty, weightless, ever-changing clouds towering up and sailing on it, but it has a blue vigour in it, and at a short distance it painted the ranges of hills and the woods a fresh deep blue. In the middle of the day the air was alive over the land, like a flame burning; it scintillated, waved and shone like running water, mirrored and doubled all objects, and created great Fata Morgana. Up in this high air you breathed easily, drawing in a vital assurance and lightness of heart. In the highlands you woke up in the morning and thought: Here I am, where I ought to be.

Someday—I don't know when—I will look out of my office window at the glass canyons of Madison Avenue and know the time has come. And I'm sure Sim will be ready when I call her up and say, "Let's go, where we ought to be."

XXI

"Yankee Don't Go Home"

•

In the letter I wrote the President in March, I told him I was resigning "with mixed feelings." Let me try to explain them.

I had enjoyed working for the government for a number of reasons. It was creative work, and I am one of those people who believe that to be reasonably happy you have to be able to say, from time to time, and about something worthwhile, "I did this—I made it happen." And when that something has social or historical value, if it's something that may endure, so much the better. It was satisfying to know they were making better bricks in Machakos, and Sim, too, felt good about having started the American Women's Association, knowing it would continue doing useful work after we were gone.

I also enjoyed my job because I believed in our policies, even though I sometimes questioned the way they were carried out. Say what you will, our national motives are honorable. We are not out to oppress or to conquer anybody, or even to impose our way of life on others. We have used our power with restraint, not to hurt but to help mankind. Only inside the government, I think, can you fully appreciate to what extent the Good Guys, if you will, are in charge—in all agencies concerned with foreign policy—and how hard they work, not only to serve American interests but to keep our world on a sane course.

Another reason I liked my job was that I had seen enough of the Communist system to want to prevent its agents from extending it to other parts of the world. We are living in an era of relatively peaceful but highly competitive coexistence, and I enjoyed the competition. (I also enjoyed battling our own bureaucracy when it interfered with our efforts.)

So my decision to leave the Foreign Service had nothing to do with disenchantment. "As an American," I wrote the President, "I have been proud to have played a part in carrying out our consistently progressive and enlightened policies, particularly in this part of the world."

But it was time to come home. Our family had been scattered and separated for so long that we all wanted to settle down in our Connecticut acres for a while. Sim and I felt that we'd done about all we could in Kenya, and the diplomatic routine was growing stale. Also, interesting things were happening in the United States —alarming things, too—and, somehow, I was no longer content to be an expatriate who just read about them. I looked forward, in journalism, to helping enlarge public understanding of what we were up against, as a nation, and what we needed to do. In some ways, the action, for anybody who cared about the future, was now at home rather than abroad.

The weeks just before you leave a post are always hectic, but the spring of 1966 in Nairobi was a busy time for us even without the farewell calls and farewell parties. We had a National War College seminar and a Peace Corps conference on our hands at the same time. Sim put on a two-day, fund-raising African art show at the residence that was visited by over two thousand people. We went to Dar and Kampala to talk shop, and flew on to Zanzibar to play nine holes at the nationalized People's Golf Club and to Kasese to see the Mountains of the Moon. With the political situation stabilized, we were also meeting regularly with Kenyatta's economic ministers to decide how to utilize the funds accumulated by PL 480 sales most effectively.

Kenyatta, meanwhile, invited the chiefs of state of eleven East African nations to come to Nairobi for an old fashioned *baraza,* without Telli Diallo, the OAU or even a formal agenda. The meeting enhanced his prestige as an African statesman; under his chairmanship old grievances were aired (and some of them evaporated), while practical bases for wider regional cooperation, both political and economic, were quietly and seriously discussed. It was encouraging to see the Somali Prime Minister (whose tribesmen were fighting the Kenyan Army) reviewing a Kenyan guard of honor at the airport, and Julius Nyerere (who had been giving aid and comfort to the Congolese rebels) posing arm in arm with General Mobutu, the new Congolese President.

Nkrumah had just been overthrown in Ghana, and a delegation from the new regime came to see Kenyatta before the eleven-nation meeting to explain what had really happened—that the military coup was, in fact, the expression of a genuine popular uprising against a corrupt and arrogant dictatorship. The lesson of Ghana, and the revelation that both the Russians and Chinese had helped construct Nkrumah's repressive police state apparatus, made a deep impression on the leaders who gathered in Nairobi. Because he had neglected the real needs of his people, Nkrumah, like Ben Bella the year before, had become a nobody overnight, and not even his Communist Big Brothers had been able to save him.

The White House announced my resignation on April 19, and the next two weeks were a blur of farewell speeches, calls and parties. In my speeches, I managed to silence the inevitable specu-lation that I was leaving the government because of some disa-greement over policy or because I didn't like Kenya. I explained that good journalism and good diplomacy in the modern world had the same objectives—to dispel illusions and prejudice and help people understand each other better—and that my leaving the Foreign Service did not mean I was retiring to the sidelines. And the fact that we had become landowners in Kenya pleased all our friends. It was a gesture of confidence in Kenya's future and made our farewells easier; we now had a *shamba* (a farm), so naturally we'd be coming back.

The Diplomatic Corps gave us an inscribed cigarette box at a reception to which everybody but Wang came. (K. K. Panni, the Pakistani who had become Dean, tried to get me and Wang to-gether for a cup of tea and some mah-jongg at his home; I didn't mind but I bet him twenty shillings Wang would refuse—and I won.) Joe Murumbi gave me a big stag lunch at Parliament; he was about to be made Vice President in place of Odinga and seemed to be looking forward to having less to do. I missed saying good-bye to Odinga, who was out of town, but sent greetings, via his associates in the KPU—who jokingly invited me to join their party when I returned to Kenya. I saw most of the other ministers individually and also at a party we gave for three hundred friends and colleagues. And I made a special point of calling on Lavrov at his home. He was waiting in the garden at a table laden with candy, cakes, coffee and brandy. After a couple of hefty toasts to the preservation of civilization, I told him I had often sympathized with him because of the problems he'd faced in Kenya. He shrugged philosophically, blaming the British "monopolists" for blocking the Soviet arms shipment and conceding that Odinga had been a disappointing politician—"not clever like Mboya." I gathered that Lavrov was bored with Kenya and with Africa. He preferred to talk about Germany and Vietnam—the two "main obstacles" to Soviet-American friendship.

"You should be glad we are fighting in Vietnam," I said. "After all, we are trying to prove that you are right and the Chinese are wrong. We can coexist because you have found out we are not paper tigers and will not yield to threats. The Chinese still aren't convinced. We are really convincing them for you."

Lavrov just smiled and refilled our glasses. After our last toast we strolled to my car, arm in arm. (Brandy can be unsettling out in the midday equatorial sun.)

"Moy dom," he said in Russian, *"vash dom.* My house is your house. When you come back to Nairobi, stay with me."

My last official call was out at Gatundu on a Saturday morning. Kenyatta had been out walking among his coffee trees and greeted me at the door of the farmhouse. We sat inside, where Mama Ngina served us coffee and cakes, and talked of the future. For it was always the future, not the past, that concerned *Mzee.* That's what made him young in heart. He spoke of starting colleges in every province. He wanted practical curricula adapted to Kenya's needs. He liked my suggestion that the Lumumba Institute be turned into a teacher-training center for students returning from abroad and that they be required to devote two years of national service to relieving the teacher shortages in primary schools. We also discussed agriculture and the need to develop idle land; he didn't feel that any more big farms should be taken over if they were productive and well managed. We spoke of the importance of family planning and of tourism to Kenya's economic development. And I repeated President Johnson's invitation that he visit the United States.

"You understand," he said, "that I could not go away these past two years. But tell the President that I haven't forgotten his invitation. Someday I would like to come."

He was pleased I had bought land in Kenya. "Come back and become a Kenya citizen," he said with a laugh as we shook hands, "and maybe we will make you Ambassador to Washington."

The next afternoon, at the airport, there were more farewells, a few tearful. Somebody came with a sign that said "Yankee don't go home."* We posed for a picture, and then Njonjo, McKenzie, Mboya, Sam Ayodo and other friends walked us to the plane. As we rose up, circling the city, I looked down at the Ngong Hills and the sunset colors of the plains. It was good to know that someday we'd be coming back.

Remembering my arrival twenty-six months before, I couldn't help thinking that the viewers-with-alarm had been wrong, as they usually are. The Zanzibar crisis had petered out and the East Germans and Chinese were stuck with commitments to go on building a showcase that nobody was looking at on an island neither of them any longer controlled. White fears of black power in Kenya had proved to be unfounded; a white Kenyan was still Minister of Agriculture and seventeen hundred Englishmen still worked in various branches of the Kenya Government; there was less tension between the races than before *uhuru*. Odinga and the demagogues were out of office. The men moving up, like Moi, Ngala, Mwai Kibaki and James Nyamweya, were unemotional, hard-working and practical-minded. When they talked about Kenya's agricultural revolution they sounded like Walt Rostow; they spoke of available credit, fair prices, technical assistance and the cash purchase of tools and consumer goods.

Nor were Kenya's plain people as backward as they might look from a tourist bus. In 1964 a carefully conducted public opinion survey of fifteen hundred mostly illiterate farm families would have warmed the heart of Horatio Alger. They overwhelmingly rated education and hard work as the keys to a better life. Eighty-

* This one hand-lettered sign must have sparked the vivid imagination of an Italian correspondent, for the *Coniere della Sera* of Rome reported my departure as follows: "A large crowd, almost the entire population of the city, saw off at the airport U.S. Ambassador William Attwood, who was returning to the States. People cheered with emotion; hundreds of banners, held aloft by young people, proclaimed 'Yankee don't go home!' "

two percent wanted their children taught in English. While 75 percent liked their tribal customs, only a minority still favored witchcraft. Their main desires were money to buy things, a better house and some land of their own. They didn't aim their sights too high; only 6 percent even dreamed of a car in their future.

The problem for Kenya's leaders was to provide the educational facilities the younger generation craved and then to produce enough jobs to employ their talents when they got out of school. It wouldn't be easy, but with the right kind of help and more foreign investment it *could* be done.

And in this respect we Americans had been helpful. We had urged Kenya's leaders to concentrate on their own problems and to tackle them in a practical way. We had reassured potential American investors and smoothed their way through the local bureaucratic brambles. We had been sympathetic but also tough when we had to be—tough about how our limited aid funds were used and tough about setting the record straight when we were maligned. We didn't need a National Policy Paper, "without which," according to a department airgram, our efforts were "likely to suffer from lack of direction or purpose." We knew our policy and what to do from our day-to-day experience without having to consult a handbook written back in Washington.

I was lucky to have had a good staff. People like Jim Ruchti, Bill Wild, John Hogan, Bob Ware, Yvonne Fonvielle, Russ Heater, Dick Drain, Bev Carter, Tom and Maria Linville, Paul O'Neill and Jean Grayson—and so many more—made my job a lot easier. As I told the President in my letter of resignation, "I have never been associated with a finer group of men and women than those who work in the Foreign Service." I only wish more of my fellow citizens had an opportunity, as I did, to learn how ably—with few exceptions—our country is represented abroad.

We also benefited in Kenya from the mistakes of our ideological opponents—not only from what they did but from what they said. Communist propaganda was generally too heavy-handed, too prone to anti-Western invective, to seem plausible even to unsophisticated Africans. We didn't bother to retort; our USIS bulletins ignored the Communists unless they said something we considered worth quoting. USIS did publicize our own contribution to Kenya's development—so well, in fact, that a 1965 poll showed that 50 percent of the Kenyans interviewed thought America had done the most to help their country (as against 42 percent who picked Britain—whose aid was many times greater than ours).

I have already mentioned the contribution of unofficial Americans—the businessmen, missionaries and tourists—to our total diplomatic effort. I don't know how it happened—because we seem to have a good many racists and other kooks back home—but I don't recall ever having to apologize for any American in Kenya except for Ronald Ramsey and Malcolm X. And they weren't there very long.

Americans and Africans had learned a lot about each other in the five years I'd been professionally involved with this continent. An ever-growing number of Americans, both in and out of government, had been posted in Africa, and the flow of African students, diplomats and visitors to the United States was steadily increasing. The best of our Foreign Service people preferred the activity and relative hardship of an African assignment to the comfortable routine of our overstaffed European embassies. One of our ambassadors in Africa told me he was horrified in 1961 to learn he was being sent to a remote sub-Saharan capital. Two years later he was transferred back to Paris. "I was moving a lot of important papers around," he told me, "but I didn't feel I was really accomplishing anything. And I wasn't having any fun. When I got a chance to come back to Africa this year, I jumped at it."

More and more Africans have been discovering the real America too. Among some "intellectuals" whose travel abroad has been confined to Europe and the Communist countries, you can still hear stale gibes at pre-New Deal capitalism, the "Invisible Government" and McCarthyism. A good many Africans who have no use for Communism are still prone to equate it with capitalism, as though Karl Marx and Adam Smith were still the high priests and active leaders of two sinister, monolithic ideologies.

But travel, education and mass communications are breaking up the stereotypes and shibboleths. Africans who come to the States expecting to find American Negroes oppressed and impoverished are almost invariably surprised to discover that there is more equality than injustice in our society, imperfect as it may be. And Africans often feel more at ease with white Americans than with other whites; perhaps our own multiracial experience at home, for all its torment, has enabled us to be less self-conscious, and less color-conscious, than Europeans in the presence of black Africans.

We don't bear the psychological burden of having been colonialists in pith helmets like the British, French and Belgians; nor do we react to Africans with that mixture of contempt, curiosity and distaste that the Russians and Chinese never fully conceal with forced smiles and flattery. (The failure of the Communists in Africa, I am convinced, stems in part from their behaving like strangers in town who are trying too hard and too fast to ingratiate themselves with the community leaders.)

Africans who have been exposed to Americans are also getting over the notion that we are all hot-eyed cold warriors obsessed with the Communist menace and lusting after new military bases. To people unfamiliar with Communist techniques, it is always a revelation to contrast our own words and actions with the devious shenanigans of Soviet and Chinese diplomats. And guided tours behind the Iron Curtain were effective only with the more gullible young Africans: Those who had already seen Western Europe or the United States were chilled by the drab austerity and the police-state atmosphere and bored by the stilted speeches about consolidating nonexistent bonds of friendship with people struggling against nonexistent American imperialism.

African visitors to the States were spared the speeches. They met people rather than officials. I remember an African judge telling me about an American lady lawyer who had been on the plane with him to New York. She had taken him around the city, introduced him to her family and friends. "Such a nice lady!" he told me when he got back to Nairobi. "She treated me as if I were a guest not just in her country but in her home. Are all Americans like that?"

It so happens that a great many are, as our visitors from abroad have been finding out.

We knew a lot more about Africa and Africans in 1966 than we did in 1961. The State Department no longer relied, as it used to, on Paris, London and Brussels for information and policy guidance. We now had a cadre of Africanists with firsthand knowledge and experience.

We—and I am speaking for most of us in the State Department who were involved with Africa—now knew that the concept of "Eurafrica," which intrigued even Adlai Stevenson as late as 1955, was a fiction. Africans were not hostile to their former colonizers, but they did not want to be tied by economic or political apron strings to any single foreign country. Commercial and cultural ties with other nations, such as the Soviet Union, West Germany or the United States, were an affirmation of their independence.

We knew now that Africans were far less racist than the colonialists had thought. With so many reasons to be bitter, they had surprised their former white masters by being forgiving instead of vengeful. It is worth noting that fewer than a thousand whites died in the great historical convulsion that brought independence to thirty-six countries of black Africa in a period of nine years.

We knew now that Africans, like most people, were better politicians than they were economists and that they wanted to develop institutions based on their own tribal and communal traditions. We had learned that in Africa parliamentary rituals borrowed from Europe did not necessarily ensure democracy, just as a one-party system did not necessarily produce a dictatorship.

President Kennedy, in his second State of the Union message, expressed our growing sophistication about the world's diversity when he said: "Our basic goal remains the same: a peaceful world community of free and independent states, free to choose their own future and their own system, so long as it does not threaten the freedom of others. Some may choose forms and ways that we would not choose for ourselves, but it is not for us that they are choosing."

So we now knew better than to judge African democracy by our own standards. (For example, majority rule, which is sacred to Western democracy, is often offensive to the African tradition of decision by consensus.) We could understand that a two-party system can be a wasteful luxury in a young country short of trained manpower where any man with the education and skill to be a political leader can put his talents to better use inside than outside the government. (Men like Ngala and Moi could certainly serve Kenya more effectively in Kenyatta's cabinet than as part of a sterile parliamentary opposition.) What is important to a young country is that it be governed effectively and with the consent of the governed, and consent can be expressed in many ways other than by the ballot box where a majority of the people are illiterate. Consent can also be abruptly withheld, as we have seen in Ghana, Algeria, Dahomey and other countries whose leaders lost the confidence of the people.

We also knew (though some of our labor leaders did not) that the role of trade unions is different in a developing country than in an affluent industrialized society—that education, welfare and vocational training are more important than strikes and political action. We had learned that dividing African leaders into "moderates" and "radicals" makes no sense; to be realistic in Africa is to be radical. The distinction is rather between the radicals like Kenyatta's team, who want to promote a *constructive* African revolution, and those like Odinga, whose idea of revolution is to Africanize and nationalize as quickly as possible regardless of the economic consequences.

Finally, we now knew that Africa is fluid, volatile and everchanging. Its nations are never "lost" or "safe" from any outsider's point of view. Ghana, the 1965 problem country, is now being governed efficiently; Nigeria, the 1965 model of orderly progress, now appears to be breaking up. Ethiopia looks stable today, but what will happen to its feudal system when the Emperor dies? All we can be sure of is that Africa will be different next year and every year for a long time to come, and that the pace and nature of its evolution depend in large part on how much attention it gets from the rest of the world.

Those of us who were stationed in Africa have also learned a good many things about the people we met there, things that don't appear in briefing books. I used to tell new arrivals at the embassy to be prepared for ulcers if they didn't have patience and a sense of humor. For it is easy to become exasperated in Africa and easier still to make fun of African shortcomings. Exchanging jokes about African inefficiency is a favorite pastime among some "Europeans." But the laughter is the kind that doesn't last. It's like laughing, when you're young, at the wallflower or the boy without a dinner jacket at the prom, and later on feeling ashamed. It takes a while, in Africa, to appreciate the qualities of courtesy, kindness and stoicism that often lie hidden behind the primitive mask.

The burden of humiliation carried by most Africans over thirty is enormous. Is it any wonder that they overcompensate for their sense of inferiority in the presence of whites? In the Congo, black soldiers would often make their white prisoners do acrobatics at gunpoint and then, having equalized their status, cheerfully invite them to a beer party. In Burundi, the government delayed signing a

PL 480 agreement with us because it would be an embarrassing confession that the country was short of food. At international African conferences, the stentorian resolutions—against Rhodesia, for example—manage to give the delegates a feeling of power that they don't really have; as do the elaborate conference halls, the de luxe hotels and the honor guards and national anthems at the airports. Of course you can say that the money spent on these conclaves should be used for internal development, but it's a mistake to pretend that we are living in a rational world where psychological imperatives don't matter.

It's also a mistake to underestimate Africans. Literacy is not synonymous with intelligence, and a man who can't read or write isn't necessarily stupid. In fact, like blind people, illiterates often seem to develop and sharpen other perceptions to make up for their handicap. But many are understandably insecure in a society that seems to be passing them by. They will go to great lengths to conceal their handicap; they will lie to please. One of our servants in Guinea would pretend to read recipes in French, not realizing that they were written in English. My secretary in Kenya once asked her houseboy if he'd washed her dress.

"Yes, *memsab,*" he said.

"You shouldn't have washed it! I'm wearing it tonight."

"But I did *not* wash it, *memsab!*"

It's hard not to become chronically exasperated in Africa, at home when the cook never tells you he is out of butter until he is, or in government offices where decisions are endlessly delayed because no one is accustomed to taking the responsibility of making them. You can watch six Africans, as I remember doing in Guinea, take three hours to unload a small truck and wonder whether Africa is ready to join the modern world. You can deplore hasty Africanization of the public services, knowing the deterioration and inefficiency that will follow. But you can avoid exasperation by being realistic, by asking yourself a few questions: Is it reasonable to expect people with chronic dietary deficiencies to be energetic? Would an American raised from birth in the easygoing communal atmosphere of an African village show any more drive or tension? How critical can we be of people whose vitality has been sapped not only by a debilitating climate and endemic diseases but also by a savage slave trade? Aren't independent Africa's achievements more surprising than its failures? Aren't its leaders more impressive than they seemed in the advance billing we got from their colonial overlords?

If you accept Africans as they are, you can work with them without being exasperated. Our Peace Corps volunteers have found that out. You do need a sense of humor because getting mad at an African doesn't help—not unless he expects you to get mad —and also because humor is the quickest way to communicate with people who are, with good reason, both shy and suspicious.

Humor. Strange things happen in Africa. One day in 1965 I got a call from Sammy Maina, a professional agitator who had organized one of the pre-Stanleyville, hang-Johnson, anti-American demonstrations. Sammy said he wanted to call on me.

"Sammy," I said, "how many people are you bringing this time?" He laughed. "This is a personal call," he said, "not political." So he came over and told me he was getting married. It would be a big wedding, the social event of the season up in Nyeri, but he didn't have enough buses to transport all the guests. He was forced to ask his friends, like me, to help him out.

I told him I was sorry but we had no funds for social events; also, it could embarrass him politically if it was known he had taken money from the American Embassy.

"Ah, but no one has to know," he said.

I was adamant. But I did agree to provide a bottle of bourbon for the reception, since we were friends.

"That would be fine," said Sammy with a broad grin, and away he went.

Humor. Also dignity, courtesy, pride. These are the words to remember when you are dealing with Africans. And you must never forget that they are groping for identity, trying to adjust the ways they've been taught to the realities of a world shaped and dominated by powerful strangers. They want to preserve their own traditions—and no wonder. Many basic African qualities are precious to any kind of society: strong family ties, respect for age, mutual help and cooperation, free speech. Some of their customs look odd to us; some of ours—such as children talking back to their elders—look odd to them. In the Congo, long ago, the missionaries ran into resistance when they tried to get the women to wear clothes; only prostitutes, said the tribal elders, covered their nakedness. Does that sound so uncivilized today?

I hope the Africans find the identity they are groping for, the blend of cultures that will permit them to remain African while adapting to the modern world. Until they do, we should not be hasty in our judgments nor yield to exasperation.

Predictions about Africa are risky; nearly everything you say must be qualified with an "if" or a "but." Even so, I can't resist making a few.

There will be more political upheavals in countries where the present leadership is weak or corrupt or both. The leaders who will survive are those who understand that economic progress is a political imperative and who look for practical, rather than ideological, solutions to their problems. Already a younger generation of cool but concerned intellectuals, mostly educated in the West, is coming to the fore, especially in the British African countries. President Kennedy is their hero; they liked his style and imitate it. They are Africa-firsters, doers rather than talkers, socialists without being doctrinaire. In several countries many of them are already moving into the power structure, into the army, into journalism, into government. The old clichés about Africans don't apply to them any more than the Deep South clichés about "darkies" apply to the American Negro of today. We'll get along with the new breed.

It is also safe to predict that Africa will need economic and technical assistance and outside capital investment for a long time to come. Not only is per capita income less than 30 cents a day, but Africans are getting *relatively* poorer every year. At present growth rates, our per capita income will go up $1,500 by 2000 A.D., while Africa's will increase by only $50. Seventy percent of Africa's children are not even in primary school, but more and more want to be. People don't eat enough, yet productivity per farmer is about one-twentieth of what it is in America.

In short, Africa's leaders confront staggering problems. But most of these have to do with people—training them, feeding them, giving them a national as well as a tribal identity. Those of us who wish to help must therefore concentrate on these immediate needs. The purpose of the Marshall Plan in Europe was to rebuild the economies of existing nation-states, but in Africa everything, political authority as well as economic structures, must be developed and built up virtually from scratch.

Finally, it looks as if the Communist thrust into Africa, both Soviet and Chinese, will continue to lose momentum. The Russians especially are backing away from this (to them) baffling continent where no nation has accepted their tutelage and so many of their myths and theories have been disproved.* (The embattled African freedom fighter is as much of a propaganda-poster fiction as the square-jawed Ukrainian tractor driver sending him fraternal greetings.) Chinese pledges of aid to Africa dropped from $111 million in 1964 to $15 million in 1965. Since their plunge into Zanzibar their diplomacy has met with nothing but rebuffs and reverses. For their part, the Africans are learning that the Communist powers not only lack the resources to help them effectively but are, in effect, meddlesome missionaries whose gospel is even more alien to them than Christianity. The constant sniping and polemics between the Russian and Chinese branches of the movement have further repelled African nationalists. A remark to a Russian by a Kenya delegate to the 1964 Afro-Asian People's Solidarity Organization meeting at Algiers summed up the feelings of many Africans I have since talked to:

"We are not Marxist-Leninists, and most of us have never read a single line of *Das Kapital*. So what interest do you have in our participating in your doctrinal quarrels? I have had enough, when I am eating a sandwich, of being accosted by someone who asks me what I think of the Soviet position and, when I am drinking

* The extent to which the Russians are becoming more realistic and objective about Africa can be gauged by these extracts from a lecture delivered in Moscow on May 5, 1965 during an academic seminar on Africa's problems: "1960 was the first Africa Year. Seventeen countries gained independence in that year. Five years have passed since then and all our expectations have not been fulfilled. Some of the countries do not vote for us in the United Nations but for the former colonizers. Why? Why has Tshombé turned out to be stronger? Why has reaction won in Nigeria? What is going on in Kenya, where an anti-Soviet campaign is beginning? . . . One of our difficulties is that we too often represent the world to ourselves as we wish it to be rather than as what it is. We need to have a more realistic approach. . . . The majority of leaders who are talking about socialism are in fact following a pro-Western policy. . . . Ideological and political struggles are going on everywhere and it is impossible to predict the outcome in individual countries. Only generally can we say that the forces of progress will come out on top." In reply to a question about the Congo, the lecturer said: " . . . We made a good many mistakes. For example, we sent 10,000 tons of wheat which was moldy when it landed. We sent lorries which were just wrecked and embezzled by the drivers. We did not realize that there was

coffee, by someone who questions me about the Chinese arguments. I would like to be able to eat in peace."

While Africa's problems may seem overwhelming, there are valid reasons for being optimistic about the future—apart from the fact that the optimists have generally been proved right over the past few years. Africa has no reform-resisting feudal class, as does Latin America; its population growth is not yet out of control, as is India's. (For example, the Congo, which is two-thirds the size of India and probably possesses two-thirds of its resources, has a population of only 15 million, compared to India's 490 million.) Africa will also escape the worst of Europe's industrial revolution —for capitalism is not what it used to be—and the worst of Western civilization's devastating wars and civil wars—for no black African nation has yet displayed either the capability or the inclination to divert precious resources to building a war machine. Quarrels between African states, even between black-ruled Zambia and white-ruled Rhodesia, have remained mostly verbal. Africa, compared with other continents, is not encumbered by a burden of old grudges, chronic rivalries and unsettled scores. The historical slate in Africa is fairly clean.

And so we reach the question that always comes at the end of such a summing up: What should we Americans do about Africa and its problems?

I said there was reason for optimism. Mine is qualified by a large "if." Africa will make it *if* the rich nations of the world look upon this continent as a test case of their ability to think in North-South rather than East-West terms. In other words, we must face the fact that the No. 1 problem of our planet in the years ahead will no longer be the cold war but the war on poverty; our world *could* live in peace half-slave and half-free, but it cannot live in

---

no discipline. We were very ignorant in 1960. But the West, the British, Americans and Belgians knew all about this. They also knew that the Congo was the heart of Africa and that a chain reaction could start there. . . . The Chinese are causing a lot of harm by urging revolution and exploiting extremists. There are extremists everywhere, of course. They distribute pamphlets in English and French and claim that they are acting under the banner of true Marxism. The African people do not understand the real situation. They have also delivered arms, though I do not know whether they have sent any to the Congo." Finally he was asked, "How many of all Africans are on our side?" He replied: "An insignificant number, really."

peace, not in this age of mass communications, one-third rich and two-thirds poor.

Assuming that we in the industrialized and developed North begin to think in these terms, then there are several things America can do to help Africa move ahead constructively. (My assumption, of course, may be unjustified; as I write these lines, the Congress has just voted our smallest foreign aid appropriation in nine years. But we have to hope for the best.)

First of all, our posture: We should not worry too much about whether people like us; the richest man in town is seldom beloved. It's more important to be trusted and respected. Nor should we appear to worry too much about what the Soviets and Chinese are up to. If we go about our business, which is helping sensible governments solve their problems, the Communists will eventually trip over themselves. The record shows that when nationalism and Communism come into conflict, nationalism sooner or later prevails. And let's bear in mind that we would have to fight worldwide poverty, ignorance and disease even if Marx had never been born.

We should have some kind of aid or Peace Corps project going in every country, not only because they are needed everywhere but because they give people a chance to get to know Americans and our diplomats a reason to talk to government leaders.

We should join forces with the World Bank, the UN and other Western countries to raise the capital needed for long-range development in Africa, and we should look forward to the day when the Soviet Union, as a developed nation, will want to take part in these multilateral endeavors.

We should disassociate ourselves progressively from South Africa, so long as it pursues lunatic and immoral racial policies; and from Portugal, so long as it refuses to follow the example of the French and British, who decolonized in time. For white minority rule is doomed in the long run, and all who seem to support it today will eventually be hurt in Africa.

We should encourage regional economic cooperation among African nations, since many can never be viable alone, but we should not try to press African leaders to adopt different political or economic institutions. They know their own people better than we do.

We should be careful about selecting personnel to staff our embassies and other missions in Africa. We need people who are young—in heart if not in years—who enjoy politics more than protocol, who like to get things done and to see results.

In our dealings with Africans, we should keep four words in mind: firm, frank, friendly and fast.

By firm, I mean making it plain to leaders who are corrupt, disruptive or hostile to African stability and American interests that we will not make it easier for them to stay in power or to foment trouble, that our assistance will go only to those countries that mind their own business and observe genuine nonalignment.

By frank, I mean discussing our objectives and actions in Africa and elsewhere candidly and, if need be, bluntly with African leaders. Only by admitting our own errors and being constructively critical of theirs can we establish good personal relations and dispel lingering suspicions of our motives.

By friendly, I mean emphasizing the coincidence of our interests and being prepared to lend a helping hand when asked to, especially in areas like education, agriculture, communications and low-cost housing.

By fast, I mean concentrating our bilateral aid on small-impact projects that can produce visible results and satisfy popular expectations with a minimum of bureaucratic delay.

Call this a 4-F policy if you will. It's what will work in Africa, as anybody who has read this far should realize. And Africa is a place where we have neither old alliances nor commercial pressures to cramp our diplomatic style.

The time, of course, is propitious for us to pay more attention to Africa. The Communists are discredited, and new leaders who are activists rather than phrase-makers, pro-African rather than anti-Western, are moving up. They need help and are receptive to advice.

"The essential thing," said the London *Economist* recently, "is that the West should use this period of grace intelligently. Will it?"

This question was posed in March, 1966. I have not seen much evidence since then that our policy-makers have tried to answer it.

XXII

A Hard Look at the Establishment

•

I think it was Ernest Hemingway who said that the only way you can really get to know a foreign country is to earn your living there. In my work and my travels up until 1961 I had been in and out of the State Department and a good many of our overseas missions. I had friends in the Foreign Service and knew of their frustrations. Abroad, I had sweated out the McCarthy period with them; in Washington, I shared their laments about the red tape and deadwood in high places that impeded action and stifled initiative. But it wasn't until I joined them on the payroll—until I began earning my living there—that I really began to understand what went on in the State Department. Not many Americans do—which happens to be one of its problems.

I have come away, after more than five years, a loyal alumnus. I feel loyal to all the overworked and underpaid men and women of our Foreign Service, especially when they are maligned by the radical know-nothings of the left and right as stuffed shirts, pinkos, cookie-pushers—and worse. I get annoyed at people who imply that Foreign Service officers are not like other Americans (maybe because they speak foreign languages), and I get tired of explaining that American ambassadors don't all live like the Hervé Alphands and that their wives don't spend their days arranging flowers and looking stylish.

But I am also a critical alumnus, and this chapter will be mostly critical—I hope constructively. For the State Department could perform much more effectively if it were not saddled with a bureaucratic system that smothers its people under an avalanche of paper, discourages their initiative and imagination and offers little but a nomadic, penny-pinching existence to young men thinking of diplomacy as a career. The only reason the department works as well as it does is that enough skilled and dedicated people have been willing up to now to serve their government in spite of the system and to go on scoring goals, as somebody said, like stunt soccer players wrapped up in nets.

Some of State's shortcomings are its own fault, some could be corrected by Presidential action and others are the result of Congressional suspicion and niggardliness. Unlike several other branches of the government, State has no constituents—nobody who wants to increase its annual appropriation, no aircraft companies or farm lobbies or veterans' organizations to fight its battle on Capitol Hill. And State never seems to put its own case across either to Congress or to the public. Reasonable requests for more funds somehow come out sounding like a cookie-pusher's plea for a bigger booze allowance.

And so, while this chapter may sound critical, its purpose is to shed some light on what goes on in the labyrinths of Foggy Bottom—and hopefully to stimulate some concern about how to induce qualified and talented people to go to work for their government and help formulate and carry out an intelligent foreign policy.

The State Department is relatively small. Its 25,700 employees (of whom 3,520 are Foreign Service officers) and its annual budget of $393 million make it the second smallest department of the government. (Labor has fewer people and Justice a smaller budget.) It is also the most far-flung—with 117 embassies, 69 consulates-general and 79 consulates scattered around the world—and the most verbose: a large embassy, on an average day, will receive more than 400,000 words, the equivalent of an 850-page book, and in Washington the department's distribution section makes copies of 70,000 incoming messages a day. So perhaps the best way of explaining what's wrong with the State Department is to start with the paper.

Paperwork is invented by bureaucratic-minded people who, like

Dr. Frankenstein, later become its victims. These are people to whom an overflowing in-box is a daily challenge and an empty one a daily achievement; for whom a satisfying week's work consists in initialing as many reams of paper and deferring as many decisions as possible; with whom you can talk of "action" only in terms of setting up a committee, hopefully one that will spawn subcommittees. The chief considerations of a bureaucrat are to abide by the letter of the regulations whatever the consequences, to keep a clean desk and never "make waves."

There are fewer bureaucrats in the State Department than in other swollen government agencies—AID, for example—but enough to make you wonder at times how a new idea ever bubbles to the top. The reason it does, of course, is that there are generally a few activists at every echelon who enjoy results and do not regard moving paper as an end in itself. Keeping these activists in the bureaucracy and recruiting new ones should be a priority objective of every incoming administration.

The production of paper is excessive at both ends and self-generating. Reporting requirements from the field keeps embassy officers desk-bound when they should be getting out and around. Most of these reports are copied, distributed and filed away without anybody reading them except—possibly—some specialist in the Bureau of Intelligence and Research. Telegrams get more attention because they are shorter, but only a few percolate up to the sixth and seventh floors or to the White House. (Ken Galbraith once told me the only way to get a telegram read in the White House was to put a four-letter word in it.) Since so much of what is reported is of no practical or immediate use, I have often wondered why Washington does not deal with its overseas missions the way a wire service editor deals with his overseas bureaus—which is to ask for special reports when the need arises rather than to expect correspondents in the field to keep filing everything they can find out about anything. Conversely, the men in the field should be spared the eyestrain of having to read or even glance at most of what comes from Washington by pouch. (Our weekly CIA summary—naturally stamped "secret"—seldom contained anything we hadn't already seen in the *New York Times* Sunday news digest.) Perhaps the only way to stop the flow of paper is to penalize anybody who writes reports that could possibly be avoided. But it won't happen;

there are too many people who need to produce paper in order to justify their presence on the payroll. (A Foreign Service officer named Holmes Welch recently defined the Welch corollary to Parkinson's Law as follows: *Every producer of paper added to the government roster creates the need for an additional consumer of paper.* But the latter, when hired, turns out to be a producer too.)

What happens to all the paper? It piles up. One of my fellow ambassadors told me that, on arriving at a new post, he asked how long it would take, in an emergency, to burn all the accumulated classified papers. The answer: six weeks, if the incinerator was in operation day and night.

Aside from reports, there are other kinds of paper that clog the machinery and waste time, money and manpower. Travel and expense vouchers are just two examples. When a Foreign Service officer goes from point A to point B, he must make out a form accounting for every minute of his time in transit. (0916— departed terminal. Airport tax: 70 cents. 0955—arrived Chancery. Bus: $1.25.) Per diem rates vary, depending on where he is and whether he happens to be stationary or in motion. The resulting voucher is both complicated and time-consuming for everyone involved in preparing and reviewing it. It has been estimated that the government spends about $10 to process an average voucher— which can easily double the cost of the reimbursement. (It can even more than double it, as in the case of a junior officer I knew in Spain whose quarterly entertainment allowance, which had to be accounted for, was only three dollars.)

The obligation to justify every penny spent is not only wasteful but can be embarrassing. A senior officer who is trusted to handle top-secret documents does not have his government's confidence where a dollar is concerned. I remember being invited to a meeting with the Guinean Foreign Minister while serving at USUN. The taxi fare to the Guinean Mission and back came to $2.40. A few days after submitting the required voucher, somebody from the administrative section called me about my taxi ride. "We have no record, Mr. Ambassador," said the voice archly, "of any reception being given at the Guinean Embassy on that day."

My favorite story is about the Foreign Service officer returning to Washington on orders. His mother, who was not on government orders, traveled with him. In making out his voucher, he carefully separated his own from his mother's expenses. But the last item was a taxi from Union Station to his hotel. In Washington there is a different fare if two people occupy the cab. Back came a query: "Did your mother ride in the cab with you?" His reply made bureaucratic history: "No. I took the cab. My mother walked and carried the bags."

The sensible and economical way to handle this kind of paperwork would be for the government to calculate the cost of moving an employee from point A to point B. Anyone traveling that distance would then be given a flat sum to travel as he wished just so long as he got to his destination on time. Time and money would be saved. But it might be necessary to get rid of a lot of people whose jobs depend on processing the paper under the present system. The Deputy Under Secretary of State for Administration told me he was not even able to introduce air travel cards as an efficiency measure; the General Accounting Office has a vested interest in keeping the system cumbersome.

Similarly, ambassadors should be given representational funds to use at their discretion without having to make out forms in quintuplicate listing and justifying every social function for which they and their staffs require reimbursement. No diplomatic missions have such big administrative staffs as ours; other countries generally treat their ambassadors like men of integrity and judgment—as George Washington treated Benjamin Franklin when he sent him to Paris with 50,000 francs and no budget and fiscal officer to bird-dog him. But that was back when the U.S. Government was too small to afford a bureaucracy.

The average Foreign Service officer is forty-one and makes $13,900 a year. When you take into account the education, the training and the wide range of skills that the State Department requires of its officers, and when you consider what private industry offers talented executives in the way of salary and advancement, the wonder is that our government is still able to induce young people with drive and imagination to make diplomacy their career. Despite occasional directives commending boldness and courage, most FSO's have become convinced from experience that the way to move up the ladder is to play it safe. As Harriman has said: "I have seen men's careers set back and, in fact, busted because they held the right views at the wrong time, or for accurately reporting facts that were not popular at the time." Caution, of course, becomes a habit as well as a necessity for a man in his forties who needs that next promotion to put his children through college. A good many of our senior FSO's are also suffering from the McCarthy syndrome; they have never quite recovered from the experience of seeing some of their patriotic colleagues hounded and persecuted by the late Senator without either the President or the Secretary of State willing to stick up for them. Moreover, a potential executive, who, because of the seniority system, is not given the opportunity to exercise his executive ability in his middle years becomes bleached out. If he does get to be a chief of mission, he has often lost the capacity for controlled indignation—for sticking his neck out—that is vital to effective leadership.

A system which rewards seniority rather than ability can produce absurd situations. I have a friend who was made an FSO-1 at thirty-nine. The next rung on the ladder is career minister. According to existing regulations, he could not become a CM until he was fifty. Yet the regulations also state that an officer who is not promoted for ten years is subject to "selection-out"—a euphemism for being fired.

From what I have seen of the State Department, the greatest concentration of executive talent can be found in the 35-45 age bracket. But most of these men and women are FSO-3's and -4's. Above them in the hierarchy—as of December, 1966—were 7 career ambassadors, 52 career ministers, 313 FSO-1's and 452 FSO-2's. With not more than 36 ambassadorships available each year, of which a quarter are filled by political appointees, the chances of a substantial number getting top jobs in their most productive and vigorous years are practically nonexistent. (In private industry, a promising young executive doesn't have to wait for his seniors to retire before being made a vice president; I wonder how far Bob McNamara would have gone at Ford if they promoted executives as the State Department does.)

What is also discouraging to talented middle-grade officers is that the higher echelons are cluttered with deadwood—with people who drifted up the ladder because somebody on a promotion panel wanted to give good old Joe or Charlie a break. (I know of one of these good old Joes who was finally moved out of an African post—he had refused to entertain Africans in his house—and transferred to a bigger post commensurate with his rank.) The deadwood are usually officers with bland records, with no black marks on their efficiency reports, with no history of ever having gotten out of line, rocked the boat or questioned their instructions. A good, energetic officer, on the other hand, can be passed over for promotion—if he lacks friends in the Establishment—on the basis of one negative efficiency report written by one superior who might not have liked the way he dressed. (I personally interceded in one such case.)

Some officers who manage to reach the top after long years of patient subordination tend to become martinets, like British Public School boys hazing their juniors because they were once hazed themselves. And their wives can be even more dictatorial: I have known of some who ordered the wives of staff members around like servants; one who put a hairdresser off limits to other wives because she didn't like him; one who insisted the staff speak to her in French; one who would whimsically appropriate a cook or a piece of furniture from subordinates. A book could be written about the dragon-ladies who have dominated some of our embassies in the past.

Wives, of course, don't figure prominently on the data by which people are selected for assignment. (They do figure under one of several headings in efficiency reports, but the reporting officer usually calls them "gracious hostesses" and lets it go at that; a member of a promotion panel told me that after reading hundreds of efficiency reports he concluded that all Foreign Service officers were married to the same wife.) In fact, a good many intangible qualities don't show up in the personnel files. In Guinea it took me four months of correspondence to get a perfectly capable officer transferred to another post without prejudice to his career; he and his wife were wrong for Africa, and didn't even speak adequate French besides. Obviously, no one familiar with our problems interviewed them before they were issued orders.

But that's how the system seems to work. Orders are issued when personnel of appropriate rank are available to fill available slots. An ambassador often has to intervene personally to block a bad appointment or get the right man assigned to his staff. And not enough ambassadors are temperamentally conditioned to raise hell. In fact, many are themselves transferred without prior consultation or regard to their preferences, and successors are then named to replace them without benefit of their counsel.

The State Department, in short, is people. It will be as competent as the people it attracts and effective to the degree that its people are properly assigned, fairly treated and promoted for ability rather than seniority. The Foreign Service is not so big that it has to be computerized and depersonalized, and it is too small to afford to keep deadwood in its upper echelons without impairing its efficiency. The Department of Defense is big enough and rich enough to be able to find parking places for its surplus colonels; State is not.

Hans Morgenthau has said that elimination of half of State's employees "could by itself not fail to improve the operation of the Department." His figure may be high; I would say a fourth could be spared to good advantage, particularly in Washington and Europe. For State is both over- and understaffed. It is overstaffed, for example, in Foggy Bottom committees where ten people will spend twenty man-hours preparing a paper that one able man could prepare in two; and it is understaffed in places like Africa where substantive officers usually work a sixty-to-seventy-hour week. If deadwood could be got rid of, there would still be a problem of maldistribution of personnel, both in Washington and in the field. On the sixth and seventh floors, our top officials are too busy every day of the week to do much original thinking; down below, the thinking is collective—a new idea must be vetted by several bureaus before it goes upstairs—and the results are papers and reports that reflect the lowest common denominator of judgment.

Anyone who has served on a committee understands the problem. Most people who attend committee meetings have no definite ideas of their own; they come prepared only to pass judgment on what somebody else suggests—to support or knock down a new idea, depending on how they think the man they want to impress feels about it.

In general, new ideas are not popular among the committee-minded layers of personnel that lie between desk officers and Assistant Secretaries. (These are the layers where senior deadwood stacks up in Washington.) A new idea is likely to require revisions of existing policy papers, guidelines and contingency plans. This means additional work—real work, not just going to meetings; it also implies that present policies, which everyone has spent years defending and justifying, might be faulty. (Guinea, we may recall, was labeled "lost" back in 1961.) Thus new ideas run into a kind of vested, automatic resistance. Chester Bowles was unpopular in the Establishment not only because he promoted younger men on merit but because he generated too many fresh and unsettling ideas.

The layers of fat in State's midsection also hold up action on all kinds of requests from the field. Clearances often take time because officers initialing a paper feel obliged to suggest some changes if only to show they have read it. When we asked Washington three weeks in advance for a letter from the President to *Mzee* on Kenyatta Day, nothing happened—even though we had sent along a proposed draft—until Wayne Fredericks personally went to the Secretary's office and got it out to us by telegram just in time. I was told later this letter was "an example of the Department at its collective worst."

Our European embassies are not unlike Washington. Most are overstaffed with paper-producers. Austria, for example, may be a small neutralist country that isn't making any history these days. But we continue to maintain a diplomatic establishment in Vienna appropriate to a major power or to an important listening post—which is what Vienna was twenty years ago. In Paris there are 21 people in the Agricultural Attaché's office just to cover France; in Nairobi we had one man and a secretary reporting on seven countries and handling PL 480 sales as well. Four economic officers are assigned to The Hague; we had one in Nairobi. A junior administrative officer on my staff in Conakry was transferred to a large embassy in Europe; he wrote me later complaining he could finish his day's work by ten A.M.—there were fifty-two people employed in the embassy's budget and fiscal section alone.

I never talked to anyone in Washington who didn't agree our European posts were too big. Yet nothing is done about them. The department's top brass is largely Europe-oriented: they spent a good part of their careers there and tend to regard anything that happens in the rest of the world as being of marginal significance, the way it was in the thirties. I remember talking to one of our senior ambassadors, a long-time member of the State Department Establishment, when I passed through Europe on my way home from Nairobi. He asked me in all seriousness what was the capital of Kenya and who was its President. An aide later told me the ambassador had no interest in anything south of the Mediterranean.

The overworked FSO in Africa and the less meaningfully employed FSO in Europe have one thing in common: they are both underpaid. The average forty-one-year-old FSO earning $13,900 a year would, with his background and talents, be in a much higher income bracket had he chosen to go into business instead of government. Only ten percent of our FSO's make $20,000, which itself is not high by corporate executive standards. And the expense accounts which embellish the average businessman's way of life don't exist in the Foreign Service. The seventeen-dollars-a-day per diem allowance an FSO or ambassador gets on consultation in Washington barely covers his hotel room; there is nothing left over for meals, laundry or taxicabs. In the field, representation funds, in my experience, never fully covered legitimate entertainment, and our embassy officers were always out of pocket. In Nairobi we were the only diplomatic mission too poor to give a party on our national holiday. Travel was also restricted for lack of funds. I do not know of a company whose overseas sales managers come home as infrequently as our ambassadors return to Washington.

Even if surplus and superannuated personnel were weeded out of the State Department, the savings would not begin to meet the diplomatic requirements of a nation with such world-wide interests as the United States. If you compare the budgets for State and Defense, you will note that we are spending about 150 times more money on our military establishment than on the agency of government whose job is to defend and advance our interests without war.

One reason that our nonmilitary agencies are on short rations—while Defense generally gets even more than it asks for from Congress—is public relations; State, as I have pointed out, has no constituents and no lobbies. The Pentagon spends nearly $40 million a year on its own public relations. State's budget for explaining U.S. foreign policy to the American people is only $3.1 million.

And the Pentagon, unlike State, has companies with Defense contracts, veterans' organizations and governors and other local officials continually pressing Capitol Hill for larger military appropriations. The cumulative effect of all this public relations effort is to make it hard for a Congressman to vote to eliminate waste in the Pentagon, but easy for him politically to attack "extravagance" in State, USIS, AID, the Peace Corps and other agencies whose missions seem less dramatic than that of our uniformed services. Most Americans are still prone to regard our "boys" (as politicians call our men in uniform) in Germany or wherever as deserving of everything we can give them, preferably at the expense of the dudes in striped pants. The "boy" may be in charge of the bar at an Officers' Club in Spain and the dude may be working a sweaty sixty-hour week in Burma, but the images persist and are reflected in the Congressional appropriations.

Many career FSO's have become resigned to this state of affairs; they develop an air of shabby gentility and give the impression of approaching Capitol Hill with dignity but with hat in hand. Congressmen regularly visit our embassies, but they nearly always go to Europe, where our diplomats, figuratively speaking, don't often get mud on their boots. (In 1965 no fewer than 90 members of Congressional delegations went to Paris, and 84 to Rome; but only four made it to Nairobi in all the time I was there). Little effort is made, as we have seen, to arrange for ambassadors and other senior officers from hardship posts to tell their stories and explain their work personally to the legislators who hold the purse strings. Regular conferences in Washington with community leaders, such as those so successfully conducted at USUN by the Foreign Policy Association, have been proposed to but never acted upon by the department. Only recently has the Bureau of Public Affairs encouraged FSO's to make speeches to civic groups when home on leave or consultation.

It wasn't so long ago that a venturesome young man interested in foreign affairs and willing to live abroad would tend to think of a career in the Foreign Service. This is no longer true. With U.S. firms opening branches all over the world, opportunities for working overseas have multiplied. In Nairobi we had men in their thirties representing American companies who not only had the satisfaction of contributing to Kenya's economic development, but were making twice the salaries of embassy officers of equivalent age and ability, and benefiting from tax advantages denied government employees. Not only that; they were treated with consideration by their home offices.

Under the circumstances, I don't see how we can expect creative, enterprising and strong-willed people to continue to enter the Foreign Service at the bottom of a ladder that is arduous to climb and not very rewarding when and if you reach the top. What we may get are prospective civil servants looking for a kind of respectable security—paper-producers who will bring neither imagination nor verve to the conduct of our foreign policy.

I do not have the competence (for I did not serve any length of time in Washington) nor, indeed, the inclination to turn this chapter into a detailed critique of the State Department and to suggest specific reforms to correct its shortcomings. This is both a narrative and impressionistic book, and whatever conclusions and recommendations I make here are the outgrowth of a limited though concentrated experience. But I have found few professionals who do not agree that the State Department needs an infusion of new talent at the top as well as at the bottom of its hierarchy. In fact, it needs it at the top if it is to get it at the bottom.

The Secretary and Under Secretaries are now too burdened with substantive responsibilities to direct enough attention to reforming the department's administrative practices and procedures. The Secretary needs a deputy with full authority—and White House backing—to retire, discharge, hire and promote people on the basis of merit and promise. I would like to see more qualified outsiders brought into the department, both in Washington and in the field, for limited tours of duty—men of proven ability from politics, journalism, teaching and industry who would not take bureaucratic routine for granted. They would improve the system and leave government, as I did, with greater understanding of and sympathy for public servants. And they could be influential in helping pry needed appropriations out of the Congress so that government service would no longer be synonymous with personal and financial sacrifice.

Younger career officers should welcome an infusion of fresh talents. Even if the proportion of career to noncareer ambassadors is kept at its present four-to-one ratio, opportunities for becoming a chief of mission would be increased if the promotion system were reformed and more attention paid to factors other than seniority. By and large, career officers are highly competent. But career ambassadors are often handicapped—compared to political appointees—by lack of access to the White House. (This is something which the President should correct.) Their other weaknesses, as I have observed them, are a predilection for analyzing a situation rather than taking action; a tendency to shy away from reporters—with whom it is usually wiser to level than to be evasive—and to regard nonofficial Americans as nuisances (visas, lost passports, etc.) rather than as potential Country Team assets; a preference (justified by protocol) for dealing exclusively with governments and keeping opposition elements at arm's length—which, as in Cuba, the Dominican Republic and Vietnam, can turn out to be self-defeating; a reluctance to engage in discussions of American politics (about which foreigners expect you to have some opinion); and a certain resentment about the activities of other government agencies on the Country Team—as though the function of the once-exclusive Foreign Service were being encroached upon by parvenus and interlopers.

There is naturally some resentment of political appointees in the State Department. A 1965 *Fortune* article about a career ambassador reflected the attitude of the Establishment by contrasting him and his "low-key, even-keel but rigorous form of diplomacy" with "the new politicized breed who have a zest for commotion and coup-making." In all fairness to political appointees, the record shows that the coups and commotion of the past six years have been largely confined—except for Vietnam—to countries where career men ran our missions. (This is not to suggest that the accusation should be turned around, since commotion seldom results from anything an American ambassador does or does not do.)

The advantages in having some qualified noncareer people scattered throughout the Establishment are that they prevent bureaucratic barnacles from accumulating, they can raise hell about red tape and personnel inequities, they can argue with the department about policy decisions without fear of jeopardizing their careers, and they are likely to see crises as opportunities rather than headaches and to appreciate the value of all Country Team elements to contemporary diplomacy. The problem is making government service rewarding enough to attract them.

State's problems and shortcomings are shared in varying degrees by most other agencies of government directly concerned with foreign policy.

AID, as State's chief operating arm in developing nations, is the most important. Without economic and technical assistance programs our diplomats in most nations of Africa, Asia and Latin America would have far less influence or leverage than they do. Unfortunately, AID is even more smothered in paper and hobbled by Congressional red tape than State, and its proportion of timid bureaucrats, no-sayers and nit-picking lawyers far higher. The good work AID does is obscured by its public image: to most Americans it is the "give-away agency." The same week in 1965 that we were talking with Kenyan officials about applying PL 480 proceeds to the irrigation of idle land, the St. Louis *Globe-Democrat* ran a cartoon showing Uncle Sam on bended knee offering a bag of gold labeled "foreign aid" to an arrogant, pot-bellied dictator.

Instances of waste and scandal in our aid operation—mostly in the fifties and mostly in a few countires like Laos, Pakistan and Korea—have discredited the whole program in the eyes of many Americans already burdened by rising domestic prices and taxes. AID is an easy and popular target for any politician who wants to appear economy-minded. The fact that our foreign aid appropriation is down to less than one-half of one percent of our Gross National Product and that the bulk of it is spent here in the U.S. on American products is one of our best-kept national secrets. And the belief that foreign aid has failed even to create goodwill for the United States is one of our most popular national myths.

If we are going to save foreign aid from being progressively whittled away by the Congress, I believe drastic reforms are needed. The first is to start dismantling the cumbersome and expensive bureaucracy that administers the program. For example, the organizational chart of AID's Bureau for Africa contains no fewer than twenty-seven boxes: there is a Program Management Division under the Office of Capital Development and Finance, a Programming Division under the Office of Development Planning, a Management Support Division under the Office of Management Operations—and so on. By simplifying existing procedures and giving the ambassador more authority and flexibility to disburse aid funds, we could save at least $50 million a year in AID administrative costs and a larger chunk of its $102 million payroll.

Second, foreign aid should be divided into short-term and long-term programs. The purpose of the former, which would be confined to education, agriculture, communications, birth control and community development, should be to create conditions of political stability that will attract substantial capital investment. An African government that is able to build high schools and roads and help its farmers develop new land and increase production will avert the unrest that alarms investors. Long-term aid, the kind that develops a country's resources, should be undertaken by the U.S. Government in cooperation with individual firms, industrialized countries, the United Nations, the World Bank and other international lending agencies. The government should also give every encouragement to private investors assisting African development through investment-guarantee agreements.

The advantage of dividing foreign aid into two categories is that the funds required for short-term, political-impact projects are relatively small, could be administered by a small staff under the direction of U.S. ambassadors and would be easier to explain to the Congress and the public. Americans are on the whole compassionate; they are ready to help people in need of books, food, roads, medicines and so forth when they see their needs in specific human terms. (One of my last official acts in Kenya was giving a $200 check to a member of Parliament from the town of Russell, Kansas, to put roofs on two self-help schools.) What Americans object to is the vague and impersonal nature of foreign aid as it is now presented to the Congress.

I mentioned birth control. It is worth emphasizing that whatever progress is made in Africa over the next few years could be wiped out unless population growth is held down. That's why it has been estimated that a dollar spent on birth control in a developing country can produce more economic benefit in the long run than a dollar spent in any other way.

USIS, like State, needs more money. With a budget of less than $170 million, USIS cannot hope to satisfy the world-wide demands for its services. The Voice of America now broadcasts 845 hours a week, up 348 hours from 1950. This sounds impressive until you look at the competition's comparable figures: the Soviet Union, 1,374 hours (up 841); China, 1,027 (up 961); Eastern Europe, 1,385 (up 973); Cuba 461 (up 461). In short, Communist propagandists know that radio is the best means of reaching the largely illiterate masses in the developing countries (90 percent of Africa's 10.5 million radios are short-wave), and they make it a budgetary priority. We know this too, but the Congress, for all its patriotic cold war oratory, isn't willing to spend the money that would enable us to compete on equal terms. A bigger USIS budget would also mean higher salaries to attract a more professional staff, libraries and reading rooms where none exist and American books on the shelves of thousands of schools. In a society that will spend $50 million to promote the Ajax White Knight, or $10 million to launch a new filter cigarette, the stinginess that now muffles our government's information programs at this time in history is inexcusable.

I have already praised the Peace Corps. Its success can be gauged both by the welcome accorded its volunteers, even in countries otherwise critical of some of our policies, and by the vilification heaped on them by Soviet and Chinese propagandists. At home, it has surprised detractors like President Eisenhower, who once dismissed it as "a bunch of 15-year-old kids in the jungle." I think the Peace Corps will go down in history as the most enduring achievement of the Kennedy administration.

I have also said a few kinds words, in the preceding chapters, about the CIA. It is the easiest of all government agencies to attack because it is usually unable, for security reasons, to defend itself. It's true that some of its unevaluated reports from the field sound like cocktail party gossip, and that the CIA has occasionally gone off on a tangent, especially when it was on a loose leash. (Its advocacy of the Bay of Pigs operation was politically idiotic.) But it has managed to recruit and retain better people than most government agencies (perhaps because its budget, being confidential can be used more flexibly to minimize bureaucratic frustrations); and I have found that with proper supervision the CIA is and will be an essential instrument of our foreign policy so long as we are confronted with conniving and unscrupulous opponents.

As for the Department of Defense, I was impressed, during my excursion into government, by the political maturity of our senior officers in the Pentagon, and depressed by the extravagance and prodigality of our military establishments. The old breed of general who looked at the world exclusively in military terms—the Le-Mays and the Twinings and the shoot-firsters—is fading away and being replaced by men who have learned from study, travel and experience that the problems of this revolutionary world are much too complex to be solved by superior firepower alone. What is regrettable is that so many of the Defense Department's resources and talents are not being employed to full advantage. Even when we are involved in limited military operations in Vietnam, the Pentagon is hard pressed to find ways of spending its money and keeping its people usefully employed. In a busy embassy (and most embassies are) it can be embarrassing and demoralizing to everybody concerned to have large army, navy and air attaché sections around with no real work to do and bigger entertainment allowances than the ambassador. In Kenya, Pentagon-financed studies of esoteric subjects like "Nandi expansionism from 1870 to 1905" were under way shortly before I left, but I could not tap the Defense Department's tremendous engineering potential to help build needed roads. I know U.S. civic action programs would be welcomed in many countries if the signing of military assistance agreements, with its overtone of "alignment," were not a prerequisite. And I am sure that most of our military men would welcome the opportunity to take part in the global war against poverty. For the frustrations of our Defense establishment are those you would expect among any group of vigorous executives and technicians sitting around a lavish firehouse, polishing their equipment and waiting for that three-alarm fire that no one really wants or even expects.

I have already described how the activities of most of these agencies are coordinated in the field within the Country Team. What is lacking in Washington is the Country Team approach. There is some liaison between the various departments and agencies concerned with foreign policy—often on an *ad hoc* basis—but I have also seen all too many instances of unnecessary duplication and even of conflicting policy decisions. (For example, I sometimes feel that Defense has never quite accepted the fact that we oppose Portuguese colonialism.) Considering the magnitude and variety of our involvement in world affairs, it is essential that the government at least integrate its own efforts more effectively. Foreign policy can no longer be separated from domestic policy. It is not something simple that can be turned over to the State Department the way national parks can be turned over to Interior. Commerce, Agriculture, Labor, Treasury and Interior, too, are all doing things that influence our foreign relations. Today a rise in the interest rate, a drop in wheat production or a change in established trade patterns can affect those relations far more than the wording of a diplomatic *aide-mémoire*. Foreign policy will never again be the exclusive province of State in this smaller, faster, more interdependent world of ours; and we should be reorganizing our governmental structure accordingly.

I said this chapter would be critical. In fairness to State, I cannot conclude it without adding that our Foreign Service represents us more ably and keeps our government better and more fully informed than that of any other major power. It does not generate many new ideas—as it did in the pre-Dulles era—but this is a fault of bureaucratic procedures, ingrained routines and seventh-floor leadership that tolerates mediocrity and overstaffing so long as the wheels keep turning and the paper gets processed. Revitalizing State would be difficult (have you ever tried scraping barnacles off the bottom of a keel?), but it would not be impossible over a period of five years under a reform-minded Secretary with full White House backing and a sympathetic Congress. Bob McNamara's gradual efforts to streamline the far bigger and more cumbersome Pentagon bureaucracy are an example of what can be done.

The recommendations I have made in the foregoing pages can be summarized as follows:

1. Get rid of deadwood and trim overstaffed posts and bureaus.
2. Promote FSO's on merit rather than seniority.
3. Make salary scales comparable to those offered by private industry.
4. Minimize the production and distribution of paper.
5. Personalize (i.e., decomputerize) personnel assignments.

6. Dismantle the AID bureaucracy and put foreign economic assistance under the State Department.
7. Separate foreign aid into short-term bilateral and long-term multilateral projects.
8. Coordinate the activities of all federal agencies concerned with foreign affairs.

The support of Capitol Hill will be essential; that's where the money comes from. This support depends in turn on greater public understanding of government operations and why reforms are needed, for people elect Congressmen. But unfortunately the American people, whose lives are most directly affected by our foreign policy actions—who are regularly taxed, drafted and killed because of our world-wide diplomatic and military commitments —often seem as confused and uninformed as ever, in this age of mass communication and instant news, about the world we live in and America's role in shaping the one our children will inherit.

XXIII

Postscript to a Long Journey

•

The westbound jet left Nairobi in the late afternoon, and by the time they served dinner we were passing over Stanleyville. There was a refueling stop at Lagos, and we got to Robertsfield, Liberia, about 1 A.M. It was the west coast again, damp and sticky after the Kenyan Highlands. The air-conditioning in the terminal hotel felt good.

I had a two-day layover before making a connection to Conakry, where Sékou Touré was expecting me; I had sent a message saying I wanted to see him before leaving Africa. So I spent the day resting and making notes for our talk. In the evening, a junior officer from our Monrovia Embassy came out in a car and we drove the fifty-five miles into the city through the rubber plantations to have dinner with Ambassador Brown. I had never met the Browns, but after more than five years in the Foreign Service I didn't feel like a stranger with any American ambassador. We could talk shop and exchange news of mutual friends: so-and-so had been transferred to Rangoon, somebody else was being considered for an ambassadorship and whatever had happened to X? Being in the Foreign Service is like belonging to a small and congenial lodge with clubhouses all over the world. Coming into a residence, you feel right at home among the government-issue furniture, the crested glassware, the ornamental tea service and the standard stereo console. The shop talk is stimulating and the small talk comradely and familiar. It was a club into which I'd been accepted, and I was going to miss it.

The next morning I caught the PanAm jet to Conakry. I noticed it was May 3, the anniversary of the inaugural flight I went to meet three years before when Sarge Shriver came to open our fair. This time Pierre Graham, our chargé, was at the airport to meet me. He said Touré understood this was a private call, since my resignation had been accepted, and was pleased I was coming.

Commissaire Paul, the hero of the Svetlana case, was no longer at the terminal, but other officials recognized me and came over to shake hands and to go through the conventional Franco-African greeting:

"*Alors, ça va?*"

"*Ça va, et vous?*"

"*Ça va bien. Et madame?*"

"*Elle va bien, merci.*"

"*C'est bien, ça. Et les enfants?*"

"*Tout le monde va bien. Et chez vous?*"

"*Eh bien, ça va.*"

"*C'est bien, ça.*"

Then a pause, a smile and your hand is finally released.

"*Ça va, alors?*"

"*Ça va.*"

We made our way through the terminal and drove into town. The road had been widened and the potholes filled in. A Swiss motel had sprouted up. The Russian stadium and Polytechnic Institute were completed. New trees had been planted along the Avenue de la République. Otherwise, Conakry looked about the same. The American Embassy had been enlarged, and an AID comptroller now occupied my old office. Our mission now had its own commissary, doctor and school, and a second floor had been added to our former residence. Nearly all the people I'd worked with were gone, but our servants—Mamadou Diallo, Mamadou Diop and Mamadou Barry—were still around, and we spent a congenial five minutes before lunch performing the *ça va* ritual.

Guinea was still limping along, plagued by mismanagement, a worthless currency and a shortage of skilled manpower. Touré had severed relations with Britain over Rhodesia and with France because of an alleged plot to overthrow his government. But the Russians were still in the doghouse and making no special effort to reingratiate themselves. The only new Communist project was a small dam being constructed upcountry by the Chinese.

Guinea's economic prospects had nevertheless brightened with the resumption of operations at Boké under the agreement signed with Harvey Aluminum. Other Western companies were now again interested in forming a consortium to help mine and market the bauxite. Our AID vocational training programs were doing well, as were the Peace Corps volunteers, whose arrival had helped double the American population—to about four hundred. Our embassy officials told me they were impressed by the younger Guineans who had returned from study abroad, but that the latter were as frustrated as we were by the bureaucratic inefficiency and inner-circle intrigue that pervaded the upper echelons of government. Touré's impulsive invitation to Nkrumah a few weeks earlier to come to Conakry as Guinea's co-President after the coup in Accra had also upset and embarrassed a good many Guineans; even our servants, who rarely talked politics, were complaining about having to attend public rallies to hear this stranger making speeches in a language they didn't understand.

In short, nothing much had changed in Guinea—which wasn't too bad from our point of view. What I wanted to know was how much Touré himself had changed.

In the late afternoon, I met Karim Bangoura, who was back on consultation from Washington, at the entrance to the palace, and we went upstairs to Touré's office. It seemed like old times. Touré was wearing a white *boubou* and cap and had lost none of his diffident charm. I told him I had not wanted to leave Africa without saying good-bye to him, whom I had long admired and defended as a true nationalist.

We talked about recent events in Kenya. He deplored the split in KANU. "I know that Odinga at heart is loyal to Kenyatta and not a Communist," he said. "They should have resolved their differences within the party." He seemed surprised when I pointed out that Odinga had received more than a million dollars from Communist sources—which was hardly evidence of loyalty to Kenyatta.

The Guinean Ambassador to Peking had just made a violent anti-American speech, and I asked him about that. (It really did seem like old times.) Touré hadn't seen it, but said anyone attacking us wasn't speaking for Guinea. He asked me to get him a copy of the speech.

As to his own deteriorating relations with his neighbors, Touré asserted that Senegal and the Ivory Coast had been plotting with the French to overthrow him, so it was up to Senghor and Houphouët-Boigny to initiate any reconciliation. "Liberia and Guinea don't agree on everything," he said, "but Tubman is a good neighbor who doesn't meddle in our internal affairs. Why can't the others follow his example?"

When I brought up the subject of Nkrumah, Touré suggested we continue our talk in the morning, as he had another appointment at his residence.

"Drive out with me," he said. "People have been saying I am afraid of a *coup d'état* here. You will see that I am not. I told you once I am a fatalist. I don't expect to die in bed. Perhaps I will be shot. But I will never put guards between me and my people."

His Citroën was parked in the courtyard. Saifoulaye Diallo was waiting there, and we all got in the car, with Touré at the wheel. He drove slowly down the Avenue de la République and then along the south *corniche*. Whenever we stopped at a red light, somebody on the sidewalk would run over to shake hands with him. I couldn't help wondering if the windshield was bulletproof. It seemed like a terribly long drive.

That evening I met some government officials who told me they were worried about Guinea's growing isolation in Africa. Nkrumah's presence bothered them too. But Touré apparently wasn't taking anyone's advice; he seemed obsessed by the idea that he was surrounded by enemies. "Be tough when you talk to him," they said. "He might listen to you." I agreed to try.

We met again at the palace at eleven. I told Touré I'd be very frank, as friends should be. I said I was especially disturbed by his eccentric behavior with respect to Nkrumah and the implications in his recent speeches that the United States was somehow involved in alleged plots against Africa. I said this was nonsense; our policy today was the same as it had been under Kennedy. We were ready to help leaders who were serious, who had the interests of their people at heart and who were genuinely nonaligned—but only if mutual confidence existed and our assistance was welcomed. Personally, I was no longer sure if he was still the thoughtful, rational man I'd known or if Guinea still wanted good relations with the United States.

Touré, who until now had been taut and reserved, suddenly became quite animated. He went to the phone and asked Saifoulaye and Mamady Kaba to come over. While we waited for them, a pretty Guinean girl came in with some fruit juice. I looked up at her and Touré laughed.

"Come back to Guinea," he said. "You can see we have the prettiest girls."

When the others arrived—Kaba wearing a Chinese tunic—Touré launched into a long, rambling sermon about the family of man and morality and the importance of never sacrificing spiritual values for material gain.

"Guinea may be poor," he said, "but we have remained faithful to African ideals. People like Houphouët have abandoned them for temporary economic advantages."

As for Nkrumah, Touré said he'd been "emotionally" shocked by the military coup in Ghana, as he had been by President Olympio's assassination in 1963. He had invited Nkrumah to Guinea as a matter of principle—to prove his devotion to "legality." It was not personal; they disagreed about many things. But Nkrumah was an African patriot and still a legitimate chief of state "regardless of whether he had committed any crimes."

Touré was clearly convinced that Nkrumah's downfall had been engineered by the West—chiefly Britain. When I mentioned the universal rejoicing in Ghana after the coup, he said it was always easy to mobilize a few thousand demonstrators. We argued back and forth. At one point, he slid off the couch onto one knee to emphasize a point. Finally he said he would be persuaded the revolution was genuine if the new regime held a referendum.

"Let them give the people of Ghana a chance to reject Nkrumah legally," he said. "I would then accept their verdict. Nkrumah could stay here if he wished but only as a private citizen. He could get a job, like anyone else."

I remarked that Nkrumah didn't really need a job—he had looted enough from Ghana to live comfortably for a long time. But I said I was surprised that a revolutionary like himself was now opposed to a popular revolution.

Our talk finally ended when I said I had to catch a plane. I told him I was glad to see he was still rational and logical, though I regretted his premises were based on erroneous information. He smiled. "I am just true to my principles," he said. "I will be proved right."

We parted cordially. He gave me an armful of autographed books and said he hoped I'd keep in touch with Bangoura in Washington. "I'm glad you spoke frankly to me," he said. "That's how friends should talk."

Thanks to the new highway, I managed to make the Air Afrique jet with minutes to spare. Alpha Diallo, the Deputy Foreign Minister who had come to see me off three years before, was there again, along with other Guinean friends. There were French-style embraces and then we were off, circling up over the coast, past Dubreka—where Senator Hartke had played the drums, past Boffa —where Sim and I had been given the elusive goat, and on to Dakar—where I had once been carried off the plane on a stretcher. Thinking now of those days, I had to agree with Touré: he hadn't changed. He was still earnest, intense, sincere—still a dreamer living his dream and articulating his own quasi-religious philosophy. It was Africa that was changing and passing him by. Touré was becoming anachronistic—a talker in a continent where the doers were taking over. He was no longer in the mainstream of African evolution, and I felt sorry for him. For he had been a trail blazer whose defiance of De Gaulle in 1958 gave Black Africa a sense of pride and confidence in its own destiny; and now he was just a nice but erratic guy who was beginning to look as if he might finish last.

Conakry–Dakar–Paris–New York–Washington. In Washington I went through the strenuous debriefing-and-lobbying exercise for the last time. The Kenyans badly needed a $3 million development loan to help tide them over the next two years, and I argued— perhaps in vain—in favor of giving them some budgetary support through additional aid projects. (The hard-pressed Chinese had just managed to give Tanzania $7.4 million in grants and interest-free loans.) I saw all the usual people and found that Vietnam was more than ever monopolizing our attention and our resources. (Even Bill Wild, my AID Director in Kenya, was suddenly transferred to Saigon, to the dismay of the Kenyans he had come to know so well.) Vietnam had priority over everything else; the sideshow of 1961 had become the main event of 1966. While the Congress slashed the foreign aid appropriation to about one-third of one percent of our Gross National Product, it had added an extra billion dollars to what the Pentagon asked for. I read that eleven television vans, each costing $200,000, were being shipped to Vietnam so that our troops could see "Bonanza" and "The Beverly Hillbillies," and I thought of all the schools we could be building in Kenya with that money.

But there were nevertheless good reasons, for those of us who cared about Africa and looked beyond Vietnam, not to feel discouraged about the future. Joe Palmer, who had taken over from Soapy Williams, was a career officer and former ambassador with long African experience; and Wayne Fredericks, the most capable Africanist in the government, was still Deputy Assistant Secretary of State. So the African Bureau was in good hands. At the White House, Walt Rostow, who had replaced Mac Bundy, showed me an LBJ memo urging his top advisers not to be unduly diverted by Vietnam from the problems of Africa, Latin America and the rest of Asia. At a White House reception marking the anniversary of the OAU, I listened to the President speak with perception and understanding about the continent I had just left. Bob Kennedy, who was on his way to Africa, was still the most attentive listener in town, except for Bill Moyers; I liked Kennedy's suggestion that we cut down aid to countries that squandered their resources on useless military hardware. It was good to hear Senator George McGovern demanding that we let America's farmers produce as much as they could in a world that was two-thirds hungry. And I left Dean Rusk's office, after my farewell call, feeling, as I usually did, that President Kennedy picked a better man as his Secretary of State than many people suspect.

I was glad to learn that my successor in Kenya would be Glenn Ferguson, a former Peace Corps representative who had been running the VISTA program. He was young and energetic and had the White House connection he would need if things got rough again. (At this writing, Kenya is still on a stable and progressive course. Odinga's party is disintegrating: Jaramogi himself was recently intercepted by the police after slipping across the border into Uganda under an assumed name to collect funds from Communist embassies in Kampala, and Oneko finally lost his seat in

Parliament. But Ferguson would have plenty to do just to keep our aid at its present minimal level.) I was also pleased that Bob McIlvaine, a career man who knows Africa, got my old job in Guinea. (He played it just right—tough and cool—in October when Touré, in another emotional outburst, accused us of conniving with Ghana in the arrest of his Foreign Minister in Accra.)

My farewell call on the President was brief—and interrupted by several phone calls. He hoped I'd talk to Senator Fulbright about foreign aid and Vietnam (I did but without much success) and asked me to suggest names of people who might be brought into the Foreign Service. And I left him feeling, as I had before, that he is the most unappreciated President of our time.

And then my Washington consultation was over, except for some final administrative disentanglement. Tully Torbert, who had been my neighbor ambassador in Somalia, drove me to the shuttle at National Airport. It was just six and a half years since Adlai Stevenson and I, on one of these flights, had had the talk that started this whole adventure.

"Get some rest," said Tully. "You look tired."

Tired I was, and anxious to get home.

Home. The house is a mess after two sets of tenants. You mow the lawn and clean out the basement. You start seeing old friends. You give the commencement speech at the high school. At parties you get into conversations and sometimes arguments. You read the papers and watch television. At first, you get discouraged about a lot of things; and then, as time goes by, you begin to feel more hopeful.

Let me try to explain what I mean before this long journey comes to an end.

What first struck me was how little my fellow Americans seemed to appreciate the way the world has changed in the last few years—and to what extent the changes have been in our favor. This was disturbing, because a democracy like ours can't act fast or update its policies without the support of public opinion. Yet most people don't bother to stop and think about the trouble spots of a few years ago—Berlin, Cuba, Lebanon, Panama, Indonesia, the Congo —or consider how much better they look today.

Everybody worries about Vietnam—with good reason. But even

there it could be worse. Of course we should never have become so deeply involved; but once we were committed, there was no turning back. At least the Asian Communists are learning what the Russians have already found out: that the Americans are not paper tigers. It has been a costly, bloody lesson. But it may be averting a greater tragedy later.

More important in our endangered world, Soviet-American relations have quietly but steadily improved since the 1962 crisis over Cuba. The Vietnam war notwithstanding, we have a tacit agreement to avoid a direct military confrontation. A test-ban treaty with the Russians has been signed; a nuclear nonproliferation treaty seems to be in the works. The long, grim deadlock is broken, and the first tentative steps away from disaster have been taken. This may be, as President Kennedy once said, only the first step on a thousand-mile journey on the road to peace; but every sane man can rejoice that we have made a start.

And the once-monolithic Communist movement has cracked wide open. We may have our family quarrels in the West, but what is going on between Russia and China is no mere quarrel; it's a feud of such proportions that the cold war as we knew it will never be the same again. Whatever challenges lie ahead, they probably won't include coping with an aggressive, single-minded, billion-strong Communist empire stretching from the Iron Curtain to the Yellow Sea.

None of this is to say that all's well with the world. For most of mankind, poverty is still the rule and freedom only a dream. But on balance, the state of the world looks considerably more hopeful than it did six or seven years ago. This you would not suspect from listening to some commentators and reading some columnists, or from talking to your neighbors. What you hear all too often is that the Communists are scoring all the points, while we're committing all the blunders; that foreign aid is wasted because it doesn't reach the people and that nobody likes us anyway.

A lot of this nonsense gets disseminated by the professional, self-styled anti-Communists who make a comfortable living scaring people over the airwaves and on the lecture circuits. But a good deal also comes from the press, where bad news always rates the most attention and good news is usually no news. American reporting from Africa, for example, frequently seems designed to perpetuate Soviet myths: Africans are more often than not portrayed as racist, anti-Western and susceptible to Communist blandishments. Month after month, hope fades, violence flares, whites flee and targets ripen for Communist takeovers. I have a collection of clippings that don't make me proud of the profession I have returned to. Quoting them all would add a chapter to this book. An April, 1965, syndicated column by Robert Allen and Paul Scott is not untypical. Citing an alleged CIA report that Kenyatta backed the Lumumba Institute, they pointed out that Odinga, as "Kenyatta's chief aide," had received Russian money and warned of "Kenyatta's close ties with the Kremlin and dedication to spreading Russian Communism in Africa."

Some of what appears in print is funny, like the magazine piece portraying the plush New Stanley Hotel as a kind of frontier inn where white settlers exchange the news "in this land of primitive communications"; some could be troublesome, like the New York *Daily News* story sneering at some Cameroon UN delegates as near-cannibals the same day they had supported our China position in the General Assembly; most of it is simply superficial and inaccurate, deepening and crystallizing public ignorance about Africa.

As for the conduct of our foreign policy, popular novels and television serials often make life in the Foreign Service seem like a kaleidoscope of cocktails and karate. I never realized what I'd been missing in the State Department until I read the blurb on a Pyramid pocketbook called *Embassy,* a novel that "rips through the flag-shielded façade to expose those exotic bits of America where a Congressman can turn a diplomat into a lackey . . . where wealth can transform a fool into a policymaker . . . where adultery becomes an obsessive temptation—and a hint of scandal is material for blackmail. . . . Not since The Ugly American have you seen such sham-stripped closeups of the men and women who make 'the Foreign Service way' a way of life."

So far as Africa is concerned, the problem is essentially that most editors, like most senior Foreign Service officers, are Europe-oriented. Newspapers, wire services and networks bunch their foreign correspondents in Europe (and now Vietnam) and generally cover Africa and even South America with stringers and an occasional roving reporter looking for the kind of story ("Race War

Looms") that will make page one and justify his expense account. The result is that a good deal of the history now being made abroad never gets reported at home, while relatively insignificant political developments in Europe get more attention than they deserve. During the Kenyatta-Odinga showdown in 1966, when eleven Communist intelligence agents were expelled from Kenya, I found no Nairobi dateline in either the *New York Times* International Edition or the New York *Herald Tribune* European Edition; but the Belgian cabinet crisis was reported in detail, and the *Trib* even had a half-column on the reduction in Luxembourg's armed forces.

The press is not entirely to blame for our clouded view of the world in general and Africa in particular. The scholars and professional intellectuals on the far right, the far left and even in the political middle often contribute to the confusion. In 1964 as distinguished an Africanist as Professor Arnold Rivkin could write in as eminent a periodical as *Foreign Affairs:* "Only after Guinea withdrew from the tightening Soviet embrace in 1962 did we take an active interest in them . . . partly because De Gaulle had relented enough in his attitude toward Guinea to allow the United States to enter the scene." *Vide,* as the scholars say, Chapters II through V of this book.

The far rightists are more clamorous than numerous, but their propaganda probably upsets a good many otherwise decent and clear-thinking people. The John Birch Society magazine, for example, publishes a fascinating kind of fever chart each month showing the degree of Communist control in various countries of the world. Guinea, in 1963, was rated as 96 percent "Red." I understand that the State Department is given a 2 percent Communist-control rating—which sounds encouraging until you learn that in Birchspeak 3 percent is sufficient for takeover. The kind of people who believe this nonsense seem to want to believe it. They resent hearing that we are doing well or that the Russians and Chinese are at odds; they are constantly looking for evidence that the Communist conspiracy is still in high gear, that Fidel Castro is a major menace, that American diplomats are incompetent and that country after country is turning against us (preferably countries on whom, to use a Chicago *Tribune* phrase, "we have been lavishing goodies"). The fact that they have been consistently wrong, because they lack a sense of history, does not diminish their zeal or dim their vision of an apocalypse where a posse of Arizona vigilantes gallop into Red Square to the cheers of ragged Russian slaves.

"My goodness," said a lady on shipboard to whom Sim and I had been introduced. "You both seem so nice and *normal* to be in the State Department. Do you read *Human Events?* Well, I get it every Monday morning and it scares me to death. Of course, you wouldn't know what goes on in Washington because the Communists are just *using* nice people like you."

Mostly you can smile and shrug them off. The only time I'd get mad at the radical-right kooks was when they made our job harder. I remember Telli Diallo showing me a letter he and other African delegates to the UN had received from a group called the "Friends of Senator Ellender." The letter minced no words; it called the recipient "a nigger, a cannibal and a Communist." It didn't help us at the U.S. Mission.

On the other end of the political spectrum we now have the New Left groups repeating the stale clichés of the Wallace Progressives of 1948. They don't like the State Department either. The pinko Foreign Service of the Birchers becomes the fascist Foreign Service —stuffy, reactionary and enamored of dictators. To the disciples of the New Left, the CIA is villainous, but the KGB is never mentioned; Soviet imperialism is a myth, and universal peace and harmony would prevail if the United States would just withdraw from its world-wide commitments into an impossible kind of Yankee-go-home neo-isolationism. (Impossible because we are too big, too rich and too strong to be irresponsible.) Reading some magazines, I sometimes think that fatuity is growing faster on the pixilated left than on the pathological right.

In between, we have politicians who should know better sounding off on foreign policy in terms that only compound public confusion. The list is long, but none do this as consistently as Richard Nixon. In recent months he has suggested that we withhold aid from countries unless they agree to sign military agreements with us (even the Chinese don't go that far); he has managed to becloud our noncolonial role in Vietnam by comparing us to the French; he has complained that our major allies have deserted us by trying to work out a settlement from the sidelines instead of plunging after us into the Vietnam swamp.

As if all of this weren't enough to keep the American people confused about foreign affairs, there is also the fact that history is moving too fast these days for the average man to keep it in proper focus. To understand what is happening in the world today, and to avoid getting confused or discouraged, we Americans in particular need to keep three things in mind:

The first is that we are living in one of the most revolutionary periods in human history. The old colonial order—and with it, the supremacy of the world's white, Christian minority—is vanishing. New nations—and new imperialisms—are rushing into the vacuum. This is the political revolution.

All these new nations want to break through the sound barrier of modernization in a few years. Hundreds of millions of people are hungry for the things we take for granted. This is the economic revolution.

But they are trying to do this in the midst of a population explosion that will double the number of people in the poor countries of the world during the next generation. This is the biological revolution.

Meanwhile, supersonic flight, atomic energy and the intercontinental ballistic missile have made the world much smaller and much more dangerous. No place on earth is far away any more, and no one is safe. Never in history have so many people been at the mercy of so few. This is the scientific revolution.

Together, these revolutions have already made the world a far different place from what it was as recently as World War II. But we are only just beginning to realize that its conflicts can no longer be settled by armed force, but with bricks and bulldozers, with medicines and teachers, with rice and respect.

The second thing we have to understand is that a lot has happened, is happening and will happen in the world, regardless of what the United States does or does not do. Too many people still believe that when things don't go our way, somebody in Washington must be at fault. But the fact is that while our policies can help guide the course of history, they can't alter it or dam it up. Castro and Mao Tse-tung came to power because their countries were ripe for revolution. Eastern Europe is Communist because the Red Army chased out the Nazis during World War II. Charles de Gaulle may be a hard man to deal with, but there he is.

In Africa the tide toward independence can no more be reversed than the tide toward full equality in the United States. Those who think so, whether they are Portuguese colonialists or Southern segregationists, are living in a dream world. The choice today is either to curse the tide or to see to it that what is bound to happen, happens with a minimum of harm.

In short, being the strongest power on earth doesn't mean that we can impose our will, our system or our way of life on other countries. That's what the Russians and Chinese have tried to do, and that's why they have made so little headway among the newly independent nations. Fortunately, our aim—and our strength—is that we stand for free choice and not coercion. Slowly but surely, people are beginning to understand this all over the world. For our part, we should be satisfied to make the world safe for diversity. That's already a lot.

The third thing to remember is that the cold war slogans and attitudes we've lived with since 1946 have become obsolete.

In Western Europe the threat of Soviet armed aggression has diminished to the point that we should start talking about a general political settlement, including troop reductions. In Eastern Europe the brutal discipline of the Soviet empire is not what it was under Stalin, and life is becoming tolerable. The Iron Curtain is still there, but not so tightly drawn.

The Atlantic Alliance is no longer the only cornerstone of Western strength and influence. In the United Nations, the NATO allies are outnumbered by thirty-eight African countries alone, to say nothing of the Asians. Winning the support of these nations, even at the risk of annoying some former colonial powers, is important to our long-range interests as well as those of the world organization.

And all around the globe, we are beginning to see that the big problems of the next generation, as I have mentioned earlier, will be less East-West than North-South ones. After years of nuclear stalemate and a balance of terror, the Soviet leaders—if not yet the Chinese—may have concluded that exporting Communism by force is a futile exercise; already the younger generation of Russians is far more interested in buying cars and TV sets than in Communizing the world. But the problem of closing the gap in living standards between the rich and the poor countries is rapidly becoming the biggest challenge the world has ever faced.

Thus, if we can keep in mind that the world is in revolution, that the United States is not omnipotent and that the nature of the cold war is changing, we Americans will be in a better position to know where we stand and what we have to do. We may also conclude that there is more reason for satisfaction than for despair. That is certainly the mood among people in government whose job is working on foreign policy on a day-to-day basis. Yet the professional agitators and headline seekers are those whose voices are more often heard in the land.

The wonder is that we manage to do as well as we do, as a nation, given the barrage of nonsense to which we are subjected from so many sources. Maybe most people don't listen. Maybe they're too busy bowling or watching television in their spare time to pay attention to the kooks, and thus preserve their common sense about the world at large. Read the polls and you can't help concluding that Americans often sound more reasonable than some of their elected representatives: They support the UN. They want a negotiated settlement in Vietnam. They're not against foreign aid when they feel it's doing good. They join the Peace Corps.

They are curious and questioning, especially on the campuses. A good deal of the ferment may be negative and unproductive—the protests about our involvement in Vietnam are several years late—but at least something's going on. In the fifties you couldn't even start a good argument about foreign affairs on a university campus, but at a college reunion a few weeks after returning from Kenya, I found an overflow crowd of alumni and undergraduates coming to hear a symposium on Africa.

It is easier than it used to be to talk frankly about real issues. The fictions are fading. Hardly anyone pretends that Formosa is China any more, and you can now question the need for our huge ($2.6 billion a year) military establishment in Europe without being accused of appeasement. And ideology is fading too. The crusaders, both Communist and anti-Communist, are dwindling on both sides of the Iron Curtain; except in China, the cool generation —the atomic age generation—is moving up, setting the pace, taking over. The reason for the world-wide posthumous popularity of Jack Kennedy is that he was the first spokesman of this generation to come to power.

As time goes on we will be hearing less and less about the cold war and more and more about the real problems facing mankind—poverty, population and nuclear proliferation. So there will be work to do for all of us—in business, in the professions and in government—who like to take part in the history of our time; for the next few years are going to be decisive in shaping the kind of world our children and grandchildren will inherit. There will still be dangers. But at long last those of us reaching middle age can begin to see beyond the tensions that have been the trademark of our generation to the opportunities and challenges that lie ahead.

I have been luckier than most of my contemporaries during this transitional period in having had a chance to work for three men who, despite differences in style and temperament, understood this changing world and cared enough to use all their vitality and energy to make it better. Adlai Stevenson, who was ahead of his time, Jack Kennedy, who was so much a part of it, and Lyndon Johnson, who is carrying on what they began—each made me proud to be an American at this time in history.

Because of their leadership, we Americans have done remarkably well since President Kennedy summoned us, on that wintry morning in January, 1961, "to bear the burden of a long twilight struggle, year in and year out, 'rejoicing in hope, patient in tribulation,' a struggle against the common enemies of man: tyranny, poverty, disease and war itself." Whether we continue to do as well, year in and year out, will depend on our ability, as citizens of a powerful country, to look at the world as it is, and not as some of us would like it to be; to act with wisdom and compassion, and to be unafraid.

Index

AFRICA

● Capital cities

0   MILES   1000

PORTUGUESE GUINEA
GAMBIA
Bathurst
Dakar
Nouakchott
Bissau
SENEGAL
SPANISH SAHARA
CANARY IS.
Conakry
PORTUGUESE GUINEA
SIERRA LEONE
Freetown
Monrovia
LIBERIA
Abidjan
Kumasi
Accra
GHANA
IVORY COAST
UPPER VOLTA
Ougadougou
Bamako
Mopti
Timbuktu
MALI
MAURITANIA
El Aiún
IFNI (SPAIN)
MOROCCO
Rabat
STRAIT OF GIBRALTAR
SEE ENLARGED INSET
Lomé
TOGO
DAHOMEY
Porto Novo
Lagos
NIGERIA
Kano
Niamey
NIGER
ALGERIA
Algiers
TUNISIA
Tunis
Tripoli
MEDITERRANEAN SEA
EUROPE
FERNANDO POO
CAMEROON
Yaoundé
CENTRAL AFRICAN REPUBLIC
Bangui
Fort Lamy
Lake Chad
CHAD
SAHARA
LIBYA
SUDAN
Khartoum
White Nile
Blue Nile
Nile
U.A.R. (EGYPT)
Cairo
Suez Canal
RED SEA
ASIA
ETHIOPIA
Addis Ababa
FRENCH SOMALILAND
Djibouti
SOMALIA
GULF OF ADEN
Lake
Uele
Benue
Niger
Senegal
20°
20°
40°
20°